Praise for
Capitalism 4.0

"Hugely ambitious . . . The overall impression is startlingly original. Kaletsky offers a genuinely new take on the credit crunch."

—JEREMY WARNER, *Literary Review*

"A path-breaking insight into the next stage of the way we manage the global economy." —GORDON BROWN

"Anatole Kaletsky sometimes seems like the Stephen Hawking of economics. . . . [He] leave[s] most current economic wisdom stretched flat on the carpet. . . . He goes—wisely, lucidly, above all confidently—where no experts have gone before. You know you're in the presence of a master."

—PETER PRESTON, *The Observer*

"Idiosyncratic, entertaining and contrarian."

—DAVID SMITH, *The Sunday Times*

"Few writers are trying to address future concerns with a new and more hopeful economic agenda. One . . . is the respected British financial journalist Anatole Kaletsky. In *Capitalism 4.0*, he makes a thoughtful but moderate set of proposals which [rely heavily] on faith in the ingenuity of capitalism as an adaptive mechanism. His recommendations often make sense."

—JEFF MADRICK, *New York Review of Books*

"At a recent conference of worried bankers I was asked if political hostility to big business was the precursor of a significant "regime change." . . . Had I read *Capitalism 4.0* beforehand I would have been able to produce a better answer."

—HOWARD DAVIES, *The Times*

"The surest way to be taken seriously as an economist is to predict disaster . . . [but Kaletsky] does a lot more than doom-saying in this outstanding work. . . . The narration is brilliant, especially where it blends theory with crises. . . . This is a must-read book."

—Madan Sabnavis, *Business World India*

"A good starting point for any meaningful debate on the kind of economic system the world wants after the crisis, and how to achieve it."

—Rajesh Kumar, *Outlook India*

"Fascinating and resists simple summary ... He is unfashionably optimistic about the ability of capitalism, particularly its American form, to reinvent itself to meet new challenges. At a time of great anxiety about the apparent paralysis of the American democratic system and faltering economic recovery, it takes some chutzpah to be so optimistic"

—Paul Seabright, *Times Literary Supplement*

"Kaletsky shines with erratic brilliance. He opens up a fertile field for thinking about the future of our political economy. He offers a scathing critique of conventional economics"

—Robert Skidelsky, *New Statesman*

Capitalism 4.0

The Birth of a New Economy

in the Aftermath of Crisis

Anatole Kaletsky

BLOOMSBURY

LONDON · BERLIN · NEW YORK · SYDNEY

First published in Great Britain 2010
This paperback edition published 2011

Copyright © 2010 by Anatole Kaletsky

The moral right of the author has been asserted

Bloomsbury Publishing Plc
36 Soho Square
London W1D 3QY

www.bloomsbury.com

Bloomsbury Publishing, London, New York, Berlin and Sydney
A CIP catalogue record for this book is available from the British Library

ISBN: 978 1 4088 0973 0

10 9 8 7 6 5 4 3 2 1

Printed in Great Britain by Clays Ltd, St Ives plc

MIX
Paper from
responsible sources
FSC® C018072
FSC
www.fsc.org

In memory of my late parents,

Jacob and Esther Kaletsky,

who experienced true calamities and crises—
the Russian Revolution, the two world wars,
the Holocaust, the purges of Stalin—
but whose joyful and indomitable spirits lived on.

Contents

Part III
Market Fundamentalism Self-Destructs

Part IV
The Great Transition

Part V
Capitalism 4.0 and the Future

Preface to the Paperback Edition

THE WAY TO WIN FAME and fortune in economics is always to predict disaster. Perennial pessimism, regardless of the true conditions, may not be a winning strategy in business, politics, or finance; but in economic forecasting, as in other branches of prophecy since Jeremiah and Cassandra, instilling fear with fervor is the only reliable formula for success. Nobody remembers the prophet who predicts, correctly, that there will be no plague of locusts or that the Ides of March will pass without event.

When *Capitalism 4.0* was written, in late 2009, its moderately optimistic message was ahead of its time—and intended to be. "Ahead of its time" can, however, be a euphemism for "plain wrong," and many of this book's arguments seemed close to this embarrassing position in mid-2010, when it was first published. With the U.S. economy apparently sinking back into recession, with consumers crushed by debts denominated in trillions, with Britain and much of Europe allegedly facing bankruptcy, with the Obama presidency seemingly failing, and with demagoguery displacing reasoned argument in politics around the world, the measured optimism of *Capitalism 4.0* seemed Panglossian and far-fetched.

For Americans in particular, bound up as they were in the vicious politics of their culture wars, a strong economic recovery and a consensual political settlement seemed out of the question. And indeed the U.S. economy failed to live up to the unrealistic promises of quick recovery made at Barack Obama's inauguration. More surprisingly, Obama turned out to be a leader who polarized American politics, belying this book's optimism about more constructive relationships between government and business. In Britain, meanwhile, the coalition government proved as politically pragmatic as expected, but surprisingly ideological and dogmatic in its economic approach.

But despite these important caveats, the arguments in this book have generally been strengthened by the passage of time. In fact, many of the ideas and predictions dismissed as almost impossible in 2009 may be so obvious and inevitable a year later as to appear banal. Such intellectual inversions often happen in revolutionary periods—events can move straight from impossible to inevitable, without ever passing through improbable. Consider the most important claims in this book.

The world economy has *recovered—and strongly.*

Global capitalism did not collapse, and nobody, except a few hysterical TV pundits, believes any longer that it will. Instead, the United States, Britain, and most of Europe definitively came out of recession. The emerging world, led by China and having hardly missed a beat in the crisis, enjoyed its strongest-ever year of economic growth. In America, GDP had regained its peak by the end of 2010 and the total length of the slump turned out to be somewhat shorter than the double-dip recession of 1980–82. The outlook for Britain was less rosy, owing largely to the government's surprisingly ideological approach to fiscal, monetary, and industrial policies, a dogmatism strikingly at odds with the coalition's centrist politics as well as the arguments in this book. Even Britain, however, will benefit from the global economic recovery and should be able to avoid a double-dip recession if the government and the Bank of England rediscover the economic pragmatism and ideological flexibility that are the characteristic features of Capitalism 4.0

Banks have *survived and repaid their governments.*

Banks in most of the world—with Ireland, Spain, and Germany as the main exceptions—have repaid all of their government loans well ahead of schedule. By early 2011, the official estimate of U.S. taxpayer losses from the government financial support operations was only $20 billion—just 1 percent of the $2 trillion figure widely quoted in the U.S. media as recently as late 2009. By the time the remaining bank shares and securities owned by governments and central banks are returned to the private sector, it is almost certain that U.S. and British taxpayers will make substantial profits, instead of suffering the crippling losses expected a year before.

The crisis has hit Europe harder than the United States.

The process whereby countries with excess savings—such as China, Japan and Germany—financed unsustainable consumption in the United States, Britain, Spain, and other debtor countries turned out to be even more destabilizing and dangerous for Europe than it was for the United States. While everybody had recognized for years that China was lending money to the U.S. mortgage market in order to finance the shoppers who bought Chinese goods at Walmart, there was far less understanding of the a similar chain of "vendor financing" that allowed Greek and Spanish consumers to borrow from German banks or sell villas to German autoworkers and then use the proceeds to buy German cars. This Circle of Manipulation, described in Chapter 16, was acknowledged in Europe only in early 2010, when Greece slid toward default. As a result, the survival of the euro was threatened and the existence of a single currency, far from insulating Europe from trouble, increased the financial risks. But Germany decided to support its neighbors by agreeing to unprecedented collective responsibilities for national debts. As a *quid pro quo*, Greece, Spain, and other Mediterranean countries agreed to previously unthinkable market-oriented reforms and reductions in government spending. The result was a convergence of politics and economics across Europe that nobody had imagined possible even a year before.

The reinvention of economic theory has started.

Predictions of a second Great Depression gave way to a new cliché in 2010: the Great Recession. But the truth is that the world in 2010 embarked on a Great Transition comparable to the transition forty years before from the Keynesian era to the Reagan-Thatcher market fundamentalism era and the even bigger transition forty years before that, from classical free-market capitalism to the Keynesian New Deal. It is not just the interaction of governments with markets that is changing, it is also the debate about fundamental political and economic ideas.

Orthodox economic policies have *been abandoned.*

Economic policies have been permanently transformed by the crisis. The huge fiscal and monetary stimuli introduced in 2009, derided and denounced by market fundamentalist skeptics, have worked very much as planned. China, Germany, and Britain introduced bigger fiscal stimuli earlier in the crisis than the United States did, and their economies rebounded more quickly. The relationship reversed by early 2010, with the U.S. economy accelerating well ahead of the others, in response to monetary stimulus, which by its nature acts more slowly than fiscal policy and was much bigger in America than elsewhere.

Near-zero interest rates, considered a bizarre and dangerous aberration when introduced as a panic measure in the post–Lehman Brothers emergency, have been accepted as a quasi-permanent feature of economic life. This book's prediction of interest rates below 2 percent throughout America and Europe for the best part of a decade no longer looks crazy or even particularly bold.

Despite zero percent interest rates and the unprecedented printing of central bank money, inflation has not accelerated (except marginally in Britain). The dollar and the pound have not collapsed as was widely predicted by monetarists. And bond markets, far from panicking, have enjoyed big gains for the reasons explained in this book. Stock markets, meanwhile, have risen at near-record rates and profits are at all-time highs less than two years after their biggest-ever plunge. In short, the unorthodox postcrisis measures of monetary, fiscal, and credit stimulus have worked more or less as intended.

Government has *simultaneously expanded and contracted.*

Public spending is on a declining path everywhere, yet the whole world is demanding that governments accept new responsibilities, especially for "creating jobs." Governments are therefore being forced to reduce their spending on what used to be considered core public functions. The public financing of pensions, education, and health care is being reconsidered, and privatization of public-owned assets is accelerating around the world. Government is therefore expanding and contracting at the same time, very much as described in Chapter 17.

A new version of capitalism has *begun to evolve.*

Although the global economy and financial system have survived the crisis, the need for a new model of capitalism is almost universally acknowledged all over the world. In Barack Obama's 2011 State of the Union speech, in David Cameron's concept of a Big Society, in the reconstruction of the eurozone and, not least, in the surprisingly successful managed capitalism of Asia (especially China), an important part of the message is the same: there must be new partnerships between the public and private sectors and new thinking about the way that governments and markets interact. Even the Tea Party in America demands a transformed relationship of politics and economics, albeit one diametrically opposed to the proposals in this book.

But what if capitalism fails to reinvent itself? What if the global economy reverts to business as usual? It is tempting to suggest that such a failure of imagination would trigger another, even greater, financial collapse. Indeed, the prophets of doom who monopolized public debate in 2009 with their predictions of Armageddon are regrouping behind this concept. When the end of the world failed to arrive on schedule, they responded in the time-honored manner of all millenarian cults—by delving back into their sacred texts and discovering some minor miscalculations. The new consensus among the prophets of doom is that the crisis of 2007–09 was never supposed to be the Big One; it was merely the precursor of another, even greater crash. And that impending apocalypse really will mark the end of the world.

If capitalism fails to reinvent itself, will the prophets of doom finally be proved right? Without fundamental reforms, the next financial crisis really could be far worse than the last one. And in the event of another economic meltdown, China really could seize the standard of global leadership irrevocably from economically discredited democracies of America and Europe. But such calamities are unlikely. The global capitalist system shows every sign of an ability and willingness to reinvent itself in the coming decade, but if this does not happen, the reason will be that the reinvention has turned out to be less urgent than this book suggests.

Therefore, the most likely alternative to this book's central argument about the evolution of a new version of the capitalist system is not that the world economy will sink into permanent stagnation or disintegrate in some sort of apocalyptic crisis. It is that capitalism will turn out to be even more successful than I have suggested by simply muddling through.

Introduction

THE WORLD DID NOT END. Despite all the forebodings of disaster in the 2007–09 financial crisis, the first decade of the twenty-first century passed rather uneventfully into the second. The riots, soup kitchens, and bankruptcies predicted by economists and pundits never materialized—and a year after the crisis nobody any longer expected the global capitalist system to collapse, whatever that emotive word might have meant.

Yet the capitalist system's survival does not mean that the precrisis faith in the wisdom of financial markets and the efficiency of free enterprise will ever again be what it was before the bankruptcy of Lehman Brothers on September 15, 2008. A return to decent economic growth and normal financial conditions is likely by the middle of 2010, but will this imply a return to business as usual for politicians, economists, and financiers? Although globalization will continue and many parts of the world will gradually regain their prosperity of the precrisis period, the traumatic effects of 2007–09 will not be quickly forgotten. And the economic costs will linger for decades in the debts squeezing taxpayers and government budgets, the disrupted lives of the jobless, and the vanished dreams of homeowners and investors around the world.

For what collapsed on September 15, 2008, was not just a bank or a financial system. What fell apart that day was an entire political philosophy and economic system, a way of thinking about and living in the world. The question now is what will replace the global capitalism that crumbled in the autumn of 2008.

The central argument of this book is that global capitalism will be replaced by nothing other than global capitalism. The traumatic events of 2007–09 will neither destroy nor diminish the fundamental human urges that have always powered the capitalist system—ambition, initiative, individualism, the competitive spirit. These natural human qualities will instead be redirected and reenergized to create a new version of capitalism that will ultimately be even more successful and productive than the system it replaced.

To explain this process of renewal, and identify some of the most important features of the reinvigorated capitalist system, is the ambition of this book. This transformation will take many years to complete, but some of its consequences have become discernible already. And with the benefit of even a few years' hindsight, it is clear that these consequences will be very different from the nihilistic predictions from both ends of the political spectrum at the height of the crisis. On the Left, anticapitalist ideologues seemed honestly to believe that a few weeks of financial chaos could bring about the disintegration of a politico-economic system that had survived two hundred years of revolutions, depressions, and world wars. On the Right, free-market zealots insisted that private enterprise would be destroyed by precisely the government interventions that proved necessary to save the system—and as soon as the crisis was over, started to claim that all the trouble could have been avoided if governments had simply allowed the financial systems to collapse. A balanced reassessment of the crisis must challenge both left-wing hysteria and right-wing hubris.

Rather than blaming the meltdown of the global financial system on greedy bankers, incompetent regulators, gullible homeowners, or foolish Chinese bureaucrats, this book puts what happened into historical and ideological perspective. It reinterprets the crisis in the context of the economic reforms and geopolitical upheavals that have repeatedly transformed the nature of capitalism since the late eighteenth century, most recently in the Thatcher-Reagan revolution of 1979–89. The central argument is that capitalism has never been a static system that follows a fixed set of rules, characterized by a permanent division of responsibilities between private enterprise and governments. Contrary to the teachings of modern economic theory, no immutable laws govern the behavior of a capitalist economy. Instead, capitalism is an adaptive social system that mutates and evolves in response to a changing environment. When capitalism is seriously threatened by a systemic crisis, a new version emerges that is better suited to the changing environment and replaces the previously dominant form.

Once we recognize that capitalism is not a static set of institutions, but an evolutionary system that reinvents and reinvigorates itself through crises, we can see the events of 2007–09 in another light: as the catalyst for the fourth systemic transformation of capitalism, comparable to the transformations triggered by the crises of the 1970s, the crises of the 1930s, and the Napoleonic Wars of 1803–15. Hence the title of this book.

The first of these great transitions—the period of social and economic upheaval that started with the political revolutions in America and France and the industrial revolution in England—created the first era of modern capitalism, running roughly from the British victory over Napoleon in 1815 until the First World War. This long period of relative systemic stability and rising prosperity ended with the First World War, the Russian Revolution, and finally the Great Depression in the United States. These unprecedented political and economic traumas destroyed the classical laissez-faire capitalism of the nineteenth century and created a different version of the capitalist system, embracing Franklin Roosevelt's New Deal, Lyndon Johnson's Great Society, and the British and European welfare states. Then, forty years after the Great Depression, another enormous economic crisis—the global inflation of the late 1960s and 1970s—inspired the free-market revolution of Margaret Thatcher and Ronald Reagan, creating a third version of capitalism, clearly distinct from the previous two. Forty years after the great inflation of the late 1960s, the global economy was hit by another systemic crisis, in 2007–09. The argument of this book is that this crisis is creating a fourth version of the capitalist system, a new economy as different from the designs of Reagan and Thatcher as those were from the New Deal. Hence the *birth of a new economy* in the subtitle of this book.

The concept of capitalism as an evolutionary system, whose economic rules and political institutions are subject to profound change, may seem controversial and even subversive from the standpoint of precrisis thinking. The Thatcher-Reagan revolution of the early 1980s was widely proclaimed as a rediscovery of true capitalism after the cryptosocialist heresies and deviations of the Keynesian period—and this worldview is still held by most conservative politicians and business leaders. In the great scheme of things, however, the dominance of free-market fundamentalism from 1980 until 2009 was just one thirty-year phase in the long history of modern capitalism's development since the late eighteenth century. Viewing recent events in this historical perspective reveals the crisis and its consequences in a new light.

Many politicians and business leaders consider, for example, that any government interference with market forces is inimical to the free-market system. They oppose all such interventions on principle as the thin end of a socialist wedge. Given the long and triumphant history of capitalism before anyone had heard of Reagan and Thatcher, this is an absurdly narrow-minded view. The changing relationship between government and private enterprise, between political and economic forces, has been the clearest feature of capitalism's evolution from one phase to the next—first in the early nineteenth century, then in the 1930s, then in the 1970s, and again today. And after each of these evolutions, the capitalist system has emerged stronger than it was before. To understand the new politico-economic model emerging from the crisis, it helps to consider the changing relationships of governments and markets in these three previous phases.

In the classical laissez-faire capitalism that dominated the world from the early nineteenth century until 1930, politics and economics were essentially distinct spheres. The interactions of government and markets were confined to collecting taxes, mainly to pay for wars, and erecting tariff barriers, mostly to protect powerful political interests. Then, from 1932 onward, came the New Deal and the social democratic European welfare states. In reaction to the Russian Revolution and the Great Depression, this second version of capitalism was defined by an almost romantic faith in benign, all-knowing governments and an instinctive distrust of markets, especially financial markets. The third version of capitalism, created by the Thatcher-Reagan political revolution of 1979–80, took the opposite view. This version romanticized markets and distrusted government. The last variant of this species—the financially dominated market fundamentalism described in this book as Capitalism 3.3—took this position to its extreme. Capitalism 3.3 did not just distrust governments; it demonized government, ridiculed regulation, and treated public administration with open contempt. This extreme antigovernment ideology, not only in politics but also, and just as importantly, in theoretical economics, triggered the 2007–09 crisis. As Karl Marx might have predicted, Capitalism 3 was destroyed by the contradictions of its own antigovernment ideology.

The self-destruction of Capitalism 3.3 has left the field open for the next phase of politico-economic evolution: the emergence of Capitalism 4. As in the 1930s and 1970s, this transformation will redefine the relationship between politics and economics, between governments and markets. The dominant ideology from the 1980s until the 2007–09 crisis assumed that markets were always right and governments nearly always wrong. The previous phase of capitalism, from the 1930s until the 1970s, assumed that governments were always right and markets nearly always wrong. The most distinctive feature of capitalism's next era will be a recognition that governments and markets can both be wrong and that sometimes their errors can be near-fatal.

This recognition of fallibility may, at first sight, seem paralyzing. In fact, it should be empowering. It creates scope for leadership, creativity, and experimentation in both politics and business—concepts that the preceding version of capitalism was reluctant to accept. Acknowledging that both governments and markets make mistakes implies a collaboration between politics and economics, rather than the adversarial relationship of Capitalism 3. The extraordinary opportunities created by technology, globalization, and social change in the dawning era of Capitalist 4 suggest that, if the rising generation of American and European politicians and business leaders play their cards well, the new economic model will be more prosperous than the last one. Perhaps it will one day be described as Obamanomics. If not, however, and America and Europe cannot show the ideological flexibility required to make Capitalism 4 succeed, the political economy of the coming decades will probably be shaped by China and other authoritarian neocapitalist nations, instead of by Western democracies.

If the West is to rise to this challenge, the 2007–09 crisis, along with its antecedents and its aftermath, need to be seen as a phase in the dynamic process of capitalist evolution. This is the picture presented in Part I.

Part II then discusses the crisis and the boom that came before it from this historical and evolutionary perspective. This book rejects the conventional wisdom that the global boom in housing and credit before the crisis was simply a debt-fuelled illusion. Instead, Part II argues that much of the

increase in consumer borrowing and asset values from the early 1990s onward was a rational response to benign economic trends that began in the
late 1980s. All these trends were driven ultimately by four tremendous
technological and geopolitical transformations that converged in 1989: the
breakdown of communism, the reemergence of Asia, the revolution in electronic technology, and the worldwide acceptance of pure paper money that
was not backed by gold, silver, foreign exchange reserves, or any other objective symbol of value.

The benign trends of the precrisis period inspired excessive speculation
and produced a damaging boom-bust cycle, but this in no way contradicts the
argument that most of the growth in credit and asset prices before the crisis
was fundamentally justified and will prove sustainable in the long-term.
Boom-bust cycles have always been and will continue to be a feature of the
capitalist system. The events that led up to the crisis were quite typical of previous boom-bust cycles and less extreme than many in the past. Why then
did this particular boom-bust cycle climax in such unprecedented disaster?

This is the question addressed in Part III. The explanation centers on an
exaggerated and naïve interpretation of economic theory that took to absurd extremes the free-market economic policies applied more pragmatically in the Thatcher-Reagan and Clinton periods. This market
fundamentalist approach to economic policy turned a fairly standard, if severe, boom-bust cycle into the greatest financial crisis of all time. More
specifically, market fundamentalism was behind the unforced errors of the
Bush administration, especially of its treasury secretary, Henry Paulson,
that were the proximate cause of financial catastrophe. How could the most
powerful and best-resourced government in the world have made so many
ruinous mistakes? Much of what went wrong could be attributed to a per-
nicious interaction between academic economics and political ideology,
which magnified each other's faults and biases, like a pair of distorting mir-
rors. As a result, the classical economics of Adam Smith and David Ricardo
were turned into the ludicrously exaggerated doctrines of efficient markets,
rational expectations, and monetarist central banking that monopolized
economic thinking in governments, regulatory institutions, and financial
businesses worldwide. Part III concludes with the argument that new forms
of economics, moving beyond the mathematical pedantry and ideological

assumptions of rational expectations and efficient markets, need to be urgently invented if a reformed model of capitalism is to succeed.

On the foundations established by reinterpreting the past and present, Parts IV and V examine how Capitalism 4 is evolving in the postcrisis decade ahead. What will be the main features of the new system?

If one common theme linked many of the troubles that converged on the world economy in the autumn of 2008, it was the quasi-religious doctrine of perfect markets and the related belief that effective government and free markets are Manichaean opposites, unable to coexist in the same world. After the worldwide bank bailouts and the U.S. government's takeover of General Motors, the dogma that government intervention is always inimical to private enterprise can no longer be sustained. Freer markets and smaller government can no longer be presented as a credible answer to every challenge facing the capitalist system.

The symbolic confirmation that, for serious policymakers, the love affair with market fundamentalism was over came in August 2009, in the famous Congressional testimony of Alan Greenspan, a proud disciple of the quintessential free-market ideologue, Ayn Rand. Asked whether his free-market beliefs had proved dangerously flawed, Greenspan replied: "Yes, I have found a flaw. I don't know how significant or permanent it is, but I've been very distressed by that fact . . . Yes, I found a flaw. That is precisely the reason I was shocked, because I'd been going for forty years or more with very considerable evidence that it was working exceptionally well . . . Those of us who have looked to the self-interest [of private companies to promote the capitalist system]—myself especially—are in a state of shocked disbelief."[1]

Appropriately enough, the nature of this flaw was identified by Ayn Rand herself in an essay on her objectivist philosophy that had inspired Greenspan and other American conservatives for two generations: "The ideal political-economic system is laissez-faire capitalism . . . In a system of full capitalism, there should be (but, historically, has not yet been) a complete separation of state and economics, in the same way and for the same reasons as the separation of state and church."[2]

Most serious political philosophers, sociologists, and economic historians have long realized that the opposite is true. Any society driven purely by market incentives will fail catastrophically, in economic as well as political

terms. The freest, most incentive-driven market economies in the world are
not the United States or Hong Kong or even tax havens such as the Cayman
Islands but failed states and gangster societies such as Somalia, Congo, and
Afghanistan.[3] The overriding importance of political institutions in creating
the conditions for successful capitalism has been established in great works
of social scholarship going back to Adam Smith's *Theory of Moral Sentiments*
and Max Weber's *Protestant Ethic and the Spirit of Capitalism.*[4] But after the
Thatcher-Reagan revolutions of the 1980s, business leaders, academic economists, and conservative politicians decided to ignore the historical realities
described by sociologists and political scientists in favor of the oversimplified assumptions of market fundamentalist ideologues such as Ayn Rand.
The result was the quasi-religious dualism between politics and economics
that finally became unsustainable during the Lehman crisis.

Politicians forced to support private banks with public money could no
longer deny that government safety nets are a natural and necessary feature
of social reality, whether in financial markets, or fire fighting, or the provision of defibrillators in public places.[5] Banks driven to the brink of failure
could no longer pretend that their reckless disregard for risk and "eat what
you kill" bonus culture was purely a private matter between their shareholders, directors, and employees. Investors ruined by relying on theories of efficient and rational financial markets could no longer pretend that
market-based financial regulations and accounting rules were always more
reliable than political and regulatory judgments.[6] The upshot was that the
market fundamentalist opposition between government and private enterprise could no longer be seriously maintained.

The new kind of capitalism now emerging is essentially reversing Ayn
Rand's objectivist ideal. Instead of separating the State and private economy, Capitalism 4.0 is bringing them into a closer relationship. If markets
and governments are both imperfect mechanisms for achieving social objectives, systems of checks and balances reflecting both private incentives
and political decisions will often give better results than market or public
mechanisms on their own.

Capitalism 4.0 is recognizing that governments and markets make mistakes not only because politicians are corrupt, bankers greedy, businessmen
incompetent, and voters stupid, but also because the world is too complex

and unpredictable for any decision-making mechanism to be consistently right, whether it is based on economic or political incentives. Experimentation and pragmatism must therefore become the watchwords in public policy, economics, and business strategy, even if this means a loss of consistency and coherence.

The ability to operate by trial and error, to correct mistakes before they do too much social harm, is the greatest virtue of the market system. A similar pragmatism will have to be extended in the years ahead to political decisions and to the interaction of government with business. Political and business leaders already seem to be embarking on this learning process. Jeffrey Immelt, the chairman of General Electric, for example, reacted to the crisis by calling on his managers to "become systems thinkers who are comfortable with ambiguity."[7] Meanwhile, President Obama has advocated "a new, more pragmatic approach that is less interested in whether we have big government or small government [than] in whether we have a smart, effective government."[8] But while political and business leaders are recognizing the shift from a world of rationalist predictability to one characterized by ambiguity, unpredictability, and fuzzy logic, economists will be more stubborn in defending the precrisis ideas of rational and efficient markets. The gap between economic theory and business practice is therefore likely to widen before it begins to contract.

Mainstream economics before the crisis assumed that competitive markets move automatically toward equilibrium, that financial cycles have little or no effect on long-term economic performance, and that a properly functioning private-enterprise economy will always remain near full employment, leaving only one important role for government macroeconomic policy, which is to keep inflation under control. The crisis has refuted all these market fundamentalist assumptions. The world will now have to recognize that financial cycles, occasional banking crises, and self-reinforcing economic slumps are natural and recurring features of any market system. And that, in turn, implies that governments and central banks will have to take greater responsibility for managing growth and employment, as well as maintaining financial stability and keeping inflation under control.

These enormous new responsibilities might suggest that government will grow ever larger, at the expense of taxpayers and private businesses, but the opposite is actually happening in Capitalism 4.0. Government is starting to shrink in size, even as its responsibilities and influence expand. Part of the reason is simply the size of deficits created by the crisis and the political resistance to taxes, which appear to be approaching the limits of public acceptability in many countries. A deeper cause of the shrinkage of the public sector in Capitalism 4.0 will be the inability of bureaucratically inflexible big government to meet society's ever-changing demands. These complex demands, ranging from universal health care and energy independence to stable mortgage financing and rising wages, can be satisfied only by the profit motive acting through competitive capitalist markets. What is changing, however, is the role played by government in managing these markets and creating incentives for profit-seeking businesses to achieve politically favored objectives.

Clearly financial regulations are being tightened, but Capitalism 4.0 also means a host of other reforms and shifts in the boundaries between the market and the state. Black-and-white dividing lines between the responsibilities of government and business are turning into shades of grey. Making the picture even more complex, governments and markets are being forced to move in different directions in different parts of the world. To gain control over exploding health costs, for example, America is moving towards more government regulation. In the very different circumstances of Britain, by contrast, more private financing and market competition are needed to deliver the same ultimate objective of cost control. Mortgage financing will need more regulation in Britain but less government intervention and subsidy in the United States. Education is likely to become more market-driven in every advanced country (with the possible and ironic exception of supposedly socialist Sweden and Denmark, where private schooling is widespread), whereas in developing countries such as China, India, Brazil and South Africa, free state education still has a long way to expand.

Some of these paradoxes, for example, the convergence of health care toward a mixed public-private model, may suggest a bland Third Way approach that simply splits the difference between America's market system and Swedish social democracy. But this is not the case. The idea that some countries or sectors may need more market and less government in a particular historic context while others need less market and more government is no more paradoxical than the idea that a kitchen needs both a refrigerator and a stove.

Creating appropriate criteria for the government's relations with the market—for example, in subsidizing alternative energy without unacceptable inefficiencies, regulating trade without resorting to outright protectionism trade, or regulating health care and education without denying free choice—will create big problems for public policy in Capitalism 4.0. And although there will be no simple answers, the problems of rebalancing public and private interests will have to be confronted if Western democracy is to overcome the challenge from a different model of capitalism rising in the East.

China's tremendous economic growth and the success of its state-controlled economic model in coping with the 2007–09 crisis have cast doubt on the theory that capitalism and democracy will always be mutually supportive. The optimistic slogan of the Thatcher-Reagan period that "free markets create free people" can no longer be taken for granted. The hopes of a durable convergence between the Chinese and Western models of capitalism also appear increasingly illusory. Whether we look at business practices, economic policies, political rights, or geopolitical interests, China and the West appeared to be drifting apart after the crisis. Serious conflicts might not occur for years or decades, but the two models of politico-economic development are proving incompatible in many ways. In business practices, Chinese regulations and industrial strategies increasingly favor domestic industries over Western investors and exporters. In economic policy, China's determination to run huge trade surpluses and maintain an undervalued exchange rate while it offers cheap products to American and European consumers implies ever-rising international debts and the continued loss of semiskilled manufacturing jobs. China's economic self-assurance is making it more stubborn in its rejection of Western-style democracy and human rights. Finally, and perhaps most seriously, China's growing confidence in its model of authoritarian, government-led economic development is creating inevitable frictions with Western geopolitical interests and offering emerging nations a genuine alternative to democratic market-led development.

The West thus has a choice. One option is to acknowledge respectfully that China has been a more cohesive, durable, and successful society than Western Europe or America for most of the five-thousand-year span of recorded history. From this perspective, twenty-first-century China is

merely reclaiming a natural position of global leadership for its cultural values and national interests. Another, less defeatist, option is the one suggested in this book: We can demonstrate by our actions that Western
democratic capitalism is more adaptive and durable than the Chinese authoritarian version. To do this, however, the West will have to acknowledge
the challenge to its entire worldview presented by a self-confidently authoritarian China and recognize that, after the 2007–09 crisis, a reinvention of the Western socio-political model is required.

If the necessary reforms happen, American-led democratic capitalism
will reemerge as the most successful and attractive politico-economic
model for nations and peoples the world over—subject to one crucial proviso: The Western world will have to return to full employment and robust
economic growth after the 2007–09 crisis. If Western democracies are to
meet the challenge from authoritarian state-led capitalism in China, predictions of a long period of slow growth and stagnant living standards in
the United States, Britain, and other advanced economies will have to be
proved wrong.

In 2009, Mohamed El-Erian, a prominent academic and financier,
coined the phrase New Normal to describe the depressed economic conditions he expected to prevail for many years, or even decades, after the crisis.
The new economic environment, he argued, would be marked by permanently weaker activity, employment, and profits, as the artificial stimulant
of excess borrowing was removed. If this prediction turns out to be right, it
will raise serious questions about the long-term survival of a free-market
capitalist system.

The argument for permanently weaker economic growth rests on the assumption that much of the extra wealth created in the precrisis period was a
mirage. This assumption is now widely shared. Yet the many conservative
politicians, financiers, and business leaders who vehemently denounced the
precrisis credit expansion as a fraud and illusion never seemed to consider
the logical implication: If most of the wealth created from the 1980s onward
was a fraud, the same must be true of the free-market reforms that supposedly created this imaginary wealth.

Ronald Reagan and Margaret Thatcher have been admired for reversing the structural deterioration of Anglo-Saxon capitalism by creating the

free-market system described in this book as Capitalism 3.0. But postcrisis conventional wisdom implied that the Thatcher-Reagan reforms merely disguised the capitalist system's malaise behind a froth of financial bubbles. Once the phoney speculative froth was blown away, it seemed as if very little genuine wealth was created by the new model of financially driven capitalism of the 1980s. A logical corollary was that the genuine wealth created by the free market period must have been much *smaller* than the wealth created by the government-led high-tax capitalism of the 1950s and 1960s.

On this reading of history, even the apparent resolution of class conflicts in the 1980s was a conjuring trick, because the true living standards of working people fell for most of the free-market period, with their pauperization disguised by a fraudulent inflation of property values and buildup of mortgage debt. As this tower of debt collapsed, the middle class and the poor were told that they gained little or nothing from free-market reforms. And if, as the New Normal asserted and still asserts, economic conditions after the crisis were bound to be even worse, then the middle class will have to conclude, *a fortiori*, that the free-market reforms of the Thatcher-Reagan period made them much worse off than their parents in the Keynesian Golden Age.

This view of the world seemed to imply that the free-market system was doomed and the next phase of capitalism's political development would be a swerve to the left. Why then was this interpretation of the crisis promoted with greatest enthusiasm by conservative economists and politicians? How was it possible to extol the virtues of the Thatcher-Reagan era, while deriding its claims to have raised living standards as a cruel deception?

Some conservative politicians and economists claim that free-market prescriptions were never properly applied. They argue that growth would have been much stronger and more stable if bureaucracy, regulation, and welfare had been attacked even more aggressively than by Reagan, Thatcher, and George W. Bush. But such arguments will fail. After a thirty-year experiment with free markets and minimal government has been exposed as a failure, it is hardly conceivable that democratic societies will react by supporting even more radical policies of deregulation and laissez-faire. Much more likely than another experiment in free-market radicalism would be a return to some modernized version of 1970s-style government-led capitalism, perhaps accompanied by a shift in ideological leadership from Washington to Beijing.

Before giving way to this depressing prospect, however, we must recall that this view is based entirely on an unproved conjecture: that the postcrisis New Normal *will* be a period of stagnant living standards, depressed asset prices, and weak growth. This book argues, by contrast, that the world economy will be able to achieve a rapid recovery, provided central banks and governments redirect their macroeconomic policies toward growth and keep interest rates at rock-bottom levels. This book argues also that the benign long-term trends that created the precrisis financial boom will ultimately be more powerful and enduring than the mood swings and policy errors that caused the bust. In that case, the New Normal will turn out to be a period of *faster* growth and *higher* living standards than in the precrisis decades. In the shadow of the deepest recession in postwar history, with consumers, homeowners, and governments still crushed by debt, this may seem a preposterous prediction. But is it really so far-fetched?

Even though private businesses and households were reluctant to spend in the immediate aftermath of the crisis, politicians and central bankers rediscovered the powerful tools at their disposal to boost economic growth— zero interest rates, open-ended credit guarantees, fiscal stimulus, and a limitless ability to print money. According to the fundamentalist economic doctrines of the precrisis period, such tools were useless because government efforts to boost growth with monetary and fiscal policies were always doomed to failure. But as capitalism began to reinvent itself, such fundamentalist assumptions gave way to a more pragmatic understanding of economics. Policymakers worldwide realized that they could keep interest rates at or near zero for many years or even decades. They could direct public spending toward infrastructure and job creation. They could manage exchange rates to promote export-led growth. And they could ignore taboos against subsidies and tax incentives to encourage investment and preserve jobs.

In a speech in January 2010, Lawrence Summers, the head of the U.S. National Economic Council, made the following prediction: "When historians look back on the economic figures for 2010–19, I will be very surprised if they are not much better than the figures for 2000–09. If we renew our failing systems, we can provide much better outcomes to the American people than we did in the last decade."[9] No one at the time paid much attention, because a New Normal of stagnant living standards and weak growth was generally believed to be inevitable—perhaps even morally imperative—after the financial excesses of 2007–09. But if governments and central banks continue to use the economic tools at their disposal—and if political and business leaders seize the opportunities presented by the emergence of a new capitalist system—the optimism expressed by Summers will prove to have been justified.

If the postcrisis decade does indeed prove more prosperous than the one before, the world will conclude that the reforms of the Thatcher-Reagan era, while they were not the universal panacea claimed by market fundamentalist zealots, were not a deception either. Financial capitalism was not just a Ponzi scheme. The wealth created by financial markets may not have been as great as some imagined, but neither was just a figment of collective madness. The demolition of communism, the technological revolution, the rise of Asia, and the abolition of the gold standard were not just daydreams but genuinely earth-shattering events which transformed humanity's capacity to create wealth. These are essentially the conclusions of this book.

But what if these conclusions are wrong? What if the world economy stalls instead of continuing its recovery, and what if the evolution of capitalism just described does not occur? In that case, the shift in wealth and power from America and Europe to Asia will surely accelerate. The Western financial system will remain crisis-prone and unstable. Political consensus will prove impossible to achieve in an environment where conservative business sentiment demands ever-greater freedom for private enterprise, while workers and voters are told to tighten their belts to pay for more free-enterprise reforms of the previous thirty years that brought about disaster. In that case, a different species of capitalism from the one described in this book—one based on Chinese authoritarianism rather than Western democratic values—will rise to dominate the world.

So WHICH FORM of capitalism will prevail? In the immediate aftermath of the deepest economic slump since World War II, no one can say for sure. By early 2011 the early optimism of the Obama administration had been replaced by political gridlock. Hopes of a new political direction had dimmed in the United States. In Europe, the single currency zone seemed to be on the brink of breakup. Britain's political outlook was more uncertain than ever and Japan was sleepwalking into its third lost decade. Among the world's biggest economies, China alone had emerged from the crisis more confident and powerful than before. In this environment, to believe in the ultimate success of a new form of democratic capitalism demanded a leap of faith.

Nothing is preordained in history and nothing is immutable in economics. In the past forty years, dozens of relatively small events could have changed the course of history and transformed economic conditions the world over. Imagine if Deng Xiaoping had died in the Cultural Revolution alongside his mentor Liu Shaoqi. Or if Gorbachev had been passed over for the Soviet leadership. Or if John Hinckley's bullet had been aimed an inch higher at Ronald Reagan's chest. Or if Argentina had not invaded the Falklands, saving the government of Margaret Thatcher. Or if the hanging chads in Florida had fallen for Al Gore instead of George W. Bush.

Any of these events would certainly have transformed the pace of change, but would they have moved history in a different direction? No one can say for certain, but an inexorable logic in both capitalism and democracy appears to favor self-improvement over self-destruction. This logic implies that economic progress, political consensus, and systemic evolution are inherently more probable than economic collapse, anarchy, and disintegration. And a life-threatening crisis, far from dashing hopes of progress, makes forward motion all the more likely. This is the creative logic of survival now driving the world economy toward Capitalism 4.0.

Part I

Capitalism and Evolution

CHAPTER ONE

Mr. Micawber and
Mad Max

Something will turn up.

—Mr. Micawber's endearingly self-deceiving
refrain in *David Copperfield*

DEMOCRATIC CAPITALISM is a system built for survival. It has adapted successfully to shocks of every kind, to upheavals in technology and economics, to political revolutions and world wars. Capitalism has been able to do this because, unlike communism or socialism or feudalism, it has an inner dynamic akin to a living thing. It can adapt and refine itself in response to the changing environment. And it will evolve into a new species of the same capitalist genus if that is what it takes to survive.

In the panic of 2008–09, many politicians, businesses, and pundits forgot about the astonishing adaptability of the capitalist system. Predictions of global collapse were based on static views of the world that extrapolated a few months of admittedly terrifying financial chaos into the indefinite future. The self-correcting mechanisms that market economies and democratic societies have evolved over several centuries were either forgotten or assumed defunct.

The language of biology has been applied to politics and economics, but rarely to the way they interact.[1] Democratic capitalism's equivalent of the biological survival instinct is a built-in capacity for solving social problems

and meeting material needs. This capacity stems from the principle of competition, which drives both democratic politics and capitalist markets.

Because market forces generally reward the creation of wealth rather
than its destruction, they direct the independent efforts and ambitions of
millions of individuals toward satisfying material demands, even if these
demands sometimes create unwelcome by-products. Because voters generally reward politicians for making their lives better and safer, rather than
worse and more dangerous, democratic competition directs political institutions toward solving rather than aggravating society's problems, even if
these solutions sometimes create new problems of their own. Political competition is slower and less decisive than market competition, so its self-
stabilizing qualities play out over decades or even generations, not months
or years. But regardless of the difference in timescale, capitalism and democracy have one crucial feature in common: Both are mechanisms that
encourage individuals to channel their creativity, efforts, and competitive
spirit into finding solutions for material and social problems. And in the
long run, these mechanisms work very well.

If we consider democratic capitalism as a successful problem-solving
machine, the implications of this view are very relevant to the 2007–09
economic crisis, but diametrically opposed to the conventional wisdom that
prevailed in its aftermath. Governments all over the world were ridiculed
for trying to resolve a crisis caused by too much borrowing by borrowing
even more. Alan Greenspan was accused of trying to delay an inevitable
"day of reckoning" by creating ever-bigger financial bubbles. Regulators
were attacked for letting half-dead, "zombie" banks stagger on instead of
putting them to death. But these charges missed the point of what the
democratic capitalist system is designed to achieve.

In a capitalist democracy whose raison d'etre is to devise new solutions
to long-standing social and material demands, a problem postponed is effectively a problem solved. To be more exact, a problem whose solution can
be deferred long enough is a problem that is likely to be solved in ways that
are hardly imaginable today. Once the self-healing nature of the capitalist
system is recognized, the charge of "passing on our problems to our grandchildren"—whether made about budget deficits by conservatives or about
global warming by liberals—becomes morally unconvincing. Our grand-

children will almost certainly be much richer than we are and will have more powerful technologies at their disposal. It is far from obvious, therefore, why we should make economic sacrifices on their behalf. Sounder morality, as well as economics, than the Victorians ever imagined is in the wistful refrain of the proverbially overoptimistic Mr. Micawber: "Something will turn up."

One condition, however, must be satisfied to "turn up" new solutions, whether for stabilizing financial markets and managing the economy or for eliminating global pollutants and curing diseases: Capitalism and democracy must themselves survive. That is why sacrifices to protect democracy and private enterprise against the military challenges of communism, fascism, and religious fundamentalism are rational and morally admirable, while sacrifices on behalf of our grandchildren's purely economic prosperity are not (at least at the level of society as a whole).

But capitalism's survival depends on more than military protection. Modern capitalism is a complex social system that has been incredibly successful in expanding the wealth, technologies, and life span of every generation since the late eighteenth century, but like every complex system, it is delicate. Many self-organizing complex systems operate on what evolutionary biologists and mathematicians call the "edge of chaos," a constantly shifting line of balance between potentially disruptive forces that the system itself creates. Karl Marx was right that capitalism, by its nature, creates internal contradictions that inevitably lead to crises threatening its survival. What Marx and his followers missed, however, was the capacity of politics, especially democratic politics, to resolve these contradictions, overcome the crises, and enable capitalism to survive.

What, then, does democratic capitalism require for its survival? The lesson from history, evolutionary biology, and everyday common sense is that one condition has to be satisfied for any complex system to survive in an unpredictable and constantly changing world: The system itself must be adaptable, that is, it must have internal mechanisms allowing it to undergo radical change.

The crisis of 2007-09 marked the fourth time in the history of democratic capitalism that the system faced the challenge of comprehensive change. The question is whether it will again adapt, as it did at the turn of the nineteenth century, the 1930s, and the1970s. Experience suggests that it will—and that the main mechanism for this survival will be the Micawber Principle: the seemingly improvident assumption that a problem postponed long enough is, effectively, a problem solved.

Hoping that "something will turn up" may sound like deluded wishful thinking, but it is really just an extension into politics and macroeconomics of Adam Smith's arguments about the self-organizing dynamics of the capitalist economy. Smith showed how the "invisible hand" of competitive markets automatically coordinates the actions of millions of individuals pursuing their own self-interest so that they satisfy each other's needs, despite the fact that no one is thinking consciously about the common good.

This same invisible hand steers individual initiative and creativity toward solutions of society's collective problems, provided two conditions are satisfied. First, the process of spontaneous self-organization must be given enough time to produce new adaptations after each of capitalism's periodic crises. Second, the right incentives must exist for business competition and human creativity to address society's common problems, as well as meeting individual material desires. As Joe Stiglitz, the Nobel Laureate economist, has repeatedly argued, private markets cannot necessarily be relied on "to align private incentives with social returns"[2]—and this is particularly true during dramatic technological or political change.

For example, consider carbon emissions. Market incentives today make it much more attractive to use coal and oil than any other energy source and, therefore, rule out the possibility that the private sector will invest in developing and scaling up solar, wind, nuclear, and other low-carbon energy technologies. These market incentives could be changed, but only through political decisions. To change the incentives, governments could impose much higher taxes on fossil fuels or physical ceilings on carbon emissions, similar to the bans introduced in the past on dangerous chemicals such as lead, tobacco, DDT, and CFC refrigerants, which had created a "hole" in the earth's ozone layer.[3] If governments took such initiatives, market mechanisms would reduce carbon emissions to whatever level the political system might prescribe and would probably do it more quickly and less expensively than anyone imagines. If incentives are not changed through the political process of one-person one-vote, however, there is no prospect that private enterprise would spontaneously create a low-carbon world through the market mechanism of one-dollar one-vote.

One of the biggest mistakes made by market fundamentalism is the assumption that markets will always create the necessary incentives for private enterprise to solve urgent social problems. In reality, many challenges—mass unemployment in the 1930s, inflation and labor unrest in the 1970s, financial instability and climate change in the present period—can be addressed only if politics creates new economic incentives and new institutions to stimulate the problem-solving, innovative capacities of private enterprise.

As societies progress, they always face new challenges—and over time, the reforms made by previous generations create new problems for succeeding generations, necessitating further reforms. Sooner or later, a crisis occurs and the need for reforms becomes so urgent that conservative opposition is overwhelmed, but this process normally takes years or decades rather than months. It is in adapting incentives and institutions to changing social conditions that the troubles for the capitalist system often arise. For example, the U.S. government could readily reduce the cost of medical insurance, which is almost double the level of other countries with similar standards of healthcare, by making a political decision to change market incentives—but to do this would mean overcoming powerful opposition from the entrenched interests benefiting from the status quo. In each of the great transitions of modern capitalism, new institutions had to be created and economic incentives have to be realigned in the face of intense opposition. When the requirements for new incentives become too radical for the existing politico-economic arrangements, capitalism reaches an evolutionary breakpoint, as it did in the 1930s, in the 1970s, and today. The next two chapters describe this process of systemic adaptation in detail, but to introduce the argument, consider briefly the two great transitions of capitalism in the twentieth century.

In the 1930s, democratic capitalism faced unprecedented threats from communism, fascism, and the Great Depression. The response was a previously unthinkable expansion of government spending, social insurance, redistributive taxation, and employment rights. But in the late 1960s and 1970s, these responses to the earlier crisis had themselves begun to threaten the system's survival. From the 1980s onward, the Thatcher and Reagan revolutions responded to the new challenges of inflation and mass unemployment by curbing government, deregulating financial markets, and transforming economic incentives at the top and bottom of the income scale. These reforms were successful in overcoming the challenges of the 1970s, but they too began to create distortions, which finally triggered the near-fatal crisis of 2007–09. This crisis, in turn, is forcing the next systemic transformation, one that may well have to be as radical as the Roosevelt and Thatcher-Reagan revolutions.

The transformation of capitalism always seems most difficult to achieve when it is most needed—at the moment of near-breakdown. The interest groups that thrived under the old system then fight ruthlessly to prevent change. They insist that the only conceivable mode of economic organization is the version of capitalism that endowed them with wealth and power and that any attempt to change the system is doomed to failure. They warn that attempting reform is far too risky with the entire economy on the brink of failure. These were the arguments of business organizations opposing the New Deal and Keynesian economics in the 1930s. They were the arguments of the labor unions and public employees fighting Reagan and Thatcher in the 1980s. And they are the arguments of the banking and financial lobbies today.

The lobbyists for special-interest groups are not the only ones who warn that the model of capitalism on the point of disintegration must be supported because it is the only one that can work. The media, influential academics, and the political establishment usually hold the same view. These powerful opinion-formers have risen to prominence under the old system. Their intellectual conservatism is often even more entrenched than lobbyists' pragmatic economic interests. In the 1980s, the liberal academic and media establishment felt almost as threatened by the Thatcher-Reagan revolution as the union leaders and government employees whose jobs were directly affected. The same was true of the predominantly conservative media and academics of the 1930s, and the same is broadly true today.

It is not surprising, therefore, that at these historic moments, when the capitalist system appears to be in its death-throes, it also seems incapable of radical reform. But these are exactly the moments when the genius of democracy comes forward to play its role. Just when the economic system seems to be ineluctably failing, politics kicks in to shake up institutional structures. New incentives are created and, after a period of transition, a reformed version of capitalism takes shape. "Something will turn up" is therefore a perfectly valid principle in capitalist democracies, provided the political economy is flexible enough to adapt—and is given the time to do so.

The caveat about time is crucial because evolution can be a slow process. That is why appeals for immediate sacrifice and demands to stop delaying an inevitable day of reckoning are siren songs luring capitalism to its destruction, not bugle calls for its defense. Time, far from "running out" as alarmists always proclaim in the depths of the crisis, is generally on the side of the system. If capitalism can be held together for long enough, it will find a way to adapt and survive. Yet impatient demands for purging and liquidation always dominate public debate at capitalism's moments of crisis. At such times, the attitudes of Andrew Mellon, the notorious U.S. treasury secretary under President Hoover,[4] seem irresistible to the overzealous proponents of free enterprise. These market fundamentalists are actually a greater danger to capitalism than Marxists revolutionaries—and at least as deluded. The common themes of their demands are that capitalism must return to its historic roots, contracts and debts must be implacably enforced, free enterprise must be unshackled, and political interference with market forces must be restrained more rigorously.[5]

Luckily for our societies, this is when democracy intervenes. Market fundamentalist politicians may claim, especially when they are out of government, that capitalism can save itself by reverting to a mythical Golden Age of untrammelled free enterprise. But voters are generally wiser. They realize, if only subliminally, that capitalism survives by moving forward, not backward. And in moments of crisis, voters and practical politicians understand that capitalism needs time to adapt to new conditions. This is why an ultraconservative politician such as George W. Bush committed more money than all previous presidents put together to government interventions in the free market. The scorched-earth economics always demanded by free-market ideologues at times of crisis are rejected, and central bankers ensure that the day of reckoning for past excesses is postponed.

In short, democracy usually offers capitalism a breathing space that allows the system and its institutions to evolve. Capitalism doesn't break because it bends.

What does this approach imply about the crisis that reached its climax in the weeks after the collapse of Lehman Brothers on September 15, 2008? Rather than destroying or permanently crippling the international financial system, as many commentators suggested at the time, this crisis probably marked the start of a fourth great transition in the 250-year history of modern capitalism. Far from suffering extinction, the capitalist system has started evolving into a new species, which will presumably be better suited for life in the early twenty-first century. This process of evolution will transform economics, politics, and business in the years and decades ahead. Part V gives specific examples of these impending changes in politics, business, and economics. It illustrates how this fourth major variant of capitalism, described here as Capitalism 4.0, is likely to be different both from the market fundamentalism of the Reagan and Thatcher period and from the faith in government that beguiled the world from the 1930s until the 1970s.

In speculating about the future, however, it is foolish to make dogmatic predictions. Indeed, a key distinction between Capitalism 4.0 and its earlier variants is likely to be a recognition that the world is a far more complex and unpredictable place than we assumed. Experimentation, rather than certainty, will be the watchword in both political and business life. Intellectual humility and self-doubt, especially among economists and politicians, are likely to be more fashionable in the coming decades than they were in the three decades of market fundamentalist zealotry ushered in by the Thatcher-Reagan revolutions or in the four decades of bureaucratic overconfidence that began with the New Deal.

The emerging worldview of Capitalism 4.0 will need to recognize that the world is too complex and uncertain to be understood, let alone managed, by a naive reliance on markets, as in the last version of capitalism, or by excessive faith in benign and omniscient government, as in the model before. In Capitalism 4.0, experts who claim to divine the future according to immutable economic laws are likely to be dismissed as charlatans, because the one thing we will know for certain about economics and public policy is that nothing is certain.[6]

Moreover, the public may increasingly appreciate that incorrect forecasts about economic growth or financial conditions, and the misguided policies that they inspire, are not always due to the ignorance of economists and other experts or the dishonesty of politicians. Neither is the problem, to quote the standard disclaimer of academic papers, that "more research is required."

Unpredictability is inherent in human behavior, and this is as true in economics as in politics, psychology, diplomacy, or even warfare. It is even more true of financial markets, whose movements depend not just on what will happen in the future but also on what people believe will happen and on how those beliefs, in turn, might affect the behavior of other investors and then reality itself. This complex and unpredictable feedback between reality and beliefs was called "animal spirits" by Keynes and has been elaborated in greater detail by George Soros in his theory of reflexivity.[7] Its consequences for finance, politics, and economics are a key issue throughout this book.

The recognition that the world is intrinsically unpredictable and impossible to control might suggest that Capitalism 4.0 will be a deeply pessimistic era. But this isn't necessarily so, partly because of the systemic adaptability of capitalism and democracy described previously as the Micawber Principle. Another reason why uncertainty need not imply pessimism is a curious feature of economic and political life that might be called the Mad Max Paradox.

The 1979 film *Mad Max* is set in a dystopian future after the collapse of civilization. Violent motorbike gangs roam the Australian outback, fighting for food, weapons, and fuel. The king of these gangs is the vicious Mad Max, played by Mel Gibson, who controls a disused oil depot and munitions dump. I was reminded of this film in March 2009, at almost the exact low point of the financial crisis, in a conversation with a client of my consulting firm, the managing partner of a hedge fund that had just made a billion dollars by betting on the near-bankruptcy of every financial institution in the world. Despite the terrible news from the banks, signs that market sentiment might be turning and sporadic evidence of growth, *green shoots* in Wall Street parlance, were starting to appear in economic statistics. I asked my client what he thought about these green shoots. His response stunned me:

> It took thirty years of madness to create this mess and that's what it will
> take to get out—not months or years, but decades. I saw this building up
> long ago and that made me a billion dollars. So I reckon I understand

what's going on. I may be a farm boy from Texas and I'm no economist, but that billion dollars says I can see the difference between green shoots in a cornfield and green slime on a pile of horse manure.

You know, I don't even bother to look at the figures anymore. Whatever the statistics say, we are looking at ten years of depression, maybe twenty. What interests me is not if this depression will last ten years or twenty; it's whether democratic societies can survive that long. My hunch is they can't.

So I don't care about economic figures or government stimulus plans or ups and downs in the market. What I'm looking for as an investor is the next big thing—maybe the *last* big thing, really, once all this chaos gets to the point of no return. That last big thing, I reckon, will be the U.S. government going bust and the Chinese cashing in their Treasury bonds. When that happens, the dollar goes down the pan and a sack of greenbacks won't buy you a roll of bathroom tissue. So for me, the only things to own today are assets that will keep their value when the dollar and the U.S. government go up in smoke: that's gold, oil, and farmland—plus the guns and ammo to protect them.

As I listened to this tirade, it struck me that my overexcited client differed only in style, not in substance, from many respected commentators, celebrity financiers, and Nobel laureate economists who were appearing during the nadir of the crisis in March 2009 in the world's most serious media—the *Financial Times,* the *Wall Street Journal,* business television, and the BBC. It also struck me that what made this fashionable hysteria so persuasive was also its fatal flaw: the tone of absolute certainty, the simple logic, and the appealing extrapolation of recent events. These are the standard tricks of demagoguery that make dogmatism so convincing and so misleading.

In early 2009 there was another reason why the prophets of doom acquired an irresistible appeal. Not only had the doomsayers apparently been proved right in the terrible autumn of 2008, but some had made fortunes betting on their own grim predictions. In a world that still equated profits with wisdom, this was the rhetorical trump card my Mad Max client threw down as he reached the climax of his diatribe. His superior understanding and foresight had earned him the right to watch the end of civilization from the comfort of his very civilized mid-Manhattan office with its mock Louis Quinze furniture and spectacular view of Central Park. Yet the incongruity of his wealth and his grim forebodings made his argument so absurd. My client had made his money because capitalism was an extremely volatile and unpredictable system. How then could he be so sure that the future was now irrevocably and clearly predetermined?

The private enterprise system, by its nature, guarantees against straight-line extrapolations. Anyone who is certain that events can move in only one direction is almost sure to be wrong. Moreover, even if the Mad Max predictions were plausible, what was a rational way to react?

If the world really was about to implode into anarchy, how would a slight, balding, middle-aged financier with no special skills in martial arts or survival, benefit from hoarding oil and gold? After the breakdown of law and order, his apparent wealth would quickly vanish into the hands of trained commandos and Mafia hit men. The collapse of civilization and a Hobbesian "war of all against all" would bury hedge-fund billionaires along with poorer physical weaklings.[8] If, on the other hand, civilization survived, a billionaire with no military skills but a good nose for financial speculation could hope to make another billion or two. He could continue to play the markets in comfort and rely on the law, the police, and the army to protect his property rights, instead of hoarding his own "guns and ammo." Given this balance of potential rewards, he was clearly irrational to "invest" in the end of civilization, whatever his theoretical analysis suggested. In such extreme conditions, the Micawber Principle that "something will turn up" to save the system is the only reasonable basis for action by businesses and investors, even if no one can predict exactly what *deus ex machina* will appear to save the day.

It struck me that this Mad Max Paradox was really the financial equivalent of Pascal's Wager, the famous utilitarian argument for belief in God invented, with a touch of irony, by the French philosopher and mathematician Blaise Pascal:[9] Suppose that God exists. If you believe in Him, you will be rewarded in heaven and will lead a happier life on earth. If you do not believe in Him, you will suffer eternal damnation and torture. Now suppose that God does not exist. If you believe in him, you will be proven wrong when you die, but this will cost you nothing because you will be dead by the time the truth is revealed. And if you do not believe in Him, you will be proven right, but this vindication will profit you nothing, either in death or in life. The conclusion seems inescapable: It is rational to believe in God, whether or not He actually exists.

The Mad Max Paradox is a far more powerful argument for entire societies than Pascal's wager is for individuals because economic beliefs can change economic and social realities, but religious beliefs cannot affect the existence or otherwise of God. If everyone thinks that the global economic system is doomed and they can do nothing to save it, this belief will itself bring about the anticipated apocalypse—and no one, not even the prophets of doom, will gain anything from their foresight. If, on the other hand, businesses, consumers, and investors all decide that prosperity and growth will resume at some point, the actions they take in accordance with this conviction will help bring about a recovery. Those who believed in the economic system's survival will then be rewarded—as investors, businesses, or employees—while those who ran for the hills will have nothing but their hoards of "guns and ammo." This economic version of Pascal's logic relates to Barack Obama's trademark slogan in the 2008 presidential election: the Audacity of Hope. And it points to a final broad conclusion about the likely zeitgeist of Capitalism 4.0.

Far from paralyzing political action, recognizing uncertainty can be empowering. Suppose we acknowledge that all forecasts are bound to be inaccurate, that public behavior is extremely unpredictable, and therefore that both market judgments and government regulations will sometimes be spectacularly wrong, triggering costly financial crises. At first sight, this seems a counsel of despair, suggesting that all efforts at economic management, investment strategy, and political leadership are futile. But on closer inspection, the opposite is true.

The more uncertain the environment, the greater the need for intelligent leadership and strategic, but flexible, thinking. A proper understanding of uncertainty implies a new kind of interplay between politics and economics, between government and markets, between one-man one-vote and one-dollar one-vote. The last part of this book illustrates some possibilities of such a worldview by looking at how Capitalism 4.0, with its skeptical preference for experimentation over doctrine, and its willingness to steer market incentives to achieve politically determined social ends, could respond to some of the biggest challenges of the coming decades: financial regulation, energy and climate change, the burdens of healthcare for aging populations, and the global competition with China's authoritarian state-capitalism.

In line with the spirit of Capitalism 4.0, the conclusions are optimistic but guarded. All these challenges can in principle be tackled by the creative powers of human ambition, creativity, and the competitive spirit acting through markets but also under the guidance of political forces. In the new model of capitalism, market forces are not merely unleashed, but intelligently harnessed, like all nature's other powerful energy sources.

Capitalism must be allowed to work, but it must also be shaped by politics, though not by the overweening politics of the Social Democratic–New Deal era.

The politics of the future must recognize that capitalism is prone to crises, clouded by uncertainties, and dependent on government support for its survival; but it must also recognize that government decisions are riddled with bureaucratic conflicts, fall prey to entrenched lobbies, and are often motivated by political, not public, interest. To believe in democratic capitalism but also acknowledge its many flaws and contradictions takes a combination of scepticism and intellectual courage that seems to defy logic, especially in moments of crisis. This courage might be called, with apologies to Rev. Jeremiah Wright and Barack Obama, the "audacity of doubt."

CHAPTER TWO

Political Economy
and Evolution

The King is dead. Long live the King!

—Traditional proclamation on the
death of an English monarch

IN THE WINTER OF 2008–09, twenty years after the collapse of communism, capitalism seemed also to be on the brink of collapse. Karl Marx's prediction that capitalism would be destroyed by its own internal contradictions appeared to be coming true. The result was the intellectual equivalent of a nervous breakdown. As all the major banks of America, Britain, and Europe suddenly required government support for their survival, as General Motors was nationalized, and as the personal wealth accumulated in the decade of capitalism's global triumph went up in smoke, believers in free-market ideology were intellectually shattered.

From Presidents Chavez of Venezuela and Sarkozy of France to the editors of the *Wall Street Journal*, everyone agreed that the era of Anglo-Saxon capitalism was over. American conservatives, politically disenfranchised by the crushing defeat of George W. Bush, far from supporting the U.S. government's attempts to save the economy and financial system, formed an unholy alliance with neo-socialists and unrepentant Marxists to declare that free-enterprise capitalism was dead. Instead of the American Century, proclaimed by neo-conservatives a few years earlier, China's rise to global dominance in the decades ahead now seemed as inevitable. Around the world, finance ministers and diplomats prepared to abandon the Washington Consensus presented to developing countries throughout the previous twenty years as the only way to achieve economic progress.[1] The Beijing Consensus was the new buzzword, even if no one was quite sure what it meant.[2] Yet within a few months of the collapse of Lehman and the election of a new American government, it had become obvious that reports of capitalism's death were exaggerated and premature.

Capitalism had not collapsed, banks had not lost the trillions of dollars predicted, and the highly leveraged U.S. and British economies had suffered no more damage than the supposedly prudent Germans and Japanese. So what was the world to conclude as finance returned to normal and economies started to recover? Was it possible that Anglo-Saxon capitalism would survive and might even reestablish its global leadership in defiance of the apocalyptic prophesies? The answer was "Yes and no." And that is still the answer. The rest of this book will show why this answer is neither vacuous nor evasive.

Yes, capitalism will survive and global financial markets will be restored to their precrisis dominance, probably under American leadership. But no, this will not be the same capitalism and the same American leadership that dominated the world for three decades up to 2009.

With the benefit of hindsight, the schoolchildren of the future may be taught that the history of the twenty-first century really started in 2010, after the astonishing financial crisis that transformed global capitalism in 2007–09, just as the history of what we now think of as the twentieth century started after the Great War in 1918, , and nineteenth-century history started in 1815, after Wellington's victory over Napoleon at Waterloo.

Capitalism is an adaptive system. It is formed and reformed by a constantly shifting interaction between an arrow of technological progress and a ring of repetitive financial cycles. As a result, its economic and political arrangements are continually evolving. This is why capitalism, despite its natural propensity to suffer financial crashes, has defied all Marxist, Malthusian, and neo-fascist predictions of terminal crisis—and will doubtless continue to defy them for decades or centuries to come. The irony of capitalism's amazing resilience, however, is that this same ability to mutate keeps subverting the conservative ideologies most zealous in their devotion to each successive variant of the system. These votaries of the social status quo invoke the iron laws of economics to claim apolitical legitimacy for prevailing social conditions, be they wide disparities of income or so-called entitlements to government-financed healthcare and public sector jobs for life. Yet there is nothing objective or permanent about such inherently political arrangements.

Marx was right in believing that capitalism and the "bourgeois democracy" it created are full of internal contradictions. But he misunderstood both history and economics when he jumped to the conclusion that such contradictions would prove to be capitalism's fatal flaw. In fact, the ability to cope with internal contradictions is the greatest strength of the capitalist system. Because capitalism is always in the process of self-destruction, it is always recreating itself and, like a species evolving through natural selection, this protean creature emerges from each mutation stronger than it was before.

Focusing on the evolutionary nature of capitalism draws attention to the inevitability of radical change in political institutions, as well as in economic life. This mutability is the key condition for capitalism's prosperity and long-term survival. Yet politicians, businesspeople, and economists to the right of the ideological spectrum, the people supposedly most dedicated to capitalism's historic triumph, are mostly blind to the most important reason for its success. They extol the virtues of Joseph Schumpeter's process of "creative destruction,"[3] whereby dying industries are replaced by previously unimagined new technologies and managerial systems, but they wilfully ignore the same process of creative self-destruction that renews the system as a whole.

Why should the politico-economic structure of the capitalist system be considered immutable, while its microfoundations are in constant flux? This mystery has never been properly addressed. Why, for example, do conservatives predict that any increase in taxes will destroy all initiative and enterprise, when previous versions of the capitalist system worked quite successfully with taxes that were much higher? And why does the Left proclaim with equal confidence that any reductions in government spending will irreparably fracture society, when many state "entitlements" did not exist in the stable and orderly societies a generation ago? Why do both sides not accept that institutional and political flexibility are natural and necessary features of the capitalist system's evolutionary progress, just as the flexibility of technologies, skills, and managerial practices have been natural and necessary features of capitalism's microeconomic progress, driving the replacement of stagecoaches with jet aircraft, stevedores with telecommuters, and telegraphs with mobile phones? The purpose of this chapter is not to resolve this intellectual puzzle but to examine the flexibility of capitalism's politico-economic arrangements and argue that this has been the key characteristic allowing the system to survive crashes, revolutions, and wars.

Every few decades, the institutions of capitalism have had to be dismantled, carefully examined, and then, where necessary, replaced. The reason why the system has survived the recurrent crises that Marx correctly predicted can be summarized by a simple sentence from the preceding chapter: Capitalism doesn't break because it bends. Specifically, history shows that the capitalist system has experienced big swings in the balance between politics and economics, between the power of government and the power of the market, between one-man one-vote and one-dollar one-vote. These swings can be illustrated by two ideologically opposite examples.

Until the late nineteenth century, the idea of a progressive income tax was widely considered to be incompatible with the basic principles of capitalism and private property rights. In the United States, income tax was declared unconstitutional by the Supreme Court in 1895 and could not be levied by the federal government until the ratification of the Sixteenth Amendment, in 1913. At that point, a top tax rate of 7 percent was applied to incomes above $500,000 (roughly $10 million in today's money). This tax was denounced at the time as an expropriation of property and a threat to the existence of the free-enterprise system.[4] In Britain, the People's Budget of 1909, in which Lloyd George, backed by Winston Churchill, proposed the first progressive income tax in the country's history (with a top rate of 11.25 percent), was considered so revolutionary that it precipitated a constitutional breakdown that led eventually to the Parliament Act of 1911, ending the power of the hereditary House of Lords.[5] Yet despite these apocalyptic contemporary views, few would deny today that the

United States and Britain both survived as capitalist countries after the introduction of income tax. And the few conservative extremists who assert that the United States ceased to be a truly capitalist economy when it adopted progressive taxation must explain the remarkable success of America's crypto-socialist system in the decades after World War II, when even Republican administrations kept income tax rates as high as 91 percent.[6] Some market fundamentalists may maintain that capitalism narrowly survived in the 1950s and 1960s *despite* such handicaps as progressive taxation and the growth of government spending. But the truth is that capitalism has survived *because* of these reforms—not because they were economically beneficial but because they were necessary in specific historical conditions to create the political consensus for the survival of free enterprise.

Now consider an example from the other end of the ideological spectrum. In the 1970s, European advocates of progressive mixed-economy capitalism believed almost unanimously that governments, rather than markets, should be responsible for managing exchange rates, running utilities such as electricity, telephones, and water, and even controlling wages and prices across the economy. The capitalist system was considered too fragile and unstable for such important decisions to be left to unpredictable markets. Yet in the 1980s, politicians all over the world, led by Margaret Thatcher and Ronald Reagan, abandoned these roles, defying warnings that society could not survive such radical reforms. The predicted collapse of society never happened, but for many years, progressives and social democrats continued to believe that the postwar consensus in favor of mixed-economy capitalism only narrowly survived despite deregulation and privatization. As the new market-oriented system prospered, however, it became obvious that the postwar welfare state had survived *because* progressives made the historic compromises involved in privatization, deregulation, and reduction in trade union power.

Systemic transformations in capitalism are, by the hectic standards of financial markets and modern politics, a slow, almost geological, process—so far, three truly fundamental changes have occurred in 250 years. But the correct geological analogy is with seismic, rather than glacial, changes. History shows that systemic evolutions of the kind described generally occur through discontinuous, not gradual, changes.

Andrew Gamble, the Cambridge political scientist, distinguishes between such truly transformative crises *of* capitalism and mere crises *in* capitalism,[7] the regular financial cycles that have produced busts and crashes throughout economic history and have helped to reorganize businesses through Schumpeter's process of "creative destruction." In a crisis *of* capitalism, what is reorganized is not just a group of businesses and industries but the capitalist system itself. Such events are rare and, as Gamble says, "intensely political in nature . . . they become the occasion for far-reaching change both within states and between states. They create conditions for the rise of new forms of politics and policy regimes . . . new institutions, new alignments, new policies, and new ideologies." Gamble points out, consistently with this book's classification, that there were only two such general crises of capitalism since the nineteenth century: in the 1930s and the 1970s. Far from destroying capitalism, as many contemporaries from both ends of the political spectrum had expected, these upheavals "can be seen in retrospect as creating the conditions for [the capitalist system's] renewal, and for a further period of expansion."[8]

The distinction between crises *in* capitalism and crises *of* capitalism, between humdrum cyclicality and extreme instability leading to regime change, is all-important but often overlooked. The question, then, is which kind of crisis occurred between February 2007 and March 2009? Was this upheaval so fundamental that it would alter the entire system? Or was it merely a cyclical event, leading to the reorganization of just one or two industries, for example, house building and international finance?

In the depths of the crisis and for a year or so after, there seemed to be no doubt. Entire libraries could be filled with the books predicting the death of the market system, the demise of America, the rise of China, and so on. But by early 2010, a very different mood had settled on the world. Oddly, the people most convinced of the total collapse of the global economy during the crisis were the ones who migrated fastest to the complacent camp who sneered that nothing much had really changed.

Cynics on the Left started to complain that the crisis had been a non-event because the banks were never nationalized, finance was not tamed, and human greed was not abolished. Like Jehovah's Witnesses or votaries of Nostradamus who keep revising their calculations about the Day of

Judgment, they began to predict that the 2007–09 crisis was merely preparing the way for another even more catastrophic crash—and that this really, truly would be the final crisis that brings the world to an end. The prophets of doom on the Right showed even more chutzpah when their jeremiads proved wrong. Having predicted that the free-market system would be ruined by government interventions and that fiscal stimulus plans were doomed to failure, what did they say when government interventions saved the system and fiscal stimulus revived economic growth? They insisted that unfettered free enterprise had proved its resilience, *despite* all the government interference, and that the postcrisis recovery would have been even stronger if only the politicians had refrained from meddling and allowed markets to solve the problems on their own.

As memories of the crisis recede, will public opinion begin to accept this diagnosis? It seems unlikely. Business and financial lobbies have, of course, regrouped their forces to oppose new regulations and argue that only minor tinkering is needed to restore the free-market status quo. But the economic consequences of the crisis, though less catastrophic than the zealots of the Left and the Right had predicted, have nonetheless proved extremely costly. They will be felt for decades ahead. More importantly, the crisis has shaken deep-seated economic assumptions and political beliefs. A generation who saw their jobs destroyed and their savings almost wiped out by the impending failure of every major bank in the world, can never again rationally believe in unfettered freemarket capitalism and minimal government. It is almost certain, therefore, that 2007–09 will turn out to have been one of the historic crisis *of* capitalism—the kind that creates a new version of the capitalist system. Why call this new version Capitalism 4.0?

Chapter 4 explains in greater detail capitalism's evolution before the crisis went through three broad stages, each initiated by a period of upheaval. Identifying each stage with the politicians or economists who codified and then destroyed it, these three historical stages can be defined as follows:

Capitalism 1: from Adam Smith and Alexander Hamilton to Lenin, Hoover, and Hitler

Capitalism 2: from Roosevelt and Keynes to Nixon and Carter

Capitalism 3: from Thatcher, Reagan, and Milton Friedman to Bush, Paulson, and Greenspan

The most important distinctions between these three phases concern the relationships between politics and economics, between governments and markets, between decision-making on the basis of one-man one-vote and one-dollar one-vote. To oversimplify an oversimplification (a practice with long and distinguished provenance in economics, as discussed in Chapter 11), the three stages of capitalism's evolution thus far can be briefly characterized from the following point of view.

Capitalism 1 lasted from 1776 until the 1920s and went through several lesser variations described in the next chapter as Capitalism 1.0, 1.1, 1.2, and 1.3. This system of social organization treated economics and politics as two almost unrelated spheres of human activity. Its most articulate spokesmen advocated keeping markets and government far apart. But, they also took it as axiomatic that the capitalist economy and polity would rise or fall together. Either both capitalist politics and economics would progress in parallel toward the sunlit uplands of ever-greater prosperity and human happiness, as implied by the optimistic "Whig view of history."[9] Or injustice, poverty, and class wars, which were unavoidable by-products of free markets, would doom both the capitalist economy and polity to collapse and revolution, as communists, fascists, and some pessimistic conservatives of the Malthusian school averred. The idea that the systemic tensions created by unbridled capitalism might be resolved by political reforms effective enough to control class conflict, yet moderate enough to preserve the fundamentals of the private enterprise system, hardly figured in theories of economics, even though pragmatic action to ameliorate the harshest excesses of free markets—slavery, illiteracy, child labor, pauperism, and so on—dominated political debate throughout the nineteenth century. The unifying ideology of this long historic phase, therefore, was that the iron laws of market economics required that government intervention in business activity be strictly a last resort.[10]

This separation of politics and economics ended with Capitalism 2, the social democratic Keynesian approach that started in the Great Depression. Economics became essentially a branch of politics in Capitalism 2, which started with the New Deal of the 1930s, passed through military Keynesianism and ended with the spectacularly successful postwar Golden Age, before disintegrating in the stagflation of the 1970s. The chief theorists and political leaders of this forty-year period assumed that market forces were often wrong and that the single most important function of government was to manage the economy, by taming and controlling unstable market forces.

Capitalism 3, the Thatcher-Reagan monetarist counterrevolution that culminated in the Bush–Greenspan market fundamentalism described in this book as Capitalism 3.3, adopted the opposite approach. Instead of treating economics as a branch of politics, it treated politics as a branch of economics. Its most important leaders believed that governments were usually wrong and always inefficient; therefore markets should be empowered wherever possible to discipline and control venal politicians.

Assuming that the era of market fundamentalism ended with the 2007–09 crisis, what should we expect as the defining characteristic of Capitalism 4? It will probably be a recognition that governments and competitive markets can both be wrong and that the world is too unpredictable and complex to be managed by any immutable institutional structure. This conclusion may seem paralyzing and depressing, but it is actually empowering. If markets and political institutions are both recognized as fallible, the rational response must be a willingness to experiment and a preference for reversible policies and business decisions, initially conducted at a modest scale and in a decentralized way. Luckily, such decentralized experimentation is consistent with both modern technology and social trends. The benefits of small-scale reversible experimentation are already becoming visible in business, social policy, and even diplomacy. The postcrisis transition from the hubristic dogmas of neo-conservative market fundamentalism to the humble scepticism of Capitalism 4.0 should promote and accelerate these trends.

Before imagining how capitalism might evolve in the future, however, we need to look more closely at the present and the past. We have to do this to answer the question left hanging earlier in this chapter: If economic history does progress through once-in-a-generation seismic changes, has the world just witnessed such a sudden break? Part II tries to answer this question by putting some historic and theoretical context around the extraordinary events of 2007–09. To prepare the ground requires a fuller stylized history of capitalism, which the next chapter provides.

CHAPTER THREE

The Four Ages
of Capitalism

The lion, the tiger, and the leopard are three species of the same genus—obviously different and obviously alike.

THE WORD *capitalism* in its modern sense is only 150 years old.[1] But the two human characteristics on which it is founded are universal, stretch back into the mists of history, and explain why efforts to replace the chaos and injustice of the markets with more rational or moral systems have always failed. These two basic human qualities are the competitive spirit (ambition) and the desire for sensual gratification and mastery of the material world (which can be described pejoratively as greed). These instics, however, are not sufficient to define capitalism. Max Weber first noted in *The Protestant Ethic and the Spirit of Capitalism,* there were two additional requirements for modern capitalism's success: social acceptance of profit and wealth accumulation as legitimate and respectable motives for human behavior, as opposed to deplorable, albeit ineradicable, vices; and the recognition of voluntary exchange and cooperation, rather than heredity and coercion, as the main organizing principles of economic life.[2]

These concepts emerged from the Calvinist ideology of the late seventeenth century, according to the standard view of social history pioneered by Weber. But they were crystallized by Adam Smith in *The Wealth of Nations,* producing some astonishingly counterintuitive revelations. Smith

observed that a market economy, although it involves millions of uncon-
nected individuals who work at highly specialized and narrow tasks, is a
naturally self-organizing mechanism provided a few simple rules of commerce and mutual trust are generally obeyed and enforced. This self-
organizing system produces mutually satisfactory outcomes as if it were
guided by an "invisible hand," but without the need for supernatural or divine intervention. And individuals, as long as they act predictably within
this mutually agreed social framework, can satisfy each other's material
needs simply by pursuing their own self-interest. To provide useful services
to other people, we do not need to know them, love them, or anticipate
their desires. As Smith said: "It is not from the benevolence of the butcher,
the brewer, or the baker that we expect our dinner, but from their regard to
their own self-interest."[3]

The miraculous efficiency of the market system, taken for granted
everywhere today, was far from obvious to half of humanity just a few
decades ago, as illustrated by the famous, though probably apocryphal, an-
ecdote about Nikita Khrushchev's first trip to the United States. The Soviet
leader, after visiting some supermarkets in Manhattan and finding them
filled with fresh food, in contrast to the empty shelves of Moscow, turned
to his host, Vice President Richard Nixon, and asked, "Who is responsible
for the supply of bread to New York City? I want to meet this organiza-
tional genius." In *The Company of Strangers*, a brilliant book about the roots
of economic cooperation in the biology of human evolution, the Anglo-
French economist Paul Seabright delightfully describes the wonder that
market forces ought to inspire:

This morning I went out and bought a shirt. There is nothing very unusual
about that; perhaps twenty million people did the same. What is more remarkable is that I, like most of those twenty million, had not informed any-
body in advance . . . Yet the shirt I bought, although a simple item by the
standards of modern technology, is a triumph of international cooperation.
The cotton was grown in India, from seeds developed in the U.S., and the
material in the dyes came from at least six other countries . . . the machinery for cutting it came from Germany and the shirt itself was made up in
Malaysia. The project of making a shirt and delivering it to me has been a

long time in the planning. And yet nobody knew I would be buying a shirt of this kind today . . . If there were any single person in charge of supplying shirts to the world's population, the challenge facing them would bring to mind the predicament of a general fighting a war. One can imagine an incoming president of the United States being presented with a report entitled 'The World's Need for Shirts,' trembling at the contents and immediately setting up [a] Presidential Task Force. . . . The Pope and the Archbishop of Canterbury would issue calls for everyone to pull together to ensure the world's shirt needs were met.

Citizens of the industrialized world have lost their sense of wonder that they can go out spontaneously in search of food, clothing, furniture, and thousands of other useful items and . . . somebody will have anticipated their actions, and thoughtfully made such items available for them to buy. For our ancestors, who wandered the plains in search for game, or scratched the earth to grow grain under a capricious sky, such a future would have seemed truly miraculous, and the possibility that it might have come about without the intervention of any overall controlling intelligence would have seemed incredible.[4]

Adam Smith's pioneering analysis and explanation of this miracle was published in the spring of 1776.[5] By a telling coincidence, it was on July 4 of the same year that the U.S. Continental Congress issued its Declaration of Independence, creating the first self-consciously capitalistic nation—one that was quickly to become the incomparably successful paragon of economic and social progress and eventually to set the standard for political development for all other nations around the world.

To establish the dominance of the broad politico-economic model created by these breakthroughs took forty years of war and revolution—the American War of Independence, the French Revolution, and the Napoleonic Wars. But from the Battle of Waterloo in 1815 onward, the increasingly liberal political and economic systems established in America and Britain spread rapidly to Europe and, by way of the age of imperialism, to the rest of the world. This system of classical imperialist capitalism, underpinned by British and American politico-economic thinking, prospered for roughly one hundred years, until the period of disintegration that started with World War I in 1914 and climaxed with the Great Depression and World War II. This age of classical capitalism could be subdivided into several subperiods, marked out by financial and military crises:

Capitalism 1.0: from 1776, the U.S. Declaration of Independence and *The Wealth of Nations*, to 1815, the defeat of Napoleon at Waterloo

Capitalism 1.1: from 1820 to 1849

Capitalism 1.2: from 1848–49, Europe's Year of Revolutions, the repeal of the Corn Laws, and the Navigation Acts, until the late 1860s, during the aftermath of the U.S. Civil War and the Franco-Prussian War

Capitalism 1.3: from 1870 to 1914, the United States' Gilded Age or the Second Industrial Revolution

Capitalism 1.4: from 1917 until 1932, the period of disintegration, when capitalism came closer to genuine collapse than ever before or since

Some of the upheavals that punctuated the transitions from one of the subperiods to another were bloody and traumatic—for example, the American Civil War and the slaughter of the Paris Commune—but they did not turn out to be systemically transformational crises of capitalism, as described in Chapter 2. Nevertheless, serious historians will justifiably point out that the 150 years from 1776 to 1929 saw more radical political and economic changes than any previous period in human history and thus it is ludicrous to lump them together into a single epoch—and if this were a work of history they would be right. But economics relies on simplifications and stylized facts. And one consistent theme ran through all the politico-economic variations of the nineteenth century and justifies, at least for this discussion, the single label of Capitalism 1.

This entire epoch had in common a clear and unquestionable ideology: a belief that the capitalist system based on private property and the profit motive was an elemental force of nature, governed by iron laws of economics that were as immune to human manipulation as a hurricane or a tidal wave.

The general philosophy of laissez-faire[6]—a belief that economics and politics are two distinct spheres of human activity and emotion that must remain as distinct as possible in the interests of both economic and political progress—was dominant throughout this 150-year period. Government intervention in the economy was quite extensive, mainly through high and variable trade tariffs and excise taxes. These were used not only for raising revenues, but also for what would now be described as protectionist industrial policies to favor influential industries or social interests, such as textile manufacturers or yeoman farmers. But economic thinkers were virtually unanimous in believing that such government interventions were relics of a precapitalist feudal period and were destined to disappear.

Protectionist or paternalistic precapitalism was seen not as a serious long-term rival, but as a temporary roadblock to the onward march of liberalism and free trade.[7] The only alternative to classical laissez-faire capitalism—and one that was viewed seriously as a potential rival—appeared to be the abolition of private property, money, and even mankind's competitive instinct, predicted not only by Marxists but also by anarchist revolutionaries, Utopian Christians, and socialists of many stripes.

In one crucial respect, however, the friends and foes of capitalism were alike. Neither side had any concept of a governmental duty or capacity to create jobs, support private industries, guarantee the soundness of financial institutions, or stabilize economic cycles. To the extent that government impinged on private business, it was as a judicial disciplinarian or sometimes a predatory looter. A strong and well-organized state was needed to enforce contracts and protect private property, but an overweening state would stunt economic progress by favoring politically powerful vested interests and by squeezing private enterprise for revenues to support aristocratic luxury or to fight wars.

For most nineteenth-century thinkers, therefore, government was considered most legitimate when confined to what the French called the regalian responsibilities of the state: justice, lawmaking, and national defense, to which liberal thinkers gradually added the provision of basic education and relief from extreme poverty and physical exploitation.[8] Managing economic activity and employment was emphatically not among these regalian duties—and this disconnect between government and the economy was something everyone could agree on, from bourgeois liberals and conservative oligarchs to Marxist revolutionaries and Utopian social-democrats.

The last, most successful phase of Capitalism 1—and the one that came nearest to the laissez-faire ideal—began around 1870. More precisely, it can be dated from the late 1860s, a remarkable period that witnessed the end of the U.S. Civil War and the abolition of slavery (1865), Britain's Second Reform Act (1867), which dramatically extended voting rights, and the start of the Second Industrial Revolution, a period of dramatic economic acceleration from around 1860 onward, based on the new technologies of electricity, chemical engineering, and petroleum. This triumphant decade of accelerating progress was also, ironically, the age when classical capitalism suddenly seemed under the greatest threat. Despite the technological and social progress, this period also saw an upsurge of anticapitalist thinking and action with the publication of Marx's *Das Kapital* (1867); the foundation of the first American trade union (1869), the Knights of Labor; and the revolutionary uprising of the Paris Commune in 1871.

These social and technological upheavals, far from undermining capitalism, laid the foundation for a period of unprecedented prosperity and peace that Keynes described in a poetic passage suffused with his characteristic blend of irony and affection: "After 1870, there was developed on a large scale an unprecedented situation [of rising living standards and expanding production] . . . In this economic Eldorado, in this economic Utopia, as the earlier economists would have deemed it, most of us were brought up."[9] It is impossible to better Keynes's wistful evocation of capitalism's exuberant spirit in this prelapsarian Golden Age:

What an extraordinary episode in the economic progress of man that age was which came to an end in August, 1914! The greater part of the population, it is true, worked hard and lived at a low standard of comfort, yet were, to all appearances, reasonably contented with this lot. But escape was possible, for any man of capacity or character at all exceeding the average, into the middle and upper classes, for whom life offered, at a low cost and with the least trouble, conveniences, comforts, and amenities beyond the compass of the richest and most powerful monarchs of other ages. The inhabitant of London could order by telephone, sipping his morning tea in bed, the various products of the whole earth, in such quantity as he might see fit, and reasonably expect their early delivery upon his doorstep; he could at the same moment and by the same means adventure his wealth in the natural resources and new enterprises of any quarter of the world, and share, without exertion or even trouble, in their prospective fruits and advantages; or he could decide to couple the security of his fortunes with the good faith of the townspeople of any substantial municipality in any continent that fancy or information might recommend. He could secure forthwith, if he wished it, cheap and comfortable means of transit to any country or climate without passport or other formality, could despatch his servant to the neighbouring office of a bank for such supply of the precious metals as might seem convenient, and could then proceed abroad to foreign quarters, without knowledge of their religion, language, or customs, bearing coined wealth upon his person, and would consider himself greatly aggrieved and much surprised at the least interference. But, most important of all, he regarded this state of affairs as normal, certain, and permanent, except in the direction of further improvement, and any deviation from it as aberrant, scandalous, and avoidable. The projects and politics of militarism and imperialism, of racial and cultural rivalries, of monopolies, restrictions, and exclusion, which were to play the serpent to this paradise, were little more than the amusements of his daily newspaper, and appeared to exercise almost no influence at all on the ordinary course of social and economic life.[10]

As he wrote those words in 1919, Keynes clearly saw that classical capitalism was dying after the mortal blow of the Great War. But even he did not fully imagine how venomous were the serpents that had bred in the lost Eden he evoked. Far more insidious than the monopolies and cultural rivalries he mentioned were the monsters of communism, fascism, and class conflict, fed by the widening inequalities of nineteenth-century capitalism, which finally become intolerable after the shared sacrifices of the World War. As Keynes's bourgeoisie were sipping their tea in bed and chancing their fortunes on foreign ventures, the working classes in the prewar Golden Age were growing restive and then being crushed by Knickerbockers, Special Constables, and Cossacks. During and after the war, they started to fight back in earnest.

Marx had predicted correctly, albeit prematurely, that laissez-faire capitalism would succumb to its internal contradictions, even as it grew stronger. And he had been proved right. The newly enfranchised working classes were organizing in unions and political parties—and where the right to organize legally was denied them, political oppression was inspiring revolutionary movements and anarchist bands. These movements were reinforced and ultimately led, again much as Marx had predicted, by middle-class intellectuals and anarchist romantics repulsed by the crass, inhuman materialism of their age. One of the characteristic media images of the golden period was the caped, black-hatted anarchist with a fizzing bomb under his arm. And this was not just media hysteria, as Keynes's description suggested, because the revolutionary groups of the 1880–1915 period far exceeded in their destructive political impact anything achieved in our age by the terrorists of the PLO, the IRA, or even Al-Qaeda.[11]

By 1914, the classical free-market capitalism of the Victorians was already declining. Never could it return to the happy complacency that Keynes described before World War I and the Russian Revolution. Never could it reverse the growing power of the working classes, the result of democracy and the steady expansion of voting rights.[12] The internal contradictions identified by Marx were moving inexorably toward a systemic breakdown, though how or when this crisis might happen was impossible to predict. In 1919, when Keynes was warning of the economic catastrophe foreshadowed by the Versailles Treaty, the danger was still invisible to less acute observers.[13]

It was not until the financial earthquakes of hyperinflation in Weimar Germany and the Great Depression of the 1930s that the rest of the world began to understand what Keynes was elegantly dissecting in his papers and what communist and fascist radicals had been shouting from the rooftops since 1918: The nineteenth-century politico-economic system was in its death throes. Capitalism had to reinvent itself or become extinct. The system opted for reform and survival.

The new species of capitalism born out of the economic disasters of the interwar period is what I call Capitalism 2. It can be dated from Britain's abandonment of the gold standard on September 21, 1931. It gained strength with Franklin Roosevelt's election as president in November 1932. Its intellectual symbol was Keynes's *General Theory*,[14] whose publication in 1936 crystalized the new economic and political ideas that were gaining influence in the same way that *The Wealth of Nations* had codified the ideas of Capitalism 1 in 1776. And it grew to horrifying force as Hitler revived the German economy from 1933 onward with what can be seen with hindsight as the only wholehearted attempt to implement the policies that Keynes had been vainly recommending to the British government for the previous five years.[15]

This new species of capitalism thrived for roughly forty years and passed through the following four stages:

Capitalism 2.0: from 1931–38, the abandonment of gold and New
   Deal experimentation
Capitalism 2.1: from 1939–45, government-led militarism
Capitalism 2.2: from 1946–69, the Keynesian Golden Age
Capitalism 2.3: from 1970–80, inflation, the energy crisis, and the
   breakdown of the postwar gold-backed currency system

Of the many transformations that occurred in the 1930s, one of the most remarkable and historically resonant was the invention of a heroic government economist. Robert Skidelsky aptly subtitled the second volume of his magisterial biography of Keynes "The Economist as Hero." And soon there were odder juxtapositions: the heroic central banker and the heroic finance ministry bureaucrat. The newfound importance of government economic policy would have been inconceivable to anyone who lived just a few decades before. The interactions between the government and the market in Capitalism 1 had been considered incidental to economic activity and generally damaging to it: Governments needed to raise revenues through tariffs and taxes, mainly for fighting wars. Guilds, landowners, and manufacturers lobbied for tariffs to protect them from low-cost foreign competition. And artisans tried to sabotage factories and mass production. Governments chose sometimes to satisfy such special interests and other times to resist them, but that was the limit of economic politics.

Until the 1930s, almost no one, especially those in the nerve center of the global economy that was nineteenth-century Britain, believed that politicians could or should do anything to improve or stabilize the workings of the market. The cycles of finance and economic activity were treated as forces of nature, which politicians could no more moderate than they could influence the tides. Even the interventions of the Bank of England to quell panics in the money markets were seen mainly as private matters, motivated by the self-interests of the City of London and British finance, rather than a core responsibility of the state.[16] Prime Minister Gordon Brown has described in several speeches a document in the Treasury archives that shows the government's reaction to Keynes's early proposal to lift the British economy out of the Great Depression. His advocacy of what would now be described as demand management was dismissed by the permanent secretary of the Treasury in three scribbled words: *Extravagance, Inflation, Bankruptcy.*[17]

The view that government had no responsibility for macroeconomic conditions such as unemployment changed gradually after the First World War and was transformed by the collapse of global trade and industry in the early 1930s. As public outrage intensified over mass unemployment, the twin threats of socialist revolution and fascist dictatorship forced democratic politicians to engage with the economy in ways that classical economist had never imagined. At the same time, the breakdown of the gold standard suddenly offered governments a freedom of action never imaginable before. "Nobody told us we could do that" was how Sidney Webb, the founder of the London School of Economics and a prominent Labour politician, famously described the sudden sense of liberation for Ramsay MacDonald's government in Britain after its decision to abandon gold in September 1931.[18]

The upshot was that economists, politicians and voters gradually realized that markets and governments were enmeshed in ways that no one had previously understood. This realization led, in turn, to the defining characteristic of Capitalism 2: a belief that capitalism, if unguided by government, was ruinously and intrinsically unstable. Electing benign and competent governments to protect the public and the economy from the inevitable chaos of free markets thus became the most important function of politics, at least in peacetime.

The philosophy that the market was usually wrong, while the government was always right, reached its apotheosis in the Golden Age of Keynesian economics, from 1946 to 1969. This was the most successful period of economic management, in terms of living standards, technological progress, and financial stability, in the history of the world. But like the Edwardian Golden Age eulogized by Keynes in 1919, this "economic Eldorado" also came to an abrupt end.

From the late 1960s onward, the world was hit by a succession of economic crises. Arguably, these started with the inflationary financing of the Vietnam War and Great Society welfare spending under Lyndon Johnson, but other countries, including Britain, Italy, France, and even Germany, also faced severe disruptions, ranging from inflation to assassination and terrorism from the extreme Left and the extreme Right. The deathblows to Capitalism 2 were the breakdown of the international monetary system in 1971, when President Nixon unilaterally closed the U.S. Treasury's "gold window,"[19] and the 1973 Arab embargo, which quadrupled the price of oil. The result was a lethal combination of high inflation and mass unemployment that came to be known as *stagflation,* an economic malady the world had never seen before. By the time of the second oil shock, after the 1979 Iranian Revolution, capitalism faced the same dilemma as it did in the early 1930s: It had to transform itself or become extinct.

What emerged from the wreckage of stagflation was Capitalism 3. This period began with the election of Margaret Thatcher in June 1979, closely followed by Ronald Reagan's election in November 1980 and the taming of inflation by Paul Volcker's application of monetarism in 1981–82. The intellectual inspiration for this great transition came from Milton Friedman and his monetarist followers at the University of Chicago. Monetarism was closely related to other "new classical" economic doctrines, which revived the assumption that free, competitive markets, provided they were not distorted by state intervention, would always keep a capitalist economy in balance, producing efficient and rational outcomes, including economic stability and full employment.

According to modern economic orthodoxy, the fundamental cause of the great inflation of the 1970s was loose monetary policy, especially in America, as Presidents Johnson and Nixon printed money to finance the Vietnam War and the Great Society welfare programs. But many other countries, including Britain, Italy, Germany, and France, experienced even greater turmoil, ranging from inflation and labor unrest to student uprisings, cultural revolutions, and political assassinations, committed by both Left and Right. To explain the crisis of capitalism in the 1970s simply as a consequence of errors in monetary policy is therefore naïve. There were deeper reasons for the great inflation and the breakdown of state-led Keynesian capitalism than the financial profligacy of the U.S. and other governments. Conservative explanations of the breakdown stress the disincentive effects of high taxes, the stifling of private enterprise by overbearing governments, and the militant unions they empowered. Marxist accounts, ironically, emphasize some of the same factors, especially the class conflict and pressure for income redistribution promoted by an increasingly powerful labor movement. Indeed, the great inflation can be viewed more accurately as a symptom of the breakdown of Keynesian capitalism in the 1970s, rather than the cause. Economic theory today treats inflation as a purely monetary phenomenon, determined by the amount of money created by central banks. But there were deep political and sociological reasons why monetary expansion began to produce inflation in the late 1960s, instead of fueling rapid growth of employment and real output, as it had in the previous twenty years.

The Keynesian full-employment policies of the postwar period sowed the seeds of their own destruction. In an economic system built on natural tensions over the distribution of wages and profits between workers and capitalists, unemployment, or at least the fear of unemployment, has a crucial disciplining effect. By the late 1960s , a postwar generation of workers had grown up with no experience of mass unemployment and no memories of the Great Depression. As a result, labor militancy intensified and pay demands escalated; and in an economic system where the top priority of government policy was maintaining full employment, companies felt confident that enough money would be printed to accommodate whatever pay offers were needed to stave off labor militancy and strikes. Inflation was the inevitable result. The only way to stop this inflationary spiral and restore discipline in the labor market was for governments to abandon full-employment policies and create conditions in which millions of workers would lose their jobs. This is exactly what happened after 1979.

The self-destruction of Keynesian full-employment policies was anticipated in 1943, in one of the most prescient economic papers ever published. The Polish economist Michal Kalecki, who had collaborated with Keynes in Cambridge and Oxford in developing the policies that had solved capitalism's crisis of unemployment, argued that this solution would itself create a new crisis of capitalism, triggered by labor militancy and inflation. This inflationary crisis would, in turn, force the capitalist system to reinvent itself again—and economic theory would devise retrospective justifications for whatever new policies the survival of capitalism demanded:

> The assumption that a government will maintain full employment in a capitalist economy if it knows how to do it is fallacious . . . Under a regime of permanent full employment "the sack" would cease to play its role as a disciplinary measure. Continuous full employment would cause social and political changes which would give impetus to the opposition of business leaders . . . The self-assurance and class-consciousness of the working class would grow. Strikes for wage increases and improvements in working conditions would create political tension . . . Popular pressure for jobs would reach its height at or near election times, leading to government-induced preelection booms. The workers would get out of hand and the "captains of industry" would be anxious "to teach them a lesson" . . . A powerful bloc is likely to be formed between big business and *rentier* interests, and they would probably find more than one economist to declare that the situation was manifestly unsound.[20]

The economist found to "declare the situation manifestly unsound" was Milton Friedman. The transition from Capitalism 2 to Capitalism 3 proceeded almost exactly as Kalecki had foreseen. The Thatcher-Reagan political revolution was paralleled by the monetarist revolution in economic theory, and between them they overturned the faith in active government inspired by Keynes. Like the previous phases of capitalism, this new era could be roughly divided into several subperiods:

Capitalism 3.0: from 1979–83, early monetarism and confrontations
   with unions
Capitalism 3.1: from 1984–92, Volcker and Greenspan, Thatcher-
   Reagan booms
Capitalism 3.2: from 1992–2000, the Great Moderation
Capitalism 3.3: from 2001–08, market fundamentalism under
   Greenspan and George W. Bush

This thirty-year epoch started with Thatcherism in 1979 and ended with the crisis of 2007–09. As Capitalism 3 dies out, a new creature, related but distinct, could be seen emerging from the undergrowth and preparing to become the dominant species.

We will consider the characteristics that Capitalism 4 will need to develop to prosper in the new politico-economic landscape in Parts IV and V. But before turning to the development and survival of the new species, let us consider in detail the reasons for the extinction of the previously dominant species. This is the subject of Parts II and III.

Part II

The Arrow and the Ring

ALL GREAT FINANCIAL CRISES begin with the belief that the world has changed forever. They all end with the realization that the change was not what it seemed. A cliché among professional investors is that the four most expensive words in the English language are "This time it's different." But while it is dangerous to ignore the cyclical nature of financial markets, and of human behavior more generally, we must also recognize that the driving forces of economic and business activity—technologies, social structures, and political institutions—can and do change. It is a fashionable conceit, especially in the midst of crises, to claim that the secular trends of historical progress can have no permanent effects on the fundamentals of capitalism: the emotions of greed and fear, the balance between government and business, the speculative behavior of stock market investors, and so on. However, such cynicism is even more deluded than the faddish enthusiasm that imagines every new technological gadget to mark the dawn of a new age. In short, four words even more expensive and foolish than "This time it's different" are "Everything's always the same."

A proper understanding of the dynamics of capitalism requires us to recognize both the long-term trends that change the world and the financial cycles that sometimes exaggerate and overwhelm these secular trends. To put this more graphically, history and economics are driven by a rivalry between what can be called the arrow of progress and the ring of repetition. I choose these metaphors because the arrow and the ring are among the most pervasive symbols in the mythologies of any nation. Every civilization has understood the dualistic interplay between change and permanence, between the male and female principles, between the yang and yin of creativity and preservation. And this creative tension is as much a driving force in politics and economics as it is in every other aspect of human psychology.

Yet this all-important dualism of life and society is rarely mentioned in economic discussions. Instead of trying to understand the interplay between repetition and progress, economists and financiers are typically divided into two mutually hostile camps. Some declare that the lessons of previous experience are irrelevant because the Internet or globalization or the credit-crunch has changed everything: Technology shares will rise to infinity; all the goods in the world will be made in China; credit will contract or expand forever. Others insist that all cycles are the same. The boom-bust cycle in housing was essentially the same as the speculation in technology stocks in the 1990s, the Japanese bubble in the 1980s, and Tulipmania in seventeenth-century Holland. But why should we adopt either of these extreme views?

Some features of human life do permanently change history, for example, the abolition of slavery, the invention of antibiotics, or the harnessing of electricity or computer power. Others, ranging from love and hate to financial panic, are repeated in every generation with uncanny precision. Only by thinking about *both* the arrow of progress and the ring of repetitive behavior can we understand how they interact to create the risks and opportunities of economic life.

In the specific case of the 2007–09 crisis, we can see how several genuinely unprecedented trends dating to the late 1980s coincided with a powerful, but not unusual, financial cycle. This overlay of cycle and trends produced a boom until 2006. This boom was followed by a cyclical bust that was amplified by a series of extraordinary policy blunders (described in Chapters 9 and 10) and led to the near-destruction of the world capitalist system in the autumn of 2008. Contrary to predictions, however, the system did not collapse, because the next phase of the cycle, again interacting with long-term uptrends that had been forgotten during the period of panic, created the conditions for a rebirth and evolution of capitalism in 2010 and beyond.

Because economics is driven by both secular trends and cyclical patterns, we need to start by looking at both sets of forces separately and then consider how they interact. Only in this way can we properly understand why recent events happened and where they may lead.

CHAPTER FOUR

Annus Mirabilis

Why did I free Nelson Mandela in February 1990? Because of the Berlin Wall. Once Communism collapsed in 1989, I felt sure that the ANC would abandon its revolutionary aspirations. This meant we had a chance to negotiate a peaceful end to Apartheid.[1]

—F.W. de Klerk, president of South Africa, 1989–94

You ask me why India broke out of the Hindu rate of growth in 1991. It is quite simple really. When we saw what happened to the Soviet Union in 1989, we realized that our reliance on central planning had been an historic mistake. The only alternative was to liberalize the economy. We started to do that in 1991.[2]

—Jaswant Singh, foreign minister and finance minister of India, 2004–06

IN SEPTEMBER 2006, at the Annual Meeting of the World Bank and International Monetary Fund (IMF) in Singapore, the IMF's chief economist, Ranghuram Rajan, presented probably the most optimistic *World Economic Outlook* in this august institution's sixty-year history.[3] Unaware that the first tremors of the 2007–09 crisis were about to shake the world economy just six months later, in February 2007, he began his presentation with a self-deprecating joke: "I have been told to smile more often. Now, since my natural disposition is to be serious, I might seem a little schizophrenic. But this in a sense accords well with the state of the outlook."[4]

Dr. Rajan's cheerful schizophrenia was understandable. The surest way to be taken seriously as an economist is always to predict disaster, regardless of what is going on. Finance ministers are expected to be dour and stingy. Central bankers pride themselves on their pessimism and repeat as often as possible their sadomasochistic catchphrase: "I am paid to worry." Although economics was invented by Adam Smith as an optimistic study of the boundless possibilities of human freedom and its ability spontaneously to create prosperity, by the early nineteenth century its reputation had changed. Economics came to be viewed as a miserly obsession with money and a devotion to everything in Victorian society that was destructive of the human spirit. Its symbols were the "dark satanic mills" of William Blake, the sadistic workhouses of Dickens, the hypocritical bourgeois of Balzac, and the starving match girl of Hans Christian Andersen. No wonder economics was nicknamed "the dismal science."[5] This miserable view of economics was pithily summarized by J. K. Galbraith in 1977: "We all agree that pessimism is a mark of superior intellect."[6]

Yet this cynical conventional wisdom about the fundamental nature of economics, as well as about the capitalist system economics seeks to understand, is wrong. Most great economists—Smith, Ricardo, Mill, Keynes, Schumpeter, and Hayek—had an optimistic outlook about human creativity and the capacities of the market system. They were fundamentally optimistic for both practical and intellectual reasons.

The main intellectual goal of economics set out by Adam Smith, and partly achieved by him in *The Wealth of Nations*, was to explain the miracle that led millions of unrelated individuals, all working freely in pursuit of their own desires and personal interests, to serve the needs of others and promote the prosperity of all. After Smith, other great economists enriched this understanding with unexpected and counterintuitive detail. Ricardo showed how nations could benefit from free trade even if it seemed initially to hurt many of their businesses and workers. Mill showed how spreading prosperity to the working class could serve the interests of business, even though profits might appear to be squeezed by higher wages. Keynes showed how slumps could be avoided, even when companies and consumers lacked the confidence and financial wherewithal to invest and spend. Schumpeter showed how the destruction of some industries would lead to the creation of others that would create better products and more jobs. Hayek showed how the "spontaneous order" of an apparently chaotic market system would always be better at serving humanity than the calculations of central planners armed with the most powerful computers.

Even more amazing than this intellectual history, and a better reason for economists to smile, was the market system's practical success in satisfying material needs and desires. The advances in living standards, nutrition, education, health, and every other indicator of human well-being during the 250-year ascendancy of market economics could be described as the human achievement in history. Later chapters return to some of the unwelcome by-products and social costs of this wealth creation—environmental damage, wars for resources, social inequality, and so on. But judged by its own materialistic standards, the reign of market economics has been a spectacular triumph. This long-term triumph of global wealth creation has been interrupted by financial crises and wars, but in the early years of the twenty-first century, just before the 2007–09 financial crisis, there appeared to be more reasons for confidence in the unstoppable growth of the global economy than ever before.

This brings us back to why Dr. Rajan was smiling in 2006. Why wasn't he fretting, as usual, about the risks of a global recession and reiterating the IMF's standard denunciations of profligate governments, unsustainable trade deficits, and the crushing burdens of consumer debt? It is tempting to say with hindsight that Dr. Rajan and his IMF colleagues, along with all the other well-paid economists who failed to predict a financial disaster, were stupid or blinded by dogma or hog-tied by institutional interests. There is some justice in such claims, as discussed in Chapter 11. However, a more important reason why so many well-informed experts were so misled about the outlook was that the world economy genuinely was in remarkably good shape just months before the crisis erupted.

As Dr. Rajan explained to that IMF meeting in late 2006, economic activity all over the world was expanding briskly but not too strongly; inflation and interest rates were stable; employment and incomes were rising; and these healthy trends seemed set to continue almost wherever one looked around the globe, even in the recently war-torn depths of sub-Saharan Africa. Moreover, the reasons for this remarkable performance seemed clear.

Most economists had long been enthusiastic about free trade, globalization, and technological progress, but the benefits of these forces were usually hedged with warnings about the concomitant risks of financial leverage, economic instability, job insecurity, and so on. In the years leading up to the crisis, however, the evidence appeared to be mounting that the technological and structural advances of the preceding decade were generating even greater benefits than expected, and doing so with rather lower costs. Thus, when the IMF's researchers considered the familiar long-term hazards in the global outlook—the trade deficits in America (and to a lesser extent in Spain and Britain), the danger of boom-bust cycles in housing, the threats to financial stability from speculators and hedge funds—they concluded that these risks were all *less* disturbing than they had appeared a year or two before. Hence, the smiling faces in Singapore in September 2006. How differently economies—and IMF physiognomies—were going to look just twelve months later!

The fact is that the arrow of progress was soaring higher than ever in the months just before the crisis. Why was this so? The rest of this chapter and the next two will try to answer this question. Chapters 7 and 9 will then explain how the ring of financial cyclicality, spinning relentlessly in the background, suddenly brought the arrow down to earth. Part III will show how the combination of these cyclical and secular forces interacted with the political ideology of Capitalism 3.3 to trigger a crisis of a kind never seen before.

Five vast and irreversible changes transformed the world in the two decades before the crisis, starting in the pivotal year of the late twentieth century—the *Annus Mirabilis* of 1989. The reason for choosing this starting point will be obvious from the first of these transformations.

One, the seventy-year experiment with communism came to an end in November 1989, when the Berlin Wall was demolished. Even more important than the physical break-up of the Soviet bloc was the ideological collapse of Marxism as a political doctrine and of central planning as an idea for organizing economic activity without markets. From 1989 onward, all nations, regardless of their political institutions, their stage of development, or their local traditions, were forced to acknowledge private property, the profit motive, and the voluntary exchange of goods and services through competitive markets as the only plausible basis for economic life. As revealed by the epigraphs to this chapter, the aftershocks from this sudden and unexpected implosion spread far beyond the Soviet bloc—to India, China, South Africa, and every country and political movement that had been beguiled by the deceptive logic of socialist delusions.

Two, Asia, and especially China, emerged as a significant part of the global economy. In theory, China's gradual transformation into one of the most fiercely competitive and profit-oriented systems of private enterprise the world had ever seen began with Deng Xiaoping's introduction of "Socialism with Chinese characteristics" in 1978.[7] However, these reforms only began to deliver impressive results about a decade later, in the late 1980s, turning China into a serious commercial power, transforming the global trading system, and shifting the center of gravity of the world economy toward Asia.

Three, a technological revolution accelerated in the late 1980s and did for human memory and intelligence what the steam engine and electricity did in the nineteenth century for muscle power. In March 1989, Tim Berners-Lee, a British physicist working at the CERN laboratory in Geneva, wrote a proposal for a "world wide web" of documents written in a standardized "hypertext language" that would reside on computers dotted around the world and communicating through phone lines with what he called "browsers." Berners-Lee predicted that his world wide web would quickly allow "the creation of new links and new material," making "authorship universal" for computer users everywhere. In addition, in the late 1980s and early 1990s, the time and cost of data processing and global communications was reduced to virtually zero by the ubiquitous adoption of personal computers.[8] As a result, by the early 1990s, communication, data storage, and computer processing had become almost free goods. Parallel though less spectacular improvements in air and sea transport technologies reduced the cost of long-distance physical communication for goods and people to about one-third their level in the 1950s.[9]

Four, the end of the Cold War produced a "peace dividend," substantially reducing defense spending in America, Europe, and the Soviet Union. More importantly, the peace dividend seemed to confirm a new era in which global wars were out of the question. The World Wars of the first half of the twentieth century had consumed or directly destroyed much of the physical wealth created by three successive generations. As a result, each of these generations was forced to save a large share of its income to invest in the reconstruction of houses, factories, and physical infrastructure that their parents had destroyed. The postwar baby boom generation suffered no such depredations—and the dismantling of the Berlin Wall implied that no such disaster was going to occur in the near future. Even localized wars became far less likely after the end of proxy conflicts in Africa and southeast Asia between the United States and Soviet Union. Meanwhile, the declining value of natural resources and farmland, especially in comparison with the products of technology and intellectual property, reduced the economic incentives for territorial expansion. The one aberrational case, when such territorial expansion was attempted—Saddam Hussein's invasion of Kuwait in August 1990—was quickly reversed by an international community showing unprecedented unity. With homes, factories, and roads no longer threatened by military destruction, the habits of saving and frugality imposed on previous generations by the needs of postwar reconstruction, receded into the past.

Five, the demystification of money was a less widely noticed but equally unprecedented event. This process began with the collapse of the Bretton Woods international currency system in 1971. On August 15, 1971, President Nixon closed the "gold window," where the U.S. Treasury had always stood ready, at least in theory, to convert into gold any dollars presented by foreign governments. Because the dollar had become the sole standard of value for all currencies—even in Communist countries such as China, Russia, and Cuba—after World War II, the decision to sever its official link with gold was momentous. For the first time in five thousand years of recorded history, every country in the world was now using pure paper money that was not linked to gold, silver, land, slaves, salt, cowrie shells, or any other "natural" or God-given standard of value. This unprecedented event transformed the global economy in ways that no one understood at the time—and which are still not fully appreciated forty years later. It deserves a longer explanation.

While most nations had abandoned their gold standards during the depression of the 1930s, they all did so reluctantly and as a temporary measure. After the war, as part of the settlement agreed by the allied powers at the Bretton Woods Conference in 1944, all national monies, even those of the communist countries, were linked to the dollar and, hence, at least in theory, to gold. If a peasant in China or a miner in Britain wondered why his yuan or pound note had any value, he could be assured by his government that it was worth an equivalent sum in dollars and thus in gold. After August 1971, this concept of value no longer applied.

From that day onward, anyone who asked why a dollar bill was worth more than the paper it was printed on could not get a satisfactory answer. The dollar was valuable because the U.S. government said it was. As the text on the dollar bill declares, "This note is legal tender for the settlement of all debts public and private." But the debts to be settled were themselves denominated in paper dollars, so the concept of value was circular, dependent solely on the U.S. government's assertion, or fiat. In Britain, the curlicue text on a five-pound note made this circularity even more obvious: "I promise to pay the bearer on demand the sum of five pounds," the governor of the Bank of England states on the note. But what would "the bearer" receive if he went to the Bank of England to redeem this "promise"? Nothing more than a choice between another identical five-pound banknote or five single-pound coins.

After the dollar had become a pure paper currency, representing nothing more than the fiat of the U.S. government, the idea that other currencies could acquire some intrinsic value by linking to the dollar lost its allure. Every form of money in the world was now an abstract symbol of confidence in the government that ordered its issue. No currency anywhere in the world represented an objective kind of value. This situation had never existed before—and its economic consequences were vast. As governments realized that they had broken their age-old servitude to gold, silver, or another externally imposed financial standard (such as the dollar), their initial confusion was quickly replaced by a sense of astonished liberation. In principle, any government could now print any amount of money at will. Not surprisingly, the initial result was an outbreak of inflation that greatly aggravated the fear and confusion that had started to haunt financial markets in the late 1960s and this escalated steadily throughout the next ten years.

By the late 1980s, however, governments in the main advanced economies had become surprisingly responsible with their newfound monetary freedom—inspiring a degree of faith in pure paper money that no one would have imagined possible when the gold link was abandoned in 1971. In the United States, the arrival of Ronald Reagan at the White House and Paul Volcker at the Federal Reserve reduced inflation to moderate levels by 1982, and the skillful handling of the 1987 stock market crash by Volcker's successor, Alan Greenspan, inspired tremendous confidence in the Fed's monetary management. An even clearer symbol of the burgeoning belief in paper money was the upsurge of confidence in the German mark and the Japanese yen, which culminated in two of the most extraordinary events in economic history, both occurring in 1989.

European governments resolved in the Delors Report of April 1989 and at the subsequent Rome Summit to create a synthetic new currency, the euro, which would derive its value neither from gold nor the fiat of any sovereign government, but merely from the reputation of Europe's central bankers. The staged progress toward the European Monetary Union, which began in 1990, was initially greeted with skepticism but quickly gained credibility in the financial markets. Even more remarkable was the worldwide faith in Japan's yen. This produced the greatest financial boom in history, which climaxed in December 1989. Such was the world's demand for the trillions of paper yen flying off the Bank of Japan's printing presses that the garden of the Emperor's Palace in Tokyo was calculated in 1989 to be worth more than all the land in California.[10] The Nikkei share index, which peaked on December 31, 1989, at 39,000, had become so overvalued that twenty years later it was still 75 percent below the levels it had reached in that fateful year. These figures, incidentally, illustrate a point we will come to later: The U.S. housing and mortgage boom, by the standards of history's great financial bubbles, was actually a modest affair.

The incredible bull markets that occurred in 1989 in all sorts of paper assets confirmed something that would have been unthinkable to politicians and economists of previous generations. Less than twenty years after President Nixon severed the link between gold and the dollar, the world had learned to manage successfully a system of pure fiat money of a kind that had never existed before. In the 1920s, Keynes had denounced the global monetary system's dependence on gold as a "barbarous relic," but even he never imagined that governments would be liberated completely from this age-old servitude and freed to print paper money, unconstrained by international agreements or external disciplines of any kind.

Rightly or wrongly—and we will return to the pros and cons of pure fiat money in Chapters 6 and 15—the demystification of money from the late 1980s onward offered governments a new ability to manage (or mismanage) their national economies. The world's learning experience with pure fiat money, which started with the breakdown of Bretton Woods in 1971, took almost twenty years to complete. By the time this learning process was finished in the late 1980s, money had been transferred from the divinely ordained realm of nature and turned into a pure human construct, subject to political control. This revolutionary demystification of money did to economic policy what the French Revolution did to state religion. As in the case of political secularization, the transformation of money from a mysterious natural substance created by God into a mundane human artifact churned out by printing machines was an earthquake that reverberated for decades. Along with the other great historic transformations that converged in the Annus Mirabilis of 1989, the unexpected triumph of paper money was still shaking the world twenty years later. Between them, these irreversible, once-and-for-all events created powerful and long-lasting economic trends that ultimately set off the financial crisis of 2007–09. This is the story the next chapter takes up.

CHAPTER FIVE

The Four Megatrends

Basic change is the result of a confluence of forces, rarely just one force. Al-
ways ask yourself if there are enough different forces pushing in the same
direction before you make a judgment.[1]

—John Naisbitt

THE WORD *megatrend* was coined in 1982 by John Naisbitt, an Ameri-can management consultant and best-selling author, to describe some of the irreversible structural changes that he expected to transform the re-maining years of the twentieth century. Although such "futurology" is fash-ionably derided in sophisticated economic circles, Naisbitt's main arguments—about shifts from industrial to information societies, from na-tional economies to a unified global economy, and from hierarchical busi-ness organizations to networking—turned out to be broadly correct.[2] Certainly, the efforts to identify qualitative structural changes made by self-styled futurists such as Naisbitt and Alvin Toffler[3] offered far better guid-ance about events in the last two decades of the twentieth century than the supposedly scientific forecasts of academic economists and official institu-tions such as the IMF, World Bank, and OECD. In the rest of this chapter, the word *megatrend* will therefore be used without further apology, even though it will provoke condescending smirks.

From 1989 onward, the apparently distinct and one-off events described in the last chapter, began to interact in four powerful and enduring trends.

These trends dominated the global economy for the subsequent two decades and will probably continue to do so for several more decades, perhaps even generations. The four megatrends discussed in this chapter and the next two are as follows.

One, 3 billion new consumers, producers, and savers joined the global capitalist system from the late 1980s onward, roughly doubling the potential size of the world economy and vastly increasing its potential growth rate for decades ahead. What set off this dynamic megatrend was the interaction between three historic events described in the last chapter—the breakup of the Soviet bloc, the opening up of China, and the end of proxy wars between communism and capitalism in the developing world. The result was that almost the entire world's population found their lives guided for the first time by the invisible hand of market forces, instead of being ruled by the iron fists of communism and feudalism or the clumsy robotic grip of central planning.

Two, globalization transformed almost every economic activity in every country, as the principles of market competition, private enterprise, and free trade won universal acceptance after the breakdown of central planning and state ownership. In effect, the entire world economy started moving toward a NAFTA-style free trade area, if not quite a European-style single market. As this policy change interacted with the new technologies of zero-cost communications and cheap transport, the classical economic principles of specialization and comparative advantage began to operate with unprecedented effectiveness across the world. The result was an upsurge of productivity growth and wealth creation, especially in China and other previously backward Asian countries. This process of globalization transferred many manufacturing industries from the advanced economies to the developing world, vastly increasing the world's productive capacity. This transfer of industrial activity made the world economy more prosperous but also more stable, for the reasons described in the next chapter.

Three, the Great Moderation—a period of unprecedented stability in inflation, unemployment, and economic cycles—created twenty years of almost continuous growth throughout the world economy that lasted right up to the recession of 2008–09. As the world began to recover from the recurrent crises of the 1970s and learned to live with pure fiat money, governments and central banks gained previously unimagined freedom to manage their economies and stabilize both inflation and unemployment. Policymakers gradually reverted to the active demand management that had been abandoned in the monetarist counterrevolution described in Chapter 11. Moreover, globalization stabilized the world economy by suppressing inflation and shifting many volatile manufacturing industries from America and Europe to China and other emerging economies. This transfer of industry made advanced economies less susceptible to inventory and capital investment cycles, but it also helped to stabilize emerging economies by reducing their dependence on subsistence agriculture, the most volatile industry of all.

Four, a financial revolution resulted from the adoption of a free-market philosophy, the buildup of savings in the rapidly growing Asian economies, and the stability created by globalization and successful demand management. With risks of bankruptcy and unemployment diminished in the stabilized economies of the 1990s, businesses and consumers felt that they could borrow more than ever before and banks were more willing to lend. Meanwhile, the demystification of money meant that debt ceased to be a moral or theological issue and became just another consumer product. Financial innovation also meant that savings previously locked up in property and other illiquid assets could be used as collateral to support consumer and business borrowing. This attractive new feature of property, summed up in the saying "my home is an ATM machine," led to an increase in the value of homes in relation to other more traditional investments such as stocks and bonds. The result of this revolution was that ordinary homeowners and small businesses gained opportunities to smooth their spending over their entire lifetimes and to manage their finances in ways that had been available only to large multinational companies and wealthy family trusts. This financial revolution was responsible for the boom-bust cycle that exploded in the 2007–09 crisis, but the changes in traditional attitudes to debt, in property values, and in views about reasonable levels of borrowing are unlikely to be fully reversed even after the crisis.

The first two of these four megatrends—the emergence of three billion new capitalists, both producers and consumers, in Asia and the unification of the world economy into a single market—have been discussed at length in many excellent studies, such as Martin Wolf's *Why Globalization Works*.[4] The transformative power of the other two megatrends, by contrast, has not been as widely recognized. In fact, the most enthusiastic chroniclers of globalization and the rise of Asia, such as Wolf, have mostly failed to grasp the intricate links between these two megatrends and the parallel revolutions in financial markets and monetary policy. The next two chapters will look in detail at these less familiar issues. The theme in the background of this discussion will be the way that all four global megatrends were mutually reinforcing, first in creating the period of remarkable economic stability that came to be known as the Great Moderation and then snapping back with a vengeance in the crisis of 2007–09.

CHAPTER SIX

The Great Moderation

Practice moderation in all things, including moderation.[1]

—Gaius Petronius

THE GREAT MODERATION was the title chosen by Ben Bernanke for a speech he delivered in February 2004. The speech was given to celebrate and explain the U.S. economy's escape from what had been widely expected to be a serious and prolonged recession, following the boom and bust in technology shares. His speech began with this sentence: "One of the most striking features of the economic landscape over the past twenty years or so has been a substantial decline in macroeconomic volatility."[2] These words continued to ring true right up to the bankruptcy of Lehman on September 15, 2008.

Bernanke's speech built on the work of two MIT economists, Olivier Blanchard and John Simon, who in 2001 decided to investigate economic volatility in the postwar period.[3] They found that industrial output and employment had become much less variable since the mid-1980s. Economic volatility had fallen by half in relation to the period before 1980, while the variability of inflation had been reduced by two-thirds. What explained this sudden macroeconomic stability? This was the main question Bernanke raised in his speech and went on to answer:

"Three types of explanations have been suggested for this dramatic change; for brevity, I will refer to these classes of explanations as structural change, improved macroeconomic policies, and good luck. . . . Explanations of complicated phenomena are rarely clear-cut and simple, and each of the three classes of explanations I have described probably contains elements of truth. Nevertheless, sorting out the relative importance of these explanations is of more than purely historical interest."

Not surprisingly, Bernanke gave priority to his second explanation—the improvement in the policies of the Fed and other central banks. But before focusing in detail on this argument, which relates to the last two megatrends described in the preceding chapter, it is worth considering a less familiar change that was brought about by globalization and whose supporting role in the Great Moderation has been underplayed. Had this structural change been fully appreciated by policymakers around the world and by academic economists, some of the predictions about the end of globalization that followed the collapse of Lehman might have sounded less apocalyptic.

The Platform Company: A New Business Model

A fact that corporate managers long ago recognized, but macroeconomists still disregard, is the way that interactions of free trade and free communications transformed the business models of large international companies, first in the United States, later in Britain and Europe.

As trade grew by leaps and bounds and Asia opened up for business from the mid-1980s onward, multinational companies became increasingly aware that globalization was changing the way their businesses created the wealth that produced profits for the shareholders and wages for the employees. Broadly speaking, the *value chain* in any business consists of three links—first, the conception and design of a product or service; second, its manufacture or preparation; and third, its marketing and distribution. Traditional management models emphasized the second link in this chain—the manufacturing process—as the point where successful businesses generally located their key competitive advantage. The classic example in the preglobalization economy was Henry Ford. His ability to build cars more cheaply and quickly than anyone else created a multinational manufacturing business that conquered the world.

But globalization and communication technology transformed this analysis. As these megatrends intensified, the production part of the value chain became the link that was most susceptible to low-cost competition from emerging markets. As a result, manufacturing for many businesses became a losing proposition. As American, British, and European companies watched the profits from their manufacturing operations squeezed by international competition, their solution was to outsource these operations to emerging markets. Over time, many basic nonmanufacturing activities, such as bookkeeping and routine customer relations, experienced the same fate.

When companies decided to outsource, they converted from multinationals, such as Ford or Exxon, which sell everywhere and produce everywhere, into what the French economist Charles Gave has dubbed Platform Companies. These are businesses such as IKEA, Nokia, Apple, and Nike, which sell everywhere but seem to produce nowhere.[4] The essence of the Platform Company, or Platco, is that it no longer sees its core competence as the middle part of the value chain, production. Instead, these companies create platforms for the products they design, which they then buy cheaply from factories in emerging markets. The Platcos then profitably distribute these products, bought from low-cost manufacturers, to relatively affluent consumers, first in America and Europe but also increasingly in the emerging world.

This process of outsourcing is familiar and platitudinous in business-school management models, but its macroeconomic implications have been less widely discussed. The most obvious implication is the way that outsourcing has helped control inflation—not just because goods made in China or Mexico are less expensive, but also because the transfer of production to these low-cost countries has broken the power of labor and intensified competition within the United States and Europe.

A second consequence of the Platform Company model has been to reduce the significance of global trade statistics. As more businesses transform themselves into Platcos, the visible part of the value chain—manufacturing—appears as a trade deficit for countries such as the United States and Britain, which took the lead in this managerial transformation. On the other hand, the "invisible" value—design, technology transfer, managerial know-how, and customer servicing—is frequently lost in the internal accounting of global purchasing contracts designed to maximize financial flexibility and minimize corporate taxes.[5] Yet these invisible parts of the value chain are often far more profitable than visible manufacturing, as well as a source of better paid and steadier employment. A $1,000 computer made in China, for example, will register as a $1,000 debit in the U.S. import statistics, but most of this value will flow back to America through the profits and royalty receipts of Apple, Intel, or Microsoft.[6] Depending on how the internal accounting at Apple, Intel, and Microsoft treat these profits and royalties, they could appear in the statistics as U.S. service exports, be omitted for many years from the trade figures, or even be classified as loans from the Chinese subsidiaries of these companies back to their parents in the United States.

The third and most important macroimplication of the new business model, has been the unexpected contribution made by Platform Companies to economic stability, as well as to growth. Linking globalization to economic stability may seem absurd. The public usually associates globalization with job insecurity, factory closures, and general economic angst. However, globalization is one of the most important reasons for the steady reduction in economic volatility that Bernanke mentioned but never explained in the introduction of his speech on the Great Moderation.

Platform companies have generally outsourced the parts of the production process that involve the greatest volatility: heavy capital spending, physical inventories of materials and finished goods, and unionized industrial employment. The outsourcing of capital and labor resulted in the outsourcing of a large amount of economic volatility from the United States and Europe to the Third World. This was not, however, a zero-sum game because the globalization process enabled developing countries, most obviously China, to transform themselves with amazing and unprecedented speed into industrial, rather than agricultural, economies. While they imported industrial volatility from America and Europe, developing countries reduced the overall instability of their economies by becoming less dependent on primitive farming—the most unreliable business. Gone are the days when the probable strength of the monsoon was the most important issue economists had to ponder when they tried to forecast India's GDP growth.

That the stabilizing effect of Platcos is not just a hypothetical speculation is suggested by the calculations on volatility quoted by Bernanke in his speech. The clear decline in industrial volatility from the mid-1980s was a near-universal phenomenon among industrial countries, with just one exception. That was Japan—the advanced economy in which the Platform Company model was most strongly resisted and industrial outsourcing to emerging markets was for many years a managerial taboo.

Having established how globalization contributed to the remarkable stability of employment and output in the two decades before the 2007–09 crisis, we can now return to Ben Bernanke's most important claim about the Great Moderation: that the main reason for economic stability from the mid-1980s onward was the skilful management of monetary policy by the Fed and other central banks. This was almost certainly true, but not in the way claimed by Bernanke and other policymakers.

The Reinvention of Demand Management

The main argument presented by Bernanke in his speech was that the Fed's success in maintaining low inflation from around the early 1980s onward was the key to the stability of the U.S. economy and the world. But observing central bankers' behavior, as opposed to their rhetoric, suggests that this is only half the truth. The Fed and other central banks were not only targeting and achieving low inflation but also doing something more important and controversial, at least in the worldview of Capitalism 3. They were doing something forbidden by the monetarist prescriptions that they were claiming to follow from 1979 onward. They were using interest rates not just to control inflation, as required by the monetarist orthodoxy, but also, quite consciously and deliberately, as a tool to minimize unemployment and promote economic growth.

According to the monetarist doctrine, a central bank that solely targets inflation will, by doing this, indirectly stabilize unemployment. By contrast, a central bank that aims to stabilize unemployment directly, as recommended by the Keynesian approach, is committing a mortal sin. This difference may now be dismissed as a pedantic quibble, as Capitalism 4.0 takes shape and the monetarist orthodoxy of the Thatcher-Reagan generation is replaced by more pragmatic and eclectic views of macroeconomics. But in trying to explain why the world economy suddenly settled into a period of unprecedented stability from the early-1990s onward—and also why, despite all the apocalyptic prophecies during the crisis, this Great Moderation is likely to return now that financial systems have been stabilized—the distinction between what central bankers such as Bernanke were saying and what they were doing is all-important.

Moreover, in the aftermath of the 2007–09 crisis, with inflation at a satisfactory level and showing no signs of accelerating or falling, it is critical to know whether governments and central banks will set policies merely to stabilize inflation—and hope for the best in terms of unemployment and economic activity—or take positive action to stimulate job creation and growth.

We saw in Chapter 3 that during the last great transition of capitalism, from the government-led Keynesian Golden Age of the postwar years to the market fundamentalist era of Reagan and Thatcher, a dramatic change occurred in economic thinking. The monetarist orthodoxy, which insisted that the only legitimate role of government in macroeconomic management is to control inflation, was not just an optional intellectual bagatelle but the most essential part of the new ideology that created a social and political revolution.

The political revolution led by Reagan and Thatcher would have been impossible without the parallel revolution in economic thinking—or rather the counterrevolution, as the monetarists described it, arguing that the Keynesians of the 1930s were the misguided and illegitimate revolutionaries who had subverted the sound economic ideas of nineteenth century classical capitalism. Monetarist theory was ideologically vital because the exclusive focus on inflation it recommended had an important political corollary: Societies would have to learn to tolerate whatever unemployment levels the markets dictated. Any attempt by central banks or governments to stimulate growth and reduce jobless numbers below what Milton Friedman called the "natural rate of unemployment" would cause inflation to spiral out of control.[7]

In the conditions of class conflict and labor militancy prevailing in the period after 1968, when Friedman posited his "natural-rate hypothesis," the idea of tolerating high unemployment had tremendous political appeal, because unemployment was the only effective way of curbing the excessive union power that seemed to be threatening the existence of the capitalist system. But the unavoidable, and conscious, implication of monetarism was that governments and central banks were forced to pull out completely from the business of trying to manage economic demand and stabilize their economies.

Abandoning demand management would not matter, according to the monetarist doctrine, because a market economy would automatically stabilize itself, as in classical theory, if governments stopped interfering with market forces. Unfortunately, this theory simply did not accord with the facts, as the experience of the interwar period and the analysis of Keynes and his followers clearly showed. Thus, the result of governments abandoning the responsibilities for managing economic activity and unemployment, which they had embraced from the 1930s onward, was a return to the tremendous economic and financial volatility of the pre-Keynesian period.

The crucial point elided in Bernanke's monetarist explanation of the Great Moderation—and in almost all official accounts of economic policy—was that central banks and governments quietly restored active demand management from the mid-1980s onward, carefully balancing the risks of high inflation and unemployment. Moreover, the central bankers had two great advantages compared to their Keynesian predecessors. They had learned from the bitter experience of the 1970s that greater weight must be attached than in the past to the risks of accelerating inflation, and they had more effective tools for macroeconomic management at their disposal, because of the unexpected triumph of pure fiat money after the breakdown of Bretton Woods.

The result was the spectacular success of macroeconomic stabilization described as the Great Moderation—at least until the crisis of 2007. Had governments truly followed the narrowly antiinflationary policies described by Bernanke (and still embodied in the official targets, though not the practice, of most central banks other than the Fed), the Great Moderation would probably never have happened. A much more likely outcome would have been something akin to the twenty years of stagnation in Japan. The return of active demand management was thus among the most important changes in the world economy from the late 1980s onward. But because of the totemic significance of monetarist economic ideology—an ideology that could almost be described as the Thatcher-Reagan era's "creation myth"—the comeback of Keynesian-style demand management is almost never discussed or publicly admitted by politicians and central bankers. The rest of this chapter offers a brief outline of this immensely powerful mega-trend.

The decade that followed the breakup of the Bretton Woods monetary system in August 1971 was one of the most traumatic periods in the 250-year history of capitalism. The damage to political and business confidence from the unprecedented phenomenon of stagflation—a combination of rising inflation and unemployment that appeared inexplicable in both Keynesian and monetarist economics—was comparable to the collapse of confidence in liberal laissez-faire capitalism that occurred in the Great Depression of 1929–39. That traumatic decade, characterized in Part I as the transition from Capitalism 1 to Capitalism 2, was a period of tremendous upheaval in economic thinking as well as in politics, society, and financial markets—and the same was true of the 1970s.

When the 1970s began, policymakers everywhere subscribed to the predominant ideas of the Keynesian–New Deal consensus. In every advanced capitalist country, the application of monetary and fiscal policy to regulate economic activity and minimize unemployment, an idea that had not occurred to economists until the 1920s, came to be regarded as probably the most important function of government. In the twenty-five years from the end of World War II until the early 1970s, this belief was held as strongly among conservative politicians and business leaders in the United States and Japan as it was among trade unionists and social democrats in Germany, France, and Britain.

The main arguments about economic policy during this period, which is often described as the Golden Age of Keynesian economics, and which I have characterized as Capitalism 2.2, were hair-splitting disputations over the precise levels of unemployment that governments ought to target. In Britain, for example, the Treasury spent most of the period of Conservative government during the 1950s and early 1960s absorbed in an arcane argument over whether the optimum level of unemployment was 2.3 percent, as calculated by traditional civil servants, or 1.8 percent, as postulated by the

"Young Turks" from the Economics faculty in Cambridge University.[8] In the United States, the commitment to full employment was equally fervent. Arthur Burns, the most respected and influential conservative economist of his generation—chief economic adviser to President Eisenhower and later the chairman of the Federal Reserve Board—was able to state in 1946 without qualification: "The principal practical problem of our generation is the maintenance of employment, and it has now become—as it long should have been—the principal problem of economic policy."[9] In a later description of the economic philosophy, which he and the Eisenhower Administration felt bound to follow, Burns went even further. It could never be acceptable, he argued, for unemployment to rise above 2.5 percent. Whenever this happened in the 1950s, "the federal government, in its new role of responsibility for the maintenance of the nation's prosperity, deliberately took speedy and massive actions to build confidence and pave the way for renewed economic growth."[10]

How different from the rhetoric of economic policymakers today! After the inflationary traumas of the 1970s, the monetarist revolution in economic thinking imposed a strict taboo on any claims that governments could stabilize employment or growth. If a politician suggested a numerical target for reducing unemployment, he would be committing treason in the war against inflation. A central banker would rather tie himself in verbal knots than admit that he sets interest rates in order to create jobs.

Even after the crisis, inflation is the only macroeconomic variable for which governments are allowed to set public targets. And central bankers must focus solely on price stability in every speech. If central bankers can control inflation, states the official orthodoxy, then jobs and prosperity will take care of themselves, or more precisely, will be achieved automatically by market forces. To the extent that central bankers and finance ministers do act on jobs and economic growth, these actions still have to be repackaged and disguised as arguments about long-term inflationary prospects. When the economy is in a slump, central bankers cut interest rates, if necessary all the way to zero, just as they would if they were aiming at a 1950s-style job-creation target. But officially they still pretend that they are acting to prevent deflation, or even to *increase* inflation, instead of stating openly that they are trying to reduce unemployment or support economic growth. Chapter 11 explains the economic ideology behind this strange rhetorical deformation. What matters in the present discussion is how the central bankers started actually to behave in the Great Moderation and how this behavior evolved after 2008.

If we focus on actions, rather than rhetoric, it is clear that the Great Moderation began when policymakers, first in America and then in other countries, returned to the traditional Keynesian objectives of minimizing unemployment and stabilizing growth. In the United States, the return to demand management began as early as the summer of 1982, when a three-year recession and the bankruptcy of the Mexican government persuaded the Fed that its experiment with monetarism had gone too far. That, in the chronology of Chapter 3, was the moment of transition from Capitalism 3.0 to Capitalism 3.1. By the early 1990s, almost every major economy had quietly followed America in resurrecting neo-Keynesian policies of fine-tuning demand to stabilize growth and employment.

To see why this happened and to understand the consequences, which resonated more powerfully than ever after the Lehman crisis, we must return to the *Annus Mirabilis* of 1989.

By 1989, globalization had helped to weaken trade unions, commodity cartels, protected national monopolies, and other structural obstacles to competition that had been largely responsible for the stagflation of the preceding decade. As a result, inflationary pressures around the world had subsided, especially in Margaret Thatcher's Britain and Ronald Reagan's United States, countries that had embraced the new free-market model most enthusiastically. Over time, the achievement of low inflation began to transform the attitudes of governments, voters, and central bankers. With prices relatively stable, governments and central banks could again start using interest rates to support employment and growth instead of using all their monetary firepower against inflation. High unemployment had been viewed by monetarists as a "price worth paying" to keep inflation under firm control,[11] but after inflation had subsided, voters and central bankers wondered whether this payment was still required.

Until 1989, however, one big obstacle, at least outside the United States, prevented a decisive redirection of monetary policy in favor of stabilizing growth and employment. That obstacle was the totemic mystery of gold—

or, to look at the same phenomenon from the other direction, the almost superstitious fear of pure paper money.

The decision by President Nixon to abandon the gold standard in 1971 had left the world, as explained in the last chapter, with no objective or "natural" standard for the value of money and no constraint on the ability of governments to print money at will. This was an irreversible historic event of potentially cataclysmic proportions, comparable to the invention of the atom bomb, penicillin, or the birth control pill. Although ordinary people and businesspeople may hardly have noticed, the mental universe of economists and central bankers was transformed in ways that few at the time understood.

A natural response to the fears of inflation engendered by the sudden freedom of governments to print money at will was an effort to tie the hands of politicians and central bankers with strict monetary rules. The trouble was that no one could say with any confidence what those rules ought to be. When inflation became politically alarming in the 1970s, the quantity theory of money, which argued that inflation would accelerate more or less at the same rate as the government printed money, became increasingly attractive because it did suggest simple rules to keep politicians under control. On closer inspection, however, the proposed monetarist rules turned out to be far from simple. There were many ways of measuring, and even defining, money, which often gave conflicting answers about whether the printing presses should be accelerated or slowed. Moreover, a perversity that came to be known as Goodhart's Law showed that when central bankers measured money in a particular way and set this as a target, financial markets would quickly hoard or dump that kind of money, thereby guaranteeing the breakdown of whatever relationship had previously existed between this definition of money and inflation.[12]

To make matters worse, businesspeople, financiers, and ordinary citizens outside America had relied since the war on the gold-backed dollar as a gauge to value their own national currencies, which had proved unreliable and volatile in countries such as Italy, France, and Britain. Given the low esteem in which these countries generally held their government institutions, skepticism was only natural about the promises of monetary self-restraint from national politicians, even if these promises were backed by supposedly irrevocable monetarist rules. A strong conviction therefore developed in Europe, as well as in parts of Asia, that money would only command public confidence if it were linked to an external anchor that was beyond the control of national politicians. With gold no longer taken seriously, this meant attempting to anchor, or peg, domestic money to some foreign currency that commanded more respect, usually the dollar or the German mark. But this approach proved even more flawed and unreliable than the one based on preordained monetary rules. A country that pegged its currency to the dollar or the German mark exposed itself to currency speculation. If the country suffered a bout of economic weakness in relation to the United States or Germany, it quickly became a sitting duck. As a result, Britain, France, and Italy, along with many other economies, were in an almost continuous state of siege in the mid-1970s, as their governments vainly tried to defend the pound, franc, and lira against speculative attacks from the currency markets, repeatedly plunging their countries into recession with extremely high interest rates.

Amidst all this chaos, the greatest surprise of the post-Bretton Woods period—and perhaps the greatest testament to capitalism's powerful instinct of self-preservation—was that the restoration of global monetary order after the 1971 breakdown took only twenty years.

The United States was the first country to emerge from the chaotic learning period, largely because of its sheer economic dominance, as well as its long history of monetary independence. Unusually for such complex historic events, the breakthrough can be dated precisely. It occurred on August 24, 1982, when Paul Volcker unexpectedly slashed the Federal Funds rate from 12.5 percent to 9 percent and announced that he had suspended the Fed's money supply targets. At this point, the U.S. economy had been stuck for three years in its deepest and longest recession since the 1930s.[13] A week earlier, the Mexican government had declared itself effectively bankrupt, and it was soon to be followed by Brazil, Chile, Argentina, the Philippines, and many other developing countries.[14] These defaults effectively ended the monetarist experiment in America, and from 1982 onward, the economic policies of the U.S. government reverted to the dual mandate first suggested in the 1946 Employment Act and clarified in the Humphrey-Hawkins Act of 1977: "to promote effectively the goals of maximum employment, stable prices, and moderate long-term interest rates."[15] The Fed returned with gusto to this traditional task after the brief interlude of strict monetarism that was needed to complete the extinction of the failing postwar Keynesian model I describe as Capitalism 2.3 and facilitate the emergence of President Reagan's Capitalism 3.0.

Outside the United States, the transformation of economic philosophy from strict monetarism to a reformed version of active demand management had to wait a few years longer. In Britain, the change was triggered by the pound's expulsion from the European Monetary System in 1992. This forced Britain to abandon the quixotic quest for a reliable external anchor for the value of sterling, a quest that had obsessed the Treasury since Ramsay Macdonald abandoned the gold standard in 1931. From September 1992 onward, the British government accepted, for the first time in history, a full and unqualified responsibility for managing Britain's own paper money, with no reliance on external anchors or other artificial props. The surprising result, which left the Treasury more baffled than ever, was a strengthening of the pound and the longest period of growth and stability in Britain's three hundred years of recorded economic history.

In the rest of Europe, the route back from monetarism to demand management was more indirect and complex. In 1989, the European Union laid out a plan of breathtaking audacity to create the euro, the first ever currency with no tangible backing, either from a commodity standard or from a government with clear sovereign powers. Many experts believed the euro would never happen, but by 1994, the progress toward monetary union had eliminated the recurrent currency crises in France, Spain, and Italy. After the euro was formally created in January 1999, the European Central Bank acquired the same freedom of action in monetary policy that the Fed enjoyed. Initially, the ECB clung firmly to the monetarist traditions of the German Bundesbank. But over time, its policies became increasingly pragmatic, with France, Italy, and Spain gradually gaining influence over the euro project, while German banks and export industries became increasingly exposed to financial conditions in the rest of the eurozone. By the outbreak of the subprime crisis, the ECB was providing even more liquidity than the Fed or the Bank of England, and by 2010 it was lending without limit to insolvent banks and governments to avert a breakup of the euro.

In the period after the *Annus Mirabilis* of 1989, therefore, the governments and central banks in every major economy gradually shifted from the exclusive focus on inflation demanded by the monetarist counterrevolution. Instead, they started using all the instruments of economic policy to stabilize growth and employment, much as their predecessors had done in the period between the end of World War II and the breakdown of Bretton Woods. This transformation in the objectives and methods of economic policy—effectively the reinvention of postwar Keynesian demand management with the additional opportunities and challenges implied by pure paper money—accounted for the extraordinary economic stability of the subsequent twenty years.

Ben Bernanke, in his speech about the Great Moderation in 2004, still felt obliged to pay lip service to the official doctrine that maintaining low inflation had been the key to the Fed's success in stabilizing employment and economic growth. The truth, however, was that the Fed and other central banks gradually returned to the broad economic philosophies, if not the exact policies, abandoned in the 1970s. These policies were again directed, as they had been in the 1950s and 1960s, to achieving a reasonable balance between price stability, full employment, and steady growth. And for most of the twenty-year period after demand management was reinvented, the central bankers were remarkably successful in walking the tightrope between inflation and unemployment.

Their success lasted right up until the autumn of 2008, when the Lehman crisis blew up the tightrope, the safety net, and most of the spectators in the circus tent. With this observation, it is time to consider the last and most controversial of the four megatrends: the financial revolution that triggered the Great Moderation's spectacular demise.

CHAPTER SEVEN

The Financial Revolution

Neither a borrower nor a lender be;
For loan oft loses both itself and friend,
And borrowing dulls the edge of husbandry.

—Oft-quoted speech by Polonius, possibly the
most misguided character in Shakespeare

AFTER THE BURSTING of the property and credit bubbles, it became an article of faith that the change in attitudes to risk in the 1990s was a symptom of monstrous greed, stupidity, and incompetence. Equally fashionable was to ridicule the frenzy of property investment, especially in America and Britain, as the most extreme and deluded example of "irrational exuberance" in history. But much of the buildup in credit was fundamentally justified and irreversible. It was, in fact, a rational response to transformative economic trends of the kind described in the last two chapters.

During the Great Moderation, workers and companies were becoming less vulnerable to the risks of the economic cycle—to bankruptcy and unemployment at the extreme. The recognition that cyclical volatility was subsiding had a dramatic effect on the assumptions that bankers, businesses, and individuals made in managing both personal and corporate finances. An increase in borrowing and lending was a reasonable and predictable response. The same could be said of the so-called speculation in housing. Most people who bought houses in what is now described as the bubble period were behaving quite sensibly. And as the dust settles after the 2007–09 financial meltdown, it looks increasingly probable that people who invested in property during the early phase of the bubble period will get get the last laugh over the financial pundits who predicted, even at the bottom of the 2009 slump, that prices would fall by a further 20 percent or even 50 percent. Property owners, provided they financed their investments carefully enough to avoid becoming forced sellers during the period of market panic, have remained well ahead of investors in equities and bonds in most of the world once tax benefits and implied rents from owner-occupied houses are taken into account.

These are controversial statements in the immediate aftermath of the greatest financial crisis in history, a crisis generally believed to have been brought on by insane property speculation. But they are backed by statistical facts.

Let us begin with the supposedly crazy personal borrowing. It is true that by 2007, personal debt levels in many countries were much higher, relative to income and total wealth, than at any previous point in recorded history. But does this mean the borrowing boom was mad? If economic growth is more stable, jobs are more secure, and interest rates are lower than they have been for generations, is it not reasonable to borrow more?

Workers who are less likely to be fired and businesses that are less likely to suffer sudden losses can reasonably afford to take on more debt or cut back on the savings they would normally set aside. If a buildup of savings in China and Japan causes interest rates to fall and then remain at very low levels for a decade, borrowing becomes even more attractive. If at the same time money has been demystified and stripped of its quasi-religious golden trappings, debt starts to be treated as an everyday consumer product, without the free offer of Victorian morality annoyingly attached to it in the past. And in liberal societies, where adult citizens are allowed to decide on most aspects of their lifestyle, paternalistic regulations to protect borrowers and lenders from their own supposed imprudence naturally erode. Thus, some of the financial deregulation often blamed for allowing the crisis was a reasonable and predictable response to long-term social progress.

The result of all these changes was a natural increase in the use of credit and, eventually, of other more sophisticated financial products. This was

FIGURE 7.1 U.S. HOUSEHOLD DEBT AS PERCENT OF DISPOSABLE INCOME

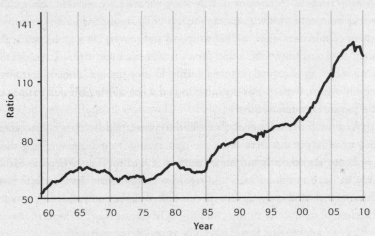

Source: Reuters EcoWin.

the story of the world financial system until the last years of the global borrowing and lending boom. It was only in that last year or so that the process went suddenly, but briefly, mad.

Until 2005, the numbers behind what later came to be viewed as a malignant, cancerous growth of financial activity were actually moderate. The first big increase in consumer debt occurred in the mid-1980s, mostly the result of the abolition of oppressive restrictions on credit, such as America's "Regulation Q"[1] and Britain's hire-purchase and foreign exchange controls.[2]

From 1984 (when most of these regulations were lifted) and 1991, the ratio of U.S. household debt to disposable income increased by one-third, from 63 percent to 83 percent, as shown in Figure 7.1. It then stabilized at around this level for about a decade, before increasing again by about a third, from 83 percent of income in 1999 to 112 percent in 2005. (Following the financial crisis, consumer debt returned to around this level in early 2011.) This second stage of the debt buildup was more of a global phenomenon than the first, involving British, French, Spanish, Scandinavian, and Australian borrowers more than Americans. This stage was driven by another broadly rational and healthy financial process: Interest rates fell in real terms to around half the level that prevailed in the first stage of the debt buildup because trillions of dollars were successfully recycled around the world from countries with excess savings or aging populations to countries where people were more willing to spend and invest. On a global scale, the main flow was from China and Japan to America and Britain. An equally large recycling of capital occurred within Europe, from Germany and Holland to Spain, Greece, Portugal, Ireland, and the newly liberated nations of the former communist bloc.

As a result of these generally welcome events, middle-class homeowners and small businesses were given the opportunity to manage not only their assets but also their liabilities in ways that had previously been available only to large multinationals and wealthy family trusts. Interest rate risk, currency risk, and even unemployment risk could be controlled and restructured through options, futures, and financial derivatives. In short, the availability of sophisticated financial products was democratized.

As these new financial products became available, people were sensible to use them. Elderly homeowners with big houses but small incomes could supplement their pensions and enjoy life in retirement, instead of leaving all their wealth locked up in real estate until death suddenly transferred it to their kids. Self-employed workers with ambitious ideas but limited earnings could raise capital against their housing wealth. Newlywed couples with modest savings, but good job prospects, could buy their own homes in their twenties instead of living with their parents or renting.

Nothing was irrational or reckless about this behavior, provided it was not carried to excess. Credit is the lifeblood of a market economy, and an increase in borrowing, combined with a loosening of credit terms, was a natural and welcome consequence of the structural improvements in the world economy that followed 1989.

Whether all this extra borrowing was reasonable and appropriate or excessive was not a matter of principle but of degree. But surely it was crystal clear that the borrowing *had* expanded out of all proportion? After all, the levels of debt in America and Britain had already risen above 100 percent of incomes by 2001. In media and political rhetoric, debts at 100 percent of income are often presented as self-evidently absurd. But a moment's thought about the lives of ordinary people, which journalists and politicians sometimes seem unaware of, reveals that the true absurdity is the cliché about the dangers of 100 percent debt.

Few families have ever managed to buy a house without borrowing two or three times their annual incomes—and such borrowing has been going on for generations with no ill effects on the capitalist system or on the finances of families and banks arranging the loans. Debt is considerably greater than 100 percent of annual income for most normal businesses and households through most of their lifespan. Even a simple car loan on a Mercedes or Cadillac will often exceed the annual income of the limousine driver who takes out the loan.

What matters in establishing the solvency or financial safety of a household or business—or an entire nation, as we will later see in discussing United States borrowing from Japan and China—is not whether debt is greater than income. It is whether the cost of *servicing* the debt—in other words, the monthly interest and capital repayments—are affordable. And that, in turn, depends on the rate of interest and the repayment terms. If interest rates fall by a third, which they roughly did between 1999 and 2005, an increase of about one-third in the level of debt should come as no surprise.[3]

Turning to the *level* of debt, as opposed to its servicing costs, what matters is how debt compares to the value of a family's assets, not the income they earn. A family earning $100,000 a year can sensibly borrow $300,000 if they own a $400,000 house; but even if their earnings were $150,000, they would be rash to borrow $300,000 against a house worth only $200,000. And no sensible banker would lend them the money to do this (although many foolish ones did precisely this in the frenzy of the subprime credit boom).

A rarely mentioned fact about the second phase of the U.S. debt buildup, from the mid-1990s onward, is that the increase in personal debts was smaller than the increase in the value of personal assets. This is shown in Figure 7.2, which is based on quarterly figures published by the Federal Reserve. The light grey line at the top is total household wealth. The bottom dotted line is all household debt, including mortgages, credit cards, and so on. The thick grey line is the measure of net wealth that results by deducting the total of all these debts from the gross wealth figure. What these statistics make clear is that in 2006, American households were far richer, even after

FIGURE 7.2 U.S. HOUSEHOLD ASSETS AND LIABILITIES AS A PERCENT OF DISPOSABLE INCOME

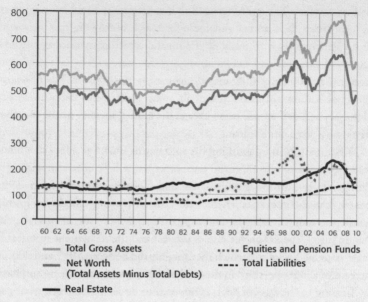

Source: Reuters EcoWin.

taking into account all their borrowing, than ever before in history. And not only were they richer in absolute terms, their wealth was much higher in relation to their incomes, which meant by any normal financial yardstick that they were more solvent than ever before and more capable of carrying their debts. Although other countries do not have statistics on wealth as detailed and reliable as those produced by the Federal Reserve in America, the figures that are available suggest that a similar story could be told about the buildup of wealth and debt in Britain, Australia, Spain, and most other highly leveraged economies. In all cases, the growth of debt during the boom period was smaller than the increase in wealth.

Some object to such calculations and state that much of the increase in wealth enjoyed by Americans, Britons, and many other nationalities during the boom times was an illusion, created by unsustainable bull markets in shares and housing. But this objection is wrong. The statistics show that even at the lowest point of the housing and stock market collapses in early 2009, American households, after accounting for all their debts, were still richer not just in absolute terms but also after accounting for price and wage inflation than at any time between 1974 and 1985. In other words, even at the bottom of the largest simultaneous slump in housing and stock prices since the Great Depression, Americans were still more solvent than they had been before the great upsurge of personal borrowing began in 1984. By the end of 2009, just nine months after the low point of the slump, the wealth of American households had recovered sufficiently to boost the net worth to income ratio above the highest levels recorded in the 1960s, 1970s, 1980s, or early 1990s.

International comparisons reveal a similar picture, confirming that the story of Americans' extraordinary imprudence and profligacy is simply untrue. At the end of 2006, which is the last date for which comparable figures are available and also more or less the high point of the global credit boom, U.S. personal debts were 139 percent of disposable income, which was almost identical to Japan's 132 percent and Canada's 133 percent. The figures in Continental Europe were somewhat lower, ranging from 105 percent in Germany down to Italy's 69 percent. The real outlier among the G7 economies was not the United States but Britain, where personal debts were 175 percent of disposable income in 2006.[4]

To cite all these numbers is not to suggest that the buildup of debt in the period leading up to the crisis could have gone on forever or was driven entirely by benign forces such as globalization. It couldn't and it wasn't, as shown by subsequent events. But in trying to understand the causes of the crisis—and its likely consequences in the years ahead—it is not enough to praise the virtues of thrift and denounce the wickedness and stupidity of debt.

Whether borrowing is sensible or harmful for a family or a business—or for a nation—is not a matter of principle. It is a matter of degree. The same can be said about the other so-called financial excesses blamed for the crisis: the allegedly wild speculation in U.S. housing; the supposedly unsustainable flows of international capital out of China; and the fad for securitizing old-fashioned mortgages and traditional bank loans into newfangled tradable bonds.

This is not the place for a detailed analysis of the last two issues. Securitization of debt is a technical business that has been adequately debated by bankers and regulators in specialized publications. Global financial imbalances are discussed in Chapters 15 and 16 from the standpoints of macroeconomics and geopolitics. Suffice it to say that a natural consequence of unifying the world economy was a substantial flow of capital from rapidly growing but politically risky and financially underdeveloped Asian countries into U.S. Treasury debt, the world's most stable and politically secure asset. The problem, as in the case of the growth of consumer borrowing, was one not of principle but of proportion. Similarly, the conversion of bank debts into tradable securities was a sound idea and had worked well in many markets for many years. Again, the problem was not one of principle but of execution, as explained in such excellent books as *The Trillion Dollar Meltdown* by Charles Morris and *Fool's Gold* by Gillian Tett, although sometimes belied by their sensational marketing (Tett's subtitle was: *How Unrestrained Greed Corrupted a Dream, Shattered Global Markets and Unleashed a Catastrophe.*)

The question of property speculation, on the other hand, demands more attention. House prices have far greater resonance for ordinary people than asset securitization or global rebalancing. Yet the public discussion of the role of housing in the crisis has been misleading and superficial.

It is taken as axiomatic in all explanations of the crisis—from tabloid newspaper headlines to learned academic articles—that the rise in U.S. house prices in the years leading up to the crisis was one of the greatest financial bubbles of all time. It is a cliché that American homeowners, driven mad by greed and herded by irresponsible or crooked bankers, bid property prices up to insane levels. This fit of irrational exuberance supposedly possessed almost every American and eclipsed all previous financial bubbles, such as the 1990s Internet mania or the Japanese property boom. The unprecedented scale of this speculative mania in American housing is generally believed to be the fundamental reason for the scale of economic catastrophe after the Lehman bankruptcy.

This story offers an exciting and morally uplifting explanation of the biggest financial crisis in history—and one that any homeowner can readily understand—but it is demonstrably false.

Housing inflation in the years leading up to the bust was modest by historic standards, and the U.S. market, even at its peak, was one of the least expensive and inflated in the world. U.S. property prices never reached levels remotely comparable to the extremes in many other countries during the pre-Lehman period, never mind the surreal levels of 1980s Japan when, as mentioned in Chapter 4, one garden in Tokyo was worth as much as the entire state of California. Meanwhile in Britain, where property prices did rise to unheard-of levels, they stabilized surprisingly quickly after the crisis, suggesting that something more durable than a mere speculative frenzy had probably been driving them up.

Part of the rise in property prices around the world was due to sound fundamental reasons connected with the long-term economic trends discussed in this chapter—and these strong fundamentals began to reassert themselves quite quickly as the financial chaos unleashed by Lehman was brought under control. Here are some solid statistical facts rarely mentioned in the conventional housing and credit story. When U.S. house prices hit their peak in 2006, they had increased by between 67 percent and 92 percent (depending on the index used) from the beginning of 2000. Taking the average of the various U.S. house price indices, the annualized increase during this entire seven-year boom was about 10 percent. Over the same period, GDP grew at an average rate of 6 percent and personal incomes per head by 5 percent. So the annual increase in house prices during this entire bubble period was about 5 percent greater than the growth in incomes available to support them. By the standards of other financial bubbles, this overshoot in relation to the fundamentals was modest—and did not last very long.

Most of this relatively brief housing boom, far from inflating a bubble, could be seen as a recovery from an earlier twenty-year slump. As shown in the chart in Figure 7.3, which is based on the National Association of Realtors' monthly index of home resale prices (the U.S. housing indicator with the longest and most reliable track record), U.S. house prices have fluctuated throughout the four decades from 1968 to 2009 around an average of 7.25 times per capita incomes—with no sign of any long-term trend, either up or down.

However, some big cyclical moves did occur during this forty-one-year period. The first was a surge in the 1970s, as inflation took off. This was

FIGURE 7.3 U.S. HOUSE PRICES RELATIVE TO PERSONAL INCOME PER HEAD

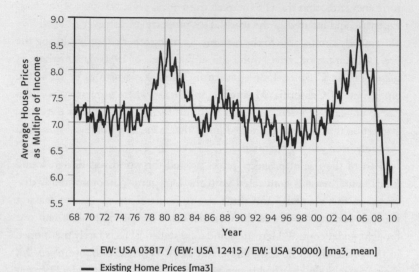

Source: Reuters EcoWin.

followed by a slump in the early 1980s caused by the sky-high interest rates of the Volcker monetarist phase. A gradual recovery from 1984 onward was stymied by the savings and loan crisis in 1990; after that, the market fell into a long hibernation. The net effect was that house prices fell by 25 percent relative to incomes in the fourteen years from 1981 to 1995. What happened in the following twelve years, from 1995 to 2005, was a reversal of this decline. Then in 2006, property prices slightly overshot the previous peak on the way up, and in 2009, they fell below the previous troughs by a wider margin.

International comparisons convey a similar message: Nothing was exceptional about the U.S housing boom. In the decade leading up to the crisis, the U.S. had the slowest house price growth among the major economies, except those of Germany and Japan.[5] According to an IMF analysis in late 2009, house prices rose 50 percent faster than general inflation in Britain from 2000 to 2006, by 60 percent in France, and by 80 per-

FIGURE 7.4 RISES AND SUBSEQUENT FALLS IN HOUSE PRICES (IN PERCENT)

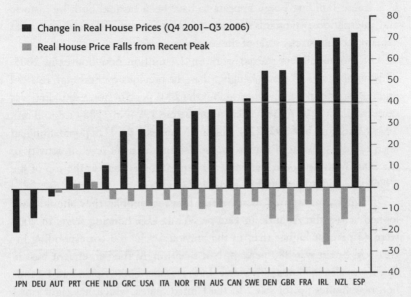

- ■ Change in Real House Prices (Q4 2001–Q3 2006)
- ■ Real House Price Falls from Recent Peak

JPN DEU AUT PRT CHE NLD GRC USA ITA NOR FIN AUS CAN SWE DEN GBR FRA IRL NZL ESP

Source: IMF World Economic Outlook, September 2009, p. 102.

cent in Spain. The corresponding number in the United States was just 35 percent (see Figure 7.4).

The U.S. property market was also less out of line with fundamental drivers of value such as income growth, demographics, and land availability. At the peak of the global property boom, the fundamental valuation of U.S. houses, as expressed by the ratio of U.S. prices to personal incomes, was 12 percent above its long-term average. In Britain, France, and Australia, this valuation gauge was 40 percent above average, while in Denmark, Holland, Spain, and Ireland it was 60 percent higher than normal.

Perhaps, then, the true excesses of the U.S. housing boom were not in prices? Perhaps the reckless overexpansion of the construction industry caused the real problems, littering America with abandoned subdivisions and empty condominiums from Las Vegas to Miami Beach. The boom in the number of houses built was, in fact, more extreme than the rise in their prices. Construction investment increased, albeit briefly in 2005, to a postwar high of 6.3 percent of GDP. On closer inspection, however, the U.S. house-building boom appears to have been normal both by historic and international standards—certainly not so far out of the ordinary as to explain the monstrous scale of the subsequent bust.

U.S. homebuilders started work on 2.1 million new houses in 2005. This number was 43 percent higher than the previous cyclical high in 1994 and may sound like a big increase. But the 2005 peak in house-building was quite similar to the three cyclical peaks before 1994: in 1986 (1.8 million), 1978 (2 million) and 1972 (2.4 million). Moreover, the U.S. population had been rapidly growing. Relative to population, the peak level of activity in the 2005 housing boom was some 10 percent lower than at the top of the 1986 cycle and 40 percent below the 1972 high.

If Americans wanted to see a real housing bubble, they should have looked across the Atlantic to Europe. While U.S. housing starts in 2005 were 43 percent higher than in the previous cycle, the corresponding increase in Spain was 280 percent. Not surprisingly, the subsequent bust in Spain was also incomparably worse. In September 2009, Spain had 1.1 million new homes up for sale.[6] In the United States, which has eight times the population and fifteen times the national income, the comparable inventory of new homes was 251,000. By late 2010 this inventory was below 200,000, the lowest level since 1968.[7]

How, then, can we explain the near-universal belief that the U.S. housing boom was a historically unprecedented and internationally unequalled outbreak of financial madness and that the reckless behavior of American consumers and homeowners was the underlying reason for the near-collapse of the entire global capitalist system?

Part of the explanation is the sheer diversity of the U.S. economy, which encompasses vast differences in local conditions. Nevada, California, and Florida suffered genuine catastrophes, but Texas and much of the midwest were hardly affected by the housing boom. The opposite happened in the 1980s, when a severe property crisis hit Texas but had almost no effect on the east and west coasts. Because media debate is naturally dominated by extremes, headline-grabbing exaggerations and misleading statistics tend to get the most attention.[8] But even in places such as Las Vegas, the inflation of property values was not as crazy as the wild excesses of previous financial bubbles. In the Internet boom of 1999, companies such as AOL and Yahoo were worth hundreds of times their annual profits, while many smaller businesses that vanished overnight without ever making a profit were valued at billions of dollars.

Nothing remotely comparable ever occurred in the U.S. real estate boom. Therefore, the enormous effect of the U.S. property bust must have been connected to something other than the size of the preceding boom. To understand what really happened, we must separate the fundamental drivers of long-term trends in property and finance from the cycles that emerged on top of these trends. The next two chapters deal with the ring of cyclical behavior. Before turning to this part of the story, however, we must finish the discussion of the four megatrends by explaining how they permanently transformed both property and finance.

Megatrends in Housing and Finance

The most fundamental cause of property inflation all over the world from 1989 onward was the sustained decline in interest rates that resulted from low inflation, economic stability, and globalization. Because houses are mostly purchased with mortgages, interest rates are a powerful driver of property prices. Thus, the interest rate effects of the post-1989 megatrends were almost bound to create house-price booms all over the world, as households and banks gradually realized that low interest rates had become a permanent fact of life.

But the interaction of rising house prices with deregulated finance had a further structural effect. As mentioned, the deregulation of finance meant that property investments could be readily turned into cash through the mortgage market. Homeowners who wanted to spend part of the capital they had invested in property no longer had to sell their homes and trade down or become renters. Instead, they could use home equity loans and other forms of mortgage equity withdrawal to cash in their property savings a little at a time. As a result of this new facility, houses, which had previously been considered an illiquid asset—meaning that it was difficult, expensive, and inconvenient to turn them into cash—suddenly became liquid.

This desirable new financial amenity made housing a more attractive investment than it had ever been before compared to bonds, equities, and other assets. The natural consequence was to make houses more valuable than in previous decades, when the liquidity feature did not exist.

While politicians and media commentators may now condemn the habit of borrowing against property wealth as irresponsible and deluded, it made good sense. Middle-class families were merely starting to live by the same financial standards that applied to governments, businesses, and aristocrats by financing themselves with "perpetual loans" on which the principal never needs to be repaid as long as the interest due is promptly met each month.

For most of the long upswing in home values that began in the mid-1990s, the broad consequences of this democratization of credit were benign. The financial revolution supported the globalization process that made the world more prosperous and stable and spread the benefits of economic development to many of the world's poorest countries. Within advanced economies, especially in America and Britain, the greater availability of credit helped to eliminate serious recessions for almost two decades. It discredited the Marxist ideology of class warfare and it gave ordinary people some of the ability to control their destinies that the rich had always enjoyed; many could now lead lifestyles different from their parents and spread income and consumption more evenly over their working lives.

There were, of course, huge mistakes made in the allocation of capital and credit. Market forces directed investment into houses in the wrong locations at the wrong prices. They steered lending toward borrowers who were unlikely to repay their loans. But markets always make mistakes like this, and usually they are neutralized by trial and error, inflicting serious losses on some businesses, financial institutions, and imprudent borrowers but doing no permanent damage to the capitalist system as a whole.

What, then, went so badly wrong? The simple answer—and one that deserved more attention than it received immediately after the crisis—is that trees do not grow to the sky. Although it was perfectly reasonable, and indeed inevitable, that the processes of deregulation, globalization, and successful demand management described in this chapter would raise borrowing to levels far above those considered normal in previous decades, that did not mean borrowing could rise forever. At some point, the burden of debt would become unsustainable, even after taking into account the new and generally healthy trends in the world economy. If the boom continued beyond this point, a painful bust was almost sure to follow.

Why didn't bankers or regulators just stop the borrowing before it reached this critical point? Part of the reason was that bankers and policymakers were consumed by greed, blinded by ideology, and corrupted by lobbying. But the main reason was the one repeatedly cited by Alan Greenspan, to general approbation while he was still Fed chairman and to universal derision after he retired. No one had any idea of where the critical limit to prudent borrowing might be, nor how it could be determined.

In a world economy transformed beyond recognition by the megatrends described in the preceding chapter, it was genuinely impossible to tell in advance what would be sustainable levels of debt. Normality or sustainability could not be gauged in this new world by applying historic yardsticks, such as the average debt levels that had prevailed in previous decades.

No one could judge, for example, whether the use of interest-only and reverse mortgages had already gone too far in 2005 or was still in a healthy period of expansion, because these facilities did not exist or were not available to ordinary homeowners a few years before. To ask in 2006 whether the natural ceiling for debt levels was 90 percent of income or 100 percent or 120 percent was like asking in 1996 whether mobile phone accounts or Internet connections would reach their natural ceiling at one hundred million, one billion, or five billion, or asking in 1956 whether American families would end up owning one TV set or two or four. When new products and services are introduced to the market, there is simply no way of guessing sustainable levels of demand.

This intrinsic uncertainty explains why the economic prophets who claim to have predicted the 2007–09 crisis were all ignored. For the previous twenty years, these people had been crying "wolf"—or at least "irrational exuberance"—every time they saw asset prices or credit levels rising to what they deemed to be unsustainable levels. Every time, the financial wolf they thought they spotted turned out to be a friendly Labrador.[9]

In most cases, these prophets of doom simply refused to acknowledge the new attitudes to debt and asset values that resulted from the structural transformations of the late 1980s. They dogmatically denied that such events could ever change the way that assets should be valued or that markets might work. The clearer it became that "this time is different," the more stubbornly they repeated that "everything's always the same." It was therefore quite reasonable for the financial world to ignore these seers who cried wolf.

Unfortunately, as the premature alarms repeatedly turned out to be false alarms, both borrowers and lenders became increasingly confident and then complacent. Eventually, hubris took over completely, and it became increasingly improbable that the financial boom would ever stop of its own accord at some reasonable equilibrium level. The biggest mistake made by bankers, regulators, and consumers was again articulated eloquently by Alan Greenspan. Their mistake was to assume that markets, while subject to occasional excesses, must surely be better than politicians or regulators at controlling the risks created by their own behavior.

Investors had no more idea than Greenspan, or anyone else for that matter, about a prudent limit of household debt and bank leverage or how far house prices could reasonably rise. The world had changed too much for either bankers or regulators to be able to make these judgments. To make matters worse, no strong incentives existed for bankers to make arbitrary judgments about the prudent limits of credit expansion that would lose them business if others believed the limits had not yet been reached. Hence, the notorious comment by Charles Prince, the chairman of Citigroup, that turned into an ironic refrain throughout the financial meltdown: "When the music stops . . . things will be complicated. But as long as the music is playing, you've got to get up and dance. We're still dancing."[10]

And despite the derision and humiliation suffered by Prince as a result of this statement, another leading banker made almost the same admission a year later, when the calamity suffered by Citigroup was well known. This time, the confession related to the wildly excessive foreign currency lending that ruined the economies and banks of central Europe: "Foreign currency lending in the short-term is a nuisance, in the long-term it is worse. When it is in the euro, it is 50 percent sin; when it's in other currencies, it is more sinful. But as long as big players are doing it, we have to do it or we would be out of the market."[11]

There could hardly be better illustrations of Keynes's most famous remark about bankers: "A 'sound' banker, alas, is not one who foresees danger and avoids it, but one who, when he is ruined, is ruined in a conventional way along with his fellows, so that no one can really blame him."[12]

Considering this unequivocal lesson of history, which should have been familiar not only to Greenspan but to every financial regulator and central banker in every capitalist country, the sensible response to an unprecedented change in the fundamental drivers of housing and consumer finance would have been for regulators to recognize that financial markets could not be trusted to control their own excesses. Markets are wonderful at harnessing human energy and creativity to solve the problems expressed by a particular structure of incentives and institutions. But they cannot always be trusted to adapt these incentives and institutions to new events. Often, new incentives and institutional structures must be imposed on markets from the outside by political decisions. After the crisis, this may seem so obvious as to be hardly worth stating. Yet the idea that public policies could sometimes establish rules and incentives better than the markets, was preposterous and unacceptable to the market fundamentalist thinking of Capitalism 3.3.

Regulators could not guess the prudent limits of household borrowing. And they were rightly reluctant to stop a process that produced clear social and economic benefits. But this didn't mean they were paralyzed. They could, for example, have taken steps to slow the rate of credit expansion and forced banks to keep increasing their capital reserves as lending expanded, recognizing that a financial bust was likely to occur eventually as credit continued to expand.

But a world in the grip of market fundamentalist thinking refused to face this dilemma. It assumed that markets would set their own limits and the more freedom they were given, the better they would do this job. As Barney Frank later noted: The rules broke down "because the people who were in charge of them didn't believe in them. Alan Greenspan, to his credit, acknowledged that . . . when he was given the mandate to regulate subprime loans, he refused to do it because he did not believe in regulation."[13]

The failure of banks to stop lending when debt levels became too high was not a failure of the market. It was a failure in the understanding of what markets could or should be expected to do. It was a failure to understand that markets can operate only in an economic and political context that is set by politicians and officials, responding to different incentives from those of the market itself. And it was a failure to understand that banks always depend on guarantees of economic stability that the state must provide, because the government, representing as it does the entire nation, has a greater interest in financial stability than the managers and shareholders of the banks.

The ideological decision to rely solely on the market to set limits on its own behavior made trouble inevitable. The boom in credit and housing was almost bound to overshoot to the point where it produced a damaging bust, for reasons clearly articulated in the 1980s by George Soros in his theory of reflexivity. Booms and busts are a natural feature of financial markets even in normal times; they tend to become more extreme in periods of radical change, driven by new technologies or by political and social transformations. The confluence of megatrends driving the world economy from 1989 onward was a spectacular case of such a historic transformation and thus it was likely to produce a boom-bust cycle. But financiers, economists, and politicians, intoxicated by the free-market ideology that was itself both cause and consequence of this historic transformation, failed to understand that the most powerful long-term trends are likely to produce the biggest overshoots and therefore the most extreme boom-bust cycles. As Soros has argued,[14] the fact that the free-market system appeared to be so successful, created an inflated belief in the economic and political theories on which this successs appeared to be based. An extraordinary boom-bust cycle in ideology was thus overlaid on the more or less normal boom-bust cycles in finance and housing.

As in a perfect storm, when the waves created by a hurricane are reinforced by a tidal surge, the overshoot in credit and the overshoot in free-market ideology were mutually reinforcing. They created a world in blank denial about the obvious and intrinsic instability of financial markets, a world convinced that financiers and investors, no matter how bizarrely they might act, always knew best—and thus that regulators and politicians would always serve the public interest by leaving markets to their own devices. This was the ruinous mistake that turned what might have been a normal boom-bust cycle into a disaster. To see why it happened and understand how this experience is likely to shape capitalism after the crisis, we must now look in detail at the ring of repetitive financial cycles.

CHAPTER EIGHT

The Ring of Finance

Technically, this is 1929. The only question is whether the Depression of 1930 will follow.

—George Soros, October 1987, twenty years before the subprime crisis

The collapse of the global marketplace would be a traumatic event with unimaginable consequences. Yet I find it easier to imagine than the continuation of the present regime. [1]

—George Soros, February 1995, twelve years before the subprime crisis

SIR ISAAC NEWTON was not just the world's greatest mathematician and scientist. He was also Master of the Royal Mint in London from 1699 to 1727, a period that took in the South Sea Bubble, perhaps the most notorious of all the booms and busts that have punctuated financial history. With his incomparable intellect and his access to what today might be called insider information, he invested in the South Sea Company and cashed out his shares with a 100 percent profit in April 1720, judging that their price had advanced too far. But Newton, supreme mathematician though he was, had miscalculated. In June the same year, he realized that he had underestimated the prospects for the South Sea Company's shares. He reinvested the proceeds of his previous speculation, adding massive further borrowings on top. When the bubble burst three months later, Newton had lost his entire fortune of £20,000, equivalent to $5 million today if adjusted for consumer prices or roughly $90 million in relation to the average wages in eighteenth-century England.[2] Newton retreated from public life and soon left London, venting his bitterness against the world of finance in a famous quote: "I can calculate the motions of the heavenly bodies, but not the madness of people."[3]

Recurrent booms and busts have shaken capitalism since its inception, with routine financial panics occurring every few decades and earth-shattering crises, such as the South Sea Bubble or the Lehman bankruptcy, every generation or two. These financial manias, going back even before the South Sea Bubble to Tulipmania in seventeenth-century Holland, often caused severe economic dislocations, especially in financially oriented countries. Such disruptions have usually been powerful enough to over-whelm, at least temporarily, the strongest of favorable historic trends. In the long run, however, the arrow of progress has always prevailed against the ring of finance. In trying to gauge the lasting consequences of the 2007–09 financial crisis, therefore, it is essential to make the correct distinctions be-tween the cyclical forces and the structural forces that are driving events.

The standard view of the crisis and its aftermath is that the near-collapse of the global financial system after September 15 represented a permanent change in the structure of the world economy, especially financially domi-nated economies in America and Britain. Because of the crisis, these extrav-agantly consuming and debt-laden nations would never be the same. Although some sort of recovery would probably occur, stimulated by tempo-rary cyclical forces such as government stimulus and inventory demand, the "new normal" in the overleveraged Anglo-Saxon economies would be differ-ent from what the world perceived as economic normality before 2007.

In other words, debt reduction and spending restraint are now the main long-term trends that will dominate the post-Lehman economy, while the forces powering recovery—extremely low interest rates, strong growth in Asia, rebounding asset prices, and world trade—are just temporary *cyclical* factors.

That, at least, is what the standard model of the crisis asserts. The idea that the breakdown in the global financial system must imply a permanent structural downshift in the momentum of global capitalism has been pre-sented most persuasively by two of the world's most prominent and admired financiers, George Soros, the world's leading hedge fund manager, in *The New Paradigm for Financial Markets*,[4] and Mohamed El-Erian, chief executive of Pimco, the world's biggest bond investor, in his book *When Markets Collide*.[5] El-Erian coined the phrase *new normal* to describe the subdued long-term outlook for the U.S. economy as it struggles with the secular trend of deleveraging and weak consumption. Soros popularized the term *market fundamentalism* and conceived the idea of a sixty-year super-bubble, inflated by misguided ideology as well as financial excess and finally bursting on September 15 to leave the world permanently transformed.

This book also tries to make the case that the crisis has permanently transformed global capitalism. But the arguments of the previous chapters suggest that the nature of this transformation may be diametrically oppo-site to the one predicted by Soros and El-Erian.

Chapter 5 showed that the world economy has been driven since the early 1990s by four powerful long-term trends: the rise of Asia, globaliza-tion, the Great Moderation created by the reinvention of Keynesian de-mand management, and a revolution in finance. The last of these trends has been broken by the crisis, at least for now, and may have been permanently reversed. The first three megatrends, however, are still very much in place and, if anything, have been reinforced since September 15.

Even if financial liberalization and credit growth were permanently fin-ished, the expected consumer belt-tightening in the United States, Britain, and other highly leveraged countries will take no more than a few years. A slowdown in debt-financed consumption is therefore unlikely to overwhelm for long the expansionary forces of globalization and demand management. More controversially, this chapter and the next one will argue that the spec-tacular reversal of fortunes in finance caused by the crisis may not have been a permanent change in trends. The revival of finance from 2010 onward sug-gests that the crisis was just a normal cyclical process, exaggerated to surreal proportions by the ideological excesses and dysfunctions of market funda-mentalism that Soros correctly identified.

The argument, in short, is that standard accounts of the crisis and its af-termath have the dynamics of trends and cycles reversed. The conventional view is that long-term structural trends were for years pushing the world economy into more and more dangerous territory. These trends, especially the ones in the financial sector, but also the imbalances between the United States and China, became unsustainable in 2007. The conventional conclusion was that the world would suffer several decades of structural unravelling as the long-term trends of 1989–2007 reversed. According to conventional wisdom, this structural unraveling will continue in the long term even if cyclical forces create a temporary rebound in 2010 and 2011.

But is this a plausible interpretation of what is happening in the modern world economy, and especially of what is structurally permanent and what is cyclically transient? Is it not more likely that the true relationship of trend and cycle is the opposite of the one posited in this standard model?

This book's argument is that three of the four structural trends that began in 1989 are still going strong and may well have been strengthened by the crisis. From 2005–2009, however, these trends were overwhelmed by a cycle of unprecedented ferocity. This cycle was created by dysfunctions in finance, which exaggerated both the upswing and the subsequent plunge. The cyclical financial collapse, exacerbated by almost incredible political mismanagement, as described in Chapter 10, overwhelmed the favorable long-term trends—but only for a while.

After policymakers got a grip on the financial crisis in 2009, the long-term uptrends in the world economy began to reassert themselves. Economic growth revived more quickly than almost anyone expected and continued to surprise on the upside in 2010. This experience suggests that instead of the recovery being a temporary cyclical aberration in a new normal now characterized by long-term stagnation and mass unemployment, the opposite may be true. It could be that the new normal will mean a continuation of the Great Moderation which, after all, had been running for less than twenty years before the crisis, accompanied by an accelerating process of globalization. Meanwhile, the cyclical aberration will turn out to have been the wild financial rollercoaster of 2007–09. In short, conventional wisdom may have confused the trend with the cycle or, to put it more figuratively, the voice with the megaphone.

It seems presumptuous to suggest that some of the most successful and thoughtful financiers of their generation may have misunderstood the nature of an extreme financial cycle. But history shows that such things often happen. If this turns out to be true, Soros and El-Erian would be in excellent company, with Isaac Newton no less.

Part II began with the investors' adage that "this time is different" are the four most expensive words in the English language and noted that all financial booms are created by a belief that the world has changed in a way never seen before. This is a good reason to be suspicious of extravagant claims made at times of financial euphoria. Often forgotten, however, is that a similar scepticism needs to be exercised in financial slumps. Although the likelihood of irrational exuberance at the top of a boom is universally acknowledged, almost no one seems to recognize the mirror image of this logic: "This time is different" can also be a dangerously misleading slogan at the bottom of a bust.

If anything, the despondency in the depth of a crisis is likely to be more exaggerated and deceptive than the euphoria at the top for two reasons: first, because fear is a more powerful emotion than greed, at least in the short term, and second, because the natural condition of any market economy is expansion, and the capitalist system has a strong, almost biological, instinct for self-preservation. Therefore, to justify the claim that "this time is different," the evidence of some unique and unprecedented change in conditions has to be even stronger in a bust than in a boom. To illustrate this point, let me quote from some articles published in leading American newspapers near the bottom of the recession:

There is no question that this is the worst economic time since the Great Depression.

Sluggish economic growth this year will cap the worst three-year period centered on a recession since the Great Depression.

The banking industry has plunged to its lowest point since the Great Depression.

The worst retail sales period on record since the Great Depression.

This recession is hitting white-collar workers more heavily than any since the Great Depression of the 1930s.

Forecasts for a weak recovery suggest the period [ahead] will be the worst for the economy since the Great Depression.

What, you may ask, is so remarkable about these quotations? After all, we now know that the recession of 2008–09 *was* the deepest since 1936— so the despondency displayed in these quotations turned out to be justified.

Not quite. All these articles were published not in 2008 or 2009, but in early 1991. And the 1990–91 recession, far from being "the worst economic time since the Great Depression," turned out to be the mildest and shortest recession on record and had already ended when these comments appeared in print.[6] Moreover, these dire prophecies (often masquerading as factual descriptions of current conditions) were followed by the greatest bull market in history and fifteen years of uninterrupted economic growth.

The record of markets and financiers misinterpreting temporary booms and busts as permanent structural changes and, therefore, extrapolating cyclical movements into long-term trends is as old as the history of capitalism. The most famous and preposterous examples of exaggerated misinterpretations of boom-bust cycles, Tulipmania and the South Sea Bubble, occurred at the very origin of the modern capitalist system. But the lessons that ought to be drawn from these episodes about the relative importance of trends and cycles are not those commonly supposed.

The bubbles of the past are usually held up as proof of human irrationality and specifically the capacity for greed to detach financial conditions from economic reality. What these episodes actually reveal, however, is that even the most preposterous excesses of irrational exuberance at the climax of financial manias often reflect genuine and momentous changes in long-term technological or political trends. The despondency at the bottom of the subsequent busts, by contrast, tends to be a purely cyclical phenomenon. Caused by an unravelling of the unsustainable credit inspired by exaggerated optimism in the upswing, the typical bust is abetted by various forms of stupidity, corruption, and fraud. But after the bust has occurred and the financial detritus has been cleared away, generally at great public expense, the favorable long-term trends that powered the boom tend to reassert themselves—and often end up exceeding the bullish speculators' wildest dreams.

The most recent and familiar example of a boom-bust cycle driven by fundamental economic progress, but vastly exaggerated by finance, was the Internet mania of the 1990s. Although the shares of companies such as Microsoft, Cisco, Amazon, and Intel have not recovered, even ten years later, to the ludicrous levels they reached in the spring of 2000—and possibly never will—the development of the Internet, mobile telephony, and computing power has justified the bullish expectations at the height of the boom. If anything, the effects of these new technologies on every part of the world economy have turned out to be more far-reaching than anyone in 1999 predicted. A broadly similar argument can even by made about Tulipmania and the South Sea Bubble.

The purchase of a single tulip bulb for the price of a townhouse in Amsterdam, at that time the richest city in the world, seems like a symptom of certifiable madness, yet even this behavior appears less bizarre when placed in its historic context. Tulipmania marked the emergence of the first free-enterprise capitalist economy in history.

In the early seventeenth century, during the Eighty Years' War of 1568–1648, the predominantly Protestant bourgeoisie of the United Dutch States were fighting for their freedom from an oppressive and obstinately feudal Spanish monarchy. By the early seventeenth century, this war was moving in favor of the Netherlands, and in 1602, exploiting their advantage against the declining Spanish and Portuguese maritime powers, the citizens of Holland founded the Dutch East India Company, quickly gaining a monopoly over most of Europe's trade with Asia. This incredible commercial opportunity inspired and financially underpinned the creation in Holland of the first mercantile capitalist nation. This was arguably the most important event in the economic history of the world up to that point. A bull market in Dutch assets of every kind understandably ensued, and by 1630, it had extended to tulips.

Tulips offered an indirect but financially efficient way of speculating on the rapid growth of incomes and asset prices in Holland. They were simply one extreme and outlandish manifestation of every investor's desire to get a stake in the Dutch boom. Tulip bulbs, ultimately bought and sold on futures contracts well before the bulbs had even germinated, were equivalent to the speculative contracts on other people's mortgages that blew up in the subprime bubble. The baroque financial structures of seventeenth-century Holland, built on the assumption of ever-rising tulip prices, inevitably collapsed, just as the mortgage-backed securities built on ever-rising prices for Las Vegas condominiums inevitably collapsed in 2007.

But the bursting of the tulip bubble in 1637 did not end Dutch economic hegemony. Far from it. Tulipmania was followed by a century of

Dutch leadership in almost every branch of global commerce, finance, and manufacturing. Holland's global dominance continued until the early eighteenth century, when another rising capitalist nation secured an even more enticing commercial advantage after another war with Spain—the War of the Spanish Succession of 1701–14.

This time, Spain's defeat by an Anglo-Dutch alliance led in Europe by the Duke of Marlborough resulted in an even greater commercial and geopolitical opportunity than the one captured by the Dutch East India Company a century before: a monopoly on most of the trade across the Atlantic. In those days, Atlantic trade consisted largely of shipping slaves, silver, and gold between Africa, Europe, and the Spanish colonies in Mexico and Peru but also included supplying and developing the North American colonies. The monopoly was granted by the victorious British Crown to the London-based South Sea Company, whose establishment in 1711 symbolized the emergence of England as the world's dominant economic power.

As in the case of Tulipmania, this structural transformation in economic conditions gave rise to an unsustainable financial boom, the South Sea Bubble. This bubble burst in 1720, exposing colossal fraud and political corruption. It brought ruin to many notable British business and aristocratic families. Financial acumen and analytical brainpower were no defense against the bubble's devastation, as Newton discovered. The indiscriminate nature of its financial devastation may explain why the South Sea Bubble, along with Tulipmania, is usually considered the quintessential case of the financial markets' detachment from reality, a view expressed in the title of probably the most famous book on the history of finance, Charles MacKay's *Extraordinary Popular Delusions and the Madness of Crowds*.

But was the South Sea Bubble, along with the Mississippi Company speculation that blew up in Paris at about the same time, really nothing more than an extraordinary delusion? It might have been if trans-Atlantic trade were set to peak in the 1720s and America were destined to become a small unproductive backwater of the world economy. It might have been if England were about to be dislodged by Spain or Holland as a maritime and economic power, instead of the other way around. It might have been if finance and trade were heading for inexorable decline in relation to European agriculture. However, the historic trends that drove Newton and his fellow speculators to apparent madness were far from over. They had only just started. The South Sea Bubble, rather than marking the end of Britain's economic dominance, was scarcely a hiccup in the country's rise to global financial power.

Just as the Dutch financial system hardly missed a beat after Tulipmania and went on to dominate the world for the next century, the British economy quickly rebounded after the 1720 crash. The financial returns from trans-Atlantic trade and investment in the American economy—the "fantasies" on which the South Sea and Mississippi Companies were founded— far exceeded the deluded speculators' wildest dreams.

Such historical examples do not prove that the speculators in property and financial derivatives before the crash of 2007 will ultimately be proved right. On the contrary. The buyers of Squared-CDOs, who were as foolish as the late investors in Pets.Com and the leveraged buyers of South Sea promissory notes, will never recover a penny of their reckless speculations. But the idiocies of CDO-2 investors do not necessarily imply a structural decline in the United States and British economies, just as the idiocies of Dutch speculators in striped-black *Semper Augustus* bulbs did not reflect the imminent demise of the Dutch economy. What they reflected was a spectacular transformation in Holland's economic fundamentals that investors had no idea how to handle or evaluate, especially in its early phase.

In the same way, it is increasingly clear that the truly fundamental long-term changes in the world economy of the past two decades will turn out to have been the megatrends that inspired the euphoria of the upswing, while the collapse of 2007–09 was a temporary manifestation of cyclical financial excesses. The next chapter explains how cyclical, rather than structural, forces were behind the 2007 bust in mortgage finance, which was then exaggerated by the astonishing incompetence of political mismanagement into the greatest financial crisis of all time.

CHAPTER NINE

Boom and Bust
Forever

We will never return to the old boom and bust.

—Prime Minister Gordon Brown, March 2007,
six months before the run on Northern Rock,
Britain's largest mortgage bank

FINANCIAL BOOMS AND BUSTS have baffled and fascinated economic thinkers since capitalism's earliest days. It is therefore no surprise that the greatest financial crisis in living memory, which occurred in the months after the bankruptcy of Lehman, elicited many different explanations. These ranged from excessive savings in China to policy mistakes by the Federal Reserve Board, from corrupt political lobbying to the immutable facts of human psychology, crystallized by the unforgettable two-word phrases from Alan Greenspan that punctuated the boom and bust: first "irrational exuberance," then "infectious greed," and finally "shocked disbelief."

Although the proponents of these differing explanations are often bitter rivals, they all may be right. Each theory of financial cycles is usually presented as a complete and unique account, to the exclusion of all others. But the pragmatic spirit of Capitalism 4 warns against false dichotomies that assert that if one point of view is right, all others must be wrong.

The Theories of Boom-Bust Cycles

No serious theory of financial cycles should ever claim to capture the complete truth and few are unambiguously false. Even two theories considered by their proponents to be contradictory—for example, the ultralibertarian Austrian interpretation and the government-oriented Keynesian approach—can be simultaneously valid. Modern academic fashion may demand that all economic theories be rigorously self-consistent, but reality is much more complex. With this proviso—that serious theories of financial cycles should be viewed as complementary rather than mutually exclusive—it is helpful to consider three ways of thinking about the causes of boom-bust processes, each of which can be subdivided into several (usually conflicting, but not necessarily incompatible) schools of thought.

Investment-Led Cycles

The Austrian model, pioneered by Ludwig von Mises, is driven by extreme investment swings caused by interest rates that are first below and then above some natural rate. In the ultralibertarian spirit of Austrian economics, these swings in interest rates are usually blamed on the meddling of incompetent governments and central banks. A period when interest rates are kept too low, often for political reasons, creates a credit boom, during which investment is artificially stimulated and capital flows into projects with low rates of return. The result is widespread malinvestment in, for example, poor-quality housing that can find buyers only because of the unnatural conditions created by a credit boom. When the wasteful investment eventually pushes interest rates above the natural rate, the result is a credit contraction and recession. At this point, investments and businesses that prospered based only on excess credit and artificially low interest rates go bankrupt. A crisis ensues, but eventually markets rebalance of their own accord and capital is reallocated to more efficient uses.[1]

Following this purgative liquidation phase, a genuinely free-market economy would return to a stable track. But governments and central banks usually panic during the liquidation phase, pushing interest rates below their natural rate again and boosting the money supply. This artificial stimulus, especially if sustained for a long period, inevitably sets off another credit boom and the cycle begins anew. This analysis has obvious appeal, especially for libertarians who instinctively oppose all forms of government interference with free markets.[2] In practice, however, the Austrian recommendation that slumps should be allowed to run their natural course and "purge the rottenness out of the system"[3] has never been followed by any government anywhere in the world since the calamitous experience of 1929–1932.

The Keynesian explanation also focuses on investment but comes to the opposite conclusion. The Keynesian cycle is explained mainly by swings in investment resulting from changes in business sentiment and profit expectations, as well as interest rates. According to Keynes, business expectations could be affected by "animal spirits" reflecting changes in technology or in geopolitical and social conditions, as well as monetary policy. Periods of optimism tend to produce high rates of investment, which increase the amount of capital in the economy and raise production at an accelerating pace. Eventually a point is reached when the economy's output potential exceeds consumption, businesspeople's profit expectations go into reverse, and investment declines. This starts a cyclical downturn.[4]

The Keynesian cycle, however, is not symmetrical, because a sharp decline in investment causes job losses, declining incomes, and a further fall in consumption. This depresses business expectations even more, causing more job losses and still lower consumer spending. The result can be a vicious circle from which market forces will not, on their own, provide an escape. Thus, although the upswing of the cycle is ultimately self-correcting, the decline may not be. At this point, government spending and borrowing, plus direct action to push credit into the economy, may be needed to prevent a prolonged slump. This was essentially what the G20 governments concluded in April 2009 when they took various measures to boost economic growth and try to force their banks to expand credit.

Cycles Driven by Investor Psychology and Uncertainty

Hyman Minsky, a great American economist based at Washington University in St. Louis, argued in the 1960s that long periods of economic stability would lead to conditions of financial overconfidence that would, in turn, promote leverage and exaggerate risk-taking and increase debt burdens throughout society. Minsky's theories were ignored by the academic establishment from the 1980s onward but came back into prominence during the 2007 crisis and received widespread attention not only in the media but also in central banks and finance ministries around the world. A key feature of what Minsky called his Financial Instability Hypothesis was that economic stability would encourage banks to innovate. When economic conditions prove surprisingly benign, banks start accepting low-quality assets as collateral and find new ways of lending to ever-riskier borrowers. These processes eventually become unsustainable. But crucially, the unwinding of leverage does not occur in a gradual way that would bring the system back into equilibrium, as assumed by mainstream academic economics.

Instead, as borrowers begin to experience debt problems, bankers seize assets pledged as collateral; but they discover that these assets are no longer worth their original values and many are impossible to sell at any reasonable price. At this point, a liquidity panic ensues because no one is willing to bid for the speculative assets that banks desperately need to sell to preserve their solvency. As the solvency of the banks is questioned, savers withdraw their money and banks are forced to sell even more assets, driving down prices still further. As this process continues, the entire banking system can be threatened with collapse, unless the government intervenes with guarantees or supportive measures of other kinds. The point of inflection in this cycle, when lenders suddenly realize that they were dangerously overoptimistic in their lending decisions and their original assumptions about asset values, is often described as a Minsky Moment. A classic such moment occurred during the Russian government default and hedge fund crisis of 1998.[5] According to many analysts, the 2007–09 credit crunch was a Minsky Moment writ large.

George Soros's Theory of Reflexivity can be seen as a generalization of Minsky's Financial Instability Hypothesis and Keynes's theory of animal spirits. Soros puts both on a different philosophical basis by emphasising the two-way interaction between people's perceptions and the events perceived. Soros argues that miscalculations made by both lenders and borrowers result from the gap that inevitably exists between reality and human understanding. Human thinking consists of two potentially discordant elements—a cognitive function, which tries to understand reality, and a manipulative function, which tries to change reality.[6] These functions can interfere with one another.

The interference between the cognitive and manipulation functions creates two problems. The first is that human knowledge—the cognitive function—is always imperfect and, therefore, market expectations will always be wrong, at least to some extent. The second problem—and the one at the heart of the theory—is that in situations where reality involves thinking participants, expectations about the future will alter reality, and this new reality will in turn change expectations. This two-way interaction between reality and expectations is the process that Soros calls reflexivity, and it can create boom-bust cycles similar to the kind Minsky described.

In the Soros theory, financial markets do not reflect the most accurate possible forecasts about the future and then move naturally toward equilibrium, as assumed in standard economics. In fact, they often do the opposite. Imagine that house prices have been rising for a period, perhaps because they are recovering from a previous bust. The rise in prices may encourage overoptimism about future housing demand and make houses appear more attractive to bankers as collateral for mortgage loans. The increased availability of mortgages then increases the demand for houses and this pushes up house prices, thereby justifying the original optimism about them. Thus, financial expectations have changed the reality they were supposed to predict—and this, in turn, gives the financial cycle another twist. As bullish investors find their expectations confirmed, they push prices even higher and encourage even more mortgage lending and housing demand, thereby validating even more optimism among both homeowners and bankers.

Soros's theory of reflexivity generalizes this simple example to a wide range of situations in which expectations about economic and political fundamentals diverge from reality and then influence reality. The changed fundamentals then reinforce the initial expectations, creating self-perpetuating cycles that can push an economy, or indeed an entire society, further and further from a balanced state. Eventually, a point is reached when expectations become so extreme and unrealistic that the fundamentals can no longer be sufficiently manipulated by the process of reflexivity. At the point that Soros calls the Moment of Truth, which is identical in financial markets to the Minsky Moment, the self-reinforcing mechanism goes into reverse—and boom turns to bust.

In his books and lectures, Soros has used reflexivity to analyze many extreme and unexpected events, including the collapse of communism and breakup of the Soviet Union. During the 2007–09 crisis, he persuasively argued that the purely financial boom-bust cycle was combined with a wider cycle in free-market ideology, starting in the late 1970s and culminating in the extreme deregulation of the precrisis phase. These two cyclical processes, in finance and in politico-economic thinking, were, in turn, mutually reinforcing. The apparent wealth created by the financial sector encouraged more deregulation, which in turn made finance even more profitable and therefore politically influential. According to Soros, the interaction between these financial and political processes, and their reflexive influence on one another, created a super-bubble that culminated in the unprecedented bust of 2008.

Behavioral finance, a blend of traditional economics and experimental psychology, became a popular theory of boom-bust cycles after Alan Greenspan coined the phrase "irrational exuberance" in a 1996 speech.[7] The idea that financial instability is a consequence of various forms of irrational behavior was elaborated and popularized a few years later by the Yale economics professor Robert Shiller in his best-selling book *Irrational Exuberance,*[8] published three months before the bursting of the technology stock bubble.

Among the sources of irrationality discussed by behavioral economists and demonstrated in their financial experiments are herd instinct, overconfidence, and anchoring. In the anchoring syndrome, people base expectations about inherently uncertain events on whatever magic numbers or trends are brought to their notice, even if these bear no rational relationship to the events they are trying to predict. Herding and projection bias seem to provide convincing and simple explanations both of irrational exuberance in the boom phase of financial cycles and of irrational despondency in the bust. But in contrast to other cyclical theories that suggest that financial markets are intrinsically unstable, behavioral finance treats trend-following behavior as a temporary, and perhaps avoidable, aberration. The behavioral view is therefore less challenging to the fundamental assumption of textbook economics that markets are, on average, driven by rational calculation and are always self-stabilizing in the long term.

Chaos theory was developed in the 1960s by Benoit Mandelbrot, one of the leading mathematicians of the twentieth century. Mandelbrot spent thirty years demonstrating that this theory, which transformed the study of biology, meteorology, geology, and other complex systems, could be applied also to financial markets. Mandelbrot's research program undermined most of the mathematical assumptions of modern portfolio theory, which is the basis for the conventional risk models used by regulators, credit-rating agencies, and unsophisticated financial institutions.

Mandelbrot's analysis, presented to nonspecialist readers in his 2004 book *(Mis)behavior of Markets,* shows with mathematical certainty that these standard statistical models based on neoclassical definitions of efficient markets and rational expectations among investors cannot be true. Had these models been valid, events such as the 1987 stock market crash and the bankruptcy of the 1998 hedge fund crisis would not have occurred even once in the fifteen billion years since the creation of the universe.[9] In fact, four such extreme events occurred in just two weeks after the Lehman bankruptcy. Mandelbrots's ideas were popularized by Nassim Taleb in *Fooled by Randomness* and *The Black Swan.*[10] These books, and the mathematical research they reflect, show that movements in financial prices are not "normally" distributed[11] and that markets are much riskier than standard models indicate. The implication is that all the standard risk-management employed by bankers, regulators, and credit-rating agencies before

the Lehman crisis were deeply flawed, and their use was bound eventually
to produce enormous losses leading to a total breakdown of the financial
system. The mathematics of chaos theory, although it has been profitably
used for trading by some sophisticated hedge funds, has been almost ignored by mainstream economists and financial regulators, largely because it
is too challenging to conventional paradigms of neoclassical economics and
efficient markets.

Cycles Driven by Income Distribution

Post-Keynesian and neo-Marxist economists have argued that the origin of
financial crises lies, at the deepest level, in the shifting distribution of national income between wages and profits. Building on the pioneering ideas
of the Polish economist Michal Kalecki, whose work in the early 1930s anticipated much of Keynes, the Cambridge school of post-Keynesian economists—Joan Robinson, Geoffrey Harcourt, Nicholas Kaldor, Robin Marris,
and Robert Rowthorn—have noted that although workers tend to spend
almost all their incomes, the entrepreneurs and investors who benefit from
corporate profits save a high proportion of what they receive.[12] The post-
Keynesians also argued that advanced capitalism generally shifts income
distribution in favor of profits and away from wages, partly because of technological progress and monopoly, and partly for political reasons such as restrictions on organized labor.

The result of widening income inequalities and rising profitability is
that a growing share of national income flows to owners of capital, who
spend less than they earn. Meanwhile wage earners are forced to run down
their savings and increasingly to rely on debt to maintain their standard of
living. The only way to keep the economy growing in these conditions is for
government to support demand with deficit financing and for the banking
system to expand credit to poorer and less creditworthy borrowers. As long
as this credit expansion creates sufficient demand, the economy can continue to operate with reasonably full employment. But if income distribution continues to move against labor, workers eventually find themselves
unable to service further borrowing and a financial crisis becomes inevitable

as working-class borrowers begin to default on their loans. The post-Keynesian economy with widening income inequality is therefore always veering between the Scylla of recession due to inadequate consumption and the Charybdis of financial crisis caused by unsustainable debt. Many of the left-wing criticisms of the Obama Administration's economic policies from U.S. Keynesian economists such as Paul Krugman, Robert Reich, James K. Galbraith, and Joe Stiglitz are linked to this school of thought.

THE THEORIES JUST OUTLINED spell out in intricate and persuasive detail how financial excesses can come about, why they are bound to hit any market-based economy, and why the resulting fluctuations can sometimes be long lasting and extreme. Rather than try to adjudicate between them, which seems to be the main objective of many partisan analyses of the crisis, it seems more sensible to accept them all, in varying degrees.

Probably the best explanation for the entire financial cycle crisis would be an amalgam of the Austrian, Soros, and Minsky theories—with the financial instability vastly exaggerated by the statistical flaws identified by Mandelbrot and the political biases of Soros's ideological super-bubble. Meanwhile, the underlying reasons for the boom in subprime borrowing, for the global imbalances between America and China, and indeed for the boom in market fundamentalist ideology are best explained by the New Keynesian–Marxist approach. Specifically, the story can be summarized as follows.

Prolonged stability caused by the Great Moderation suppressed financial risk, as explained by Minsky, and thereby transformed expectations, creating the herd behavior and reflexive changes in reality described by Soros. At the same time, the long period of low interest rates due to excess savings in Asia encouraged Austrian-style malinvestment in low-income housing, as well as the aggressive financial innovation predicted by Minsky. This happened despite the fact that low-income consumers and homeowners were becoming less creditworthy because of the widening income inequality anticipated by Kalecki and the New Keynesians. The boom in finance, meanwhile, interacted with the ideological super-bubble described by Soros and, through the process of reflexivity, created an excessive faith in markets that changed political realities. An extreme form of deregulation that had no chance of working in the long-term did seem to work for a few years in the market fundamentalist America of President Bush. The result was to exaggerate even further the faith that financial markets would automatically produce efficient outcomes to all economic and social problems. In this atmosphere of intellectual delusion, politicians and regulators refused to acknowledge the necessity of government regulation in financial markets. Even worse, they failed to understand, after the financial meltdown started, that the automatic stabilizers of market competition and supposedly rational self-interest would no longer work. Direct government intervention was by then the only way to prevent a total systemic breakdown. But policymakers found this impossible to accept until it was almost too late.

It seems, then, that all the theories of financial cycles described can shed some useful light on features of the 2007–09 crisis. Why, then, do they remain in intellectual exile, outside the mainstream of "serious" academic economics? And why is it that, apart from the tired repetition of the phrase "irrational exuberance," the inevitability of financial boom-bust cycles has almost never featured in the speeches of regulators and politicians?

The answer is clear: Any serious theory of financial cycles must, by definition, contradict the doctrine of general equilibrium that has dominated economics in the era of Capitalism 3. Mainstream economists simply *assume* that financial markets are naturally stable, that they automatically move toward equilibrium, and that they are *not* prone to boom-bust cycles. These notions became completely dominant in economic theory during the last decade, even as real-world financial fluctuations became more extreme. This is a story laid out in detail in Chapter 11. The main point for the moment is that any serious account of financial cycles must address a question once considered to be among the most important in economics and public life but deliberately ignored by the market fundamentalist economics of Capitalism 3.3: What makes finance inherently so unstable?

Why Finance Is Different from Every Other Business

The issue at the heart of all the explanations of boom-bust cycles just described is the unpredictability of the future. This is what makes finance different—and more unstable—than other economic activities. The primary purpose of any financial system is to link decisions made today with events many years or even decades ahead. Savers, investors, and businesses must resolve here and now how much to save or spend, whether to build new factories and which technologies to back, but all these decisions depend on views about the future—and those views, in most cases, can be based only on gut instincts, hopes, and fears.

In nonfinancial businesses, market prices may move more or less rationally in response to measurable changes in supply and demand, but in financial markets, prices respond mainly to subjective expectations about events in a distant future that is often unknowable, even in a probabilistic sense.[13] Modern economists sometimes pretend to overcome this problem by assuming that financiers make decisions by calculating future probabilities in the same way that normal businesses, operating in the present, count current profits and losses. But substituting probability distributions for observable facts does not solve the problem of uncertainty. It merely covers up the true problem, like a con man playing the three-card trick. Calculating probabilities may work well enough in the insurance business or in everyday banking, but in many situations, future probability cannot be assessed. Recent events have offered spectacular examples.

What was the probability that two planes would hit the New York twin towers within an hour? What was the probability that the Soviet Union would dissolve without a shot being fired? What was the probability that the U.S. government would suddenly withdraw its backing for a systemically vital financial institution that everyone "knew" was "too important to fail"?

Business life consists largely of similarly incalculable, but more banal, questions about the future that simply cannot be answered, even in a probabilistic sense. What is the probability that someone in the next hundred years will invent a soft drink more popular than Coca-Cola? This probability must surely rate at almost 100 percent, yet that would also have been true in 1910. There is no rational way of making such an assessment. It is unclear if Thomas J. Watson, the chairman of IBM in the early 1950s, ever made his widely quoted remark that "there will be a worldwide market for maybe five computers."[14] But what is certain is that even as late as 1980, no one would have put any significant probability on computer sales exceeding car sales by a factor of ten to one.[15]

The role of inherent unpredictability in finance means that the most important prices set in financial markets—interest rates, exchange rates, stock market values, and property values—will almost *never* correctly reflect conditions in the economy of today and may not create the right investment and saving incentives to keep the economy in equilibrium. Most of the time, the errors tend to cancel each other out or correct themselves quickly through normal market competition. But every so often, financial markets go haywire, succumbing to the alternating excesses of greed and fear that create boom-bust cycles. Does this mean that financial markets are pathological and immoral? The alternation of greed and fear certainly causes losses and economic disruptions in the short term, as well as suffering among innocent bystanders who have no involvement in finance, but in a longer historical perspective, financial cycles can be seen to play a crucial part in the evolution of the capitalist system.

Greed and fear, after all, are not unnatural or dysfunctional conditions. Natural selection has hard-wired these emotions into the human brain for good reasons. The great insight of Adam Smith was that greed, euphemistically described as self-interest, is the creative force that constantly drives humanity to improve the material world. Greed is what gives impetus to the arrow of progress—and this is true not only of economics. In Chinese philosophy, the creative principle of yang is associated with aggression and acquisition. In politics, Machiavelli described the accumulation of worldly "glory" as the motivating principle that drives leaders to undertake "great enterprises" and do "great things" on behalf of their fellow citizens and not just themselves.[16] But greed, whether for material possessions or for political glory, must be kept in check. Hence, the evolutionary value of fear. Fear, also known as prudence, caution, or the Chinese yin, is just as important as ambition and greed for human success.

This is why the ring of repetitive financial cycles is needed as a countervailing mechanism to control the arrow of progress. In fact, the interplay between the arrow and the ring may be necessary for the capitalist system to evolve and improve itself, just as the balance between the greed for profits and the fear of bankruptcy is needed for businesses and industries to adapt and improve.

There are times, however, perhaps only once every generation, when the financial oscillations of greed and fear get out of control. At times like this, a political force from outside the market economy must intervene to moderate the financial cycle. Governments or regulators must have the power and the self-confidence to second-guess and override market signals. They must accept responsibility for managing economic activity and employment. And they must stand ready to support the financial system if regulation fails.

The refusal of the U.S. government to recognize these obligations almost destroyed the global economy on September 15, 2008. In the last analysis, what caused the greatest financial crisis in history was not the U.S. housing boom, or the reckless greed of the banks, or the monetary policies of the Fed and the Chinese government. It was the refusal of the Bush administration and the economists who helped shape its ideology to recognize the essential functions of government in a modern capitalist economy. This is the story the next part of the book takes up.

Part III

Market Fundamentalism Self-Destructs

THE CRISIS OF 2007–09 was a cyclical event of the kind that has regularly punctuated the history of finance. What turned this fairly ordinary boom-bust cycle into the greatest financial catastrophe of all time? It was not the scale of the housing boom or the greed of the bankers or the stupidity of reckless borrowers. These were all phenomena seen many times before in previous cycles. What was unique about the crisis of 2007–09 was the part played by the U.S. government—or rather the U.S. government's refusal to play its part. The Bush administration's failure to recognize the essential role of government in stabilizing and underpinning the modern financial system brought every bank in the world to the brink of failure and threatened the global economy with an unprecedented depression.

And that failure, in turn, was not a random lapse or a casual oversight. It was a conscious decision resulting from a flawed understanding of economics. More precisely, what inspired the U.S. government's fatal procrastination in the most crucial phases of the crisis was a self-serving political ideology, masquerading as academic economic theory. This economic ideology encouraged politicians, bankers, and regulators to invent an imaginary world of financial stability and efficient, omniscient markets that could solve all problems if only the government would stand aside. As Keynes wrote with his usual eloquence two generations ago:

> Practical men, who believe themselves to be quite exempt from any intellectual influence, are usually the slaves of some defunct economist. Madmen in authority, who hear voices in the air, are distilling their frenzy from some academic scribbler of a few years back. The ideas of economists and political philosophers, both when they are right and when they are wrong, are more powerful than is commonly understood. Indeed the world is ruled by little else.[1]

The epitome of Keynes's down-to-earth practical man, exempt from any intellectual influence that he was consciously aware of, is Henry Paulson, the Secretary of the U.S. Treasury from 2006–09. His personal responsibility for the financial catastrophe has received surprisingly little attention in the post-crisis debate.

CHAPTER TEN

The Economic Consequences of Mr. Paulson

Republicans are people who believe that government doesn't work, and get themselves elected to prove it.

— P. J. O'Rourke

THE COLLAPSE OF LEHMAN BROTHERS on September 15, 2008, was the financial heart attack that turned a serious but manageable ailment in the U.S. mortgage market into a near-death experience for the global economy.[1] Even before that fateful day, many banks and borrowers were in serious trouble, but the situation seemed to be improving and certainly not spinning out of control. The credit crunch that had begun in early 2007 could still be viewed as a severe but fairly normal cyclical correction, reversing some excesses in bank lending and property speculation of a kind seen many times before. The global economy was showing reasonable resilience, and businesses and investors the world over suggested by their behavior that they genuinely believed the worst was over. Economic growth was still positive. House prices were stabilizing. Consumer and business confidence were recovering, as the price of oil fell back from the peak of $150 a

This title is a conscious echo of *The Economic Consequences of Mr Churchill*, the 1925 pamphlet in which Keynes exposed the ruinous effects of Churchill stubbornly defending the gold standard.

barrel that it hit in response to speculative fears of excessive growth in China and other emerging economies. The biggest worry on the minds of most economists and businesspeople that summer was no longer the credit crunch but the threat of inflation caused by the earlier surge in the oil prices.

A reasonable view of economic conditions before the fall of Lehman was the low-key assessment offered by Olivier Blanchard, the IMF's chief economist, just two weeks before the crash: "If the price of oil stabilizes, I believe we can weather the financial crisis at limited cost."[2]

What, then, transformed this fairly normal boom-bust cycle into the greatest financial crisis of all time? The main contention of this chapter—and probably the most controversial claim this book makes—is that the primary reason for this disaster was not the stupidity of regulators, the greed of bankers, or the improvidence of speculators in low-income real estate but a series of misjudgments made by one man: U.S. Treasury Secretary Henry Paulson.

Personalities matter in economics, as in politics and war. No one would dispute that personalities made a difference to history when Churchill replaced Chamberlain, when Lenin overthrew Kerensky, or when Napoleon ousted *Le Directoire*. The role of individuals is equally important in economic crises because, like wars and revolutions, these are historic periods when normal rules do not apply. When traditional ways of doing things no longer offer useful guidance, economic policymakers, just like generals and revolutionary leaders, have to fall back on instinct and charisma. Boldness, persuasiveness, and personal judgment can make the difference between triumph and disaster—or in the case of the 2007–09 crisis, the difference between a normal, if severe, financial cycle and a historic catastrophe.

The most amazing aspect of this crisis was the total failure of leadership and judgment in the United States. Hence this chapter's focus on the one man directly responsible for the most important errors. Henry Paulson, despite having been the chairman and CEO of Goldman Sachs—or perhaps because of it—turned out to be the most incompetent economic policymaker in U.S. history, with the possible exception of Andrew Mellon, his predecessor at the Treasury from 1921 to 1932.

Paulson's reputation, or more precisely the reflected glory of his previous position at Goldman Sachs, was so intimidating to all potential critics that no one thought of questioning the quality of his financial understanding, either during the crisis or in its immediate aftermath. Yet an objective reading of the historic record suggests that the most important decisions of the U.S. government before and after Lehman were, at best, perverse and self-defeating, and in several cases catastrophically misconceived.

Christine Lagarde, the French finance minister and one of the few policymakers to emerge from the crisis with an enhanced reputation, later described Paulson's decision on Lehman as "horrendous" and "a genuine error."[3] Alan Blinder, the former Fed vice-chairman, called it a "colossal" mistake and noted that "many people said so at the time."[4] Privately, almost all experienced policymakers, financiers, and businesspeople are even more outspoken. Yet for some reason, Paulson's "horrendous" and "colossal" errors never attracted remotely the attention and detailed criticism as the less expensive military misjudgments made by the U.S. government in Iraq and Afghanistan.

This chapter tries to fill this analytical vacuum by focusing not only on the Lehman bankruptcy but also on the policy mistakes that led to it and then greatly magnified its effects. Conventional wisdom retrospectively presented the economic slump that followed Lehman as an inevitable disaster that would probably have happened regardless, triggered by some other accident if the Lehman bankruptcy had not occurred. In the immediate aftermath of the crisis, almost all economists and analysts retrospectively declared that some other event would have acted as catalyst for global economic disaster had it not been Lehman, since a painful period of reckoning was inevitable and morally necessary after a decade of self-indulgence and greed.

This book takes a different view. There was nothing inevitable or righteous about the disaster—indeed inevitability and moral righteousness are rarely useful concepts in economic affairs. The Lehman crisis and its terrible aftermath were not acts of God, but a series of unfortunate events. They were the logical consequences of avoidable policy errors, and all these unfortunate events had one thing in common: the U.S. treasury secretary's fundamental misunderstanding of the capitalist system, especially of the critical role of government in the financial markets.

Anyone who claims that a former chairman of Goldman Sachs doesn't understand financial markets faces an obvious objection. Goldman Sachs has faced many accusations, especially since the crisis, but to link it with financial incompetence seems self-evidently absurd. And this ad hominem justification of Henry Paulson has been sufficient to discourage any critical examination of his decisions. Although there have been several gripping blow-by-blow accounts of Paulson's chaotic style of crisis management,[5] no one has seriously criticized the strategy and economic philosophy underlying all his actions. Yet even a moment's reflection suggests the strangeness of this ex officio validation of everything Paulson did.

Democratic societies aggressively question military strategies decided by generals, defense ministers, and other so-called experts in warfare. Why, then, should media commentators, politicians, and indeed armchair-generals hyperventilating in barrooms or over their morning papers be any more intimidated by the financial omniscience of a former chairman of Goldman Sachs? Should we really assume that successful bankers are better equipped for dealing with financial crises than successful generals are for devising strategies to defeat the Taliban or win the war in Vietnam? History suggests that the answer is no.

There have been at least as many cases of prominent financiers pressing for economic and financial strategies that proved catastrophic as of famous generals promoting disastrous military campaigns. In fact, the only previous time the U.S. government perpetrated a financial blunder comparable to the bankruptcy of Lehman involved a politician uncannily similar to Henry Paulson in almost every respect.

The blunder in question was the decision to put roughly one-third of U.S. banks out of business after the 1929 crash on Wall Street. The decision to liquidate the U.S. banking system, instead of printing money to bail out banks that suffered mass withdrawals, was later convincingly identified by Milton Friedman as the main cause of the Great Depression.[6] It was largely attributable to the influence of one man: Andrew Mellon, the only plausible competitor to Henry Paulson for the title of the worst U.S. treasury secretary of all time.[7]

Mellon's insistence on liquidating the banks after the 1929 crash subsequently epitomized all that was stupid, destructive, and arrogant about the policies that caused the Great Depression. This is how President Hoover recorded it in his autobiography: "The 'leave it alone liquidationists' headed by Secretary of the Treasury Mellon . . . felt that government must keep its

hands off and let the slump liquidate itself. Mr. Mellon had only one formula: 'Liquidate labor, liquidate stocks, liquidate farmers, liquidate real estate . . . It will purge the rottenness out of the system. People will work
harder, live a more moral life. Values will be adjusted and enterprising people will pick up from less competent people.'"[8]

What makes Mellon's story intriguing and surprisingly relevant to recent events is that Mellon, even more than Paulson, was the preeminent
financier of his generation. The Mellon Bank, which he had run for thirty
years before his appointment as treasury secretary, was America's second
most important financial institution (after J.P. Morgan). Mellon was the
wealthiest financier of his day and became the most powerful after the
death of Pierpont Morgan in 1913.[9] Like Paulson, however, Mellon was
neither an economist nor a deep political thinker. He was a master deal
maker (again like Paulson), using an incomparable network of business
contacts to help create astonishingly successful industrial mergers and con-
glomerations, including Alcoa, Westinghouse, Rockwell, U.S. Steel, Heinz,
General Motors, and even Rockefeller's Standard Oil. Before becoming
treasury secretary, Mellon had never spent much time considering the
macroeconomic effects of financial markets. Yet his tremendous personal
wealth and success in business gave him a boundless self-confidence in applying the views he had developed in business to the economy as a whole.

This personal history, according to later biographers, helped to explain
one of the most baffling mysteries of the Great Depression: how Andrew
Mellon, despite his immense financial acumen and business experience, became a byword for economic incompetence by the time he was ignomin-
iously bundled out of the U.S. Treasury in 1932.[10] Mellon's problem was
similar to Paulson's: He had a large ego and a small understanding of economics. His tremendous business success had instilled in him an unshak-
able belief in the strength not only of the capitalist system but of the
particular version of capitalism in which he had made his fortune. This
moral self-righteousness blinded both Mellon and Paulson to the ultimate
dependence of any capitalist economy on government support.

In Mellon, this blindness was at least excusable because, in the 1920s,
Keynes was still a voice crying in the wilderness and the concept of macroeconomics had not even been invented.[11] In Paulson's case, the best explanation of the economic incompetence chronicled in the rest of this chapter

is the point made by Paul Krugman in attacking the conservative opposition to fiscal stimulus and public spending in the wake of the crisis:[12] The free-market revolution of the 1970s and 1980s deliberately suppressed Keynes's insights about the crucial role of government in economic management, especially in crises; over time these insights were simply forgotten, in the same way that the science of plumbing was forgotten for centuries after barbarians sacked Rome. As a result, many successful businessmen and politicians genuinely believed that financial markets were automatically self-stabilizing and that government intervention in the economy would always do more harm than good. Henry Paulson, endowed with the overweening confidence of a Goldman Sachs chairman, seemed to have been a prime example of this syndrome.

Having tried, with this historical digression, to convince the reader that describing a Goldman Sachs banker as financially incompetent is not, ipso facto, an oxymoron, I can return to the narrative othe crisis.

In the summer of 2008, the life-threatening phase of the credit crunch appeared to be ending. U.S. growth in the second quarter had just been revised upwards from 1.2 percent to 1.8 percent[13] and the biggest worry was no longer the credit crunch but the threat of inflation caused by overly rapid growth in China, India, and other emerging nations.

The credit crunch was turning out to be less damaging than generally expected for several reasons. One was the continuing growth of Asia and the seemingly inexhaustible supply of excess savings in that part of the world. These savings were made available by the Sovereign Wealth Funds (SWFs) of Abu Dhabi, Singapore, Korea, China, and other countries to Western financial institutions that needed to rebuild their capital after their initial subprime losses—which helped maintain financial stability throughout the first twelve months of the subprime crisis. Another favorable factor, almost unnoticed by politicians and media commentators, was that the U.S. economy was displaying its usual flexibility in responding to the property bust. Capital and labor were shifting out of housing and consumption into the technology and industrial sectors, reducing America's enormous trade deficits and creating the conditions for an export-led growth model previously associated with Germany and Japan.[14]

A further reason for calm, even less widely recognized outside the financial markets, was the gradual deleveraging in banking that followed the government-assisted sale of Bear Stearns to J.P. Morgan. This deleveraging was doing less damage to the nonfinancial economy than generally expected for a reason suggested in Chapter 7: The really dangerous financial excesses were not in the debts taken on by homeowners and consumers but in the astronomical mutual obligations run up between the financial institutions themselves. After the winding-up of Bear Stearns in March 2008 and the regulatory forbearance offered by the New York insurance commissioner to the municipal bond insurers, these mutual debts in the financial sector were starting to be cancelled out in a fairly nondisruptive way.

The buildup of financial debt can be illustrated by contrasting two situations. The first situation is an old-fashioned home mortgage transaction, whereby a homeowner borrows $1 million from a commercial bank such as J.P. Morgan. The second is a borrowing chain, which works like this: The homeowner (0) borrows $1 million from a mortgage bank (1), which borrows from an SIV (2), which borrows from a hedge fund (3), which borrows from a prime broker (4), which borrows from an investment bank (5), which borrows from a bank (6) such as J.P. Morgan. As a result of this borrowing chain, a $1 million mortgage loan has created $6 million in total debt: $1 million in debt in the household sector plus $5 million of purely financial debt.

According to Federal Reserve statistics, more than two-thirds (68 percent) of the total growth in U.S. debt relative to GDP from 1990 to 2008 consisted of the debt owed by financial corporations to one another. In Britain, the figure was even higher.

In principle, most of the deleveraging in British and U.S. financial systems could have been achieved simply by netting out the transactions among financial institutions. However, the condition for an orderly unwinding of the debt-chains between mortgage lenders, hedge funds, investment banks, and long-term investors in the financial sector was that all participants would continue to honor their contracts. As long as they continued to do that, a high proportion of the multitrillion dollar obligations of the financial institutions to one another could simply be cancelled out with little effect on the nonfinancial economy,[15] with very little effect on the nonfinancial economy (apart from the significant but limited second-order effects of some bankers losing bonuses and jobs). The counterparty risk created by the collapse of Lehman made such an orderly unwinding much more difficult. But a proper understanding of the difference between financial and nonfinancial leverage still held out hope of protecting the nonfinancial economy from the worst effects of a credit collapse.

Deleveraging within the financial sector was proceeding rapidly after the rescue of Bear Stearns in March 2008. But if a single link in the debt-chains between financial institutions were broken, chaos would ensue. The risk of such breakdowns had been recognized by both regulators and bankers in the early days of the credit crunch and had been successfully handled (albeit at huge cost to bank shareholders) in 2007, when the mortgage-oriented hedge funds and Special Investment Vehicles set up by Bear Stearns, Citibank, UBS, HSBC, and many other major banks were bailed out by their sponsoring institutions. These bailouts were expensive to the bank shareholders but prevented systemic collapse by maintaining the integrity of all the links in the chain of mutual obligations in the financial system. This was a crucial lesson of the early phase of the credit crunch that the U.S. Treasury and the Fed recognized in the Bear Stearns deal but, in the autumn of 2008, decided to recklessly ignore.

It was only on September 15, when Lehman Brothers went bankrupt, that the world suddenly suffered a near-fatal cardiac arrest. As Mervyn King said six months later:[16] "The world economy changed after the events of Lehman, but it wasn't the failure of Lehman's as such. What changed everything was the complete collapse of confidence in the financial system around the world [after Lehman]."

Why did this happen? After all, Lehman was only a middle-sized bank with no customer deposits. It was not, by any normal definition, "too big to fail." Investment banks of comparable size had failed in the past with no catastrophic damage, most notably Drexel Burnham Lambert in 1989. In the end, the total losses from Lehman's bankruptcy came to about $75 billion.[17] This was a lot of money by the standards of normal business bankruptcies, but modest in comparison with the multitrillion dollar write-downs already suffered by banks around the world before Lehman went down. The collapse of Lehman Brothers was much more catastrophic than the raw numbers might have suggested—or Henry Paulson expected—partly because Lehman was a participant in many of the lending chains that had been gradually unraveling since the start of the credit crunch. Once Lehman defaulted, the orderly unwinding of these mutual obligations, which the Fed had tried to facilitate with the Bear Stearns bailout, become impossible. But the main reason why Lehman's bankruptcy turned out to be so catastrophic was the simple one noted by King.

Lehman precipitated "a complete collapse of confidence" among the depositors and creditors of *every* major financial institution—in effect a run on every bank around the world. Only when the world financial system suffered this unprecedented breakdown did the real economy of consumption, global trade, and industrial orders "fall off a cliff," as many industrialists and retailers immediately declared. The corollary is that the world economy would probably *not* have suffered a serious recession had the Lehman bankruptcy not been allowed to trigger the world's greatest financial panic.

This panic could have been avoided in two ways: by saving Lehman or by putting in place immediately after its failure comprehensive and unconditional guarantees for other financial institutions, which governments all over the world introduced anyway, but a crucial month too late. The decision to do the opposite—to bankrupt Lehman but do nothing to prepare for the consequences—was a case of reckless negligence easily comparable to any military blunder in Iraq. Just as the war in Iraq turned into a disaster largely because of the absence of any planning after a successful invasion, the same could be said about Lehman (and actually was by Daniel Mudd, the CEO of Fannie Mae, who compared what happened to the invasion of Fallujah[18]). But whereas the absence of proper planning and the blunders of Donald Rumsfeld were subjected to endless postmortems after Rumsfeld's resignation, the same sort of questions about the reckless negligence of the U.S. Treasury Secretary were never asked.

A partial explanation for this strange omission was Henry Paulson's daunting personal reputation. The deeper reason was an enduring belief, especially in post-Reagan American politics, that while fighting wars in foreign countries was a core responsibility of government, managing the economy and financial system was not. Indeed, government interference with the trading decisions made in financial markets was viewed throughout the crisis as politically illegitimate and economically doomed to failure. The view that politicians could be held accountable for wars but not for financial crises was a market fundamentalist confusion of the kind that will be swept away by economic thinking of Capitalism 4.0.

Consider how different the world might have looked to a treasury secretary who was willing to admit that financial markets depend on government and vice versa. First and foremost, he or she would realize that at a time of crisis all banks depend on some kind of implicit guarantee, from the government or from a quasi-public institution. Because no bank has enough ready cash to repay its depositors if they all decide simultaneously to withdraw their funds, there are only two ways to restore confidence among depositors once they start worrying about the loss of their money in a bank run. Either the bank must be able to raise a large amount of capital quickly to prove to its depositors that it remains solvent, or the depositors must be offered an unconditional guarantee from another institution whose solvency is beyond question.

When an individual bank suffers, takeover by a bigger institution is often enough. But with a run on the entire banking system, the only plausible guarantors are the government, which can tax the whole nation, or the central bank, which can print money without limit to back its guarantees.[19]

Paulson inadvertently closed off both of these escape routes in the days just before and after September 15. Through financial misjudgments motivated largely by a naïve faith in free markets, Paulson eliminated the possibility of any U.S. financial institution raising additional private capital. Then, partly through ideological dogmatism and partly political timidity, he ruled out the only viable alternative, which was temporarily to offer all American banks unlimited government guarantees.

The almost inevitable result was a run on every major bank and financial institution, first in America and then around the world. And after this generalized bank run had started, the only possible outcome was the ideological U-turn that occurred in the week of October 6, 2008, when the Irish, Greek, and Danish governments, followed by the British government, then the French and German governments, and finally the U.S. Treasury, gave the temporary guarantees that they could and should have offered on September 15. That was the week the purely financial crisis effectively ended. But the damage had already occurred and the recession in the real economy of jobs, businesses, and government budgets had only just started. The fallout from that one month of financial mayhem, like the fallout from a nuclear explosion, will continue to blight lives and nations for many years ahead.

But is it fair to blame a single man for such disaster? Although the decision to bankrupt Lehman was not a personal whim of Paulson's, it does seem reasonable to present him as the standard-bearer for the entire philosophy of government that naturally produced the long sequence of policy errors culminating in September 2008. Without a detailed analysis of this chain of blunders, it is impossible to understand the true causes of the crisis or to participate in the new economic and political thinking that will have to reshape capitalism in the years ahead.

The first big mistake was a series of regulatory blunders that began several years before Lehman with the introduction of mark-to-market accounting and risk-weighted capital requirements. Mark-to-market accounting requires banks to accept as the true values of their loans and mortgages the prices set by the financial markets for these assets. This system deliberately eliminates the role of managerial or regulatory judgment in assessing the likelihood of repayment or default. To people who believe the credo that the market is always right, this new system of accounting is a Great Leap Forward. In terms of its effect on the U.S. banking system and later the global economy it was as disastrous as Mao's Great Leap.

Mark-to-market accounting, abetted by the closely related regulatory reform of risk-based capital regulation, vastly exaggerated both booms and busts in finance, as seasoned bankers and old-fashioned, pragmatic regulators had predicted all along. In the boom phase of the cycle, these new market-based techniques created a mirage of rapidly rising market values, which allowed banks to report illusory profits, pay huge bonuses, and run down capital reserves. As a result, bank capital was much weaker at the climax of the boom than in previous financial cycles. In the bust phase of the cycle, mark-to-market accounting had the opposite effect, which was far more dangerous and dramatic.

The new accounting standards forced banks to report enormous losses as the market prices of their mortgages and other assets started falling. As each bank ran into trouble and found itself forced to sell troubled assets, the prices of all such assets fell even further, ratcheting up the apparent losses suffered by all other banks, forcing more distressed selling, and creating a vicious circle in which the apparent losses kept getting worse and worse. In the end, a large part of the paper losses reported by the banks during the crisis turned out to be illusory, just like their boom-time profits, because most assets regained a substantial part of their value after government intervention stopped the panic. Until this happened, however, the mark-to-market accounting system worked like a megaphone in the hands of a lunatic shouting "Fire!" It amplified and distorted largely imaginary losses, intensified the market's panic, and turned a series of localized credit problems into a worldwide rout.

Some accountants and most economists still claim that mark-to-market accounting had nothing to do with the credit crisis. It is hard, however, to ignore the coincidence of timing. Mark-to-market accounting became mandatory for large U.S. banks on July 1, 2007. The credit crunch began one month later, on August 8, 2007. Mark-to-market accounting was suspended on March 15, 2009.[20] The recovery in bank stocks all over the world began the same week.

The second great blunder, reflecting the same market fundamentalist mentality in the U.S. administration, occurred during the wild speculation in oil and food prices during the spring and early summer of 2008. We now know that the surge in oil prices was a purely financial phenomenon—unrelated to any physical imbalance between supply and demand—due to financial hoarding, especially by such supposedly responsible long-term investors as university endowments and pension funds.[21] Given the fragility of the world economy and financial system at that point, an oil shock was something the world could ill afford. In fact, as implied by the comment at the beginning of this chapter by the IMF's chief economist, the $150 oil price may have caused more damage to consumer and business confidence in the months before Lehman than the original credit crunch.

But because of the quasi-religious faith that the market is always right, regulators refused to intervene in the oil market to curb hoarding by financial investors. For the same reason, the Bush administration refused to negotiate with Saudi Arabia or to use the Strategic Petroleum Reserve to push down the price of oil. Despite pleas from OPEC, from the oil industry itself, and from some of the public-spirited citizens in the hedge fund and commodity trading communities,[22] American officials were determined to allow free rein to the commodity markets and financial institutions within them. As oil prices soared to $150 a barrel, central banks felt unable to cut interest rates as sharply as they otherwise would have to offset the deflationary effects of the pre-Lehman credit crunch. The market fundamentalism of regulators and accountants thus gravely weakened the world economy and banking system.

But disaster could still have been avoided had it not been for another even greater blunder: the U.S. government's refusal to intervene directly in the financial system when the credit crunch began.

Such direct intervention was what saved Britain after the Northern Rock collapse, the most serious run on a major bank anywhere in the advanced capitalist world since the Great Depression. The British government provided a temporary but open-ended guarantee to all British financial institutions, albeit reluctantly and under pressure from the Bank of England. This temporary guarantee instantly stopped the bank run, stabilized the financial system, and gave regulators the breathing space they needed to work out a longer-term solution.

Had the U.S. Treasury been prepared to think seriously about the role of government in the modern financial system, they would have seen Northern Rock as a dress rehearsal and model for dealing with the Lehman crisis a year later. By taking somewhat earlier action, the U.S. government could probably have avoided even the moderate costs and financial damage of a Northern Rock–style response. Paulson could almost certainly have saved the situation much earlier and less expensively by implementing a government-led Plan B to end the credit crunch in early 2008.

Some type of government-led anticrisis plan was widely expected in January 2008, when it became obvious that the banks' mark-to-market losses would just keep mounting and when, to make matters worse, the U.S. municipal bond market suddenly seized up.[23] The outlines of such a government-led Plan B were widely discussed in the markets at the time and could have included many of the measures ultimately adopted, but at far lower cost. For example, the Treasury, and if necessary the president himself, could have stated explicitly that the U.S. government would never renege on its implicit guarantees for Fannie Mae and Freddie Mac, the Government Sponsored Enterprises, or GSEs. Pending the necessary Congressional legislation, the president could simply have put his personal authority behind them, as the British prime minister did in the case of

Northern Rock. The Fed could have underpinned this support for the mortgage market with large-scale purchases of GSE-backed mortgages. The White House could have begun legislative preparation for authority to offer temporary unconditional guarantees for all U.S. banks. And all U.S. regulatory agencies could have suspended mark-to-market accounting. Each of these decisions were ultimately made between September 2008 and March 2009. But had such steps been taken six months earlier, the sequence of events that turned into a worldwide economic catastrophe could probably have been confined to a normal financial downturn, accompanied, in the real economy, by nothing worse than a moderate slowdown in economic growth.

Apologists for the U.S. policy response, or lack of it, may argue that all this is only obvious with hindsight, but the need for a far more active government response was apparent from late 2007 onward to many informed observers not committed to the market fundamentalist dogma that private markets could always be trusted to resolve their own problems.[24] The absence of contingency planning in the U.S. Treasury for a government-led Plan B to deal with the financial crisis was analogous, as noted, to the Pentagon's failure to make post-invasion plans for Iraq. But the Treasury's negligence was even more costly and incomprehensible. The Pentagon did, at least, start its secret preparations for war in Iraq a year before the invasion. Why did it not occur to the Treasury that defending the capitalist economy and stabilizing the financial system would be an equally demanding and urgent task? The most plausible answer is that safeguarding capitalism was never recognized in Washington as a legitimate function of government. Instead, American politicians and regulators kept delaying the necessary intervention until it was almost too late, because they were constantly waiting for some implausible market-based solution. As Paulson himself later admitted, "We've been late on everything."[25]

The procrastination and wishful thinking came to a head one week before the collapse of Lehman—on Sunday, September 7, 2008, when Paulson made his biggest mistake of all. This was the misnamed "rescue" of Fannie Mae and Freddie Mac, the multitrillion dollar mortgage companies created and guaranteed by the U.S. government.

The GSE "rescue" was an even greater blunder than the decision to bankrupt Lehman because it was an unforced error. Whereas Paulson claimed to have had no choice in closing down Lehman, he was under no such compulsion when he imposed his "conservatorship" on the GSEs. And because, as explained below, the GSE "rescue" led almost unavoidably to the bankruptcy of Lehman, this unforced error can fairly be described as the true catalyst for the entire financial collapse. Indeed, Paulson himself implicitly conceded the supreme importance of his GSE decision by starting his memoir of the crisis with a breathless account of what he himself describes as the "ambush" of Fannie Mae and Freddie Mac. The first two paragraphs of Paulson's book underline the drama of this impulsive decision:

"Do they see it's coming, Hank?" the president asked me.

"Mr. President," I said, "we're going to move quickly and take them by surprise. The first sound they'll hear is their heads hitting the floor."[26]

The word "rescue" in the previous paragraph is graced with quotation marks because the decision to place the GSEs in a government-mandated conservatorship was nothing of the kind. It was the opposite of a rescue, an act of deliberate sabotage, motivated at least in part by a political desire to clear up an ideologically ambiguous and messy collaboration between the public and private sectors of the sort abhorred by Capitalism 3.3. Dogmatic Republican free marketeers had for years been trying to shut down or neuter the GSEs because of their hybrid public-private status. And as the crisis progressed, Paulson seems to have decided that dealing once and for all with the GSEs might secure him a place in history of which he could be proud.[27]

In fact, the phrase *GSE rescue* was soon replaced by *GSE seizure*. Paulson himself emphasized that he was deliberately confiscating the shareholders' property in these companies and that he hoped to create conditions for the next treasury secretary to close down these businesses, which he regarded as unhealthy throwbacks to the Great Society era of government interventionism in private markets. The true significance of the seizure, therefore, was not that the U.S. Treasury calmed the financial markets by backing the $10 trillion worth of mortgages issued or guaranteed by the GSEs. This had already happened under the Housing and Economic Recovery Act in July 2008 (partly under pressure from the Chinese government, which was a large holder of GSE bonds).

The real significance of the rescue, which rapidly turned into paralyzing shock and awe for financial markets, was what it did to the shareholder stakes in Fannie and Freddie. These stakes were rendered essentially worth-less—including some $20 billion of new capital subscribed just a few months earlier by long-term shareholders. Among these confiscated share-holders were several foreign governments and Sovereign Wealth Funds. They had provided badly needed capital to U.S. financial institutions throughout the credit crunch and had invested in Fannie and Freddie shares with the U.S. Treasury's active encouragement and on the basis of a public statement by their regulator, James Lockhart of the Federal Housing Finance Agency, that they had sufficient capital and that their cash needs were adequately covered until at least the end of 2009.[28]

It later emerged that Paulson, to find a legal justification for his seizure, put intense political pressure on Lockhart to reverse his ruling and declare that Fannie and Freddie were in danger of insolvency, just two months after the FHFA analysis had found them to be adequately capitalized. At first, Lockhart refused to do this, arguing that there had been no substantial change in economic conditions and also that he could be sued by the direc-tors and shareholders of the GSEs. In the end, Lockhart submitted and, al-though Fannie Mae's directors were advised by their lawyers that Paulson had no legal grounds for his seizure, they were warned that they could face personal liability if they opposed the Treasury, while the terms of the seizure specifically protected them from shareholder lawsuits if they agreed. Throughout this period—and for several months afterwards—both Fannie and Freddie were enjoying positive cash flows and experiencing no difficul-ties in raising money in financial markets. Their alleged risk of insolvency, like the huge losses that banks were reporting, were largely a product of mark-to-market accounting, which the Treasury could have suspended at any time.

Paulson's decision to wipe out the Fannie and Freddie shareholders just a few weeks after their official regulator had issued a public declaration of their solvency, and at a time when they were still enjoying positive cash flows, sent a terrifying but unmistakable signal to shareholders in all other U.S. banks and financial institutions: They, too, could be wiped out by a U.S. government fiat at a moment's notice, even if the banks they owned were generating positive cash flows, had raised new capital, and had received reg-ulatory approvals as recently as a few weeks before. After the GSEs were abruptly declared insolvent by the U.S. Treasury and their new shareholders wiped out, no rational investor would put new money into any American financial institution whose solvency might conceivably come into question—and in the circumstances of September 2008, that meant every financial institution in the United States. On the other hand, speculative short sellers who attacked U.S. financial stocks in the hope that their share prices might collapse, were essentially tipped off by the treasury secretary that they would be richly rewarded if they managed to destabilize any of these companies to the point where the government felt obliged to intervene.

No one would suggest that shareholders in Fannie and Freddie or other financial institutions should have been offered government support in the same way as depositors and other senior creditors. As a last resort, shareholders must always be prepared to take a total loss, but the usual approach to serious financial crises previously had been to give troubled banks time and accounting leeway to restore their profitability. If necessary, major private banks would be offered temporary liquidity support by the Fed or implicit guarantees by the government to give them the time they needed to put themselves back on their feet. This is what happened after the Latin American defaults of the early 1980s, when all the biggest U.S. banks suffered losses much larger in relation to their capital than in the subprime debacle,[29] and also after the property crashes of the late 1980s and early 1990s. A similar combination of regulatory forbearance and slow recapitalization, along with a gradual elimination of the weakest institutions through mergers or orderly closures, could have provided an orderly way out of the credit crunch. Under such an approach, the shareholders in troubled banks or GSEs would have suffered big temporary losses—and a total wipeout if asset values never recovered—but they would also have participated in a long-term recovery, if the value of their mortgages eventually recovered, which in many cases they did.

With his GSE seizures, however, Paulson took the opposite approach. Instead of loosening accounting rules and capital requirements, the U.S. Treasury suddenly tightened them at the moment of greatest financial stress. Instead of encouraging shareholders to be patient by giving them the chance to participate in a long-term recovery, Paulson unexpectedly wiped them out overnight.

With this new regulatory philosophy, the calculus of owning shares in American financial institutions was transformed. As a result, it became impossible for any U.S. bank to raise any additional capital from private share-holders, who now quite reasonably feared a Treasury decision could wipe them out overnight. The GSE seizure thus raised a Sword of Damocles over every U.S. financial institution that might conceivably need to raise any new capital anytime in the foreseeable future—first and foremost Lehman, but also Merrill Lynch, AIG, Morgan Stanley, and Citigroup. Following the GSE rescue, it was out of the question for American banks to raise new capital from the governments or sovereign wealth funds in Abu Dhabi, Singapore, or Saudi Arabia, regardless of how hard the U.S. treasury secretary, or even the president himself, might rattle the begging bowl. Amazingly, this unintended consequence of the GSE seizure seemed never to receive a moment's consideration in the Treasury or the Fed.[30]

As a result, the GSE seizure effectively demolished the first of the two possible lines of defense discussed at the beginning of this chapter for banks facing a loss of confidence. From September 7 onward, any bank facing a sudden withdrawal of deposits could no longer hope to raise capital from private investors. The only remaining alternative was now a govern-ment-led defense. If a U.S. bank suffered a loss of confidence because of ei-ther attacks by short sellers or unexpected mark-to-market losses, only the government could now inject new capital or offer guarantees to depositors and creditors, backed up by unlimited lending from the Fed.

In the absence of such government action, the normal balance of power between long-term investors and speculative short sellers was reversed. Nor-mally, long-term investors such as pension funds, insurance companies, and Sovereign Wealth Funds are regarded in financial markets as the "strong hands" because they can afford to buy and hold their shares for long periods, betting on improvements in economic conditions that may take years to ma-terialize. By contrast, speculative short sellers are playing with borrowed as-sets, looking for rapid gains and at risk of sudden liquidation if prices move against them. In the new conditions Paulson created with his GSE seizure, this calculation was reversed. Paulson had shown that long-term investors could be permanently wiped out at short notice by regulatory whims. Mean-while, speculators who were betting on the collapse of U.S. financial institu-tions now seemed to have the U.S. Treasury on their side.

Paulson had created a financial Doomsday Machine. And, with his seizure of Fannie and Freddie, he handed speculators the key.[31]

This Doomsday mechanism began its inexorable grind within twenty-four hours of the GSE seizure. The stock price of Lehman Brothers, which had been trading in a broad but stable range of $13.00 to $20.00 for the previous two months, fell 52 percent to $7.79 in the first full day of trading after the GSE seizure.[32] With this plunge in the share price, a run on Lehman's deposits began in earnest and the only options to prevent bankruptcy were government intervention or immediate sale to a stronger institution. But the second possibility had effectively been eliminated by the GSE seizure—and this became obvious within twenty-four hours.

The Korean Development Bank, which had been talking to Lehman for months about buying a controlling stake, withdrew suddenly on September 9. The timing appeared to be linked to the GSE seizure in the way described previously. On September 8, the first working day after the GSE seizure, Jun Kwang Woo, chairman of the Korean Financial Services Commission, publicly warned of "the global finance industry losses" just suffered by Asian investors and questioned whether buying a stake in Lehman "makes sense [for KDB] in the long term."[33] The following day, KDB announced it was pulling out of all talks about buying Lehman.[34] Lehman's share price immediately fell a further 40 percent to $4.20 and its fate was sealed.

Yet Paulson, even as he watched Lehman's share price collapsing and the creditors withdrawing their funds, continued to misconstrue what was going on. Instead of realizing that his punitive treatment of the Fannie and Freddie shareholders had started a chain reaction that was going to blow up the entire U.S. financial system, he concluded that the GSE rescue had been a triumph. After all, his hard-line approach to Fannie and Freddie was drawing political plaudits from Congress and the media.[35] He therefore decided on an even tougher approach to Lehman, ruling out government support of any kind.

In Lehman's case, this meant total bankruptcy, wiping out not just the shareholders but creditors, depositors, and other financial counterparties as well. After one last frenzied weekend of attempted deal-making of the kind that had been Paulson's specialty as a Goldman Sachs investment banker with Bank of America, Barclays, and the British government, this outcome was duly announced on September 15. As a result, all hell broke loose.

After Lehman's failure, every other bank in America immediately became suspect and dealings froze between all financial institutions around the world. AIG, which had guaranteed hundreds of billions of dollars worth of bonds that were now being dumped by the liquidators of Lehman, was doomed. AIG's failure would inevitably have brought down all the other U.S. investment banks, including Goldman Sachs, plus several major banks in Europe. AIG therefore had to be rescued the day after Lehman's failure, with a huge government cash injection of the kind that Paulson had explicitly ruled out just forty-eight hours before, belying Paulson's later claim that he allowed Lehman to fail because he lacked legal authority to support nonbank financial institutions. But in setting the terms of the AIG rescue, Paulson blundered again. The AIG rescue were deliberately made as punitive to shareholders as the seizure of the GSEs. As in the case of Fannie, Freddie, and Lehman, therefore, the short sellers betting on AIG's collapse were hugely rewarded, while long-term investors who had been backing a long-term recovery in the U.S. financial system were wiped out.

The natural result was a further intensification of stock market attacks on all U.S. financial institutions, triggering more deposit runs. The speculators who had made billions out of the Treasury's decisions to wipe out Fannie, Lehman, and AIG now turned their attention to the next most vulnerable institutions: Washington Mutual, Wachovia, Bank of America, Morgan Stanley, and Citibank. Within twenty-four hours of the AIG seizure, it became obvious that as each of these stumbling giants collapsed, the next would fall like a domino, until eventually the entire American financial system would be either demolished or nationalized. The Chairman of Goldman Sachs, Lloyd Blankfein, realized even his firm would be bankrupt "in fifteen minutes" if Morgan Stanley were allowed to fail.[36]

What needs to be stressed is that this chain of disasters did *not* reflect some sudden deterioration in the world economy or the U.S. housing market in September 2008. Such economic fundamentals were, if anything, better than they had been six months earlier, when Bear Stearns was absorbed by J.P. Morgan, with government assistance, inaugurating a period of relative calm. The domino-style failure of U.S. financial institutions that autumn was *not* due to any worsening of economic conditions—it was simply a mechanical consequence of the U.S. Treasury's unpredictable and reckless handling first of Fannie and Freddie, then of Lehman, and finally of AIG.

Once Paulson had removed the option of attracting new private capital into the U.S. banking system, government intervention—through guarantees or recapitalization—became the only remaining line of defense. And the U.S. Treasury's assertion that any such government assistance would be conditional on driving share prices down almost to zero was an open invitation for speculators to attack every bank in the United States.

Even at this point, however, Henry Paulson did not seem to understand what was going on. His main preoccupation, according to his own private comments to Andrew Ross Sorkin, were still with the ideology of government intervention in private markets and with the morality of bailing out reckless bankers, preventing future bubbles, and rewarding greed. Across Washington, the main response to the crisis was a surreal argument about whose fault it was that the banks and the GSEs had got into this mess. This was reminiscent of the furious debate among French politicians in 1940 about who exactly had come up with the stupid idea of building the Maginot Line, while the German panzers rolled into Paris unopposed.

As speculators continued to enrich themselves attacking one bank after another, the financial mayhem spread from New York to Europe. In London, short sellers quickly identified Europe's biggest mortgage lender, Halifax Bank of Scotland (HBOS), as the most vulnerable institution. Within forty-eight hours of Lehman, HBOS shares had fallen almost to zero, causing a run by wholesale depositors and sending the message that this bank would fail by the weekend without support of some kind. As in America, the British government, faithful to market fundamentalist ideology despite its Labour Party label, was determined not to intervene directly (having apparently forgotten its own experience twelve months earlier with Northern Rock) and instead tried to organize a shotgun marriage with the country's biggest and best capitalized retail bank—Lloyds. Because the merger—agreed on Wednesday, September 17, two days after the Lehman bankruptcy—was presented as a pure private sector solution, without any government safety net, the speculative attacks against HBOS, instead of abating, were immediately redirected against the merged bank.

Far from acting as a firebreak against the spread of the financial crisis to Europe, the HBOS-Lloyds merger thus added fuel to the flames. By the following day, Thursday, September 18, most of the banks in Europe watched their share prices plunge toward zero, raising the prospect of bankruptcy before the weekend, as Paulson's Doomsday Machine rolled on. Back in New York, meanwhile, Morgan Stanley and Wachovia were now on the brink of failure and Bank of America, which had only just saved Merrill Lynch the preceding weekend, was under renewed speculative attack.

At last Henry Paulson, pressured by the Fed[37] and by foreign governments, realized that he had no alternative to large-scale and systemic public intervention. The plan for a $700 billion Troubled Asset Relief Program (TARP) was agreed that Thursday at lunchtime and deliberate leaks about its gigantic scale, combined with a temporary ban on short selling, triggered a near-record rally on stock markets around the world that evening and the following day. The banks threatened with insolvency just a few hours earlier were suddenly reprieved.

Even at this point, however, it emerged that the U.S. treasury secretary had not grasped the nature of the problem—as was all too apparent in his disastrous interactions with the Congress during the following two weeks, which turned out even worse, in terms of financial losses, than the immediate aftermath of Lehman. The real obstacle to successful policy was the same as it had been throughout the crisis—it was not the scale of bank losses, the absence of financial firepower, or the weakness of the U.S. and world economies. It was the U.S. Treasury's refusal to acknowledge the indispensable role of government in stabilizing financial markets—in short, it was market fundamentalist ideology.

Had it not been for this ideology, Paulson could have straightforwardly announced that he would use the $700 billion requested from Congress as a pool of new capital, to be injected into U.S. banks if and when required and on terms that promised reasonable returns for taxpayers, without being excessively punitive to current bank shareholders and without creating a bonanza for short sellers. Just over a month later, this was what the Treasury ended up doing. Alternatively and more simply, Paulson could have offered a temporary Treasury guarantee on all bank deposits and liabilities, stating that he would go to Congress in the following weeks for the necessary appropriation and adding that the U.S. Treasury would ultimately recoup any losses by levying extra taxes or fees on the banks. This would have been the most expedient solution and would have gone to the root of the problem, which was not just a lack of bank capital but an evaporation of confidence among the depositors and creditors of U.S. banks.

Guarantees would also have been the easiest form of intervention to present politically because they would have emphasized the true purpose of government assistance to the banking system: to preserve the savings of depositors—especially wholesale depositors such as corporations, foundations, savings institutions, and local governments. These depositors would have seen trillions of dollars in payrolls, pensions, and working capital evaporate if the banks were allowed to fail. Guarantees would have underlined the fact that the main beneficiaries of all bank rescues are not greedy bankers or shareholders but wholesale depositors whose money is not covered by retail guarantees. Why no political leader or banker in any major economy thought of offering this obvious explanation to calm the public frenzy over bank bailouts is a question that may baffle historians of the future, just as we puzzle over why the politicians and monarchs of the early twentieth century failed to take the obvious diplomatic steps that might have averted the First World War.

All we know for sure is that Paulson did not choose either the straightforward guarantee or the capital option. Instead, he made his final and in some ways most inexcusable mistake, refusing to offer any clear explanation of how he would spend the money he demanded from Congress and merely hinting at a convoluted scheme to buy defaulted mortgages, a scheme that no one, even in the Treasury or the Fed, could understand or explain. Again, the reasons for this perverse behavior can be traced to market fundamentalist thinking.

Paulson's hope in presenting his bizarre TARP proposal was to boost the market prices of various troubled assets, thereby indirectly strengthening the banks' apparent solvency through mark-to-market accounting. He had to offer support obscurely and indirectly because his free-market convictions ruled out straightforward capital injections or guarantees. Instead of telling regulators bluntly to suspend the mark-to-market accounting, Paulson preferred to risk $700 billion of public money on creating an illusion of higher market prices to preserve the free-market principle that accounting and regulatory decisions would always be market-based.[38] Instead of asking Ben Bernanke immediately to support all banks without limit and then using his Congressional appropriation to indemnify the Fed against possible losses, he kept the financial system in limbo for weeks while private investment bankers and lawyers negotiated the details of reverse auctions and other preposterously convoluted financial schemes.

It was after Paulson turned up at the Senate Banking Committee on the morning of September 23 and proved unable to explain his inchoate roundabout scheme that the worst of the bank runs started. Within a week of this fiasco Congress had voted down the first attempt at TARP funding, triggering the biggest-ever daily fall on Wall Street in terms of points, Washington Mutual had collapsed, the HBOS-Lloyds merger had effectively unraveled, threatening the failure of Britain's entire financial system, all the banks in Iceland had been nationalized, and the German government had been forced to throw a €35 billion ($50 billion) lifeline to Hypo RE, the country's biggest commercial property lender.

With each passing day, the panic spread to new countries and new institutions, but there was nothing irrational about it. The series of bank runs that almost destroyed the world economy were perfectly reasonable responses to the self-destructive actions of the U.S. Treasury, followed by other governments around the world. As Mervyn King noted six months earlier, commenting on the Northern Rock run:[39] "Once a run gets started, it is rational for other people to join in."[40]

Bank runs are rational because no bank has enough ready cash to repay all its deposits. Therefore, the survival of any nation's banking system depends ultimately on a belief that government or some other unimpeachable credit will stand behind the banks. The literal meaning of *credit* is *belief*.

There was much talk of a breakdown of trust at the height of the crisis, with the implication that the true cause of the crisis was a mutual distrust among selfish and greedy bankers. The real problem, however, was not the bankers' supposedly irrational distrust for one another. It was the public's very reasonable lack of trust in *all* banks and even in the concept of banking itself. Such trust could be restored only by the government because only the government, in modern societies, has the ability to levy taxes or print the money with which all debts and deposits can be repaid.

This brings us to the nub of the government's relationship with finance. The government monopoly on money creation in a modern capitalist economy is comparable to the government monopoly on the use of violence in a civilized society. The role of the finance ministry and central bank in quelling a banking panic and protecting savings is analogous to the role of the police and army in putting down civil riots and protecting property. Normally, it is sufficient if government support for the banking system remains implicit. It is even desirable for financial hygiene if some minor banks occasionally fail. But when money starts flooding out of one bank after another, the government has to stand foursquare behind the entire financial system and state unconditionally that no depositor or senior creditor of any bank will lose a penny under any circumstances—regardless of doubts about the solvency of the bank in question or the state of the economy as a whole.

This was what the Irish government did on Tuesday, September 30, the day after the failure of the first TARP vote in the U.S. Congress, with Greece and Denmark following in the next forty-eight hours. The U.S., British, and major European governments, by contrast, continued to resist any such comprehensive guarantees. For example, on Friday, October 3, the British government responded to Ireland's open-ended bank guarantees with the pathetic gesture of raising the limit on British deposit insurance from £35,000 to £50,000, adding that the government would "do whatever is necessary to ensure stability of the financial system." Needless to say, such half measures were worse than useless, simply drawing attention to the limited and conditional nature of the government's support.

In a full-scale bank run, limited guarantees and assurances about systemic stability are of no comfort to depositors, who do not give a damn about "the stability of the system" but just want assurance that they will get all their own money back, with interest and on time. The predictable result of the half-baked measures of support offered by governments unwilling to provide comprehensive bank guarantees was an accelerating outflow of deposits from U.S., British, and German banks to other countries where banks *were* fully guaranteed.

By the weekend of October 4–5, it was becoming obvious to everyone except the U.S. Treasury that this situation could not go on. Before the banks opened the following Monday morning, Angela Merkel, the German chancellor, was forced to announce a political guarantee (though not yet backed by any specific legislation) for all retail and corporate bank deposits to prevent a flight of German capital to Denmark. The same evening, Alistair Darling, the British chancellor, tried one last time to offer reassurance with his halfhearted formula to do "whatever it takes" to stabilize "the system." The predictable response the following day was another tidal wave of money rushing out of the weaker British banks. By lunchtime, it was clear that most British banks would collapse in a matter of days, if not hours.

At 7 a.m. the following day, Wednesday, October 8, the British government finally took the decisive step that everyone had been waiting for—and that Paulson should have taken three weeks, or better still, nine months before. The Treasury and the Bank of England reluctantly announced a £500 billion ($800 billion) bank support package—five times bigger, relative to the size of the economy, than Paulson's $700 billion request. Crucially, this included, for the first time in any major economy, a comprehensive and unlimited, though temporary, guarantee on all bank liabilities, including interbank borrowing, and a promise of open-ended government capital injections in the weeks ahead. This British announcement was the first clear promise of support from any major government to be backed by detailed legislative proposals and virtually unlimited central bank funding. It marked the turning point of the crisis.

By the following day, the U.S. Treasury, under pressure from the Fed, decided to follow the British example and converted Paulson's $700 billion TARP program into a bank recapitalization and guarantee plan. By the weekend, all the major European governments had followed suit. When all these guarantees and government capital injections were officially confirmed on the morning of Monday, October 13, the financial crisis was effectively over.

In that one extraordinary month, from the GSE seizure of September 7 until the British announcement of unlimited guarantees on October 8, the world financial system came closer to total collapse than ever before in history. A U.S. treasury secretary and former Goldman Sachs chairman had come closer to destroying capitalism than Marx, Lenin, Stalin, and Mao Ze Dong combined.

But there is another, more important and positive lesson. Nothing was inevitable about the calamitous outcome of the 2007–09 boom-bust cycle.

It was actively, if advertently, triggered by the U.S. Treasury and it could have been arrested at any point by the sort of decisive government actions that were finally taken by Britain on October 8, 2008, the United States on October 9, and all other major economies on October 13. Just as Iraq was a war of choice, September 15 was a crisis of choice.

Henry Paulson, along with many lesser policymakers in America and Europe, chose to foment the crisis by refusing to accept that capitalism depends on a symbiosis between efficient private enterprise and an effective government that sometimes has to override market forces. Usually, it is sufficient for the government to hover quietly in the background, defending property rights, enforcing contracts, policing the rules of the market, and ensuring that the benefits of capitalism are spread sufficiently to preserve social peace. But sometimes the government must reach into the heart of the economic system and guarantee the financial institutions whose existence is ultimately a matter of political convention. The willingness and ability of the government to intervene in this way may be tested only once or twice in a generation. But if government fails this test, the entire capitalist system can fall apart.

This was the point made brilliantly by Ricardo Caballero in his series of MIT papers comparing the financial crisis to a sudden cardiac arrest. Every few decades, any capitalist financial system, even a well-regulated and managed one, is likely to suffer a potentially fatal heart attack. To minimize the economic dangers of such emergencies, the government must provide a public safety net for the financial system, just as it provides defibrillators in public places. Caballero points out that government provision of equipment for cardiac emergencies may marginally increase the "moral hazard" of people eating too many hamburgers, but this does not imply that a better response to heart attacks is simply to blame the victims for overeating and let them die. Similar reasoning applies to government involvement in rescuing banks.[41]

Henry Paulson's inability to understand that safeguarding the financial system is a core responsibility of government had deep ideological roots. He could not believe that markets might be fundamentally wrong in guiding the economy or establishing a reasonable price for assets. He could not imagine, for example, that government judgments about solvency or the true value of mortgages and bank loans might reflect economic reality more accurately than market prices.

The ideological pendulum is now swinging. To avoid future crises, we need not necessarily more government or more detailed rules but *better* government, run by people who respect markets but also understand their limits and flaws. Markets are usually right, but sometimes they are dangerously wrong, especially financial markets, which deal in an unknowable future. Financial systems need to be regulated with a light touch, but they have to be regulated by competent public officials who have both the self-confidence to be heavy-handed in emergencies and the power to override market forces when required.

People who refused to acknowledge the essential roles of government should not have been regulating financial markets, any more than they should have been fighting wars or managing flood defenses. Henry Paulson was to finance what Donald Rumsfeld was to military strategy, Dick Cheney to geopolitics, and Michael Brown to flood control. P. J. O'Rourke, the conservative satirist, once remarked that "Republicans are people who believe government doesn't work—and get themselves elected to prove it." This should be the political epitaph for Henry Paulson and all other government mismanagers of the financial crisis.

More than the greed of bankers or the stupidity of feckless borrowers or the folly of financial rocket-scientists, it was the refusal by politicians and central bankers to understand the interdependence of government and markets that turned the 2007–09 boom-bust cycle into an existential threat to the entire capitalist system. But why were so many policymakers—not just Henry Paulson and George W. Bush but also Gordon Brown, Ben Bernanke, and Timothy Geithner—so slow to acknowledge that government intervention was the only way to prevent financial catastrophe? A large part of the explanation can be found in the sad state of modern economic theory, the subject to which we now turn.

CHAPTER ELEVEN

There Is No Can Opener

A foolish consistency is the hobgoblin of little minds.

—Ralph Waldo Emerson

AN ECONOMIST, a chemist, and a physicist are marooned on a desert island. Their only food is a can of beans, but they have no can opener. What are they to do? The physicist says: "Let's try and focus the tropical sun onto the lid—it might melt a hole." "No," says the chemist. "We should first pour salt water on the lid—maybe that will rust it." The economist interrupts: "You're wasting time with all these complicated ideas. Let's just *assume* a can opener."

This little joke, a favorite among economists, tells us more about the causes and consequences of the 2007–09 crisis than any number of ministerial speeches, Wall Street research reports, and central bank monographs. The propensity of modern economic theory for unjustified and oversimplified assumptions allowed politicians, regulators, and bankers to create for themselves the imaginary world of market fundamentalist ideology, in which financial stability is automatic, involuntary unemployment is impossible, and efficient, omniscient markets can solve all economic problems, if only the government will stand aside.

In the new economy emerging from the 2007–09 crisis, the self-serving assumptions of efficient, self-stabilizing markets have been discredited, but something must now be put in their place. Since the eighteenth century, each transformation of the capitalist system has coincided with a transformed understanding of economics—Smith and Ricardo from 1780 to 1820; the marginalist revolution of Mill, Jevons, and Walras in the 1870s; Keynes in the 1930s; and Friedman in the 1970s. The new model of capitalism will also have to build on new economic concepts—and the events that followed the collapse of Lehman must surely provoke a revolution in economic thought.

The greatest embarrassment for academic economics in the 2007–09 crisis was not the failure to predict the crisis but the failure to provide any useful analysis and guidance for politicians and the public after the crisis struck. The failure of analysis was much more damning than the failure of prediction because economics could never be taken seriously as a predictive science. Keynes never published an economic forecast, and neither did Hayek, Ricardo, or Adam Smith. What economics did claim to offer was a set of analytical tools to explain reality and suggest sensible responses to unexpected events. It was in this respect that the dominant schools of pre-crisis economics completely failed.

During and after the crisis, academic recommendations from the Left and the Right differed in almost every respect apart from one striking feature—a theoretical detachment from reality that made them almost completely useless in practice. One of the dirty little secrets of modern academic economics, for example, is that the computer models used by central banks and finance ministries to guide them in setting interest rates and regulating banks say almost nothing about finance. They generally contain no equations explaining the behavior or the financial condition of banks. They simply assume that debts are repaid in full, that financial markets always function, and that money is "neutral," having no effect on real economic activity, output, and jobs. In practice, this jargon meant that politicians and central bankers who turned to academic economists for guidance in the financial crisis were effectively told: "You are on your own since the situation you have to deal with is impossible—our theories show it cannot exist."

Despite the comprehensive failure of modern economics, many distinguished academic economists working within the existing paradigm are already regrouping to fight ruthlessly any fundamental change. Part 1 of this book described the special-interest lobbies that always mobilize in periods of transition to oppose any radical evolution of the politico-economic system.

Academic economists are a classic example of such conservative opposition. And economics theorists are already proving surprisingly influential in arguing that there can be only one true capitalist system, which is not susceptible to any fundamental change. To understand the coming struggle over the changing nature of capitalism, it is therefore essential to understand the conservative arguments of the academic establishment—and see through their mathematical flummery to the ideological roots.

Three closely related economic ideas transformed political, as well as economic, thinking in the thirty years before the crisis. The first idea, known as rational expectations, maintained that capitalist economies did not need to be stabilized by governments or central banks. The second idea, called efficient markets, asserted that competitive finance will always allocate resources in the most efficient manner possible, reflecting all the best available information and forecasts about the future. The third idea was more abstract, but equally powerful: It stated that economics, previously a largely descriptive study of human behavior, must be transformed into a branch of mathematics, requiring assumptions about this behavior that are always clear and consistent enough to be expressed in simple algebraic terms. Economic problems that could not be analyzed with mathematics were deemed unworthy of consideration.

Between them, these three ideas had profound political effects. Rational, efficient, and mathematically inexorable economics legitimized a host of highly controversial political outcomes decreed by markets. Widening income inequalities, wrenching dislocations of employment, and unprecedented riches for bankers and corporate executives could all be presented as the unavoidable, impersonal outcomes of scientific forces. Anyone who suggested that issues such as income distribution, industrial strategy, or financial regulation were legitimate subjects for government action, or even for political debate, was ridiculed as an unscientific economic ignoramus. To see how the rift between politics and economics will need to be bridged in any new model of capitalism emerging from the crisis, we must first understand how this situation came about.

In the thirty years before the crisis, almost all academic economists, notorious for their disagreement on most issues, agreed on one thing. The greatest achievement of their subject was a mathematically driven intellectual program dedicated to the refutation of the Keynesian economics that had underpinned the previous capitalist model.

This "new classical" paradigm was a conscious throwback to the ideas that prevailed in the golden age of free enterprise before the terminal crisis of Capitalism 1 in 1929–32. It became dominant in American universities from the early 1980s onward, alongside the transition of Capitalism 2 to Capitalism 3. Having taken over the academic bastions of high theory, this intellectual movement colonized central banks, finance ministries, and global economic institutions, especially the IMF, World Bank, and OECD (Organisation for Economic Co-operation and Development). The resulting approach to international economic policy came to be known as the *Washington consensus* and was spread, through IMF and World Bank programs, to emerging economies around the world.

Over time, this movement established a near-monopoly on economic thinking, suppressing dissent through its control of academic publications, appointments, and funding purse-strings. Ironically, a school of thought that glorified vigorous competition as the key to success in every human endeavor proved as ruthlessly monopolistic as a Bill Gates or John D. Rockefeller in crushing competition from other economic ideas.

What defined the intellectual monopoly of modern economics was not so much a specific theory as a mindset—a particular methodology that came to be seen as the only acceptable way for serious economists to think about the world. With a characteristic combination of false modesty and pseudoscientific pretension, the movement's central tenets were described not as theories or conclusions but merely as hypotheses—the Rational Expectations Hypothesis (REH) and Efficient Market Hypothesis (EMH). The movement's grand ambitions were revealed, however, by the power of those two value-laden words: *rational* and *efficient*.

The First Era of Economics

Every era of capitalism has produced its own economics, and to understand the full significance of the rise—and now fall—of those two value-laden words *rational* and *efficient* demands a quick review of the history of economic thought. The concept of rationality as an emergent property that evolves naturally from a competitive economic system has a long and brilliant history, going back to Adam Smith, David Hume, and ultimately to Aristotle and Plato. After Smith's discovery of the "invisible hand" of competitive markets and especially after the "Marginal Revolution" of the English utilitarians in the 1870s, economic theory came to be dominated by the rationality of *Homo Economicus,* an imaginary creature invented by John Stuart Mill in the mid-1800s.[1] *Homo Economicus* was a human calculating machine, who spent his entire life computing optimum trading strategies that maximized his own consumption. The late nineteenth century economists were able to show that this process of endless calculation could theoretically produce, through the magic of perfectly competitive markets, not only a general equilibrium in which all workers, machines, and resources were full employed, but also, under some restrictive (and unrealistic) assumptions, an optimum, or efficient, allocation of resources that offered the maximum amount of satisfaction, or utility, for society as a whole.

The notion of optimality used by economists from the late nineteenth century onward had limited practical relevance, but a huge ideological significance. Proposed by the Italian statistician Vilfredo Pareto, who later became an inadvertent hero of the Italian fascist movement, this concept stated merely that no one in society could be made better off without someone else suffering a loss. Pareto Optimality[2] deliberately and consciously ignored the critical questions of interpersonal comparisons: Could the world be improved in some sense by taking a crust of bread from Rockefeller and giving it to a starving child? Might it be better for society to offer such a child a free education if this meant imposing a modest tax on Rockefeller's wealth? Pareto Optimality, which also came to be described as efficiency, avoided all such issues of interpersonal comparisons and distribution. That was the ideological beauty of this concept. It allowed economists to relegate all questions of justice, social solidarity, and so on to what they considered the junior league of unscientific academic disciplines, such as sociology, politics, and moral philosophy. Thus was economics transformed from the radical social program for attacking feudalism, slavery, and aristocratic privileges initiated by Smith and Ricardo into a conservative ideology for justifying the status quo.

Homo Economicus was, for obvious reasons, a wonderful ideological construct, perfectly attuned to the optimistic mood of late nineteenth-century capitalism.[3] *Homo Economicus* not only made himself as happy as possible, he also helped to explain and legitimize an age in which spectacular technological progress went hand in hand with extreme inequality, grinding poverty, and wrenching social change.

This pleasure-maximizing robot, however, suffered from two fatal flaws. First, he was unable to explain why the poverty, inequality, and class struggle identified by Marx and various brands of utopian and Christian socialists were as characteristic of the capitalist system as optimal utility. After the Russian Revolution, this intellectual puzzle jumped alarmingly from economic theory into the realm of practical politics. Second, and even more disturbing from the standpoint of theoretical economics, the Great Depression demolished the gloriously self-confident Victorian concept of a general equilibrium in which perfectly competitive markets in all goods and services kept society in balance and every able-bodied worker fully employed.

The Second Era: Keynes's Government-Led Economics

In reaction to the near-total breakdown of the market system during the 1930s, classical economics, which was an idealized concept even at the best of times, became a totally implausible description of the real world. Amid the mass unemployment and hardship of the 1930s, the theory of a self-sustaining general equilibrium, in which all resources were automatically utilized in the most efficient manner and consumption was distributed in an optimal way, became a ghastly parody. Even more importantly for practical politicians, Russian communism and German fascism now presented rival models that America and Britain could not ignore.

As the socio-political system began to evolve from the first era of capitalism to the second, economics also had to reinvent itself. It did this by dividing into two distinct branches. The traditional branch, later described as microeconomics, continued to use the tools of nineteenth-century marginal theory to analyze the behavior of utility-maximizing individuals and profit-maximizing companies in competitive markets for ordinary commodities such as coal, tomatoes, or shoes.

The new branch of the subject, called macroeconomics, was invented more or less from scratch in the 1930s by Keynes and his Cambridge collaborator, Richard Kahn, along with the Polish economist Michal Kalecki. It focused not on ordinary goods but on the factors of production that create new wealth—labor, capital, and money—and especially on how the fluctuating demand for all these factors of production generates instability in the economy as a whole. Macroeconomics challenged the linear mechanical determinism of classical economics with what might now be described as postmodern concepts—an unknowable future, inconsistent personal preferences, and self-reinforcing expectations.

Keynes, in a sense, recognized the macroeconomy as what biologists, engineers, and mathematical physicists would today call a complex system. A complex structure, such as an ecological environment, the human body, or even a weather pattern, involves so many different components, all interacting in unpredictable ways, that its behavior cannot be analyzed by aggregating the individual movements of its atomistic parts.

It was an act of hubris by the classical economists to believe that something as complex as a market economy, with thinking participants who are free not only to change their own behavior but also the economic principles by which the entire system operates, can be fully understood by adding all the motives and actions of these individual businesses, workers, or consumers. Mathematical physicists proved back in the eighteenth century that it is impossible to predict precisely the long-term course of a system consisting of just three separate particles, all interacting according to the fixed laws of motion of a single gravitational force.[4] Against this background, the nineteenth century attempt to explain the entire economic system by building it up from assumptions that supposedly described the independent behavior of millions of atomistic individuals, was a case of intellectual overstretch.

Keynes and his followers realized, by contrast, that in trying to understand the aggregate, or macro, behavior of a large system, starting with microfoundations was neither necessary nor desirable. While the interactions of just three separate bodies could not be described precisely, statistical mechanics could analyze fluids consisting of trillions of atoms with astonishing accuracy by shifting attention from individual particles to the system as a whole. And biology had applied rigorous scientific methods to organisms and ecosystems infinitely more complex than that. Analogously, macroeconomics could try to understand a market economy by focusing on, and then statistically examining, simple connections that might govern the aggregate behavior of the entire system, instead of trying to analyze in detail how each individual consumer, worker, and business within the economy might behave.[5]

Two further important features distinguish genuinely complex systems such as economics, ecology, and meteorology from the relatively simple study of stable fluids in statistical mechanics. In complex systems, such as weather patterns and earthquake simulations, mathematical analysis seeking exact solutions to well-defined equations is impossible because there are too many influences. The best that scientists can do is run computer simulations offering successive approximations. Moreover, in the most interesting complex systems, such as ecological habitats, ant colonies, and human societies, individual participants can change their behavior and alter the laws of motion. This capacity for changing behavior makes such adaptive complex systems infinitely more intractable from a mathematical standpoint. But paradoxically, it can also make them more predictable and easy to understand because adaptive systems often start to organize *themselves* spontaneously into relatively orderly patterns. Such self-organizing systems are said to develop emergent laws of motion that save them from degenerating into chaos. The modern mathematics of chaos theory has found remarkable similarities between such "emergent" properties in many complex systems, ranging from patterns of industrial organization to flocks of migrating birds. Adam Smith's "invisible hand," discovered two hundred years before anyone had thought about the mathematics of complex systems, was the most spectacular example of such an emergent self-organizing property.

Keynes and his collaborators, without anticipating the study of complex systems later in the twentieth century, realized instinctively that the aggregate behavior of the economy could be understood only by focusing on different laws of motion from those governing the individual decisions of businesspeople, workers, and consumers. They noted that the markets for labor, capital, and money, far from being driven by the same dynamics as the classical markets for ordinary goods such as shoes or potatoes, could often behave in the opposite way.

For example, when businesses see wages fall in a recession, a standard classical view of markets suggests that they will hire more workers. However, they generally do the opposite. Because business expansion usually requires investment, which is motivated mainly by the expectation of future sales and profits, rather than today's profits, businesses will often respond to a fall in wages by anticipating weaker demand in the future and thus investing *less* than before. Consumers, meanwhile, will generally react to lower wages by cutting back their spending and increasing their savings. The result is a fall in both investment and consumption. This forces businesses to fire even more workers or cut their wages, which, in turn, further depresses consumer spending, causes even more damage to business expectations, and leads to still-higher unemployment.

Such vicious circles do not continue forever because a market economy contains several self-stabilizing factors, most importantly the rate of interest and the money supply. But Keynes's key point was that the nineteenth-century assumption that competitive market economies always move automatically toward a full-employment equilibrium was wildly over-optimistic.

The only possible reason for depressions recognized by liquidationists, such as Andrew Mellon, was that workers might refuse to accept pay cuts and prefer to become unemployed. But according to Keynesian economics, such "stickiness" of wages was rarely the root cause of recessions. In fact, cutting wages would generally make recessions even worse, since it would reduce workers' purchasing power.

The reasons why market economies could get stuck for years, or even decades, in conditions of mass unemployment were completely different from resistance to wage cuts. Arguably Keynes's most important insight was about the role of uncertainty and inconsistent expectations about future economic conditions. Because the future is inherently unpredictable, there can be no guarantee that businesses, workers, and households will make decisions about investments and savings that are consistent with full employment and the full use of all resources, as predicted by classical economics.

The likelihood that expectations will be inconsistent is aggravated by the divide between the forces driving aggregate and individual economic behavior. Actions that seem rational for individuals can become dangerously counterproductive when undertaken by millions of people or businesses all moving at once. This is an obvious fallacy of composition familiar in many social situations, such as crowd control, yet it is a problem that classical economics largely ignored.

The paradox of thrift is perhaps the most important of the fallacies of composition created by imbalances between reality and expectations about an uncertain future. When one household increases its savings, money flows into the financial system and from there into investment, increasing the total of personal and social wealth. But when millions of households increase their savings, their simultaneous decision to save more can *reduce* the total amount of investment in the economy by undermining growth. Thus, an increase in planned, or *ex ante*, savings can end up reducing the achieved, or *ex post*, investment, diminishing the total wealth in society.

Consider what happens when a major business fires workers or cuts their wages. Either action lowers the purchasing power of the entire economy and puts pressure on other businesses to follow suit. The underlying problem is that actions and expectations of one business affect the reality faced by others. Although changes in interest rates, wages, and prices will generally reconcile imbalances between reality and expectations, in many situations market mechanisms can have an opposite, destabilizing, effect. In financial markets, the effects of imbalances between reality and expectations can be far more extreme.

By focusing on two dissonances in human understanding—first, between perceptions of the present and expectations about the future, and second, between individual actions and collective actions—Keynes identified the most critical forces that can push a faltering economy ever further away from equilibrium. This was an outcome that classical equilibrium theory could neither predict nor analyze. As a result of this analytical success, the macroeconomics of social aggregates and dynamic instability emerged as a separate—and ultimately dominant—field of economics from the late 1930s onward. In the process, the idealized assumptions of nineteenth-century classical economics, with its Panglossian vocabulary of perfect markets, universal equilibrium, and optimal resource allocation, gradually fell into disfavor.

Even more important than Keynes's intellectual breakthroughs in this reinvention of economics was the influence of political events. The mass unemployment of the 1930s forced governments all over the world to take responsibility for macroeconomic management in ways that had never been imagined before. This political transformation changed the questions that economists were expected to answer, and the methodology of economics inevitably changed too. Instead of viewing general equilibrium as a natural, God-given property of the capitalist system, economists began to assume that government could and should intervene when required to balance supply and demand.

Keynesian economics essentially viewed a classical economy in stable equilibrium, with its perfect knowledge and consistent social expectations about the future as a theoretical oddity: an intellectually interesting but practically unimportant special case of the real world, in which markets are imperfect, the future is unpredictable, and expectations are inconsistent. Politicians and voters, after the nightmarish experiences of the interwar period, generally embraced the Keynesian view that capitalist economies are inherently unstable and that active government intervention was necessary to make them work. As a result, macroeconomic management was recognized as a core function of government from the late 1930s onward and became the most important of all political responsibilities after World War II.

Yet even as Keynes's policy recommendations were broadly adopted, his most important insights began to be overwhelmed by the bureaucratic rationalism of the postwar years. The Keynesian view that capitalist economies were prone to depressions because of inconsistent expectations, destabilizing feedbacks, and fallacies of composition was gradually replaced by a "neoclassical synthesis," which subtly changed the terms of economic debate to focus on market imperfections instead of the intrinsic instability of capitalism. The implication was that a wise and benign bureaucracy could, over time, eliminate or manage all these imperfections and achieve the classical ideal of permanent full employment after all.

The neoclassical approach brought back the concept of equilibrium as the natural state of a capitalist economy but argued that recessions were possible—and indeed likely—because of identifiable imperfections, especially a "stickiness" in prices and wages, which fail to adjust quickly enough to changes in supply and demand.

The neoclassical synthesis thus reversed the Keynesian view of what was natural and what was abnormal in the economic world. Keynes and his early followers, brought up in the turbulent interwar period, saw economic instability as the normal state of the economy and equilibrium as an unusual special case. The neoclassical economists of the 1950s and 1960s believed the opposite. They saw the perfectly competitive model economy, always naturally moving toward general equilibrium, as the theoretical norm and foundation for all serious academic analysis. The real-world economy, with its propensity to suffer unemployment and recessions, came to be seen as a dysfunctional, and theoretically uninteresting, special case.

Why did economists adopt this clearly unrealistic view of the world? One answer is the logical simplicity and mathematical tractability of the neoclassical model, which made it more attractive to economists suffering from physics envy and wanting to turn their subject into a mathematical hard science. However, the main reason for economists to adopt a new way of thinking was, as always, the political zeitgeist.

During the early Cold War years, the attraction of restoring the ideal of capitalism as a potentially perfect, or at least perfectible, system was obvious. The ideological rivalry with the collectivist Soviet Union was symbolized perfectly by the neoclassical view of the macroeconomy: a collection of independent, atomistic individuals who cooperate as cogs in a vast Fordist social machine but do this of their own free will, responding to the natural incentives of economics. Better still, the neoclassical synthesis, in contrast to the classical economics of the nineteenth-century, made room for the post-Depression political realities of welfare safety nets and active demand management to stabilize business cycles, by explaining that the Fordist economic machine needed occasional lubrication, "pump-priming," and "kick-starting" by a benignly probusiness government. Thus the new paradigm was able to co-opt both the Left and the Right. Conservatives were happy to describe the new orthodoxy as the neoclassical synthesis, while progressives such as Paul Samuelson and Robert Solow felt able to call it neo-Keynesian economics.

In this process of accommodation to the postwar ideological consensus, however, the most important insight of macroeconomics was lost: Financial instability was no longer recognized as a natural consequence of uncertainty about the future; financial cycles were now merely aberrations caused by imperfections that could, at least in theory, be ironed out by government intervention. This idea was perfectly attuned to the general optimism of the 1950s and the overconfidence of bureaucratic elites.

The Third Era: The Triumph of Rational and Efficient

As the unprecedented prosperity of the 1950s and 1960s degenerated into the social conflicts and economic upheavals of the 1970s, what remained of the Keynesian influence in neoclassical thinking came under intense attack. The target now was not just the core theoretical assertion that instability is, in principle, endemic in the capitalist system but the practical recommendation that government should play an active role in macroeconomic stabilization—the crucial point of policy that Keynes had introduced into economics and on which the neoclassical synthesis had agreed.

From the 1960s onward, conservative economists, many of them based at the University of Chicago, started arguing that macroeconomics had no proper intellectual basis. It could not be taken seriously as a scientific study unless economic models were rebuilt on precise "microfoundations," in which the actions and expectations of businesses, consumers, workers, and investors were all mathematically specified in advance. Anything economists wanted to say about aggregate concepts such as inflation, unemployment, and monetary policy had to be deduced, according to this view, from mathematically exact assumptions not only about the behavior of the millions of individuals who make up the economy but also about their understanding of how the economy works—and would continue to work in the idenfinite future.

The demand that macroeconomics had to be rebuilt on predetermined and precise microfoundations was an act of hubris. While physicists, as noted, had proved that it was impossible to solve even a simple three-body problem with analytical tools of astonishing power, developed by the world's most brilliant mathematicians, going back to Newton and Leibnitz, the microfoundations economists now wanted to find exact solutions to a million-body problem involving thinking participants and infinitely complex laws of motion.

As the only acceptable alternative, the new economic orthodoxy laid down a second methodological requirement that was even more hubristic. In the absence of precise microfoundations, which were unattainable, economists had to assume the millions of economic agents to be "rational" in a specific and peculiar sense. To qualify as "rational," the "representative agent" in the economy—who stood for every businessperson, consumer, and worker—was assumed to have a perfect knowledge of the laws of motion built into the economic model and to consistently use this knowledge to predict the future. The justification for this bizarre methodological assumption was yet another example of the circular reasoning theoretical economists enjoy.

If an economic model had correctly assumed the economy's laws of motion, it would be "grossly irrational" for people to base their behavior on any other view of the world. If, on the other hand, the model's assumptions about economic behavior were incorrect, the model was wrong anyway and therefore not worth considering. It was therefore declared that to be scientifically valid, all economic models had to comply with a Rational Expectations Hypothesis (REH): The model had to *assume* that all economic behavior, including all expectations about the future, were consistent with the economist's own theories about how the world worked.

The quixotic demands to choose between fully predetermined individual microfoundations and uniform rational expectations should have been laughed out of court. So why did this not happen? One reason was purely intellectual. Not only did these methodologies seem to turn economics into a mathematically based science, but they had the further flattering feature of allowing the model-building economist to decree the universal laws of motion be obeyed by all humanity. Rational expectations did not just raise economics to the same status as physics; they elevated economists to the role that Newton had reserved for God.

A much more important reason why the rational expectations research programs, despite obvious impracticability, had such a hypnotic influence over academic economics was that they dovetailed so perfectly with the conservative and individualistic ideology that was starting, by the early 1970s, to overwhelm the previous generation's faith in benign bureaucracy. The political attractions of rational expectations became especially powerful after this theory began to converge in the mid-1970s with Milton Friedman's monetarist counterrevolution against Keynesian policies to reduce unemployment and manage demand.

Before the confluence of monetarism and rational expectations in the early 1970s, Keynesian macroeconomics, even in the diluted form of the neoclassical synthesis, still seemed to justify government involvement in economic management in three important ways. First, neoclassical economists realized that prices and wages were not, in practice, as flexible as the classical models required. Second, they admitted that inconsistent expectations and imperfect knowledge could lead, in the real world, to financial boom-bust cycles. Third, they recognized the fallacies of composition between individual decisions and aggregate outcomes emphasized by Keynes.

The new economics of the 1970s, by contrast, rejected all these arguments—not by refuting them with evidence, but simply by assuming them away.

The new classical school, as it increasingly styled itself, demolished the first argument for government intervention with an openly political prescription—that trade unions should be weakened and business practices deregulated to increase competition—which at least had the virtue of transparency and consistency with changing ideological conditions. The other two arguments for government intervention were undermined in a more subtle way. The new orthodoxy simply inserted additional *assumptions* into economics, which it then fought ruthlessly to establish as unquestionable academic orthodoxies.

The key innovation introduced by the new classical economists was the audaciously Orwellian redefinition of the word *rational* explained previously. If, for example, an economist believed that expanding the money supply would always increase inflation, the new approach to economics entitled—indeed compelled—the economist to assume that all the consumers, businesses, and workers in his or her model would believe this too and would act accordingly. The economics of rational expectations was therefore based on circular reasoning: If it is *assumed* that an accurate model for forecasting the future exists and that everyone knows what it is, the future is predictable and the economy will always remain stable. Thus, there is never any need for government intervention of the kind advocated by Keynes to manage demand. But this chain of reasoning has assumed what it claimed to prove—like the economist in the joke deciding that he could feast on the can of beans by assuming a can opener.

Such an obvious logical fallacy became established as a new economic orthodoxy because it was so ideologically compatible with the changes that capitalism itself was undergoing during the 1970s, as it evolved from its second to its third era, but also through another intellectual subterfuge.

Promoters of REH managed to create an academic convention that economics, to be regarded as a science, could advance only through mathematical deduction from algebraic axioms and assumptions. They mocked all other ways of thinking about economics as incoherent and unscientific. According to this convention, great economic thinkers such as Smith, Ricardo, Keynes, Schumpeter, and Hayek would not be recognized as true economists because their most important works used little or no mathematics. The reason why these great economists expressed themselves in words, rather than formulas, was not because they were uncomfortable with numbers. Both Keynes and Hayek were distinguished mathematicians before they turned to economics. They realized, however, that mathematics, by its very nature, could not express the full complexities, contradictions, and ambiguities of economic life. Hence one of Keynes's most famous sayings: "It is better to be roughly right than precisely wrong."[6] Yet modern academic economics precisely reversed this maxim.

By imposing strict requirements of logical consistency and clarity on economic analysis, the overuse of mathematics actually made it logically impossible for academic economists to say anything useful or interesting about situations in which behavior is inconsistent, motivations are ambiguous, and outcomes are unpredictable—the 2007–09 financial crisis is a perfect example. Imagine if historians were subjected to similar strictures of logical consistency and precision in trying to explain the fall of the Roman Empire or Hitler's rise to power. The study of history might continue as a branch of demographics, genealogy, and some other branches of statistics, but it would cease to shed much useful light on human affairs.

Gerard Debreu, the French mathematician who more or less invented modern mathematical economics, anticipated this danger in his 1991 presidential address to the American Economic Association: "Economic theory has been carried away . . . by a seemingly irresistible current that can be explained only partly by the intellectual successes of its mathematization. . . . Values [are] imprinted on an economist by his study of mathematics. . . . The very choice of the questions to which he tries to find answers is influenced by his mathematical background. Thus, the danger is ever present that the part of economics [in mathematical economics] will become secondary, if not marginal, to that judgment."[7]

Perhaps the single most important insight emphasized repeatedly by both Keynes and Hayek, from opposite ends of the ideological spectrum, was the essential unpredictability of the economic world. The methodology that came to dominate economics from the 1980s onward effectively banned this idea. The mathematical demand for strict logical consistency made it impossible for economics to make any progress on concepts such as Frank Knight's intrinsic uncertainty,[8] Keynes's animal spirits, and Soros's reflexivity, even though these ideas referred to the single most important and interesting features of economic reality.

Because of intrinsic unpredictability, businesses, consumers, or financiers involved in the real economy would be *irrational* if they believed in some clear and unchanging model of how the economy works. Yet universal agreement on such a single "best" theory is what the methodology of rational expectations demands. By an inversion of meaning that would have done honor to Orwell's Ministry of Truth and Big Brother, the dominant economic language from the 1980s onward asserted that Keynesian models were absurd and incoherent because they considered real-world behavior that was defined as "grossly irrational" by REH.

All this may seem like an academic storm in a teacup, but the gap deliberately created between reality and economic thinking had a enormous practical effect that culminated in the crisis of 2007–09. Consider a real-world example that suddenly became extremely relevant in February 2009, in the immediate aftermath of the crisis. Keynesian economics observed that an increase in government spending and borrowing can generally stimulate an increase in output and employment—or, in a recession, can prevent them from falling as rapidly as they otherwise would.

REH models supposedly proved this prediction to be logically incoherent and therefore that government fiscal stimulus could never work. REH did this by assuming that a government stimulus would always result in an expansion of the money supply. Then they made the further assumption that all "rational" businesses, consumers, and investors would believe the simple monetarist theory that growth of the money supply invariably produces inflation. By applying some not very complicated algebra to these assumptions (along with a host of other assumptions, including perfect competition, limitless access to finance, and optimally functioning futures markets), REH theory then "proved" that businesses would be grossly irrational if they responded to government stimulus by expanding their output and that unemployed workers would be grossly irrational if they accepted jobs instead of holding out for higher wages. By contrast, the rational response, if all these assumptions were valid, would be for businesses to raise their prices and for workers to stay on the dole.

With these arguments, rational expectations theorists claimed to prove that Keynesian economics was nonsense: Government stimulus could never cure recessions, increase output, or reduce unemployment; it would merely create inflationary spirals and make unemployment and recessions even worse. This was, in essence, the "Policy Ineffectiveness Proposition" published in 1976 by Thomas Sargent and Neil Wallace. Viewed as a key scientific breakthrough, this paper supposedly refuted the policies of government spending and monetary expansion that had contributed to twenty-five years of unprecedented prosperity in the postwar period but then, in the 1970s, appeared to bring the United States and other advanced economies to the brink of inflationary ruin. In a closely related attack on government attempts to manage the economy by borrowing from the bond markets, Robert Barro, a conservative Harvard economist, came up with a theory he dubbed Ricardian Equivalence. This claimed to prove that any economic stimulus created by government borrowing would automatically be negated by private consumers, who would reduce their spending by exactly a dollar for every extra dollar the government spent.

Because Ricardian Equivalence was at the heart of furious attacks by conservative economists on government stimulus plans in America, Britain, and Germany after the crisis, a brief digression about this theory's intellectual provenance is worthwhile. Barro's theory started, characteristically, by assuming what it claimed to prove. Barro asserted that consumers with rational expectations would view any increase in government borrowing as equivalent to an increase in their future taxes. He then derived conditions under which these rational consumers would cut back their spending immediately to prepare for their future tax bills—and then assumed that these conditions would apply in a rational world.

Finally, in a public-relations coup characteristic of the new economic orthodoxy, Barro claimed support for his theory from David Ricardo, regarded by many academics as the greatest economist of all time. Ricardo had written a paper in 1820 in which he discussed whether a government involved in war would be better off raising £20 million in taxes or the same amount in perpetual bonds, on which it would have to pay interest of 5 percent, or £1m, every year in the future.[9] "In point of economy," he concluded, "there is no real difference in either of the modes, for £20 million in one payment and £1 million per annum forever . . . are precisely of the same value." This statement, which is more subtle than it may seem because of uncertainties about the future value of money, was seized on by Barro as an endorsement of his view that public borrowing was equivalent to taxation.

What Barro and other promoters of the new antigovernment orthodoxy failed to mention, however, was that Ricardo himself had poured scorn on this simplistic calculation, pointing out that it was based on assumptions about real-world human behavior that were almost certainly false: "But the people who paid the taxes never so estimate them, and therefore do not manage their private affairs accordingly . . . It would be difficult to convince a man possessed of £20,000, or any other sum, that a perpetual payment of £50 per annum was equally burdensome with a single tax of £1000." In other words, Ricardo, far from bestowing his posthumous imprimatur on the new theory, derided Ricardian Equivalence as an implausible idea.

Despite their dubious intellectual history, unsubstantiated assumptions, and circular reasoning, theories such as Ricardian Equivalence and Policy Ineffectiveness took academia by storm. Not only did they accord extremely well with the increasingly conservative worldview, but they encountered diminishing resistance. Neo-Keynesian economists, demoralized by the breakdown of the politico-economic model described in this book as Capitalism 2, were easily cowed by rational expectations and monetarist attacks. They bowed to the charge of incoherence in part because the neutered version of Keynesian economics co-opted into the neoclassical synthesis *was* intellectually weak. They therefore accepted the bizarre methodological demand that all academically respectable descriptions of real-world economic behavior had to be made consistent with the assumptions of monetarism and rational expectation, instead of the other way round.

To be fair, for a while the new theories did at least have the virtue of appearing to explain the stagflation of the 1970s and 1980s. What is strange is that their dominance remained unchallenged in the 1990s and the next decade, when their analysis and prescriptions turned out to be completely wrong. From the mid-1980s onward, businesses and consumers who believed that monetary expansion and macroeconomic stimulus would create jobs rather than inflation, far from being grossly irrational, proved to be right. Inflation declined rapidly all over the world from 1981 onward, despite rapid and variable monetary growth rates. And policymakers, first in America, then in Britain, and finally in Continental Europe, became increasingly successful in using interest rates and fiscal policy to fine-tune economic activity and reduce unemployment. Yet these empirical refutations did no damage to the academic prestige of monetarism and rational expectations. For academic economists, the internal consistency of these theories with their own assumptions was deemed much more important than their external inconsistency with the world they claimed to describe.

A third, and perhaps most notorious, member of the theoretical triumvirate that ruled economics alongside rational expectations and monetarism from the 1970s until the 2007–09 crisis was the concept of "efficient" markets. The Efficient Market Hypothesis (EMH) was a set of assumptions about financial markets that developed in parallel with Rational Expectations and thrived through a similar process of self-validation. EMH was designed to refute the instability of financial markets that Keynes and other economists of his generation, including such ultraconservatives as Hayek, believed to hold the key to the most important question in macroeconomics: Why do market economies experience booms and slumps?

Keynes and Hayek both treated financial markets as the primary cause of instability in capitalism. Although they started from contrasting ideological perspectives and arrived at very different policy conclusions, both saw that finance was governed by expectations that would always be inherently subjective and inconsistent. They therefore focused on the role of mood swings, herd instinct, self-reinforcing momentum trading, and other positive feedbacks in financial markets. The new theory of efficient markets, in a pattern that is by now familiar, simply assumed all these effects away.

EMH asserted that financial markets could never cause or amplify economic instability. On the contrary, because financial markets were the most competitive of all markets and allowed investors to trade on future events with options and other derivatives, the prices set in these markets would, by definition, incorporate the best possible analysis of all available information. If financial markets failed to reflect efficiently the best possible analysis of both current and future conditions, this could only be because of excessive regulation, or insider trading, or lack of transparency of some other kind. EMH did not claim, of course, that financial markets would always be right about the future, because unpredictable events would always occur, but it did assert that no investor could consistently outwit the market. Better still, from the ideological standpoint, EMH proved that no government official or regulator could allocate resources more efficiently, or make better guesses about the future, than the financial markets themselves.

The assumption that financial markets were "efficient" also meant that, in the absence of new and genuinely unpredictable information, financial market movements would be meaningless random fluctuations, equivalent to tossing a coin or a drunken sailor's random walk. This chaotic-sounding view was actually reassuring to investors and bankers. For if market movements were really just random coin tosses, they would be highly predictable over longer periods, in the same way that the profits of a lottery or the takings of a casino can be reliably predicted. Specifically, the coin tossing or random walk analogies could be shown by simple mathematics to imply what statisticians call a Normal, or Gaussian, probability distribution over any reasonable period of time.

This may sound obscure and academic, but like the methodology of rational expectations, the near-universal use of the Normal distribution in finance was a very important issue that led directly to the financial collapse in 2007–08. The Normal distribution is a wonderful mathematical construct because it can be analyzed with extraordinary precision. The assumptions made by the Efficient Market Hypothesis thus allowed very precise formulas to be developed for pricing options and complex financial instruments of all kinds. And these formulas, because of their mathematical precision, appeared to justify the enormous increases in leverage and reliance on risk-management systems that so spectacularly failed.

In this sense, the 2007–09 crisis could fairly be described as a simple failure of mathematical economics and its naïve application. If the Efficient Market Hypothesis had been valid, fairly simple and logically irrefutable mathematical calculations could show that most of the financial crises of the past twenty years were literally impossible. Bankers and regulators would thus have been right to ignore such risks. For example, if the daily fluctuations on Wall Street had really followed a random walk, the odds of a one-day movement greater than 25 percent would be about one in three trillion. In reality, however, at least three such statistically "impossible" events occurred during just twenty years when EMH was the dominant financial orthodoxy: in the stock market during the 1987 crash, in bonds and currencies in 1994, and in interest rate arbitrage in 1998, when Russia defaulted and the Long Term Capital Management hedge fund sensationally collapsed.

And all these earlier upheavals were nothing compared to the events of 2007–09. By August 2007, David Viniar, the chief financial officer of Goldman Sachs, claimed to be seeing "twenty-five standard deviation events," which in a normal distribution ought to occur only once every trillion years, "happening several days in a row."[10] And that was more than a year before the collapse of Lehman, when the financial markets really went wild.

By normal intellectual standards, such spectacular empirical falsification should have completely demolished the Efficient Market Hypothesis as a scientific theory. But as in the case of rational expectations, most economists, even after the crisis, remain so attached to their theories that the facts are rejected instead.[11] The financial establishment, too, has been quick to regroup in defense of EMH, since abandoning this theory would mean dismantling some very profitable, though very risky, business models. Without the Efficient Market Hypothesis, most of the trading and risk models used by major financial institutions would have to be junked. The mark-to-market profits on which banks still base their dividends and bonuses will have to be replaced by old-fashioned cash accounting, with profits recognized only as banks receive their money back from borrowers or sell assets to realize capital gains.

Worst of all from the standpoint of conservative economics, it can be shown mathematically that abandoning the assumption of the Efficient Markets will mean abandoning the assumption of automatic equilibrium in nonfinancial markets.[12] This "joint hypothesis problem" means that efficient markets and rational expectations must stand together or fall, along with all the attendant proofs used to justify with apparent mathematical rigor the ideological doctrine that government interference with market forces is always futile or counterproductive.

The Next Transition

Why has the world allowed intellectual dishonesty to infect a serious academic discipline, especially one as important to society as economics? The answer lies, ironically, in the very fact that economics is so politically important.

The pseudoscientific objectivity of orthodox economic theories has been extremely attractive to conservative politicians. Rational expectations and efficient markets claimed to prove that economic problems such as recessions, financial crashes, and unemployment were not intrinsic properties of the capitalist system but distortions and imperfections caused by human (usually government) interference with the system's natural laws. A prime example was the post-hoc rationalization of the U.S. property boom and bust. The trillion-dollar losses suffered by some of the world's most sophisticated investors in their mortgage lending clearly refuted the theories of rational expectations and efficient markets. But conservative politicians found these theories too useful to throw away. EMH asserts that competitive markets make the best possible use of all available information. If the markets make an obvious blunder, it therefore follows that some kind of government interference must be to blame. Since the crisis, conservative politicians and economists have shamelessly used such topsy-turvy reasoning to "prove" that modest government incentives for low-income mortgage lending were the fundamental cause of the financial collapse.

In sum, the power of the dominant economic paradigm arises mainly from its usefulness as ideology. Rational Expectations, along with the Policy Ineffectiveness Proposition and the concepts of Ricardian Equivalence and the "natural" rate of unemployment, "proved" that government efforts to manage economic cycles and unemployment were futile and counterproductive. General equilibrium "proved" that a capitalist economy would always achieve full employment if governments would stay out of the way. Pareto Optimality "proved" that a market economy would always allocate resources in the most productive possible manner. Efficient markets "proved" that the only constructive role of government in the economy was to deregulate and privatize. These were exactly the conclusions that politicians and business leaders wanted to hear from economists in the 1980s to validate the Thatcher and Reagan reforms.

Better still, the rational, efficient, natural, and mathematically irrefutable outcomes of market forces seemed to legitimize the distribution of income, wealth, and power decreed by whatever happened to be the economic and political status quo. Job losses resulting from laissez-faire industrial policies, ever-wider income inequalities, huge salaries for top executives and supposedly talented financial traders could all be presented as outcomes of impersonal natural forces, rather than contingent social arrangements susceptible to political reform.

When magic words such as *rational, efficient,* and *natural* were endorsed by academics festooned with Nobel prizes, their political usefulness increased. In fact, the success of the dominant economic paradigm could largely be attributed to rhetorical genius.

Imagine if the Efficient Market Hypothesis had instead been called the Casino Market Hypothesis. The bankers and regulators whose faith in efficient markets almost wrecked the global financial system might then have heeded Keynes's famous dictum: "When the capital development of a country becomes a by-product of the activities of a casino, the job is likely to be ill-done." Or suppose that rational expectations had been renamed *internally consistent expectations,* as some of its proponents originally suggested. An adequate refutation might then have been Ralph Waldo Emerson's acerbic comment that "a foolish consistency is the hobgoblin of little minds." To continue this thought experiment, try replacing *perfect competition* with *ruthless exploitation, general equilibrium* with *timeless stasis, Pareto Optimality* with *Entrenched Privilege, Ricardian Equivalence* with *Barro's False Assumption, natural rate of unemployment* with *deliberate job destruction,* and so on.

Like President Bush's Clear Skies Act, which freed polluting industries to increase emissions, the Healthy Forests Initiative, which promoted logging, and the Homeland Security Act, which encouraged paranoia, the market fundamentalist economic orthodoxy achieved its dominance partly through a clever choice of adjectives.

The 2007–09 crisis may finally have discredited this Orwellian use of language. The favored adjectives of market fundamentalism—rational, perfect and efficient—are unlikely to regain their ideological power. If so, the new economic theories introduced in the 1970s to justify the ideological transition from the big-government Keynesian era to the free-market Thatcher-Reagan model will lose their political raison d'etre.

Instead, new ways of thinking about economics will surely be developed in parallel with the evolution of a new capitalist system. For economics to be reinvented, however, the dominant research programs of the 1979–2009 era will have to be acknowledged as failures, or at least to be discarded as no longer relevant. Instead of using oversimplified assumptions to create mathematical models that bear no relation to real events, economists will have to open their subject again to a wider diversity of analytical approaches. They will have to draw insights from political science, sociology, and anthropology. And they will have to apply the methods of historians, management theorists, and psychologists, as well as mathematicians and statisticians. As economists do this, the institutional structures and intellectual outlines of Capitalism 4.0 will gradually take shape.

CHAPTER TWELVE

Toward a New Economics

To PROVIDE ANY USEFUL GUIDANCE for the development of capital-ism in the years ahead, new economic thinking will have to satisfy three conditions. First, it will have to recognize that a market economy is not a static system in equilibrium but one that is constantly evolving. The capacity for constant adaptation in response to social, political, and techno-logical change is the most important and valuable feature of a competitive market system. The second key requirement for the new economics will be acknowledgment that effective government and dynamic private enter-prise are symbiotic, not mutually exclusive. Strong government and strong markets are both necessary for the successful functioning of the capitalist system: The dream of creating a market system with no economic role for government ended on September 15, 2008. The third essential feature of the new economics, both as a cause and consequence of the other two, will be a focus on the inherent unpredictability of human behavior and eco-nomic events.

The emphasis on unpredictability introduced by Keynes, Schum-peter, and Frank Knight will be a guiding principle of the new theories competing for leadership in the intellectual marketplace during the next phase of economic thinking. In the new economy emerging from the 2007–09 crisis, the wisdom of markets can no longer be taken for granted; it must be recognized that the markets and the government are both liable to be wrong. In a world where the future is indeterminate and shaped by reflexive interactions between human behavior, expectations, and reality, the rational expectations concept of a single "correct" model that everyone believes in is obviously an absurd delusion. In the new world of indeterminacy, economic and institutional decisions will proceed by a zigzag process of trial and error. Government policies, as well as market behavior and business expectations, will evolve continuously as the economic system adapts to the changing conditions created by the system's own institutional reforms.

In short, the economy of the future will be explicitly a *mixed* economy, in the sense that both the private and public sectors will play an important role. And it will be an *adaptive* economy, where the rules of economic engagement, including the relationships between the government and private markets, will be subject to change.

Some of the policies and institutions likely to emerge from such an adaptive mixed economy are discussed in Part IV. But how will new ways of thinking about economics help to provide an intellectual and ideological foundation for Capitalism 4.0?

Despite the near-monopoly enjoyed by rational expectations and mathematical modeling in elite university departments since the 1980s, many new and interesting approaches to economics based on psychology, sociology, control engineering, chaos theory, psychiatry, and practical business insights have been developing in the shadows of the official doctrine. Some of these new ideas are springing to life after the crisis.

The approach receiving widest publicity in the immediate aftermath of the crisis was behavioral economics. Behavioral economics considers a world in which investors and businesses are motivated by crowd psychology rather than the obsessive calculation of rational expectations. It is, however, the least radical of the new ways of thinking about economics because it does not challenge the central assumption of REH—that booms, busts, and recessions are all caused by various types of market failure and thus that breakdowns in laissez-faire capitalism can, in principle, be prevented by making markets more perfect, for example, by disseminating more information or strengthening the regulations against fraud. Because behavioral economics does not challenge the subject's theoretical and ideological foundations, the academic establishment has been quite willing to embrace this approach. Indeed, the work on bounded rationality by Herbert Simon, game theory by Vernon Smith, experimental economics by Daniel Kahneman, and asymmetrical information by George Akerloff, Joe Stiglitz, and Michael Spence have all been rewarded with Nobel prizes.

More challenging to orthodox economics is the mathematical work in chaos theory and advanced control engineering, which suggests that most of the mathematical techniques used by precrisis academic economics were simply wrong. Brian Arthur, along with colleagues at the Santa Fe Institute, has spent a lifetime developing the mathematics of nonlinear complex systems and applying them to the self-organizing emergent behavior of economies and markets that involve properties defying the assumptions of standard economics, for example, increasing returns and winner-takes-all positive feedbacks. Such work has produced impressive results on industrial organization that are widely divergent from conventional economics, but these ideas have never been integrated into the study of macroeconomic policy and financial markets, where new ideas are most needed because conventional economics has clearly failed.

Benoit Mandelbrot, one of the most creative mathematicians of the twentieth century and a founder of the theories of chaos and complex systems, devoted a large part of his career to studying economics and financial markets. Many of the mathematical ideas that Mandelbrot developed and that found fruitful applications in the study of earthquakes, weather, galaxies, and biological systems from the 1960s onward were inspired by his studies of finance and economics—and could be applied to these subjects with great effect. Mandelbrot, in his book *The Misbehaviour of Markets*, described how forty years of effort to interest economists in fractal geometry were ridiculed or ignored, despite the fact that they seemed to provide a much better analysis of extreme market behavior than standard methods. Consider, for example, this paragraph written by Mandelbrot some five years before the Lehman crisis:

> The odds of financial ruin in a free global-market economy have been grossly underestimated. There is no limit to how bad a bank's losses can get. Its own bankruptcy is the least of the worries; it will default on its obligations to other banks—and so the losses will spread from one inter-linked financial house to another. Only forceful action by regulators to put a firewall round the sickest firms will stop the crisis spreading. But bad news tends to come in flocks and a bank that weathers one crisis may not survive a second

or a third . . . Most economic theorists have been going down the wrong track. When economic models fail, they are seldom thrown away. Rather they are 'fixed'—amended, qualified, particularized, expanded and complicated. Bit by bit, from a bad seed a big but sickly tree is built with glue, nails, screws and scaffolding. Conventional economics assumes the financial system is a linear, continuous, rational machine and these false assumptions are built into the risk models used by many of the world's banks.[1]

Despite the success achieved by fractal geometry and nonlinear modeling in the study of earthquakes, weather, evolution, ecology, and other complex systems, Mandelbrot always faced the same objection from economists when he proposed applying similar techniques to markets. These non-Gaussian mathematical methods could only provide approximations, as opposed to the precise answers offered by the Efficient Market Hypothesis and Gaussian statistics.[2] The fact that the exact answers of EMH bore no relation to reality did not seem to deter "scientific" economists.

Another striking example of the cognitive dissonance in the use of mathematics by scientific economists is provided by Roman Frydman and Michael Goldberg, two U.S. economists who have pioneered a research program they describe as Imperfect Knowledge Economics (IKE). This approach explicitly challenges the most important—and most implausible—assumption of rational expectations: the idea that there is one best model of how the economy works, which every rational economic agent will find out about. Instead, IKE draws on the insight of Keynes and Hayek that a capitalist economy is far too complex for anyone to be sure whether one model is better than any another, especially when it comes to predicting future events. Because of pervasive and unavoidable uncertainty, businesses and investors will rationally operate on a variety of different economic assumptions and will change these as events and human understanding evolve. Indeed, it would be grossly irrational for anyone to act like the representative agents in rational expectations theory, relying on one model when nobody can predict the furure, still less the future course of knowledge itself.

Starting from the ideas of Edmund Phelps, one of the few Nobel Laureate economists who rejected the assumption of one universally recognizable, correct economic model, IKE uses the tools of conventional mathematical economics to generate radically different results. Because the future is inherently unknowable, IKE assumes that there will always be a multitude of plausible models about the way an economy works. With this obvious but extremely controversial change in assumptions, IKE demolishes most of the conclusions of rational expectations.

More importantly, IKE shows that economists who make more reasonable assumptions about uncertainty can offer results that are much closer to real-world events than those produced by rational expectations models. To do this, IKE builds on the concept of reflexivity pioneered by George Soros—that market expectations which are initially false can change reality and become self-fulfilling. This leads to a world in which market participants who have diverse views about the true condition of the economy and indeed about the laws of economics can alter reality as they change these views. By formalizing such insights, IKE generates qualitative forecasts of currency movements—and these fuzzy numbers turn out to be much closer to actual movements in exchange rates than the sharp predictions of rational expectations models, which are precise but invariably precisely wrong.

These are just a few examples of the sort of creative new approaches to economics likely to emerge in the decade after the crisis, as the world recognizes the intrinsic limitations of market forces and economic knowledge.

Economics today is a discipline that must either die or undergo a paradigm shift—to make itself both more broad-minded and more modest. It must broaden its horizons to recognize the insights of other social sciences and historical studies and it must return to its roots. Smith, Keynes, Hayek, Schumpeter, and all the other truly great economists were interested in economic reality. They studied real human behavior in markets that actually existed, rather than making assumptions about disembodied representative agents and desocialized perfect markets of a kind that could not possibly approximate the real world.

Their insights came from historical knowledge, psychological intuition, and political understanding, which led to ever more complex explanations of social relationships, rather than abstract assumptions that atomised society and reduced human behavior to ever simpler and more unrealistic assumptions. Their main analytical tools were words, not mathematics. They persuaded with eloquence and wit, not formal logic. (One can see why many of today's academics fear the return of economics to its philosophical and literary roots.) If any of these giants of economic thinking lived today and submitted their papers to leading academic journals or applied for jobs at elite universities, they would be ridiculed and rejected.

As Thomas Kuhn explained fifty years ago in his classic study of scientific progress, *The Structure of Scientific Revolutions,* academic establishments fight hard to resist paradigm shifts, even in physics, chemistry, and other objective, empirically testable hard sciences. In economics, with all its ideological connections, a paradigm shift will be resisted even more fiercely, despite the spectacular failures the crisis revealed.

It is too flattering to economics to compare the paradigm shift that lies ahead to the one that occurred in physics a century ago. Economics is closer today to astronomy in 1543, when Copernicus realized that the earth revolved around the sun. The academic economics of the past twenty years has been comparable to pre-Copernican astronomy, with its mysterious heavenly cogs, epicycles, and wheels within wheels. Today's economists will fight for their irrational rationality as fiercely as the pre-Copernican astrologers defended their epicycles and star signs.

Max Planck observed, in the context of the revolution in physics that occurred one hundred years ago with the discovery of relativity and quantum mechanics, that "science progresses one funeral at a time." The achievements of modern economics are too meager—and its ideological importance is too great—to allow such slow progress. Either economics will reform itself quickly or the funeral will be for the discipline as a whole.

Part IV

The Great Transition

THE EFFECTIVE FAILURE of every major bank in America and Europe. The discrediting of efficient market economics. Then, most surprisingly of all, the heroic role played by left-of-center politicians in saving the free-enterprise system. These events brought Capitalism 3 to an end in 2008–09.

With market fundamentalism in its death throes, capitalism is beginning to adapt, as it always does, to the new environment. This means shedding the morbid features of the dying species and evolving a new means of survival in the world as it is, not as the previous generation imagined and hoped it would be.

Although some business leaders and politicians continue to proclaim the slogans of the Thatcher-Reagan era—"you can't buck the market," "we can't spend our way to prosperity," "the market is always right"—the repetition is mechanical and lacks conviction. The remaining free-market zealots, whether in the Chicago School, in the Tea Party, or on talk radio and in the conservative blogosphere, are like Wile E. Coyote or the septuagenarian Russian communists who parade every May in Red Square. Their belief is immoveable, but the world has moved on. Market fundamentalism has entered what George Soros, in his analysis of boom-bust cycles, calls the Twilight Period. This is the penultimate phase of a long-expanding bubble, as the air begins to leak out; the point "when people continue to play the game although they no longer believe in it."

It is now time to look in more detail at the new version of capitalism, to consider some of the ways it is adapting and to weigh its chances of success. How does the new politico-economic model differ from the previous versions? How is it performing in its first years of existence? What are its prospects of turning the postcrisis recovery into a period of durable prosperity and economic growth? The rest of this book will consider in detail how Capitalism 4.0 is likely to differ from the market fundamentalist system that has been swept away by the crisis. The three chapters in Part IV describe the economic characteristics of the new system that can already be clearly discerned. Part V then offers some more speculative views about how Capitalism 4.0 could evolve in the long term.

The feature of Capitalism 4.0 that is already clear and undeniable is that a market economy can only exist with a competent and active government. This is now obvious in the financial sector, whose survival was shown to be ultimately dependent on government guarantees.

A second essential economic function of government that has been even more clearly demonstrated and legitimized by the crisis. Governments and central banks must actively manage economic demand. The experience of 2008–09 showed conclusively that monetary and fiscal policy are highly effective tools for pulling an economy out of recession and that the market fundamentalist theories about the ineffectiveness of demand management are quite simply wrong. Chapters 14 and 15 expand on the consequences.

A third clear difference between Capitalism 4.0 and the preceding versions of the system will be an understanding that markets and governments are both imperfect and prone to error. Acknowledging this inherent fallibility will not be paralyzing, but empowering, provided the new model of capitalism encourages experimentation and proves able to adapt to unexpected events. This capacity for institutional adaptation and ideological flexibility should be one of the distinctive features of the mixed economy of Capitalism 4.0. Competitive markets operate through trial and error and quickly correct small misjudgments. In politics, democratic competition plays a similar error-correcting role. But markets can magnify errors instead of correcting them when herd instinct overtakes investors—and the same thing can happen in democracies when one ideology overwhelms all political debate. In a fast-moving, interdependent, and inherently unpredictable world, skepticism, experimentation, and flexibility are crucial. Adaptability and the willingness to admit errors will become a cardinal virtue in politicians and central bankers, as well as in businesspeople and financiers, in the world of Capitalism 4.0. This is the story the next chapter takes up.

CHAPTER THIRTEEN

The Adaptive Mixed Economy

> *Adaptive (adj): having a capacity for adjustment to environmental conditions . . .*
>
> *[The capacity] of an organism or its parts that makes it more fit for existence under the conditions of its environment.*
>
> —*Webster's Dictionary*

CAPITALISM 4.0 WILL BE an adaptive mixed economy. But what does this really mean? First, it will be explicitly a mixed economy. It will combine government and business in partnership rather than opposition and deliberately mix normal competitive markets, designed to be as transparent and efficient as possible, with a smaller number of controlled markets, consciously regulated to limit their "efficiency" in the narrow and misleading sense of Capitalism 3. Second, Capitalism 4.0 will be an adaptive system, able and willing to change its institutional structure, its regulations, and its economic principles in response to changing events.

The obvious examples of new interaction between governments and markets will be seen in the financial area, where more detailed and intrusive regulation is inevitable. Instead of trying to make markets more efficient, much of this new regulation will be deliberately designed to reduce the competition, predictability, and transparency that were the hallmarks of the previous model's obsession with perfect markets. New bank regulations will be less predictable because predictability was the very quality that allowed banks to sidestep and game the old regulations, with disastrous results. These regulations will have to be less transparent because the quest for transparency was what produced the fiasco of mark-to-market accounting.

Bankers and financiers will protest that measures of this kind make markets less efficient, but these protests will fall on deaf ears as the new economic thinking prompted by the financial crisis gains broader acceptance. Capitalism 4.0 will recognize not only that markets are often irrational and inefficient but also that efforts to make markets more efficient and perfect can sometimes produce perverse results. Reforms to make all markets more competitive, transparent, and fast-moving may seem self-evidently desirable, but there are many cases when more perfect markets would clearly be worse for the world. Markets in nuclear and biological weapons, slaves, human organs, and guns are obvious examples. The question that nobody bothered to ask until after the crisis was which financial products might fall into this pathological group. The answer turned out to be "quite a few." This was not because financial products are inherently dangerous in the same way as guns and biological weapons.[1] But trying to create more perfect markets for financial products is often counterproductive because financial products exist to deal with uncertainty—and this uncertainty is itself a market imperfection in the outdated language of rational expectations and other deceptive concepts of Capitalism 3. Attempts to make financial markets more efficient and transparent may thus create an *illusion* of eliminating risk and uncertainty, while disguising unavoidable uncertainty and hiding its true costs— or shifting this cost onto taxpayers' shoulders.

Capitalism 4.0 will also differ from previous variants by becoming a self-consciously adaptive system. To become more stable, the system will have to be more flexible, even fluid. This may sound paradoxical, but it is not. Capitalism survives by bending instead of breaking. What might be meant in practice by this quality of adaptation? Regulations will be subject to more discretionary fine-tuning. The dividing line between private and public sectors will become less clear-cut. The rules of behavior for all economic players and the structure of the economy will be more tentative and open to reform. This will be a major change from the modus operandi of Capitalism 3.

Market fundamentalism required that financial regulations, the rules of corporate behavior, and even the macroeconomic targets of central banks were set rigidly for long periods. The idea was to minimize the discretionary powers of government officials, create clear dividing lines between political and economic decisions, and provide maximum predictability and transparency for financial investors. Capitalism 4.0, by contrast, will have more variation. Rules will be altered frequently and market incentives tweaked to promote important political objectives because markets will no longer be trusted to decide autonomously on all the adaptations needed for the economic system and society to thrive in a rapidly changing world.

It may be argued that there is nothing new in the mixed and adaptive economy just described. Even in the advanced economies with the smallest public sectors, the United States and Japan, the government collects and spends some 30 percent of national income. So these economies are already thoroughly mixed. As for adaptation, this book's argument views capitalism as an intrinsically adaptive system. So what is different? The answer is a much more conscious *recognition* of adaptiveness and of private-public interdependence.

Thus, Capitalism 4.0 will create an adaptive mixed economy and will become increasingly self-conscious about the differences between this model and those that have gone before. In the old models of capitalism, the roles and objectives of government and private enterprise were fixed by long-established tradition and could be changed only through tremendous political upheavals. The main division in politics, both during Capitalism 2 and Capitalism 3, was between progressive parties who wanted to expand government and reduce the role of markets, and conservatives who wanted to do the opposite—reduce the role of government and expand markets. One question was therefore enough to establish almost everyone's political position on every issue: Do you want less government and more market or vice versa? The polarization of attitudes to business and government was as much a definitive feature of politics in the broadly progressive era from 1932 until the 1970s as it was in the subsequent conservative decades.

Not only were political attitudes to government and markets polarized for much of the twentieth century, but this polarization meant that the boundaries between the public and private sectors were rigidly predefined.

The two sides in the political debate both believed that it was their mission not only to expand either government or markets but also to entrench these changes forever if they could. Whatever the division of responsibilities between the government and the market, this allocation became fixated inflexibly in the public mind. An amusing example was the antigovernment placard displayed at one of the Tea Party demonstrations against Obama's proposals to reform health care: "Keep your government hands off my Medicare."[2] Whether the person holding up this placard was unaware that Medicare was a government program created in 1965 by Lyndon Johnson is unclear. What is certain is that, after a state-controlled Medicare system was firmly established, not even the most radical conservatives campaigned to have it abolished or reprivatized.

Such paradoxes abound the world over. Britons, for example, return from skiing holidays in France or Switzerland to bore their dinner companions with anecdotes about the wonderful medical care in those countries. Yet the same people tell opinion pollsters they would rather die, sometimes literally, than see Britain's state-controlled National Health Service replaced by a French-style mixture of private, charitable, and public hospitals. The French, meanwhile, are shocked that Britain's utilities are private companies with no obligations to heed national interests in planning their long-term energy strategies. And how many Americans, as they grumble about the miserable standards of the U.S. Postal Service, can imagine it being privatized like Germany's Deutsche Post AG, which is 65 percent owned by private investors and now the world's biggest logistics group? What all these examples illustrate is the intellectual inertia and institutional conservatism that has stifled serious debate about redrawing lines between public and private activities since the initial phase of radical reforms in the Thatcher-Reagan years.

The same ideological paralysis has descended on thinking about the *methods* by which private and public institutions should operate. A hallmark of institutional thinking in Capitalism 3 was a demand for clear rules to control both public and private behavior, backed up if possible by legally enforceable contracts. The Right demanded such rules to limit the discretion of public officials and extend the contractual principles of market capitalism to parts of society they had never reached before. In New Zealand, for example, the governor of the Reserve Bank had a contract requiring a certain rate of inflation and suffered a pay cut if it was not achieved. In Britain, the Blair government proposed contracts between schools and parents to govern homework and discipline. The Left, on the other hand, became obsessed with elaborate rules and legal contracts in the hope of curbing the private sector's ability to exploit the public and cheat.

Whatever the motivation of the original rules, regulations, or contracts defining business-government relations, all efforts to change them turned into ideological battles, almost as controversial as the positions of the public-private dividing line itself. The growing dominance of finance in the final years before the crisis made the system of governance even more rigid and therefore brittle. As stock market investors asserted their status as the ultimate arbiters of what was good for the businesses they owned, predictability and transparency became absolute requirements in all government interactions with business. In a strange twist on Charles Wilson's famous remark that "what is good for America is good for General Motors and vice versa," stock market analysts and media stock-tipsters found that transparency and predictability made life easier for them in forecasting company profits—and therefore concluded that transparency and predictability must always be good for business and for the broader economy too.

Meanwhile, political lobbyists focused their attention on defining the clearest possible rules for the interaction between business and government and then resisting all further reforms. Regulations, while limiting business opportunities, can often create valuable financial and institutional privileges for the companies involved. As a result, regulated businesses and their lobbyists can become the fiercest opponents of deregulation, while government institutions originally created to protect the public interest often, through the process called regulatory capture, become protectors of the businesses they supervise.

The dysfunctions inherent in government regulation of private activities were brilliantly analyzed by the conservative Public Choice school of economists, who contributed many genuinely valuable ideas to the Thatcher-Reagan revolution in economics. James Buchanan, one of the Nobel-laureate founders of Public Choice theory, described his school of thought as "a set of theories of governmental failure [to] offset against the theories of market failure" promoted by "the prevailing socialist mindset" of the 1960s.[3] He summarized his approach as "politics without romance."

But while Public Choice theory is often regarded as a laissez-faire ideology characteristic of the Thatcher-Reagan period, some of the most important contributors to this skeptical view of regulation[4] were progressive advocates of strong and effective governments who were trying to develop a theory on how to improve, not jettison, public choice. Even Buchanan, although a conservative in his general political outlook, maintained that he was neither for nor against government. In one of his seminal papers, he explained how the skeptical framework of Public Choice "almost literally forces the critic to be pragmatic in any comparison of proposed institutional structures."[5] This is a perfect way to characterize the attitude to government and markets in Capitalism 4.0.

The skeptical Public Choice insights about the failures of government in the 1970s and 1980s are likely to produce new conclusions under Capitalism 4.0. In the bold reforming period of Capitalism 3, the response to obvious dysfunctions in public policy was simply to reduce government, either through privatization or deregulation, and to expand the influence of markets. But what if it is clear that markets also suffer dangerous and unavoidable dysfunctions? In the new thinking that follows the 2007–09 crisis, the conclusion from Public Choice–type analysis about the flaws of politics and regulation will not be that government must be abolished. The response will be to try to overcome these problems with better institutions.

Rather than abandoning hope in regulation and simply giving free rein to markets, Capitalism 4.0 will seek more intelligent policies that take account of known dysfunctions of government such as regulatory capture, rent-seeking,[6] the political influence of special interests, and single-issue lobbies. It would be overoptimistic to imagine that such effort will be entirely successful. No one is likely to discover perfect answers to some of the deepest questions of social organization that have troubled political theorists since Plato and Aristotle,[7] but an important part of any new approach will be to increase the flexibility of public policy and try to weaken the hold of the special interests that regulations create, some of which are found in the government itself.

One small way to soften the rigidities of regulation and limit the unproductive rent-seeking that tends to be created by government is to use sunset clauses on government rules of all kinds.[8] Suppose, for example, that bank solvency regulations, employment laws, and even health and safety rules lapsed automatically and had to be redrawn every ten years. Far more thought and lobbying power would be devoted to serious debate about improving regulation and debating whether it was still needed, rather than exploiting and gaming a fixed set of rules.

To see what this could mean in practice, consider a pathological counterexample. The European Union, since its foundations in 1956, has steadily expanded its powers on the basis of a legal doctrine called *acquis communautaire*. This states that any new governmental responsibilities granted to the EU institutions in Brussels can never be taken away.[9] As a result of the *acquis communautaire*, every expansion of the EU's regulatory role, whether in competition or energy or finance or employment, becomes legally irreversible. Any new piece of European legislation therefore automatically creates a new institutional superstructure of lobbyists, lawyers, and business interests dedicated to maintaining and exploiting the new regulations. This is an obvious political scandal, yet nothing could be done about it within the ideological mindset of Capitalism 3. Opponents of regulation in Europe assumed that all government was dysfunctional and therefore that the best alternative to a permanent ratcheting up of regulation was no regulation at all—an alternative that never had the slightest chance of acceptance. For supporters of EU regulation, on the other hand, a permanent expansion and entrenchment of European government, rather than a search for time-limited solutions to specific practical problems, was always the main goal.

The concrete example in the next section will help fill in this abstract sketch of how the transition to Capitalism 4.0 could change the relationship of government and markets.

Energy Policy and the 2008 Oil Shock

The world is facing a three-pronged energy crisis. In the short term, the surge in oil prices to $150 in the summer of 2008 contributed to the financial breakdown and the recession—and the fear that oil prices could return to these levels is a major threat to global economic recovery in 2011 and beyond. In the very long-term, oil is a limited resource, as is the atmosphere's capacity for absorbing carbon. And in the middle-distance time horizon, the immense transfer of global resources to politically unstable oil-producing countries creates huge geopolitical risks. Why, then, has the United States in particular, and the Western world in general, done so little to reduce its dependence on oil?

The answer is quite simply that oil, even at $100 a barrel, is a cheaper source of energy than any existing alternative.[10] In the mindset of Capitalism 3.3, this is the end of the matter: Whatever source of energy is cheapest is the one that should be used. The market price reflects the best possible judgment about the costs and benefits of using oil, not only for individual businesses and consumers but also for society as a whole—and there is nothing that public policy can or should do to change this.

Capitalism 4.0, however, is likely to take a different view for two reasons. First, the market price may *not* in fact reflect the true benefits and costs of using oil; for example, it fails to account for the costs of pollution. Second, and more important, the market price can and should be altered if good reasons exist to do this—whether these reasons reflect political objectives, such as the desire to reduce oil revenues available to Middle Eastern terrorists, or economic ones, such as the desire to avoid another recession-inducing oil shock.

Between them, these two observations point to some obvious solutions to the long-term challenges of climate change and oil depletion—taxing oil or carbon, subsidizing alternative energy, redirecting public research funding, and offering cheap government insurance against the risks and decommissioning costs of nuclear power. The long-term response of Capitalism 4.0 to these issues is discussed at greater length in Chapter 19. But what could Western governments have done in the short-term to prevent the 2008 oil shock and the subsequent financial disaster—and what might governments do in the near future if another surge in the oil price to $150 a barrel were to threaten the global economy in the next few years?

The fundamentalist view that market prices always reflect all possible information and lead to the best possible allocation of resources blinded governments and regulators to a crucial difference between the 2008 oil shock and the ones that occurred in 1974, 1979, and 1990. All earlier oil shocks were caused by geopolitical disruptions or deliberate OPEC actions that reduced the supply of oil. The surge in oil prices in 2008 was different. It was caused not by a shortfall in supply but an increase in demand. However, this demand was not due, as widely reported, to increased Chinese consumption. China's growing use of oil was more than offset, even before the recession, by declining demand from America and Europe, as confirmed by statistics from the International Energy Agency, OPEC, and private oil companies, all of which showed almost zero growth in the world's total use of oil in 2008 and a decline in 2009.[11]

What, then, caused the extra demand that drove up the oil price to $150? The answer is aggressive buying of financial derivatives based on the price of oil by long-term investors, especially university endowments and pension plans in the United States.[12] Some of these financial contracts represented oil that was physically stored in tankers and depots in Rotterdam or Oklahoma. Other oil derivatives were simply bits of paper created by investment banks. But these banks, in turn, had to ensure that they would profit in the event of a further rise in the oil price, and they did this by buying futures contracts from oil suppliers and renewing these contracts every three months. Whether or not the financial investors received physical delivery of the oil their contracts represented made no difference. Their willingness to buy in the futures markets, and to do so at ever higher prices, ensured that the oil price went up.

As Michael Masters, a prominent commodity trader, pointed out in Congressional testimony in the midst of the 2008 oil shock,[13] the situation in the oil market in 2008 was analogous to a manmade epidemic or famine. If a contagious disease were threatening the nation and financial institutions decided to buy the entire supply of vaccines in the expectation of selling them at higher prices when people started dying, the government would rightly outlaw this behavior. The same would be true if the nation's richest citizens tried to hoard most of the wheat supply in the hope of creating a famine. Such hoarding is essentially what happened when financial institutions began to accumulate potentially unlimited amounts of oil contracts in the hope that the price would keep going up. The failure of governments to respond to entreaties for action against this hoarding, many coming from the oil industry itself, was a symptom that Capitalism 3.3 was entering its terminal stage: the stage of ideological senility, when blind faith in market forces finally brought the whole system down on September 15.

So what could have been done—and what could be done in the future by more pragmatic governments with a Capitalism 4 mindset? Outright bans on oil and commodity investment might have been the response under Capitalism 2. In the 1960s, when the Bretton Woods currency system was threatened by a surge in demand for gold, private ownership of gold was simply outlawed in the United States and most European countries.

In Capitalism 4.0, however, a more subtle and less oppressive response would be likely. Rather than banning investment in oil, governments would allow markets to keep working but would change market incentives. The U.S. government might announce, for example, that investments in oil and other physical commodities by tax-exempt institutions would in future be subject to capital gains tax. A more extreme measure would be to remove the tax-exempt status of any institutions that engaged in physical commodity investment, on the reasonable grounds that their money should be invested in productive and income-producing assets, such as the shares of oil companies, rather than stockpiles of physical oil.

Why were such interventions never attempted or even discussed? Because no one could identify a precise mechanism of market failure that was causing the explosive rise in the price of oil—at least to the satisfaction of President Bush's regulatory appointees.[14] The fact that the price increase was causing enormous and obvious damage to the world economy was considered irrelevant because it was inconceivable for regulators to act until a specific market failure could be identified. This was the identical argument used by Alan Greenspan against any regulation of subprime mortgages or credit derivatives before the 2007 crisis. But what if no particular market failure existed, and the market simply produced an unacceptable result? This kind of question could not even be asked before the Lehman crisis, but it will become commonplace in Capitalism 4.0.

Would regulatory and tax measures to curb financial investment have successfully reduced the demand for oil? Certainly. Would they have pulled oil prices back to the level of $70 to $90 believed by the oil industry to balance physical supply and demand? Perhaps, but no one could be sure in advance. In Capitalism 4.0, the fact that successful results could never be guaranteed would not discourage such intervention. If the future is recognized as inherently unpredictable, paralysis is not the rational response to uncertainty. The right response is for politicians and regulators, as well as investors and business leaders, to take reasonable decisions on the information they have before them—and then be willing to modify or reverse these decisions depending on how circumstances evolve.

This kind of bold and pragmatic policy experimentation, a hallmark of the new capitalist model, is what saved the world economy from a second Great Depression in the wake of the financial crisis. By early 2010, the new style of ultrastimulative monetary and fiscal policies had created the conditions for a much stronger recovery, especially in America, than almost anyone had imagined possible a year before, when the crisis was at its height. Maintaining this robust recovery will be the first great test for Capitalism 4.0—and it is well on the way to being passed, as the next chapter explains.

CHAPTER FOURTEEN

Irresistible Force Meets Immoveable Object

You cannot cure debt with debt.

—Apparently commonsense remark popularized by the crisis;
attributed also to Angela Merkel, the German chancellor

WHAT HAPPENS WHEN an irresistible force hits an immoveable object? Argumentative children love to needle their parents with this hypothetical question and are never satisfied with the right answer. The right answer is that there is no answer. Because there is no such thing in nature as an infinite force or an object with infinite inertia, the outcome depends on whether the force is more enormous than the object, or the other way round.

In the months after September 15, the seemingly immoveable object was the world economy, paralyzed by an unprecedented financial breakdown. By early 2009, however, it was hit by an irresistible force. More precisely, there were three irresistible forces, all marshaled by the power of governments coordinating their actions through a new global forum, the G20: zero interest rates and unlimited monetary expansion; the biggest upsurge of public borrowing in peacetime history; and open-ended government guarantees to all the world's major financial institutions.

The unprecedented deflationary power of the credit crunch and the unprecedented expansionary power of this three-pronged government stimulus program were both outside the realms of past experience. But which of them would prevail?

In the first few months of 2009, no one could be sure. Financial markets implied that there would be corporate bankruptcies in America on a scale comparable to the worst point of the Great Depression in 1932.[1] This suggested that most investors and economists were betting on the immovable object of deflation. We now know they were wrong. On October 29, 2009, the U.S. Commerce Department announced that the U.S. economy had resumed growth in the third quarter, after suffering a serious but far from apocalyptic peak-to-trough decline of 3.8 percent. By the fourth quarter, the economy was growing at its fastest rate since the boom of 2004. A catastrophe that a few months earlier had been likened to the Great Depression or the economic equivalent of 9/11 was over. The Great Recession had ended with a whimper instead of the widely expected bang.

Many people, of course, remained suspicious or even contemptuously dismissive of this rapid resolution. Surely, they argued, a crisis caused by too much debt could not have been resolved by governments borrowing even more. Surely no one could be so naïve as to believe that a seizure at the very heart of the global capitalist system could have been cured by such quick and painless measures as lending out unlimited amounts of money at zero interest rates. Surely banks that had supposedly lost trillions of dollars through reckless lending could not have been restored to solvency without even drawing on their taxpayer guarantees?

In part, this skepticism reflected moral indignation. The Great Recession was supposed to be a reckoning for past excesses. The malefactors who prospered in the good times were supposed to be punished. Yet typical punishments for bankers were a $100 million golden handshake to Charles Prince, who ruined Citigroup, and a personal tax exemption worth nearly $200 million received by Henry Paulson for his efforts at the U.S. Treasury.[2] The recession did mete out tremendous punishment—but against ordinary working people, who lost five million jobs, two million homes, and $2 trillion in foregone output in 2009 in the United States alone. Somehow, the recovery, as well as the recession, seemed unjust.

An even deeper reason for the public skepticism about the economic recovery related directly to the transition from Capitalism 3.3 to Capitalism

4.0. The theory of Capitalism 3 had insisted that a market economy was a self-regulating system that would quickly resolve its own excesses. For economists, politicians and voters still steeped in market fundamentalist thinking, a policy-induced recovery, powered mainly by government borrowing and artificially low interest rates, was something unnatural, unhealthy, and doomed to fail. Did this skepticism make sense? This is the issue we now need to consider.

The months following the crisis showed in the most convincing possible way that macroeconomics policy really does work and that it could overwhelm the most powerful deflationary forces. In any field other than economics, this experience would have been enough to refute once and for all the Rational Expectations Hypothesis, the Policy Ineffectiveness Proposition, the Ricardian Equivalence Principle, and all the other ideological assumptions masquerading as descriptions of reality that dominated precrisis economics. This was the position taken by Paul Krugman almost every week in his justly celebrated *New York Times* column, and intellectually it was clearly right.

Despite this evidence, however, many businesspeople, politicians, and ordinary voters, not just in America but also in Britain and Germany, remained deeply skeptical about the wisdom of government interventions that had pulled the world economy back from the brink. They continued to dispute its effectiveness until the evidence of recovery became undeniable. Then in 2010, as the world economy started clearly growing, they became increasingly aggressive in attacking the legitimacy of government economic intervention and exaggerating its long-term costs.

If the new model of capitalism is to prosper and win democratic support, therefore, these public doubts about the role of government in managing macroeconomic performance will have to be laid to rest. The potential costs of the stimulus policies are discussed in the next chapter, along with several other threats to the economic recovery in 2010–11. This chapter considers the issues of monetary and fiscal effectiveness and political legitimacy, which turn out to be closely intertwined.

For the public at large, the reasons for doubting the wisdom of monetary and fiscal stimulus are simple. To the extent that ordinary people think at all about macroeconomics, it is in personal or moral terms. Morality and the frustrated desire for retribution have been mentioned already, but the projection of personal experiences onto the national economy is even more important in explaining the skepticism about government stimulus plans. People naturally think of the national economy as if it were just an extended business or household—an attitude made famous by Margaret Thatcher in her frequent reflections about adding up the ledgers in her father's grocery shop.

From this point of view, the slogan that "you can't cure debt with more debt" seems to make perfect sense. As for the idea of ending a recession simply by expanding the money supply, this seems to be equivalent to writing a trillion-dollar check without the funds to back it, and it is easily presented by ideological opponents of stimulus as a Madoff-style fraud.

The appealing idea that macroeconomics can be understood by adding up the behavior of millions of individual households is the classic fallacy of composition that Keynes struggled against throughout the 1920s and 1930s. Such fallacies of composition are always hard to rebut convincingly, whether for Keynes in his analysis of macroeconomic cycles or for Ricardo in his explanations of the benefits of free trade. But politicians and economists can overcome entrenched public suspicion, if only by explaining that government debt and money supply *are* backed by something tangible—the entire wealth of the nation. The purpose of expanding both the money supply and the public debt is to allow this national wealth to keep growing—and if this exercise is successful, growth in national wealth should easily be sufficient to maintain the government's credit and to back the newly printed money.

Such an explanation, however, will only be accepted by the public under two conditions. First, there has to be clear evidence that the macroeconomic stimulus is working. Second, the government must be acknowledged as a genuine and legitimate representative of the entire nation that can call on the national wealth whenever it is absolutely necessary, whether to wage a war or to back its paper money and repay its debts.

This issue of government legitimacy seems not to be accepted by a small proportion of citizens in some major capitalist countries, most notably the United States. But the main reason for public skepticism about macroeconomic policy is more straightforward: So many experts in the markets, the media, the business community, and the universities continue to insist that the fiscal and monetary stimulus cannot work—even when it demonstrably has.

Why do these opinion-forming elites continue to deny the usefulness of macroeconomic policy, even after it has pulled the world out of recession much more quickly and with far less collateral damage than generally expected in 2009?

One factor is moral indignation and self-righteousness. Those hurt by the boom-bust cycle are outraged and want others to suffer more. Those who profited in the boom and managed to protect their wealth in the bust (which includes the vast majority of wealthy bankers and business leaders) feel guilty and do not want to gloat. Another group, illustrated by the Mad Max client quoted in Chapter 1, sat out the boom but profited mightily from the bust. They are so proud of having anticipated the economic disaster that they now feel entitled to watch an even greater disaster unfold.

Another reason for skepticism is simply a matter of timing. Even when monetary and fiscal policy are implemented with full vigor—as they were all over the world from April 2009 onward—there is a lag of a year or even two before the full economic effects are felt. The results of stimulus were thus bound initially to be declared disappointing by media opinion, which operates on a cycle of twenty-four hours, not twenty-four months.

To make matters worse, widespread misunderstanding existed, even among professional economists and investors, about the way that the stimulus might be affected by the danger of a Japanese-style deflation. The conventional view, influenced by the theory of self-fulfilling rational expectations, was that deeply entrenched fears of deflation would make monetary and fiscal stimulus impotent. In fact, the opposite was true. The more markets believed that falling prices were inevitable, the more likely the stimulus was to work. The logic is simple. In normal times, the amount of money that the central bank can print or the government can borrow is constrained by the risk of creating inflation. In the post-Lehman situation, however, the sense of collapse was overwhelming—financial markets in January 2009 implied that inflation in the United States would be *negative* for the next ten years. The Fed and other central banks could therefore print money without limit and the government could borrow all it wanted without worrying about the possibility that inflationary pressure would drive up interest rates.[3]

The last and most important reason for skepticism about economic stimulus was the resistance of a market fundamentalist society to any acknowledgment of political leadership in economics.

Government intervention, even if it did succeed in saving the economy, was seen in the precrisis model of capitalism as inconsistent with the principles of free enterprise and a first step on the road to communism. The view that all government economic intervention is politically illegitimate, which is especially prevalent in parts of the U.S. business community and Congress, is also widespread among financiers in Britain and Europe. This view is held quite unrepentantly by bankers who, just a year earlier, were themselves wards of the state.

Such hostility to government macroeconomic intervention is often taken as intrinsic to the political culture of free-enterprise capitalism, especially in the United States. But this is manifestly false. Hostility to government actions that clearly stabilize and strengthen the capitalist system does not arise from some natural conflict of interest between the government and private enterprise. It is merely the effect of thirty years of market fundamentalist thinking—or brainwashing, to use a stronger term.

The word *brainwashing* justifies a brief digression into the heyday of the previous version of capitalism in the 1950s. Communism was a clear and present danger. Russian spies, "reds under the bed," and brainwashed Manchurian candidates were widely thought to have infiltrated and subverted every American institution. Yet government intervention in the economy on a scale that would be unthinkable today was taken for granted and welcomed as a necessary condition for capitalism to thrive.

Americans in the 1950s were comfortable with the idea of their government micromanaging the economy down to the decimal place in the unemployment rate. This is how Arthur Burns, President Eisenhower's chief economic adviser, described the ultra-activist government economic policy he was pursuing in 1953: "In its new role of responsibility for the maintenance of the nation's prosperity, the federal government deliberately took speedy and massive actions to build confidence and pave the way for renewed economic growth. . . . Whenever the economy shows signs of faltering, the government must honor by its actions the broad principles of combating recession . . ."[4]

In today's conservative circles, such enthusiasm for government economic intervention would be viewed as tantamount to communism. Yet in 1953—the year when America's right-wing paranoia reached its zenith with Joe McCarthy's House Un-American Activities Committee witch-hunts against communists in Hollywood and in the U.S. Army—it did not occur to anyone to denounce the communist philosophy of the White House chief economist and indeed of President Eisenhower himself.[5]

Which brings us back to political legitimacy and leadership. The underlying reason for widespread skepticism about macroeconomic stimulus, at least in the United States and Britain, was the claim that "government cannot create prosperity." This comment is heard again and again in the markets, the media, and the academic community and among policymakers themselves—and in a sense it is true.

Printing money, issuing bonds, even writing government checks for roads or airports or electricity grids does not in itself create new wealth. But new wealth *is* created when those government checks and banknotes and bond issues finance new jobs and extra economic output. As long as millions of workers are unemployed and plenty of spare capacity exists in the economy, that is precisely how stimulus works. Printing money and issuing government bonds and checks *does* bring idle factories and workers into employment and thus creates new wealth. This is how Keynes predicted that macroeconomic policy would work. It is how macroeconomic policy has usually worked in the past, despite the claims to the contrary. And it is how macroeconomics did work after the Lehman crisis.

But what will happen when central banks start raising interest rates and governments are forced to withdraw the fiscal stimulus? Isn't the postcrisis economy just surviving on temporary life support? The next chapter discusses these questions in more detail. Suffice it to say for the moment that as the economy gets stronger, it will develop an inner momentum, as capitalism always does. Once private sector spending is strong enough to move the economy nearer to full employment, government stimulus can and should be withdrawn, but there is no reason why governments and central banks, whether in the United States or Europe or China, should withdraw their support until global capitalism is again fully fit. Inflation, as explained in the next chapter, is unlikely to be a serious risk until economic activity recovers to normal levels. And the threat of government insolvency is much exaggerated, at least in the short term, imposing no real constraints on most countries at least until 2012 and beyond.

The danger of economic stimulus being withdrawn prematurely stems from politics: the deeply entrenched belief that a country relying on its government to support and stabilize economic growth is morally rotten. This is an ideological dogma, instilled into public consciousness by decades of repetition since the early 1980s. It will take many years of new thinking under Capitalism 4.0 to fully dispel this illusion. But given capitalism's instinct of self-preservation, this ideological conversion will occur in the end, provided the economic recovery that began in late 2009 does not fizzle out prematurely. This risk of aborted recovery is the next issue to address.

CHAPTER FIFTEEN

What—Me Worry?

Bull markets climb a wall of worry.
Bear markets slide down a slope of hope.

—A venerable investment adage

THE MAIN RISKS to the world economy and the global system in the immediate aftermath of the 2007-09 crisis could be classified into three groups. The first group consists of the short-term economic threats that could still abort the global recovery and cause a double-dip recession but were largely dispelled by the end of 2010. The second set of risks are medium-term issues that are likely to dominate public policy in the three to five years after the crisis: excessive government deficits; paralyzed banking systems; a need to rebalance global growth, especially between America and China, and between Germany and southern Europe, and a possible return to the stagflation of the 1970s, with inflation and unemployment rising at the same time. Although these are all serious worries, they will probably prove more manageable than expected in the new politico-economic environment of Capitalism 4.0, as the next chapter explains. Finally, several long-term challenges, such as climate change, the cost of welfare programs for aging populations, and breakdowns in global governance and coordination, are likely to become even more daunting in the coming decades.

This chapter looks at the first set of widely feared financial problems that could still abort the global economic recovery in 2011: rising interest rates, monetary inflation, and currency crises.

These financial dangers were all exaggerated in the aftermath of the crisis, and they are unlikely to damage global growth in the early years of the new decade. Thus, the resilience of the postcrisis economy financial markets will probably continue to offer favorable surprises. The world economy and financial markets are likely to remain strong largely because interest rates all over the world will remain lower for much longer than expected.

But isn't the reduction of interest rates to near zero worldwide an unhealthy and unsustainable aberration? Won't this long period of ultrastimulative monetary policy create dangerous inflationary pressures? And is it not inevitable that the resort to printing money by governments, especially in the United States and Britain, will destabilize the dollar, the pound, or the global currency system? The answer to all these questions is almost certainly no. But the reasons for downplaying worries about monetary policy, inflation, and currency instability will become apparent only as the market fundamentalist doctrines of the precrisis period are replaced by a new understanding of macroeconomic policy in Capitalism 4.0.

Will Rising Interest Rates Choke Off Economic Recovery?

A sharp rise in interest rates from their near-zero levels after the crisis is probably the most widely feared threat to economic recovery. Big interest rate hikes, imposed before the economy had fully recovered, were responsible for all previous double-dip recessions ever recorded in the United States and Britain: 1980–82 and 1932–34 in the United States and 1974–76 and 1927–30 in Britain.[1] The double-dip recessions of the 1970s and 1980s were triggered by interest rates that rose as high as 20 percent in the United States and 18 percent in Britain. Such huge rate hikes are out of the question in the years ahead, but given the weakness of today's financial system and the generalized fears of deflation, couldn't even small rate increases be sufficient to derail economic recovery? Skeptics argue that debt levels are now so high that an increase of just one or two percent in interest rates would cause financial mayhem. But for that very reason, governments and central banks will do their utmost to delay any significant monetary tightening as long as possible—and in the post-crisis conditions that could mean many years.

To understand why interest rates are likely to remain much lower in the postcrisis period than is generally expected, it is necessary first to grasp something that goes against the grain of market fundamentalist thinking: The actions of central banks and governments are more important than the views of private investors when it comes to setting the single most important price in the entire capitalist economy—the interest rate on overnight or three-month loans.[2] In a world of pure paper money, these short-term interest rates can be set by central banks at whatever level they choose. And while the central banks may not want to keep short rates near zero forever, significant increases are very unlikely as long as unemployment remains near its post-Lehman highs. It seems probable, in fact, that short-term interest above 2 percent will not be seen in the United States, Britain, the eurozone, or Japan until at least halfway through the new decade, perhaps around 2015.

The idea of interest rates in a sub-2 percent range for the best part of a decade may seem almost inconceivable to Western homeowners and investors accustomed to 5 percent or 10 percent or even 15 percent rates. But it is worth recalling that Japanese rates have been continuously below 1 percent for fifteen years since 1995. The United States and Britain experienced even longer periods of very low rates in the 1940s and 1950s. Throughout the twenty-five years from 1930 until 1955, U.S. and British Treasury bills never paid more than 2 percent, and for much of that time they yielded less than 1 percent. These low interest rates were not symptomatic of recession or deflation. In fact, the period of extremely low interest rates from 1930 to 1955 saw some of the fastest growth ever recorded around the world. This historical experience coincided with a world war, as well as with tight financial regulation and rationing of credit and does not prove that near-zero interest rates are desirable. It does prove, however, that many years or even decades of extremely low rates can be compatible with strong noninflationary growth.

So it is *possible* for central banks to keep interest rates extremely low for many years or even decades. The more important question is: Why would they want to do this? The first reason is simply the depth of the post-Lehman recession. Even if the world economy continues to accelerate from 2011 onwards, a huge amount of spare capacity—unemployed workers, unused industrial machinery, and unoccupied offices and houses—will exist for several years. The difference between the actual level of activity and the economy's potential is known as an output gap—and all official or private estimates in late 2010 showed that this gap was still exceptionally wide, far wider than in the aftermath of previous recessions.[3]

Given this straightforward statistical fact, central bankers are unlikely to want to tighten monetary policy, even in the event of a rapid economic recovery. Instead of reacting to rapid rates of growth in the economy, they will be focusing on the *levels* of output, which would remain unusually low even after several years of recovery. This distinction between the importance of levels and growth rates was made particularly clear by Mervyn King, governor of the Bank of England, in the months immediately after the crisis, when he was asked whether he would raise interest rates to cool the economy as soon as it returned to decent economic growth. His response was a paraphrase of Bill Clinton's famous remark about what was motivating American voters in the 1992 election, "it's the economy, stupid." King declared: "It's not the growth of GDP that matters; it's the levels, stupid."[4] A similar attitude was confirmed by the Fed's communiqué of November 2009, when for the first time it spelled out the three conditions that might force it to raise interest rates: a significant fall in unemployment and narrowing of excess capacity; or an increase in inflation; or a clear deterioration in expectations about inflation.[5]

Thus, the first and most important reason to believe that interest rates will remain extremely low for a long period is that central banks worldwide are now effectively committed to a policy of supporting economic activity and boosting employment.

This embrace of demand management by central bankers everywhere is a telling indicator of the world's transition to Capitalism 4.0. Such a proactive approach to monetary policy was anathema to the economic theories of Capitalism 3, whose key injunction was that macroeconomic policy must focus exclusively on inflation control. Luckily for the self-esteem of central bankers, the blatant contradiction between their policy practice and their

economic theories, still officially based on the precrisis monetarist orthodoxy, was airbrushed out of existence by the Lehman crisis. After the collapse of economic activity and employment that resulted from the financial
seizure, inflation essentially vanished—and this allowed central banks to
pretend that they were still targeting inflation, when in fact they were
pulling out all the stops to limit unemployment and stimulate growth.

Looking ahead, the collapse of economic activity and employment after
September 15 has convinced central bankers that there is little danger of inflation until economies worldwide have enjoyed a considerable period of
strong growth. Without such a lengthy period of rapid growth, there can be
no chance of significantly narrowing output gaps—and as long as these huge
output gaps exist, inflation is not possible. That, at least, is the post-Lehman
view of most central bankers, and they are unlikely to change their minds in
the foreseeable future, despite rising commodity prices and the criticism
they face from economists still wedded to the theories of the 1980s.

A further reason why interest rates will remain very low after the 2007–
09 crisis arises, ironically, from the blowout in public borrowing around the
world. With public borrowing now running at unsustainable levels, central
bankers and finance ministers agree that reducing government deficits must
be the top economic priority when the recession is clearly over. As soon as
the economy is strong enough to withstand some tougher policy pressures,
it is clear that belt-tightening should be administered through smaller
budget deficits rather than higher interest rates.

But if taxes are raised and government spending is squeezed, this will
automatically put a brake on economic growth. As serious budget cuts are
made from 2011 onward, therefore, central banks, far from raising interest
rates, will need to offset any recessionary effects by *cutting* interest rates or
at least keeping them very low. Tightening monetary policy while also
tightening the tax-and-spending tourniquet could tip the economy back
into recession.[6] No central bank will want to take this risk.

The final argument for a long period of extremely low interest rates, especially in America, Britain, and other countries where households are
starting to save more, relates to the interaction of higher savings with economic growth. If households decide to increase their savings by cutting
back on their consumption, should this mean that growth in the national

economy slows down? This was the conventional wisdom after the crisis, yet in every previous period of economic history, it was assumed that an increase in saving should *accelerate* long-term growth. In fact, policies designed to increase national savings have been the main tools for countries such as Japan, China, and Germany to ramp up their growth rates and catch up with the United States. Savings, after all, flow into investments, and the amount of new machinery and technology an economy has to offer its workers is one of the main determinants of its productivity and its long-term rate of growth.

Why then the near-universal belief that economic growth in highly indebted countries such as the United States, Spain, and Britain will slow dramatically when their citizens decide to save more? This belief arises out of a confusion between supply and demand that was characteristic of Capitalism 3. Precrisis economics simply *assumed* that total macroeconomic demand would always be equal to total supply, without inquiring too closely about the path the economy would follow to reach this equilibrium. But consider how this process works in a little more detail. If people increase their savings (whether by putting money into bank accounts, increasing pension payments, or buying shares), they naturally cut their demand for consumer goods. Those extra savings, however, should not sit idly in the bank. Provided macroeconomic policy successfully maintains full employment, extra savings are lent to businesses for investment and expansion, so the act of saving increases the supply of goods in the economy, not just on a one-off basis but for as long as the new machines and businesses last. If the greater desire to save among households is matched by a greater willingness to invest among businesspeople, the cutback in demand for consumer goods is offset by an increase in spending on machinery, computers, factories, and so on. And as these new factories start to produce additional goods and employ more workers, the economy gets richer and people find that they can afford to save more *and* consume more at the same time.

This indeed is the magic of capitalism. But why exactly does it work? After all, an initial divergence exists between lower total demand, as households save more, and higher total supply, as investment picks up. How is this discrepancy reconciled? The answer is through an expansionary monetary policy designed to prevent depression and unemployment.

An economy in which people have permanently decided to save more needs permanently lower interest rates to ensure that all those savings are channeled into investments rather than lying idly in banks. This is especially true if the economy is suffering from excess capacity and unemployment. In such an environment, businesses will increase their investment only if financing is abundant and extremely cheap. Mention of cheap and abundant financing may sound like a sick joke in the wake of history's greatest credit crunch, but the fact that banks are reluctant to lend and demand higher profit margins only emphasizes the need for the Fed, the Bank of England, and other central banks to keep even lower the official interest rates that they set as a floor for commercial bank rates.

The combination of a weakened credit system with a rising propensity to save thus means that interest rates will have to stay even lower than they otherwise would, not just for the sake of a temporary postrecession stimulus but as a permanent fact of life in the new economy.

Very low interest rates are the best way to keep demand and supply in balance in an economy where savings are structurally high. Low interest rates, far more than Keynesian policies of deficit spending, were the key to the full employment achieved in the 1940s and 1950s, when Americans and Britons were saving roughly twice as much in relation to their incomes as they do today—and channeling these savings into the enormous investments of postwar reconstruction and the subsequent global boom. The same combination of high levels of savings and investment and structurally very low interest rates can be observed in China today. Making sure that higher U.S. and British savings again flow into strong investments will be a key task for monetary policy in the decade ahead. And the only reliable way for policymakers to do this will be to keep interest rates extremely low.

Will Printing Money Unleash Inflation?

Using low interest rates first to promote economic recovery and then to sustain a permanent boom in investment sounds attractive, but what about inflation? If central banks keep pumping out more money and offering it at zero rates, surely the result will be inflation—perhaps even the hyperinflation confidently predicted by some of the media's favorite financial experts.

In May 2009, for example, the widely followed Swiss investment pundit Marc Faber appeared on Bloomberg TV, declaring: "I am 100 percent sure that the U.S. will go into hyperinflation." What did he mean by hyperinflation? Something "close," he explained, to the rate in Zimbabwe, which was at that time 231 million percent![7]

Without going to such extremes, many respectable economists and politicians have warned that the vast sums of new money being printed, or more precisely created on computer discs, by the Bank of England and the Federal Reserve Board are bound to fuel an upsurge of inflation. Won't inflation accelerate unless central banks raise interest rates and withdraw excess money quickly from the financial system? The precrisis economic orthodoxy would say yes; but in the new economic thinking of Capitalism 4, the answer is no.

Inflation is often explained in everyday language as "too much money chasing too few goods." In economics, this simple idea is translated into Milton Friedman's famous maxim that "inflation is always and everywhere a monetary phenomenon."[8] Both statements are almost certainly right. But if considered logically, they should dispel alarm about inflation, rather than provoke it, at least until 2013 or so.

The first adage rightly emphasizes that inflation is caused by imbalances between money and physical goods. If there are too many goods—and too many workers and factories and houses—as happens at the end of a recession, inflation is unlikely to accelerate, however much money might be around. This is a simple restatement of the central bankers' sophisticated argument about the output gap. When the output gap is very wide, as it will be for at least four or five years after the crisis, the threat of inflation is slight, regardless of what monetary policy is doing.

How, then, does this square with Friedman's maxim, which seems to predict that inflation will "always and everywhere" follow rapid monetary growth? The answer is that it accords perfectly well with the true content of Friedman's research but not with the subsequent political spin, which Friedman himself encouraged as much as anyone else.

The claim that printing money always creates inflation is wrong as a matter of simple logic. What Friedman actually found in his research was that a burst of rapid monetary growth always precedes high inflation. This in no way implies the converse: that a period of high inflation always follows a burst of monetary growth. To confuse a proposition with its converse is the most elementary of logical errors: For example, all crows are black birds, therefore any black bird is a crow. This fallacy, despite its obvious absurdity, appears ubiquitously in politics as a rhetorical trick. For example: "Shooting deaths are always and everywhere the responsibility of someone with a gun. Therefore, anyone with a gun is always and everywhere responsible for a shooting death."

The claim that "printing money always and everywhere creates inflation" is a non sequitur in the same way. Yet this nonsense is repeated daily in the media and financial markets and supposedly bolstered by the prestige of Friedman's Nobel Prize. If that were really what Friedman argued, the entire corpus of monetarist economics could have been refuted by a single counterexample—for example, the fact that U.S. monetary growth was higher between 2000 and 2009 than in the previous decade while inflation was consistently lower.[9]

What Friedman actually said, however, was very different: "Inflation is always and everywhere a monetary phenomenon, in the sense that *it cannot occur without a more rapid increase in the quantity of money than in output.*"[10] In other words, a rapid increase in the quantity of money is a *necessary* condition for high inflation. This does not imply that a rapid increase in the quantity of money is a *sufficient* condition for high inflation—and the many studies of economic history inspired by Friedman's pioneering research generally confirm that the causation runs only one way.[11] An accurate, but less pithy, restatement of Friedman's maxim would be this: "When high inflation happens, it is *always* preceded by rapid monetary growth; when rapid monetary growth happens, it is *sometimes* followed by high inflation."

But isn't this mere pedantry? Even if monetary expansion does not *always* lead to high inflation, it does sometimes. So shouldn't this be a worry at present, with central banks printing money like wallpaper?

This question leads to the second fallacy in the precrisis dogmatic interpretation of Friedman's maxim. Although monetary growth is in some sense a necessary condition for rapid inflation, the precise correlation between money and inflation has never been even roughly quantified because *money* can be defined in so many ways in a modern capitalist economy and the influence on inflation of any of these ways of measuring the money supply can be observed only with "long and variable lags."[12]

Modern monetary economics initially tried to dodge this problem by looking for one correct definition of the money supply that would always correlate closely with inflation. But all attempts to find this Holy Grail broke down as inflation seemed first to correlate with one way of measuring money and then another. Eventually, Friedman's reference to an "increase in the quantity of money" had to be reinterpreted as a statement about "monetary conditions" in a vague and generalized sense.

The conventional view among economists today is that the cause of inflation is not necessarily an increase in any particular form of money but an expansion of monetary conditions in some broader sense.[13] The beauty of this assertion, from an ideological standpoint, is that it can never be scientifically tested—or indeed pinned down at all. To the precrisis economic orthodoxy, the phrase "monetary conditions" could refer to almost anything, for example, the rate of interest, the strength or weakness of the currency, the level of the stock market, the lending enthusiasm of private banks, or even the rate of inflation itself.

But if monetary conditions are entirely in the eye of the beholder, this creates a dilemma. For modern economists, the statement that "inflation is always and everywhere a monetary phenomenon" is equivalent to the First of the Ten Commandments.[14] But how can we be sure that our actions are consistent with this holy scripture if we don't know the meaning of *monetary phenomenon?* The answer is an intellectual trick characteristic of modern economics. Economists simply *assume* that the best gauge of proper monetary conditions is, by definition, whatever combination of interest rates, money supply targets, and exchange rates will produce stable inflation. They then declare triumphantly that this sophisticated new measure of monetary conditions is closely related to itself!

If that sounds like a parody from the Academy in Laputa in *Gulliver's Travels,*[15] consider the following tribute to Friedman's theories about inflation and monetary growth. It was delivered, appropriately enough, to celebrate the fiftieth anniversary of *Free to Choose*, Friedman's political credo, which could be described as the intellectual bible of Capitalism 3.3. The speaker was one of the world's top academic economists, one Ben Bernanke: "For reasons of financial innovation and institutional change, the rate of money growth does not seem to be an adequate measure of the stance of monetary policy, and hence a stable monetary background for the economy cannot necessarily be identified with stable money growth. Nor are there other instruments of monetary policy whose behavior can be used unambiguously to judge this issue . . . Ultimately, it appears, one can check to see if an economy has a stable monetary background only by looking at macroeconomic indicators such as nominal GDP growth and inflation. On this criterion, it appears that modern central bankers have taken Milton Friedman's advice to heart."[16]

An alternative version of the same self-justifying methodology in pre-crisis economics was to redefine inflation: Inflation, many economists began to assert, was whatever happens when an economy experiences rapid monetary growth. Thus, if a burst of monetary growth produces no signs of consumer or wage inflation, we can look at stock market or house prices instead. And if excess monetary growth fails to produce any evidence of property and stock market inflation, let us find something else that happens to be going up in price—for example, government bonds. By using this methodology, some economists even argue that Japan has been suffering from inflation, not deflation, for the past twenty years.

But in the wake of the Lehman crisis, even such far-fetched attempts to link expansionary monetary policies with asset inflation of some kind were unsuccessful. Despite the unprecedented printing of money after the crisis, stock market prices in late 2010 were still well below their 2007 highs and scarcely higher than in 1997. U.S. housing valuations were at their lowest-ever level, even in relation to wages artificially compressed by the recession. What else was left? Gold was rising, but was still 30 percent below its 1982 level in real terms. Was there a bubble in China? Maybe, although share prices were still far below their 2007 peak and had increased at a compound rate of only 7 percent since the early 1990s, when the Chinese economic miracle started. The only plausible asset bubbles identifiable in 2010 were in commodities and property in Hong Kon and Singapore. The increasing number of monetarist economists who warned that U.S. and European interest rates would have be raised to prevent asset bubbles were therefore proposing that the Fed, the ECB, and the Bank of England should sacrifice millions of jobs and trillions of dollars of lost output in their own economies to stabilize property prices in Hong Kong. Luckily, central banks made it clear that they would not oblige—if anything, they welcomed rising asset prices because these would strengthen bank balances, reduce property foreclosures, boost consumer and business confidence, and thus help to accelerate economic growth. In short, none of the central banks are likely to equate *any* definition of monetary growth mechanically with *any* definition of inflation.

Despite all these logical and theoretical objections, people remain uncomfortable with the idea of central banks printing money at enormous rates—since the crisis, roughly $1.7 trillion in the United States and more than £300 billion in Britain (which is proportionately more than the amount in the United States in relation to the size of the economy). So for the sake of argument, let us imagine that monetary growth really *is* linked directly to inflation, as many politicians, media commentators, and financiers continue to believe. We are still left with the question of what is meant by *printing money* and whether the new amounts printed are dangerously large.

As mentioned, *money* can be defined in myriad ways. To the extent that inflation is linked with any of these definitions, it must be with broad definitions of money that include not just physical cash but also bank deposits, money market funds, and other assets that consumers and businesses can draw immediately and without significant cost. The monetary base, which consists of physical cash and electronic deposits held at the central bank by private banks, roughly doubled in the United States (from $900 billion to $2 trillion) in the year after Lehman. In Britain over the same period, the monetary base experienced a fivefold explosion (from $50 billion to $250 billion), and in the eurozone, it increased by 33 percent but from a much higher base (from $1.3 trillion to $1.8 trillion). What Friedman would have been the first to note, however, is that this central bank money is only a small proportion of the total money supply—roughly 15 percent in most countries. The remaining 85 percent of the money supply consists of deposits held by individuals and businesses in commercial banks. These private deposits are created by commercial banks when they offer loans and mortgages to their customers—and this credit creation has, of course, drastically shrunk.

The upshot is that while the U.S. monetary base exploded by 105 percent in the twelve months following Lehman, as the Fed struggled to prevent a collapse of the economy, the broad money supply (known as M2) grew by only 6 percent, exactly the average growth rate of the previous twenty years. When economic growth recovers and financial conditions return to normal, bank lending will presumably revive, the broad money figures will begin to grow faster, and deflationary pressures will abate. At that point, the central banks may well want to withdraw some of the money they have "printed" from circulation.

Any such reduction in the central bank money, however, is likely to be modest in comparison with the huge expansion of the post-Lehman period because the cash required for the economy to function properly has been permanently increased by the crisis. To take the simplest example, people who cut back on using credit cards need more cash for their daily lives. At a more sophisticated level, banks faced with sudden withdrawals during the crisis realized that they needed far more cash and Fed deposits than they actually had. If regulators force banks to hold more cash and liquid assets in the future, as they certainly ought to, the monetary base supplied by the central banks will have to be permanently increased.

It is far from clear, therefore, how much of the extra money printed by the central banks since the Lehman crisis will ever need to be withdrawn from circulation—and there is no reason to expect all this newly created money to have an inflationary effect until and unless bank lending returns to the boom conditions that prevailed before 2007.

In sum, it is simply not true that either a shortage of goods or an excess of money is threatening to stoke inflation in the United States, or Britain, or indeed any other major economy. However, one other mechanism could, in theory, still trigger severe inflation—even in an economy that is suffering from mass unemployment and showing no obvious signs of monetary excess. That mechanism is a collapse in the currency—the last of the exaggerated postcrisis fears.

Will the Dollar Collapse?

The idea that the dollar (or the pound) will go the way of the Zimbabwean dollar is the argument most cited by people who claim to believe in an inflationary disaster for the United States and Britain. ("Claim" to believe because many proponents of the Zimbabwe thesis still seem to keep a high proportion of their assets in the United States.) If the dollar did collapse, the implications would be appalling. History shows that collapsing currencies are linked to rapid inflation much more closely than is monetary growth. If inflation started accelerating strongly, the Fed would have no choice but to raise short-term rates, the bond market would justifiably panic, the cost of government borrowing and mortgages would rise to prohibitive levels, and the economy would plunge into a second severe recession. This would be a repeat of the terrible double-dip recession of 1981–82 but on a more alarming scale.

But before getting carried away with this apocalyptic vision, note that this chain of disasters depends on one pivotal point: The dollar (or the pound) must not merely weaken a bit but must suffer an outright collapse or free fall. If the dollar merely depreciated in an orderly way by a few percent, there would be no reason to expect higher inflation, no reason for the Fed to raise interest rates, no reason for bond investors to panic, and no reason for economic growth to slow. A weaker dollar would actually strengthen the recovery by making exports more profitable and by encouraging American consumers to switch their spending from foreign goods to domestically made goods.

The critical question, therefore, is whether a dollar depreciation, if it happened (a big *if*), would trigger serious inflation. Experience shows that a genuine collapse of any currency—which might be defined as a 50 percent or more drop in a single year—invariably triggers inflation. Whether this inflation turns out to be catastrophic or controllable depends on what else is happening in the world and in the country itself. Moderate declines in the 10, 20, or even 30 percent range generally have little inflationary effect, especially in large economies with plenty of excess capacity and unemployment at the time the currency falls.

Recent examples of such noninflationary currency declines have occurred in Britain, where the pound fell by 20 percent on a trade-weighted basis in 1992 and by 25 percent in 2008, in Italy where the lira fell by 25 percent in 1992, in Japan where the yen fell by 22 percent in 1995, and in the United States, where the dollar dropped by 35 percent in 1985 and by 30 percent in 2002–03. In all these cases, inflation was slower a year after the devaluation than before and in no case did the central bank respond to the falling currency by raising interest rates.

Many people believe that the present currency predicament is far more dangerous than any in the past, because the pressure on the dollar reflects not only the financial crisis but also the weakening of America's geopolitical status. Geopolitics is certainly changing, although whether America's role will be weaker or stronger in the future is far from clear. However, we can say one thing for certain about the geopolitical argument for or against the dollar.

The strength of a currency in the modern world has nothing to do with the issuing nation's geopolitical power. The dollar's steepest-ever fall occurred under President Reagan in 1985–86, just as America was winning the Cold War. The dollar's longest decline in history began on the day President Bush delivered his Axis of Evil speech in January 2002 and lasted until March 2008. The yen has been the strongest currency in the world during the entire postwar period, despite Japan's marginal role in world affairs, while the yuan has been the weakest currency in Asia in the past ten years, just as China has emerged as a true superpower.

It could even be argued that in the postcrisis world, as evidenced by China, the ability to maintain a weak currency in the face of demands for revaluation from trading partners is evidence of geopolitical strength. In any case, the conscious preference for *weak* currencies in China, Korea, France, Italy, Spain, and many other countries offers the clearest possible counterargument to the panic-mongering on Wall Street and in the U.S. media about a dollar free fall.

China and other countries prefer weak currencies for a good reason. A weak yuan helps Chinese industries by making Chinese exports cheaper in foreign markets and by raising the prices of imports, thereby encouraging consumers to buy domestically produced goods. A weak currency also has disadvantages. For example, a weak currency makes consumers and voters feel poorer in relation to their neighbors in other countries. But for most governments (and voters), especially in periods of high unemployment, a weak currency is much more attractive than one that is too strong.

Looking around the world at the currency preferences of other countries raises an obvious question about predictions of a collapsing dollar. What currency would take off if and when the dollar went into free fall?

A currency can go down only if some other currency goes up against it. And when you start searching for another major currency anywhere in the world that might appreciate by 30 percent or 50 percent against the dollar in the next few years, the concept of a dollar collapse becomes absurd. It is inconceivable that any other major country would accept a revaluation of anything close to that amount—not Europe, not Britain, not Switzerland, and certainly not China nor Japan.

Putting the same point another way, currencies differ from all other financial assets in one crucial respect. Investors who do not like the prospects for a stock or bond can simply sell it, without thinking about what to do with the money they receive in exchange. But anxieties about a currency cannot be expressed in the same way. However nervous investors may feel about the dollar, they can sell it only by buying some other currency in which they have greater confidence. And when the prophets of doom who see the United States heading down the road to Zimbabwe are asked what other currency investors should buy in exchange for the trillions of dollars they hold, the answer is silence.

Why is there no serious alternative to the dollar as an international reserve currency? The absence of serious currency competition has little, if anything, to do with America's military hegemony, its globally dominant culture, or even the depth and sophistication of its financial markets (an argument that now looks frayed). The main reason is simply that the world has only two other very large advanced economies—the eurozone and Japan—and America, for all its problems, has generally better prospects than either.

Looking beyond the eurozone and Japan, other economies with independent currencies, such as Britain, Switzerland, Canada, or Australia, are far too small to absorb the money now invested in dollars. Whenever a significant proportion of money usually kept in America moves into a small country such as Australia or Norway, the local currency quickly becomes overvalued, causing serious damage to the domestic economy. More importantly from a financial standpoint, when a currency such as the Swiss franc or the Australian dollar becomes extremely overvalued, this sets up a high hurdle to additional investors, who start to worry that the overvaluation will be reversed at some point by a precipitous fall. Thus flows of capital out of the dollar into small currencies such as the Swiss franc or even the pound are quickly self-correcting. The same applies to gold, which is often seen as an alternative to all "currencies."

The only real alternatives to the dollar, therefore, are either the yen and the euro or the currencies of large and rapidly growing emerging countries, especially China. To say that the dollar will fall substantially over time against the Chinese yuan is a statement of the obvious, because China is still one of the world's poorest countries and is now embarked on an unstoppable journey toward much higher living standards that may one day be comparable with those of the West. Part of this catching-up process is usually a currency appreciation similar to the one experienced in postwar Japan.[17]

But the fact that the yuan is almost certain to appreciate against the dollar and every other major currency at some point is of little interest to anyone looking for an alternative now. The Chinese government is determined to control the process of revaluation, just as Japan and Germany did in the 1950s and 1960s, because it wants to maintain the advantages of a cheap currency, especially in economically uncertain times. Since the start of the crisis, therefore, the yuan was pegged to the dollar and has therefore offered no alternative to it. Moreover, the use of the yuan is strictly regulated outside China, precisely because the Chinese government wants to deny foreign investors a windfall profit as the inevitable revaluation proceeds. Thus, even investors willing to wait patiently for years as the yuan strengthens against the dollar will not have much opportunity to take advantage of this currency move.

The fact that the dollar may one day be substantially cheaper against the Chinese yuan, therefore, is of little relevance to financial conditions in the next few years. If the postcrisis transition goes smoothly, the yuan will revalue not only against the dollar but also against the euro, the pound, and the yen. Far from being a threat to the U.S. economy, this change will be a cause for celebration because it will greatly expand the Chinese market for goods and services made in the United States.

Given that the yuan is not a practical alternative to the dollar, the global currency markets offer only two options—the euro and the yen. The nightmarish vision of a global flight out of the dollar therefore comes down to the question of whether the euro and the yen are likely to rise steeply—say by 30 percent or more—in the years ahead. This is very unlikely.

The European and Japanese economies, whose exporters are already struggling with what they see as overvalued exchange rates, would be devastated by a further sharp rise in their currencies. The governments and central banks in Europe and Japan would face intense pressure to resist such a revaluation and, if necessary, to print euros and yen, respectively, even faster than the Fed is printing dollars. Already the cost of employing an average production worker is 20 percent higher in the eurozone, 10 percent higher in Japan, and 40 percent higher in Germany than in the United States. If the dollar were to depreciate substantially further, the competitive pressure on Japanese and German industries would become intolerable and it is unlikely that the euro or yen would be allowed to keep rising long enough to create the dreaded free fall of the dollar.

Moreover, since the crisis, global trade has already shifted in favor of U.S. exporters and the U.S. trade deficit has narrowed at Europe's and Japan's expense. If the euro and yen were to rise against the dollar, this process would greatly accelerate and the narrowing of the U.S. trade deficit would reduce the supply of dollars on world markets. That, in turn, would automatically slow down the process of dollar depreciation. To a large extent, such a shift has already begun, although it has remained surprisingly unacknowledged, especially in the United States. From 2006 to 2009, the current account deficit of the United States has narrowed from 6.5 percent of GDP to just over 2 percent. Meanwhile, the once-enormous Japanese surplus has almost vanished, and the eurozone has moved from surplus into deficit. Already the shift in global trade has invalidated the standard vision of America as a debtor nation, borrowing from foreigners at the rate of $700 billion a year to sustain its consumption. In 2009 and 2010, the current account deficit was about $300 billion. Thus U.S. borrowing from foreigners was down to 3 percent of the GDP. If the dollar fell much further against the euro and yen, America's trade deficit would probably turn into a large surplus. Such a surplus would mean that the United States would have started repaying its foreign debts and the eurozone would replace America as the world's biggest borrower. Under these circumstances, it is more likely that the dollar would rise against the euro, as indeed it has since the bankruptcy of Lehman, rather than going into free fall.

The final reason why a collapse of the dollar against the euro or the yen is out of the question is that all fundamental long-term problems that worry investors about the U.S. economy apply to Europe and Japan in even starker form. The money supply is larger in relation to the size of the economy in both the eurozone and Japan than it is in the United States. European banks are in worse financial condition than their U.S. counterparts, and corporate debts are higher in Europe than in the United States. Even the supposedly ultraprudent European Central Bank has been lending money on more generous terms to the European banking system than the Fed has in the United States. In September 2009, for example, the ECB lent €50 billion (roughly $75 billion) to the Irish government to fund a bailout of the Irish banks. In relation to the size of the Irish economy, this was equivalent to the Fed printing $3 trillion and giving them to the Treasury to subsidize U.S. banks. And for anyone worried about the U.S. government's profligate borrowing and spending, the levels of government debt in Japan and most eurozone countries, including Germany and France, are higher than they are in the United States.

To dwell on the economic problems in Europe and Japan may seem like a pointless exercise in schadenfreude, but in one important respect the troubles of other countries benefit the United States and Britain. Currency trading is a zero-sum game, in which the fall of one currency must automatically mean the rise of another, so the fact that the only real alternatives to the dollar are structurally weaker than the dollar is a boon to both the United States and the world.

If Europe and Japan had been structurally stronger or less affected by the 2007–09 crisis, worries about a precipitous fall in the dollar and the pound might have deterred U.S. and British policymakers from cutting interest rates as aggressively as they did. In this sense, the global nature of the

2007–09 crisis was an unexpected blessing. Everyone was in the same boat, so policymakers in every country had the freedom to cut interest rates, print money, and increase public spending and borrowing. All major economies suffered together, precluding disruptive flights of capital from weak countries to the strong.

The choice between currencies is often presented by media and financial commentators as a beauty contest, but in truth it is better described as an "ugly contest." Although investors may find all major currency unattractive, they have to keep their money somewhere, so they choose the currency that repels them least. The dollar certainly looked ugly after the Lehman fiasco. But because the yen and the euro were both at least as ugly as the dollar, the Fed and the Obama administration were able to implement unprecedented programs of monetary and fiscal expansion without worrying about a flight of capital out of the United States. By doing this, they guaranteed an economic recovery and could afford to continue doing whatever it took to sustain growth in 2010 and beyond.

The bigger challenges to the U.S. and world economies will appear from 2011 onward, as the longer-term problems of government and consumer debt, global rebalancing, and structural inflation begin to be seriously confronted. These are among the issues taken up in the last part of this book.

Part V

Capitalism 4.0
and the Future

EVEN IF THE TRANSITION to Capitalism 4.0 occurs in a more orderly and peaceful manner than the previous great transitions of the 1930s and 1970s, many genuine risks will continue to face the democratic capitalist system. The first chapter of this final part will consider the four main dangers likely to beset the world economy in the middle of the new decade, as the new species of capitalism finds it feet: government debt, financial paralysis, trade imbalances, and the threat of stagflation.

The last three chapters of this book deal with politics, finance, and international relations, which will prove even more daunting challenges to the success and survival of the new capitalist system in the years and decades beyond. To meet these challenges, the system will doubtless undergo further mutations—to Capitalism 4.1, 4.2, and so on—but the outlines of possible solutions are clearly discernible from the perspective of Capitalism 4.0.

It is impossible to touch on every issue, still less provide a detailed blueprint for possible solutions. At the same time, some specificity is essential to establish whether the model of Capitalism 4 proposed in this book differs significantly from both the free-market capitalism of the Thatcher-Reagan era and the government-knows-best philosophy of the Great Society and the New Deal.

To try to answer this question, this last part of the book gives concrete examples of changes in public policy and economics that are already emerging from the crisis or seem likely to happen in the years ahead. The chapter on economics examines four medium-term challenges in detail. In each of the subsequent chapters, ten possible reforms are outlined briefly to illustrate how new patterns of thinking could transform politics, business, and diplomacy as Capitalism 4 evolves.

CHAPTER SIXTEEN

Economic Policy in Capitalism 4.0

THROUGHOUT THE THIRTY-YEAR PERIOD up to the bankruptcy of Lehman, most governments and central banks acknowledged only one official objective for macroeconomic policy: to control inflation. The single-minded focus on inflation held even though central bankers always understood that the relationship between money and inflation was much more subtle than official slogans proclaimed. With demand management neutered by the predominant monetarist economic doctrine, only one reasonable criterion for judging the success of macroeconomic policy seemed to remain: price stability.

All the other goals of macroeconomic management that had dominated democratic politics from the 1930s until the late 1970s—achieving full employment, maximizing output growth, and keeping trade and government budgets in reasonable balance—were relegated by finance ministers and central bankers to their junior colleagues who controlled the ministries responsible for microeconomic issues such as trade policy, industry, and government budgeting.

In Capitalism 4.0, these polarized dichotomies between the monetary and the real economy, between responsibilities for inflation and unemployment, between the aims of macroeconomics and microeconomics, will no longer make sense. All economic objectives will need to be juggled in a more complex manner, as politicians and voters recognize that every aspect of policy interacts with every other.

What, then, should the central banks aim for, if not just low inflation? If a single target is to replace inflation, the best one is nominal GDP—the total spending in the economy, taking both inflation and real economic growth into account. This target was suggested in 1980 by the Nobel Laureate Keynesian economist James Tobin and James Meade[1] and popularized by Samuel Brittan, the preeminent economic commentator of his generation, on the grounds that nominal GDP is the economic statistic best correlated to the growth of the money supply and also encapsulates a combination of low inflation and adequate real growth, which is what all policymakers are trying to achieve in the long term.

Although nominal GDP is not easily understood by the public and is impossible to track accurately until months after the event, it would clearly be the best single target for monetary policy, much better than inflation on its own. But this begs the question of why central banks should have just one target. Why should they not be expected to achieve multiple objectives— low inflation and maximum economic growth—at the same time? In real life, only maniacs devote themselves entirely to one objective, be it money or fame or work or sex. Neither are politicians expected to concentrate entirely on just one enterprise, except perhaps in times of war. So why should central bankers behave in a way considered insane among normal human beings?

The answer in precrisis economic thinking was the market fundamentalist preoccupation with consistency, transparency, and clear quasi-contractual rules designed to limit the discretion of government officials. But Capitalism 4.0 will move away from these naïve abstractions, and central banks will have to accept the complexities and ambiguities of economic life. Instead of just controlling inflation or nominal GDP or any other single objective, central banks will have to aim at several targets simultaneously. At a minimum, central banks worldwide will be required to achieve low rates of inflation as well as adequate levels of economic growth and employment, as already specified in the Fed's legal magnate. Central bankers will also be expected to ensure reasonable credit growth and to collaborate with authorities in other major economies to ensure that exchange rates and trade imbalances do not get too far out of line.

The theoretical objection to such a complex set of targets is that they will at times be inconsistent and offer ambiguous guidance. That, in turn, will mean that the markets will no longer be able to form "rational" expectations about what the monetary policy will do. Part of the answer to these objections is that rational expectations are a fantasy and conceptual clarity is less important than practical effectiveness. A more constructive answer is that, at the times when monetary decisions really matter, no contradiction will exist between targeting inflation and targeting unemployment or economic growth. In a deep recession, the central bank should aim to increase *both* the price level and the rate of economic growth—and that means reducing interest rates to the lowest possible level. Conversely, in a boom, higher than normal interest rates are needed to restrain *both* inflation and economic growth. There will, nevertheless, be occasions when inflation and unemployment give conflicting signals. In those conditions, central banks must act like leaders in all other fields who face policy dilemmas and make decisions on the basis of inconsistent evidence. They have to make reasonable choices among desirable but conflicting objectives, prioritizing the ones that are most urgent at any given time. If inflation is already high—say above 5 percent—then reducing it must take priority, even if that means tolerating a period of high unemployment. If, on the other hand, unemployment is already intolerable—say 10 percent or more—that has to take priority over inflation. Such a prescription may not be entirely satisfying to theorists and ideologues, but public policy frequently involves compromises and second-best choices—and such ambiguities will need to be recognized in the pragmatic politics of Capitalism 4.0.

Governments, for their part, will have to accept much wider responsibilities for ensuring that growth is internationally balanced with much more emphasis on exports in the United States, Britain, and the periphery of Europe and on higher consumption in China, Germany, and Japan. Politicians will also have to admit that the buck stops with them, literally, when it comes to stabilizing the financial system and, therefore, they cannot subcontract ultimate responsibility for financial regulation to markets, private credit-rating agencies, or unaccountable international bureaucracies. To make life even more difficult, governments will have to accept this newfound responsibility for comprehensive economic management while setting public spending and borrowing on a rapidly declining path.

Greater complexity, broader political responsibility, and tighter constraints will be typical features of economic policy under Capitalism 4.0. The rest of this chapter will consider how these contradictory pressures could interact in dealing with some of the biggest economic challenges of the next decade.

By the beginning of 2010, as the United States reported its strongest economic growth rate since 2003, as financial markets recovered, and as banks allegedly on the point of failure suddenly announced record profits, even die-hard skeptics had to admit that a rerun of the Great Depression had been avoided. Apart from the largely irrelevant fears about monetary policy discussed in the last chapter, the worries among politicians, voters, and economists coalesced around several more serious and longer-term questions:

- Would exploding government deficits threaten national bankruptcy, especially in America and Britain?
- Would government support for "zombie banks," which were neither dead nor fully restored to health, result in a global repetition of Japan's lost decade and prevent a return to precrisis levels of growth?
- What would be done about the imbalances in the world economy, especially between the United States and China, but also within Europe, where tensions between Germany's huge export surpluses and the resulting accumulation of debts in Greece, Portugal, and other Mediterranean countries were putting the survival of the euro at risk?
- With governments everywhere focused on stimulating growth and reducing unemployment, was there a risk that the pendulum of economic policy would swing too far and too quickly, recreating the stagflation of the 1970s—the nightmarish situation in which macroeconomic policy was paralyzed because inflation and unemployment were rapidly rising at the same time?

Will There Be a Government Debt Crisis?

The worldwide fiscal stimulus plans, adding up to more than $3 trillion and announced in the immediate aftermath of the financial crisis, represented a comprehensive victory for the Keynesian view that governments should deliberately and aggressively increase their borrowing when facing severe economic downturns. With capitalism's survival at stake, all the arguments for government inaction developed by conservative free-market economists during the four decades of monetarist counterreformation were jettisoned in a matter of days. Despite some halfhearted initial protests from the anti-Keynesian theorists who still dominated the U.S. and German economic establishments—and more vehement protests from Republican and Conservative politicians in the United States and Britain—governments everywhere implemented unprecedented policies of deficit spending. These were quickly followed by revivals of growth in one country after another, roughly in proportion to the size of the various stimulus plans.

China's stimulus was the biggest and the fastest—and it helped to reverse the economic downturn within one quarter. Germany's stimulus, despite Mrs. Merkel's initial insistence that we should not try "to cure debt with debt," turned out to be the largest in Europe and produced corresponding results by mid-2009. The U.S. stimulus, while also fairly large, took longer to implement and produced slower results. Britain's modest package of discretionary tax cuts, in spite of Gordon Brown's leading role in advocating a Keynesian response to the crisis, was among the smallest in the leading economies and the initial recovery was correspondingly subdued.

Regardless of differences in detail and timing, the message of postcrisis fiscal policy was clear. Governments all over the world realized that a large increase in borrowing was necessary to protect their economies from a deflationary spiral and allow private borrowers to start paying down their debts. This was the core policy prescription of Keynesian economics and, despite the skepticism and derision from many academic economists,[2] it was universally accepted by the middle of 2009.

But even as the necessity of higher public borrowing to stabilize the economy was generally acknowledged, as the sense of crisis subsided, it became obvious that the growth of government debt would have to be stopped eventually or at least brought under control. With public deficits running at over 10 percent of national income in the United States and Britain, 8 percent in France and Japan, and 5 percent in Germany, Italy, and Canada,[3] the inexorable mathematics of compound interest showed that government debts would spiral toward infinity if these rates of borrowing persisted for more than a few years. Almost all economists and politicians—and, more importantly, a growing majority of voters—therefore agreed that urgent action to reduce deficits was needed, especially in Britain and the United

States. A political consensus for large-scale deficit-reduction thus seemed to form on both sides of the Atlantic by the end of 2009.

Probably the most important questions about the economic outlook for 2011 and beyond are whether this consensus will turn out to be an illusion or will lead to decisive action, and whether the actions to reduce government borrowing will be well calibrated or implemented too early or too late.

As the crisis subsides, unpopular tax increases and cuts in public spending could become politically impossible and large government deficits could continue for many years. In that case, more and worse financial turmoil would become almost inevitable, embracing not just the global banking system but also the government bond markets and perhaps even permanently jeopardizing the use of paper money. An opposite danger in Britain and the eurozone is that enthusiasm for budget-slashing could get out of hand. Governments could raise taxes and cut public expenditure too aggressively and too quickly. The result would be a relapse into a recession that, in turn, would make public deficits even bigger and inspire demands for further fiscal cutbacks. Such a vicious circle of policy errors could lock Britain and souther Europe into a deflationary debt trap of the kind that has paralyzed Japan for twenty years, since 1990.

To navigate between the Scylla of national bankruptcy and the Charybdis of a deflationary debt trap will be the greatest economic challenge of the postcrisis period. Luckily, this feat should be made easier by the pragmatic view of macroeconomic policy emerging under Capitalism 4.0.

But before a rational debate can begin on fiscal action, two myths have to be dispelled: Talk about national bankruptcy is a wild exaggeration, as is the claim that excessive government borrowing will burden our grandchildren with unsupportable debts. These arguments are both based on fallacies of composition of exactly the kind refuted by the Keynesian revolution in economic thinking eighty years ago but then quietly reintroduced into economics in the ideological counterrevolution of the 1970s.

The Myth of National Bankruptcy

Public finances cannot be understood by imagining the government as an aggregation of individual families or a supersized business firm. This is because governments do not borrow or spend anything in their own right. They only transfer resources from one group of citizens (the taxpayers) to others (for example, pensioners and government employees). In doing this, today's governments create obligations for future politicians to undertake another transfer of resources—from a third group of citizens (the taxpayers of the future) to a fourth group (the future owners of government bonds). All these transfers, provided they occur within a single nation, have no effect on the nation's total wealth. Thus, the concept of a country such as the United States or Britain going bankrupt is absurd.

A nation cannot go bankrupt by borrowing from itself any more than an individual can go bankrupt by writing a check for $1 billion and then posting it to himself. The possibility of government insolvency arises only if a nation, or more precisely a national Treasury, borrows from *other* countries in a currency it cannot control. This crucial issue is discussed in detail later, though it should be noted that U.S. and British reliance on foreign borrowing, contrary to widespread belief, has fallen, not risen, since the crisis. Furthermore, if present trends continue, America's borrowing from China and other foreign countries will probably stop in the next year or two, even if the government does nothing to reduce its total appetite for debt.

Another, even more significant reason why the U.S. and British governments can never go bankrupt is that they have borrowed almost entirely in currencies that they print. This means they can repay their debts without limit, simply by running the printing presses at their central banks. This is an option that did not exist for countries such as Argentina, Greece, and Thailand, which got into trouble by borrowing in dollars, euros, and yen, respectively.

Moreover, governments cannot go bankrupt in the literal sense because there is no legal mechanism to enforce debt repayment against them.[4] Why, then, are there so many examples in history of governments collapsing as a result of their debts, often causing massive economic damage to their countries? The answer is that almost all such defaults have arisen when governments borrowed in currencies they could not control, or in forms of money tied to physical commodities such as gold or silver, often from foreign citizens. Although creditors were never able to force these governments to repay their debts, they could stop lending them new money, with painful effects on countries that had become addicted to inflows of foreign capital.

Government defaults of this kind have occurred in Mexico, Brazil, Thailand, and Russia in the 1980s and 1990s and Iceland most recently. What all these countries had in common was that they borrowed from foreign banks and investors in currencies they did not control. The same was true of Germany and many European countries in the interwar period, when all government borrowing was effectively in gold. Similar foreign-currency defaults could threaten eastern European governments that borrow from Austrian and German banks in euros and countries within the eurozone, such as Greece, Ireland, Portugal, and Spain, which have limited influence on the monetary policies of the European Central Bank.

But for the United States, Britain, Japan, and other nations that borrow almost entirely in currencies that they themselves manage, default is not even a theoretical possibility—unless the definition of default is extended in some far-fetched manner to include such notions as reducing the real value of debts through inflation or increasing taxes on future owners of government bonds. Genuinely sovereign borrowers such as the United States and Britain will always repay their debts because, as a last resort, they can always instruct their central banks to print the money with which the debts have to be repaid. Such monetary expansion may or may not create inflation, but it will always be preferable from the government's standpoint to formal default. Well before governments reach the last resort of simply printing money, however, they have another line of defense through taxes.

But what happens if the government debt is owned by foreign countries? The biggest holders of U.S. debt are the Chinese and Japanese governments. Doesn't this make national bankruptcy, or at least some kind of debt servitude, a threat to the United States?

If it were true that the U.S. government is largely dependent on Chinese and Japanese credit and if the borrowing were not in dollars but in yuan or yen, default by the U.S. Treasury would indeed be a genuine threat (albeit a remote one, given the reasonably healthy state of the public finances described later). However, America's dependence on foreign borrowing is another exaggeration fostered by the gradual substitution of ideology for economics during the dying days of Capitalism 3. The facts are as follows.

According to the Federal Reserve's Flow of Funds statistics,[5] during the twelve-month period to September 2009, foreign investors bought $634 billion of Treasury bonds, which was 36 percent of the $1.7 trillion total government bond sales. So only about one-third of U.S. government borrowing was a liability to foreigners and therefore imposed a burden on future generations of Americans. The full picture, however, was even less alarming because much of the Treasury's recent foreign borrowing was offset by debt repayments from other U.S. agencies, especially the Government Sponsored Enterprises (GSEs), Fannie Mae and Freddie Mac. Including the GSEs, U.S. government entities borrowed only $352 billion abroad in the twelve months to September 2009, and taking account of additional large debt repayments by private corporations, America's total credit-market borrowing from abroad was only $189 billion, or about one-tenth of the federal government's financial deficit of $1.7 trillion.

This figure of $189 billion is a more accurate gauge of the true growth of America's indebtedness as a nation than the multitrillion dollar federal deficit quoted in shocking headlines. The figure compares with much larger national borrowings of $380 billion in 2008, $944 billion in 2007, $974 billion in 2006, and $752 billion in 2005. It seems, therefore, that America's debt burden increased much faster in the four years *before* the crisis than it did in 2009. How could this be, given that the government's deficit shot up from around $300 billion annually to $1.7 trillion during this time?

The answer is that government borrowing, despite all the attention it attracts, is only one part of the financial flows circulating around the economy—and a relatively small part, in comparison with the borrowing of private corporations and households. The true debt burden on future generations of Americans is determined by the country's borrowing from *foreign* investors, whether this borrowing is undertaken by the government or by American private companies and individuals.

The correct measure of this increase in genuine national indebtedness is not the government's budget deficit but the U.S. economy's deficit in foreign trade. Every dollar the United States spends on foreign goods and does not earn by selling something to foreigners has to be raised by borrowing from foreign investors or by selling American shares, bonds, property, or other assets. The most complete gauge of this increase in debt to the rest of the world is what economists call the deficit on current account. The current account includes not only the ordinary trade deficit in oil, cars, computers, and so on but also the surplus that America usually earns in "invisible" trade items, such as the royalty payments for Hollywood films and technology patents and profits earned by U.S. multinationals.

This truly comprehensive measure of the national debt burden is linked to the government deficit, but only in a tenuous and indirect way. If the government increases its borrowing and outlays, this results in extra spending by consumers, civil servants, defense contractors, and so on. If everything else is equal, this extra spending tends to suck in imports and increase the current account deficit, thereby adding to the nation's debt burden. But everything else may not be equal. If, for example, consumers buy fewer foreign goods because of a recession or because currency movements make imports more expensive than goods made at home, even a very large government deficit can easily coincide with a *reduction* in borrowing from abroad. This is exactly what happened in 2007–09.

While the federal budget deficit exploded from $237 billion in 2007 to $1.2 trillion in 2008 and $1.7 trillion in the twelve months to September 2009, the U.S. trade deficit[6] narrowed, from an average of $750 billion annually in 2006–08 to around $400 billion in 2009.[7] Moreover, roughly half this $400 billion trade deficit was financed by inflows of foreign direct investment into U.S. factories, property, and shares in U.S. companies. This was why total U.S. foreign borrowing in 2009—and hence the true increase in the burden on America's grandchildren—was just $189 billion, about one-tenth the size of the government deficit.

The reduction of the U.S. trade deficit is the great untold story of the 2007–09 crisis. If the recent U.S. trade performance persists, the improvement in trade deficits ought to dispel the panic about America's dependence on borrowing from China and other foreign countries. Such a calming of public anxieties is likely to occur in the first half of the new decade, more or less regardless of what happens to the government's budget deficit.

The Myth of Burdening Our Grandchildren

As misleading as the myth of national bankruptcy is the claim that government debts are immoral and unjust because they impose a burden on our grandchildren. The simplest rebuttal is the Micawber argument presented in Chapter 1: Our grandchildren will, on average, be much richer than we are[8] and thus it is far from clear why we should feel guilty about adding a little to their financial burdens if this can improve our own lives. But even if we leave aside this argument about intergenerational fairness, the fact is that the burden on future generations from public borrowing is often exaggerated in obeisance to the prevailing antigovernment sentiments of Capitalism 3.

At first glance, it seems obvious that the more we borrow today, the greater will be the burden on our grandchildren to service or redeem these debts by paying extra taxes. But we have to ask what exactly will happen to all those extra taxes our grandchildren will be paying.

The ideologically antigovernment economics of the past thirty years has sometimes implied that money paid in taxes to the government simply goes up in smoke. Taxes are often presented as a net cost to society, disappearing forever into the maws of the government bureaucracy. Whatever one's view of the effectiveness of government, this one-sided accounting is simply wrong. Every penny the government collects in taxes is spent on something, even if this spending is seen as wasteful, for example, on the salary of an unproductive bureaucrat.

How exactly, then, will future governments spend all those extra taxes they levy on our grandchildren to pay for today's government borrowing? The answer is that all the extra taxes paid by *some* of our grandchildren will be handed over by the government to some other of our grandchildren who own government bonds. This transfer of money from my grandson Peter, a future taxpayer, to my grandson Paul, a future investor in government bonds, will have no net effect on the combined income of Peter and Paul— except insofar as it may reduce Peter's work incentives or distort the investment decisions made by Paul. Thus, the net economic burden on *all* our grandchildren that results directly from government borrowing is zero. Future economic prosperity will be damaged only if government borrowing diminishes productive investment or if redistribution of income from future taxpayers to future savers discourages work. These are, indeed, potentially serious risks of a profligate fiscal policy—and they are discussed in the next section—but they are different from the myths about national bankruptcy and injustice to future generations.

The Real Case for Tackling Deficits

If governments that borrow in their own currencies face no real risks of bankruptcy, does this mean they can continue to borrow with gay abandon and simply ignore the buildup of public debt? The answer is emphatically no. Having rejected the myths about national bankruptcy and burdens on future generations, three *valid* reasons exist why public deficits will need to be reduced drastically in the years after the crisis—and why this task must start soon.

The first reason is simple arithmetic. Although nothing is unsustainable or even undesirable about present and prospective levels of public debt, which range from 60 percent to 80 percent of GDP in most advanced economies, these debts cannot grow forever without creating economically disruptive and politically divisive imbalances between future taxpayers and future savers. History suggests that government debt levels of up to about 100 percent of GDP are generally compatible with the smooth and efficient functioning of market economies. If debt levels get much higher than this, the economic distortions and political tensions created by redistributing high proportions of national income from taxpayers to owners of government bonds become so large that they endanger productivity growth and social cohesion.

To stabilize debt at about 80 percent of GDP, which has been the two-hundred-year average in America and Britain, will not require deficits to be eliminated completely, because the natural growth of the economy allows the government to safely increase its debt by a corresponding amount. But stabilizing debt would mean reducing deficits to around 4 percent of GDP.[9] For the United States and Britain, where deficit ratios in 2009 were 13 percent and 11 percent respectively, this will be a big challenge, although one they have the leeway to tackle over a period of several years. Some improvement in deficits will result automatically from economic recovery, but according to OECD estimates, the structural, or underlying, deficit ratios in both countries will still be around 9 percent, even after stripping out the effects of recession and one-off items such as bank bailouts. To get these deficit ratios down to 4 percent would therefore mean tax increases and public spending cuts equivalent to 5 percent of GDP.

Such large cutbacks have been achieved by a few advanced economies—notably Sweden and Canada in the mid-1990s—but they will pose big political challenges, requiring careful consideration of the right balance between lower public spending and higher taxes. In America, politicians of all parties have ruled out additional taxes, especially on the middle class. But without broad-based taxes that can raise hundreds of billions of extra dollars, it is inconceivable that the necessary deficit reductions can be achieved. Eliminating unnecessary government programs and painlessly improving efficiency will not be remotely sufficient because a spending reduction of 5 percent of GDP translates into $700 billion annually. This is equivalent to the entire defense budget or to *all* federal government spending apart from defense and entitlements to social security and health care. In Britain, the need for both spending cuts and tax increases has in principle been accepted, but the scale of the adjustment means that measures ruled out in the general election, such as higher energy taxes and cutbacks in health spending, will almost certainly be required.

The issue of health spending leads to the second reason why long-term deficit reduction will be essential from 2011 onward: the rapidly growing pressure on government finances from health and pension entitlements as societies get older. Public spending on health, pensions, and long-term care is projected to increase in all G7 countries by 7 percent to 8 percent of GDP from 2005 to 2050. If this extra spending is financed by borrowing, debt ratios will increase to genuinely alarming levels of 300 percent and above, as the annual health and pension deficits relentlessly compound. The IMF has calculated that the increase in public debts implied by present plans on health and pensions will exceed the effect of the 2007–09 financial crisis and recession by nine-to-one.[10] To avoid such an enormous debt buildup, which would be far greater than anything before experienced, even in wartime, taxes would have to rise dramatically. But such tax increases would mean a huge *further* redistribution of income from the taxpayers to the savers and pensioners of the future, on top of the redistribution already implied by the accumulation of public debts in the 2007–09 crisis.

Whether political consensus in democratic societies can withstand a government-directed reallocation of resources on this scale from taxpayers to savers and pensioners is far from clear. The implication is that current public policies on health and pensions are probably politically unsustainable in most advanced economies and are certainly incompatible with the present U.S. and British tax structures. We will return to these issues in Chapter 17, which deals with the politics of Capitalism 4.0. But whatever eventually happens to government health and pension obligations, the long-run unsustainability of these programs adds tremendously to the urgency of dealing with the macroeconomic deficits that emerged in the 2007–09 crisis. If these macroeconomic deficits are tackled quickly, structural reductions in health and pensions can be somewhat ameliorated and delayed. However, if no action is taken on macroeconomic deficits, the scale of cutbacks in age-related entitlements will be far greater and such cutbacks will surely be forced on governments by financial markets before the end of this decade. Thus, the real question our societies have to answer in planning fiscal adjustments is not whether we want to burden our grandchildren with extra taxes but whether we want our own pensions and health care subsidies to be paid or eliminated in the next decade.

The third, and perhaps the most urgent, reason for serious action on public finances is that big deficits restrict the freedom of governments to manage the economy. Having just rediscovered the effectiveness of Keynesian macroeconomic policy, it would be ironic if governments and central banks had to abandon demand management, as they did in the 1970s, because of the financial pressures created by out-of-control deficits.

Persistently excessive deficits can create all sorts of problems for macroeconomic management. By far the most important problem is the political constraint already faced by President Obama in 2010 as he prepared a second fiscal stimulus plan—if the deficit is already vastly higher than any sustainable level, the government loses its option to borrow even more in support of growth and employment. In addition, two standard objections are cited in pre-Keynesian economics: Ricardian Equivalence, whereby consumers supposedly reduce their spending in anticipation of future taxes, and the crowding-out effect, whereby the government's demand for savings pushes up interest rates, crowding out private investment. Neither Ricardian Equivalence nor crowding out is of practical relevance in periods of recession or weak growth, when consumers and private companies are cutting back their spending anyway. But as the economy recovers—and especially if it recovers more rapidly than expected—crowding out can become a genuine constraint on growth and productivity, especially in economies such as the United States and Britain, which need to compensate for years of underinvestment in the industries required for export-led growth.

To avoid crowding out in conditions where public deficits will remain very large for at least the first half of the new decade, close cooperation will be needed between governments and central banks. Central banks worldwide will be obliged to keep interest rates as low as possible for as long as possible, both to support industrial investment and to create conditions in which governments can reduce deficits without running the risk of pushing their economies back into recession. But central banks, especially the Fed and the Bank of England, will find it difficult to maintain very low interest rates if politicians fail to present credible plans to bring public borrowing slowly but surely under control.

Without such credible programs, the combination of uncontrolled public borrowing and economic recovery could push up long-term interest rates in the bond markets or create genuine risks of inflation. Under such circumstances, central banks would be reluctant to keep interest rates at very low levels. Higher interest rates would, in turn, slow economic growth and make fiscal consolidation impossible, potentially creating a vicious circle and a Japanese-style debt trap for the entire world economy. Central banks and governments will try hard to avoid such a disastrous outcome. To do this, however, they will have to engage in a series of complex and elaborate policy maneuvers diametrically opposed to the noninterventionist laissez-faire doctrines of Capitalism 3.3.

Their efforts would be helped if they explained clearly and frankly why reducing deficits is so important: not to avert a mythical national bankruptcy but to cope with long-term commitments on health and pensions and to preserve enough flexibility for future governments to continue actively managing demand and thereby promoting economic growth.

Japanese-Style Paralysis and Zombie Banks

Japan's experience of trying to manage an overindebted post-bubble economy, while offering government life support to a half-dead, or zombie, banking system coincided with the longest period of economic stagnation ever recorded in a modern economy. After forty years of spectacular economic growth and social development from 1950 onward, Japan fell into an economic stupor after the bursting of its property bubble in 1990. Twenty years later, Japan's economy still shows no sign of proper recovery.[11] This experience persuaded many opinion-leaders in America, Britain, and other highly indebted countries that their economies would face similar "lost decades" of prolonged stagnation, especially if they pursued financial policies similar to the Japanese.

Economists and financiers with a purist free-market worldview insisted that Western nations could avoid repeating the Japanese experience only by taking immediate and decisive action to clean up their banking systems, action of the kind the Japanese government had tried to avoid for years. Radical economists on both the Left and the Right demanded that all weak banks should be nationalized, that all dubious mortgages, properties, and other assets should be marked down in value to whatever fire-sale prices were established by financial markets, and that all overleveraged borrowers who were unable to cope with such extreme financial duress should be put into bankruptcy and liquidated at once. Of course, Western governments refused to take such radical actions and instead decided to keep their financial systems on artificial life support with Japanese-style policies of covert public assistance. The question therefore arises whether Japan is now the most plausible model for a New Normal of sluggish growth and financial paralysis in the United States, Britain, and other economies emerging from the credit crunch.

Luckily, this analogy between Japan and the Western world looks increasingly far-fetched. It is certainly true that the Japanese financial system remained paralyzed for a decade as banks and borrowers survived on government life support and failed to recognize their true losses. It is true also that the Japanese economy spent twenty years almost continuously in recession. But correlation is not causation. The question that needs to be asked about the Japanese experience is whether government support for struggling banks and overindebted borrowers caused the twenty years of stagnation or whether twenty years of economic stagnation prevented a recovery for weak borrowers and banks.

A similar question must be asked about a fascinating and much-quoted historic study, coauthored by Carmen Reinhart and Kenneth Rogoff, the IMF's former chief economist, which looked at the macroeconomic effect of financial crises in dozens of countries over the past six hundred years. This study concluded that recessions accompanied by banking crises are generally much longer and deeper than recessions in which banks avoid serious losses.[12] The question is whether this historic evidence proves that banking crises cause particularly severe recessions or that particularly severe recessions cause banking crises, which then make these recessions even worse.

One of the most famous and widely cited recent banking crises, for example, happened in 1992 in Sweden. This episode is generally presented as the epitome of skillful crisis management because the government followed the radical prescription recommended by academic economists on both the Right and the Left. It nationalized all the country's leading banks, wiped out their private shareholders, and rapidly liquidated weak borrowers. Yet, despite this textbook management by the government, Sweden suffered its worst recession in postwar history during this period. Thus, the first inference usually drawn from this experience is that deep recessions are inevitable after banking crises, even when these crises are vigorously managed. The second inference is that a banking crisis that is managed less skillfully than Sweden's will surely produce a much worse recession, as it did in Japan. Luckily for the world, neither of these commonly accepted conclusions stands up to scrutiny.

In the Swedish case, the recession actually began in 1990, almost two years *before* the banking crisis, and was caused by an extreme policy of high interest rates, which were raised at one point to above 100 percent in a desperate attempt to defend the Swedish kronor's exchange rate against the deutsche mark. This misguided monetary policy caused the deep recession and then the collapse of the banking system, not the other way round. A similar reversal of cause and effect can be seen in the Thai, Korean, Indonesian, Russian, and Argentine banking crises of the 1990s, all of which were accompanied—and caused—by extreme fiscal and monetary contractions.

Moreover, examining the causal connections the other way round, several extreme financial crises in recent history were not associated with broader economic downturns at all. The clearest such example is also one that refutes the conventional view that Japanese-style economic and financial paralysis must follow if zombie banks are kept on government life support and their losses hidden or disguised.

By far the biggest banking crisis in postwar history prior to 2007–08 occurred from 1982 to 1989, when Mexico, Brazil, Argentina, the Philippines, and many other developing countries defaulted on bank loans worth several times more than the capital of the global banks. As a result, almost every major bank in the United States and Europe was technically insolvent throughout this five-year period. Citibank, J.P. Morgan, Bank of America, Deutsche, Lloyds, and many others suffered what would now be called mark-to-market losses worth between 100 percent and 300 percent of their total shareholders' funds.[13] Yet this horrendous crisis, even bigger in relation to the bank capital of the time than the losses from subprime lending in 2007–09, did not produce a recession. In fact, the Third World debt crisis coincided with the strongest period of economic growth in U.S. history and one of the strongest in Europe.

The history of the 1982–89 crisis suggests the opposite policy prescription from the market-oriented approach proposed by almost all academic economists in 2008–09 and wisely rejected by almost all governments. The Third World debt crisis was not addressed by liquidating banks or forcing them to come clean and recognize their theoretical losses but by doing the opposite. Banks were not just encouraged, but required, by their regulators to hide their losses, valuing enormous loans to the Brazilian and Mexican governments at 100 cents on the dollar even though the interest payments had long been suspended and it was clear that the principals would never be repaid.

As one Latin American government after another stopped repaying its debts, the Federal Reserve, the Bank of England, and European regulators told all their major banks and accountancy firms simply to ignore these defaults and to issue new rescheduled loans to the defaulting governments exactly equal to whatever sums they should have repaid but didn't. The banks were thus able to preserve the fiction that they were still receiving payments from Third World governments and to continue operating as normal, even though they would have been declared insolvent under any strict application of accounting rules. In making their decision to offer this additional accounting leeway, or forbearance, the regulators assumed that over time the banks would earn enough profit from their other businesses to rebuild capital and trade their way out of insolvency. And this was indeed what happened.

By 1989, the banks had built up enough reserves to allow them to forgive most of the debts owed by the Third World in exchange for a minor sweetener from Nicholas Brady, the U.S. treasury secretary, who swapped a small proportion of the outstanding debts into so-called Brady bonds with U.S. guarantees. Although all major U.S. banks were effectively insolvent according to today's accounting standards throughout much of the period from 1982 to 1989, only one of them, Continental Illinois, failed—and its troubles had more to do with a fraud in Oklahoma than a systemic financial crisis.[14]

Far from causing Japanese-style economic paralysis and credit contraction, therefore, the decision to keep effectively insolvent banks on life support throughout the 1980s facilitated a rapid economic recovery and allowed an orderly restructuring of global finances.[15] Thus, recent historical experience from America and Europe suggests the opposite conclusion to the conventional wisdom about the Japanese lost decade: The broader economy will usually *benefit* if crippled banks are supported by the government in financial crises and encouraged to carry their loans at above-market values, rather than liquidating them quickly.

Government support for banks should not mean, however, that banks, their shareholders, and their employees are allowed to get the benefit of permanent taxpayer subsidies. Public outrage over bankers' bonuses is justifiable. And government regulation of bank salaries and dividends is politically legitimate, precisely because taxpayer support for troubled banks is likely to be needed again at some point.

The idea that banking can be neatly divided between government-controlled deposit taking and other public utility functions (sometimes described as "utility" or "post office" banks) and totally deregulated private investment functions (the "casino" banks) is a market fundamentalist illusion characteristic of the artificial public-private dichotomies of Capitalism 3. The reality, as demonstrated by the Third World debt crisis, when the institutions that went bankrupt were all strictly regulated utility banks, is that finance always and everywhere involves a combination of the utility and the casino, of socially indispensable fiduciary functions and privately profitable speculation on unpredictable risks. Rather than trying artificially to separate out the public and private characteristics of banking, the new thinking about capitalism should acknowledge that financial institutions will always be in some sense public-private hybrids, subject to the messy confusion of political and profit-maximizing incentives that infuriated Henry Paulson and the other free-market ideologues who wanted to demolish Fannie Mae and Freddie Mac.

Banks may be legally structured as private companies, answerable only to their shareholders, but they have a uniquely important social function and thus operate in the public realm, with implicit government support. Their managements, shareholders, and regulators must therefore recognize the symbiotic interdependence between private banking and government. This view of finance goes against the grain of market fundamentalist thinking, but as new, more pragmatic views of capitalism come to be accepted, financial reform and macroeconomic policy can start to be developed hand in hand. Banks can be subjected to smarter, better targeted regulations, designed to ensure that they fulfill their socially necessary functions at a reasonable taxpayer cost. And the quid pro quo for tighter financial regulation will be a greater willingness by governments to support their financial system promptly if support is required. Politicians, bankers, and shareholders will recognize that one of the main reasons for tightening regulatory structures will be to create a political climate in which governments can continue supporting weak banks with implicit subsidies and taxpayer guarantees for as long as is necessary to restore normal financial conditions and keep the world economy out of recession. This will be the surest way for Capitalism 4.0 to avoid the financial paralysis of post-bubble Japan and emerge robustly from the crisis.

The Great Rebalancing of Global Growth

The imbalances of growth and consumption—between the countries that borrowed and consumed too much during the years before the crisis and those that generated excess savings and production—are widely regarded as the most fundamental cause of the crisis. The first group of countries covers not only the United States and Britain but also Spain, France, Italy, and almost all the other countries in southern and central Europe. The second group of countries, with excess savings and large trade surpluses, is smaller in number: China, Germany, Japan, and Taiwan plus the oil exporters, including Russia. The imbalances between these two groups will present major challenges to global economic management whatever happens in the years ahead. Regardless of whether these imbalances are permanently diminished by the crisis or begin to grow again once conditions return to normal, they will drive big changes in economic and political thinking around the world.

In the decade before the crisis, China (and also, to a lesser extent, Japan, Korea, and Taiwan) powered its economy by exporting rapidly increasing quantities of goods to American consumers while manipulating the global currency system so as to thwart the market forces that would normally have limited their export growth. The Chinese government did this by forcing its citizens to exchange the dollars (and euros) they earned from exports into yuan at an artificially low exchange rate. The result was that the Chinese central bank (the People's Bank of China, or PBOC) effectively appropriated a large part of the country's export earnings, instead of allowing them to be spent by Chinese businesses and workers on consumer goods and investments from the rest of the world.

These Chinese dollar reserves, which grew from $500 billion in 2000 to $3 trillion in 2010, were then recycled by the government back to America by buying bonds from the U.S. Treasury and from the Government Sponsored Enterprises (GSEs), mainly the mortgage lenders Fannie Mae and Freddie Mac. The U.S. Treasury and GSEs, in turn, channeled these Chinese savings to U.S. households by way of cash-out mortgages and tax cuts, the latter financed by large budget deficits. Finally, American consumers completed this Circle of Manipulation[16] by using the money they received from the U.S. government and mortgage lenders to buy more consumer goods from Chinese exporters, who in turn passed their dollar earnings back to the PBOC. Like the technology companies of the 1990s, which boosted their sales and profits by lending their customers the money with which to buy their products through "vendor financing," China spent the years before the crisis providing enormous amounts of vendor financing to American consumers to ensure that the factories kept humming in Shenzen and Guangdong.

A similar, though less widely noticed and potentially more unstable, Circle of Manipulation was also spinning during this period in Europe, with Germany providing Chinese-style vendor financing so that French, Spanish, and British consumers could keep buying German goods. Germany sold cars and machinery to Spain, Italy, France, and central Europe and then recycled the revenues of its export industries by lending money to homeowners and governments in these economies. And just as the Chinese-U.S. financial recycling was necessary to keep the dollar-yuan exchange rate artificially stable, so the European Circle of Manipulation was essential to maintain the stability of the eurozone.

There were hopes that one of the positive by-products of the 2007–09 crisis would be a gradual reduction of these global imbalances. The credit crunch was clearly going to reduce consumption growth in the United States, Britain, and other high-debt economies. It therefore seemed reasonable to assume that the enormous recycling of international capital (which incidentally was responsible for most of the outsized profits and bonuses in international banking) would gradually slow. But to reduce global imbalances in a durable way, consuming and producing countries would both have to make equal and opposite changes—and as the crisis eased from late 2009 onward, the producer side showed precious little evidence of changes in behavior.

Although the credit crunch slowed consumption growth and narrowed trade deficits in the United States, Britain, Spain,[17] and smaller countries on the periphery of Europe, the export-dependent economies, especially Germany and China, seem unwilling to reduce their trade surpluses or substantially accelerate consumption and import growth. When Chinese officials speak at international meetings about their sincere intention to restructure their economy in favor of domestic-led growth and away from export dependence, what they seem to mean is that China will not *increase* its trade surplus any further beyond the level of $300 billion–$400 billion it hit in 2008–09. Considering this trade surplus increased fivefold from just $70 billion four years earlier, this is hardly a major concession. German policymakers are even more adamant that their country's economic recovery will be powered by growing exports, as it has always been.

Focusing on China, the country with the biggest and most persistent surplus, it is curious how the clearly mercantilist policy of maximizing exports and accumulating foreign exchange has been generally accepted in the United States and other countries as an inevitable fact of life—and a symbol of China's rising power, rather than its obvious vulnerability to possible trade restrictions.

For example, in the Reference Scenario drawn up by the IMF in late 2009 for rebalancing the world economy in the five years after the crisis, China's trade surplus was assumed to narrow only marginally from 10 percent of GDP in 2008 to 9.4 percent in 2014.[18] Given that the Chinese economy was certain to grow rapidly throughout this period, this modest restraint in the trade imbalance actually meant that China's export surplus would grow ever-wider in relation to the U.S. economy and the world economy as a whole.[19] A similarly mercantilist approach was evident in Germany, where the OECD, in its November 2009 forecasts, projected a widening of the trade surplus from $130 billion, or 4 percent of GDP, in 2009 to $200 billion, or 5.4 percent of GDP, in 2011. Of the great mercantilist nations, only Japan was expected to have a significantly smaller surplus in 2011 than that recorded just before the crisis.[20]

Yet it is an arithmetic impossibility for indebted countries such as the United States, Spain, and Britain to reduce their deficits unless creditor countries such as China, Japan, and Germany reduce their surpluses by the same amount. If we assume, therefore, that the United States, Britain, Spain, and other countries whose international borrowing and imports powered the global growth of the precrisis decade do decide to reduce their dependence on international borrowing and therefore their trade deficits, something will have to give. Either the surplus countries will have to abandon their policies for promoting exports, or the scene will be set for serious international clashes.

How, then, will this tension be resolved? The immediate postcrisis consensus among economists and politicians, embodied in studies such as the IMF Reference Scenario, simply assumed that the United States would return to its traditional role as the world's consumer and borrower of last resort. The U.S. current account deficit, which halved from $803 billion in 2006 to $434 billion in 2009, is assumed to widen again to $600 billion in 2011 and $800 billion by 2014. Britain and Central Europe are also supposed to continue running very large deficits to absorb the growing exports from China and the eurozone. But why should we believe this will happen?

Trade deficits were halved not just in the United States but also in Spain, the country which has consistently been the world's second biggest excess consumer and importer. In Britain, the third biggest deficit country, the trade gap has narrowed by about a third. All the factors driving these deficit reductions remained in play after the crisis. Consumer spending and borrowing, although gradually recovering in these and other deficit countries, will almost certainly remain subdued by recent standards. The dollar and the pound have both been drastically devalued against the euro and the yen, making American and British companies extremely competitive against their rivals based in Europe and Japan, while wages in Spain are being sharply reduced to cope with the delayed financial crisis unfolding there in 2010.

Most importantly, government policies and business strategies in the United States and all other deficit countries will be consciously redirected toward promoting export-led growth and debt reduction. This reorientation of political and business thinking is likely to be particularly marked in the United States. Politically, the U.S. government and American public are not going to tolerate the renewed widening of trade deficits and lurch back toward large-scale borrowing from China and other Asian countries implied by the consensus global forecasts.

This political resistance to the re-emergence of huge trade deficits is reinforced by changes in business behavior. American multinational companies, which had led the first wave of globalization in the thirty years after World War II, spent the next thirty years, from 1980 until 2010, refocusing their businesses on the rapidly growing and highly profitable American consumer market and in many cases retreating from their international ambitions. In the years after the crisis, this process will almost certainly be reversed as U.S. businesses see bigger opportunities for growth and profits in foreign markets than in serving American domestic consumers.

An interesting symbol of this strategic redirection has been General Electric, still widely regarded as one of the best-managed companies in the world. From the 1970s onward, GE transformed itself from the world's largest producer of engineering and electrical equipment into a consumer and finance conglomerate, taking over the NBC broadcasting network and buying GE Capital and turning it into the world's largest nonbank financial institution. Since 2007, this corporate strategy has been abruptly reversed. GE has sold out of broadcasting, has drastically reduced the size of GE Capital, and is reinventing itself again as a global producer of high-value investment goods, such as electricity generating equipment, nuclear technology, aircraft engines, and gas turbines.

The result of all these forces is likely to be a further narrowing of trade deficits in the United States and Britain, instead of the renewed widening of these deficits assumed by most economists. If this happens, growth in the deficit economies will be stronger than expected, as they take market share from export-dependent economies such as China, Japan, and Germany, and anxieties about their international borrowings should subside—although in Britain the benefits of stronger exports are likely to be cancelled out by the Cameron government's extremely contractionary public spending and tax policies.

If U.S. and British trade deficits narrow or disappear, while China and Germany continue to run large trade surpluses, the arithmetically inevitable result will be a pincer movement that squeezes growth in all other trading economies—especially in developing countries that naturally compete with China and in the weaker members of the eurozone, such as Greece, Spain, and Portugal. Thus, the world economy will face big problems in the decade after the crisis, whatever happens to global imbalances. If the imbalances start to widen again from 2010 onward, as conventionally expected, anxieties will mount about the international debts of the U.S. and British governments and banks. Such worries would probably weaken the dollar and the pound, while a renewed widening of trade deficits would certainly slow economic recovery in America and Britain, aggravating their unemployment and budgetary problems. For all these reasons, widening trade deficits are unlikely to be acceptable to politicians and public opinion, especially in the United States. Protectionist moves that would weaken global trade growth, and perhaps undermine the entire global trading system, would become increasingly likely.

If, on the other hand, the U.S. and British trade imbalances continue to narrow, which seems much more likely, this will present a different but equally daunting challenge. China, Germany, and Japan will either have to accept much smaller trade surpluses than currently expected or take market share from other trading nations, especially the weaker European and emerging economies. These weaker economies will then face even graver pressures of debt, unemployment, and underdevelopment.

Any possible solution to this dilemma will require major reforms of the global trade and currency systems of a kind that have eluded policymakers since the breakdown of the Bretton Woods system in 1971. Such reforms would, however, become possible and even probable as a result of the changing perception of the global capitalist system. Trade and currency policies will become legitimate issues for public debate when the government's responsibility for managing growth and unemployment is fully recognized again by politicians and public opinion, instead of being dodged or denied. This change in public perceptions about the government responsibility for balanced international growth could be benign or disruptive.

As the United States, Britain, Spain, and other European countries reduce their government and international borrowing, their leaders and voters will become increasingly aware that a proper rebalancing of the world economy depends as much or more on policy changes in the surplus countries. China, Japan, and Germany will have to redirect their economic strategies explicitly toward achieving balanced trade instead of export-led growth—and they will have to do this within several years, rather than on China's current timescale, which seems to run into decades.

In the absence of such action from China, Japan, and Germany, the major deficit countries will have to think seriously about deliberate currency depreciation or tariff protection to enforce the necessary rebalancing of global trade. U.S. legislation already provides for punitive tariffs on Chinese goods unless China frees its exchange rate.[21] Such proposals will attract increasing attention from politicians, and growing sympathy from normally free-trade economists, if the U.S. trade deficit again starts to widen, weakening the post-recession recovery and leading to a renewed increase in U.S. foreign debt.[22] Protectionist measures by the United States and other deficit countries could well result in a ruinous international trade war or even in Chinese government attempts to sabotage world financial markets by selling U.S. Treasury bonds.

In Europe, rebalancing will create a particularly stark dilemma for Germany. If deficit countries in the eurozone, such as Spain, Greece, Italy, and France, continue to rebalance their economies and reduce their trade deficits in the years after the crisis, Germany's enormous trade surpluses will vanish and its export industries will suffer large losses of jobs and output. If, on the other hand, the other European countries revert to their pre-crisis policies of running very large trade deficits, Germany will have to commit itself to transferring roughly 5 percent of its national income every year to finance the imports of less competitive eurozone countries such as Spain, Italy, and even France. The only alternative will be for the weaker economies on the periphery of the euro-zone, such as Greece, Portugal, Spain, and most of central Europe, to start defaulting on both private and government loans, inflicting Lehman-style damage on all European, and especially German, banks.

How could such worst-case scenarios of trade wars and government defaults be avoided? The best answer—and the likeliest one if the transition to a new model of global capitalism continues—involves a complex repositioning of macroeconomic policies in different parts of the world.

The United States, Europe, and Japan must move beyond the fundamentalist dogma that market forces alone should be allowed to regulate world trade, international capital flows, and currency exchange rates. Meanwhile, China and other Asian and emerging countries must overcome the statist prejudice, a holdover from Capitalism 2, that trade, capital flows, and exchange rates can be kept almost entirely under government control.

A convergence of this kind, from market fundamentalist and statist ideologies toward a more pragmatic policy consensus, will be an important feature of Capitalism 4.0, as all nations recognize that the best way to manage international trade and capital flows is through a judicious combination of market forces and government intervention. In the modern world of vast and intertwined trade and finance flows, even the most powerful countries, including the United States and China, will also have to understand that their macroeconomic objectives have big international implications—and that other countries can either accept these or resist them.

During the 2007–09 crisis, finance ministers and central bankers realized that their jobs went beyond controlling inflation and allowing market forces to do everything else. But as governments around the world acknowledge the full range of their economic responsibilities, ensuring that all these plans and objectives are consistent at an international level will become a critical component both of macroeconomic policy and of diplomatic relations.

International coordination of economic policies will be inevitable and essential if the world economy is not to degenerate into a new financial crisis or global trade wars. Such international coordination should not attempt to eliminate trade deficits altogether or to defend specific exchange rates, as overly interventionist governments tried to do unsuccessfully in Capitalism 2. But neither should it baldly insist that currency and trade flows must be decided purely by market forces. Instead, the purpose of international coordination should be to keep trade imbalances within reasonable bounds and to monitor the international effects of rising Asian savings. Such steps toward a new international consensus would remind currency markets that they are the servants, not the masters, of international trade flows and that governments have plenty of instruments available to set limits on market fluctuations that disrupt public policy. That governments must set parameters for global financial markets if economic stability is to be maintained, was recognized in the early phase of the free-market period, when Ronald Reagan and Margaret Thatcher were responsible for some of the biggest currency interventions and trade management decisions of all time.[23]

Many specific plans to influence currency movements and reduce imbalances have been proposed by prominent economists and politicians over the years. These plans have involved setting bands for acceptable exchange rate movements, automatic currency intervention under agreed conditions, integration of monetary and exchange rate policy, agreed ceilings on trade imbalances, and similar ideas.[24] But none of the ideas for managing currencies, or international capital flows, or reconciling free trade with domestic macroeconomic objectives, could receive any serious attention in the ideological environment of the precrisis years. A change in this worldview will be one of the most important consequences of the more pragmatic and empirical approach to economics emerging under Capitalism 4.0.

As long as the laissez-faire economics of Capitalism 3.3 was dominant, it was impossible for the G7, the IMF, the World Trade Organization, or any other international forum to engage in serious discussions about currencies and other issues of global management. Until the emergency meetings that followed the Lehman crisis, all that happened in such international gatherings was that the U.S., British, and German delegates felt obliged by their ideologies to preach the gospel of free-floating exchange rates and to repudiate all government intervention in currency markets at all times. By contrast, China and other emerging economies, quietly backed by Japan, France, and Italy, insisted that currencies and capital flows were government prerogatives too important to be left to turbulent and unpredictable markets. All discussions of international monetary issues were thus a dialogue of the deaf.

As a result of the post-Lehman crisis, this situation has begun to change. The G20 has emerged as a more credible forum for international economic negotiations than the G7, and the IMF has been commissioned to study the inconsistencies in national macroeconomic policies and trade objectives—and to publish explicit recommendations on how these inconsistencies should be tackled. These have been major steps in the right direction.

As Capitalism 4.0 develops, politicians and economists in the United States and Europe are again recognizing trade and currency management as legitimate issues for government policy and involvement, while China, Japan, and other interventionist or planned economies are being forced to accept a bigger role for market forces. Such reforms may seem messy, confusing, and ideologically ambiguous. Some countries are enlarging the scope for market forces, while others move in the opposite direction. Some aspects of policy, such as currency management, are being subjected to greater government intervention, while others, such as capital flows in China, are becoming freer, as the country is forced to deregulate its enormous savings. Such confusing and ideologically inconsistent arrangements are characteristic features of Capitalism 4.0.

Stagflation

The last and probably most serious worry about the macroeconomic prospects for Capitalism 4.0 is the outlook for inflation, not in the next year or two but in the second half of the new decade. As economic recovery becomes established, unemployment falls, and output gaps narrow around the world, inflation will again become a concern. Crucially, however, the reasons for legitimate anxiety about inflation will have nothing to do with the actions of central banks that are printing money. In the emerging post-crisis economic mindset, it will become increasingly clear that the genuine dangers of inflation stem not from supposedly irresponsible monetary policies but from structural changes in demographics, global trade, and public finances that could bring back the 1970s nightmare of stagflation toward the end of the decade.

As explained in the previous chapter, the fact that inflation is "always and everywhere a monetary phenomenon" in no way implies the widely accepted fallacy of market fundamentalist economics that monetary expansion causes inflation. To say that monetary policy is always the true cause of inflation is like saying that gravity is always the true cause of aircraft crashes. Monetary expansion is a *necessary* condition for inflation, in the same way that gravity is a necessary condition for planes to fall out of the sky, but it is by no means *sufficient*. In trying to gauge whether Capitalism 4.0 will eventually succumb to inflation, we must therefore look for more specific risks than the long period of very low interest rates that seems to lie ahead. To judge the true risks to price stability, we must understand why monetary expansion sometimes creates inflation and at other times promotes real noninflationary growth. In other words, we must try to identify the structural factors that can turn monetary expansion from a necessary condition into a sufficient condition for rapid inflation.

In a world economy overburdened with excess capacity in almost every industry and with millions of unemployed workers who are eager to work for competitive wages, monetary expansion should not cause inflation. Low interest rates and the growth of credit should instead create real economic growth, until excess capacity and unemployment are reduced to their long-run average levels—a process that will take three to five years in the most optimistic global growth forecasts and considerably longer than a decade according to the more common assumption of a New Normal of subdued growth. Under certain pathological conditions, however, inflation can accelerate even in the presence of mass unemployment and excess capacity. The world learned that painful lesson in the late 1960s and 1970s, when inflation soared to 20 percent in many countries, despite conditions of mass unemployment and abundant excess capacity worldwide.

Stagflation, as the lethal mix of inflation and stagnation came to be described in the 1970s, is a political nightmare, especially in a model of capitalism that views government as responsible for maintaining economic stability. Stagflation leaves politicians and central bankers with no acceptable policy options. If they cut interest rates or increase public borrowing and spending, they are rightly damned for fuelling more inflation; if they tighten monetary and fiscal policy, they are equally damned for aggravating unemployment. A return of stagflation, therefore, would quickly sabotage the new mixed-economy model of capitalism emerging from the crisis, just as in the 1970s stagflation demolished the government-led model of Capitalism 2.

Could the nightmare of stagflation come back? To answer this question, we need to understand why stagflation is an unusual and pathological condition and why this strange pathology suddenly infected the world economy forty years ago.

In theory, stagflation should never occur in a properly functioning market economy that corresponds even roughly to the competitive model. If there is an excess supply of consumer goods and most other products, wages and prices should not generally rise. If there is mass unemployment, wages should remain subdued and maybe even fall; they should certainly not rise at an accelerating rate. Why, then, did the impossible combination of inflation and unemployment suddenly become inevitable in the 1970s?

To make stagflation possible, competition must be thwarted and excess supply must be blocked by barriers and cartels of various kinds. In the late 1960s and 1970s, at least four such barriers to competition rose much higher. Unions prevented wage competition, despite high unemployment. Trade barriers protected nationally dominant companies from global competitors and allowed them to raise prices. Commodity cartels such as OPEC boosted raw material prices even though the world was awash with excess supplies. And rapid expansion of governments insulated large parts of the economy from market competition altogether.

Are these phenomena, or others of a similar nature, likely to recur in the decade ahead and create conditions for a new era of stagflation? Not yet, though the risks just listed give cause for concern. Let us consider the outlook for these four risks.

Unions and Wages

Probably the most important structural change that helped to eliminate stagflation in the 1980s was the weakening of organized labor after the upsurge of union militancy that began in the late 1960s. The 1950s and early 1960s were generally a period of peaceful labor relations, as productivity grew rapidly in the postwar recovery, while workers and union leaders still scarred by memories of terrible unemployment in the 1930s were content to moderate their wage demands. Moreover, the proportion of unionized workers in the private-sector labor force started falling gradually in the 1960s as the United States, Britain, and other advanced economies reduced their reliance on large-scale manufacturing. Toward the end of that decade, however, the accelerating growth of public-sector employment began to offset this decline in union power.

More importantly, the twenty-five years of continuous full employment after 1945 transformed the psychology of the postwar generation of workers and union leaders. Full employment began to be taken for granted and unions became increasingly militant in demanding a larger share of corporate and national incomes, as predicted by Michal Kalecki in his 1943 article.[25] Companies and governments were generally willing to concede to these demands for higher wages against the background of rapid global growth—and this labor market pressure started turning easy monetary conditions into inflation. After the power of organized labor was broken by the combined effects of tough antiunion laws and the abandonment of Keynesian full-employment policies in the Thatcher-Reagan period, inflation subsided. By 1982, the threat of stagflation had disappeared.

Will organized labor regain its erstwhile power and rapidly push up wages, now that the credibility of Keynesian policies has been restored by the crisis? This scenario seems unlikely. On the contrary, the sharp increase in unemployment, which is likely to persist for years after the crisis, even according to the most favorable economic assumptions, will stave off the day when workers can again take their jobs for granted, as they did in the 1960s. It will therefore be many years before labor regains the confidence and bargaining power to press for a larger share of the economic pie. If an inflationary threat does emerge from the labor market in the second half of the decade, it will result not from union power but from demographic changes and the growth of the public sector, a topic to which we return at the end of this chapter.

OPEC and Oil

Soaring oil and commodity prices were the second obvious factor contributing to the stagflation of the 1970s and early 1980s. The OPEC oil embargo of 1973 pushed up prices to previously unimaginable levels and was able to keep them high for several years despite falling demand. OPEC's unexpected success inspired attempts at imitation by other commodity cartels—in copper, tin, rubber, and coffee—although none of these were successful for more than a few months. Could soaring oil and commodity prices pose a similar threat to the world economy when the postcrisis recovery picks up steam? The doubling of oil prices between 2006 and the summer of 2008 suggested this, but as in the case of labor pressures, the depth of the post-Lehman recession staved off the inflationary risk for the United States and Europe. On the other hand, in China and other emerging economies that rapidly rebounded from the crisis, commodity-driven inflation has become a major threat.

In any case, the role of commodities in the stagflation of the 1970s should not be overstated. Inflation was already accelerating worldwide from 1969 onward, well before the oil embargo in 1973. And although the sudden quadrupling of oil prices seemed to be the event that set off the most spectacular part of the inflationary upsurge in 1974–75 (and again in 1979–80), the real trouble was caused by the wage increases demanded (and obtained) by workers to compensate for the rising price of oil. Wages behaved very differently after the 2008 oil shock, as workers and their unions gave greater priority to keeping their jobs than to raising wages.

Unless labor market conditions experience major changes during the next decade, wages are unlikely to rise to compensate for higher prices of oil. Labor's weak bargaining power in the postcrisis environment also means that stagflation is unlikely to occur in the long run from oil and other commodities physically running out. Even if the exhaustion of global oil supplies happens sooner than expected and sends energy prices sharply higher, this will not produce inflation unless wages rise in tandem. If labor's bargaining power remains weak, rising oil prices will simply reduce the amount of money people have to spend on other goods and services. Thus, dwindling oil supplies will lead to big shifts in *relative* prices between oil and other goods but not to an increase in the average price level of all goods. The same will be true if energy prices rise substantially, as they probably will, to promote investment in more secure and less polluting energy sources. On balance, oil and commodities seem unlikely to return as major risk factors for stagflation in the next decade.

Protectionism and Global Competition

Protectionist trade restrictions were a third significant factor in the stagflation of the 1960s and 1970s. Before the early 1970s, trade had been growing extremely rapidly as Europe and Japan recovered from the war years and American multinationals extended their technology and managerial skills around the world. But this growth of trade slowed abruptly from about 1970 and remained fairly stagnant until the mid-1980s, partly as a result of protectionism and partly because of the international financial chaos that followed the breakdown of the Bretton Woods currency system. This slowdown in world trade growth meant that many industries operating in relatively closed domestic markets—for example, steel and autos— were able to raise their prices. Wages for unionized workers in these relatively protected industries kept rising even faster, despite a global excess of steel and auto capacity and an even bigger excess supply of willing industrial workers around the world.

The global trend toward protectionism and declining import penetration was reversed in the late 1980s, as the world monetary system stabilized, the free-market philosophy of Capitalism 3 gained worldwide acceptance, and the megatrends of globalization became established. These events helped eliminate the last vestiges of stagflation from the world economy by the early 1990s. But the trend toward globalization may not be irreversible.

Another upsurge of protectionism, or at least a partial reversal of globalization, seems like a much more plausible cause of stagflation in the coming decade than either labor militancy or energy and commodity cartels. As discussed in the preceding section, it is almost inevitable that imports will decline as a share of GDP in the United States, Britain, and many southern European countries. The only question is whether this reduction in imports will be driven by normal market mechanisms, such as shifts in competitiveness, or by political decisions, such as the creation of new trade barriers against China. Whatever the mechanism that causes the slowdown in import growth, inflationary pressures are bound to intensify.

As long as unemployment remains very high, the United States, Britain, Spain, and other highly leveraged economies will probably absorb the rising cost of imports entirely through lower living standards and real wages. But as these countries move back toward full employment, the rebalancing of global growth will make them more prone to inflation than they were in the precrisis years. From this point of view, the sooner the world economy can be rebalanced, eliminating excessive trade surpluses and deficits worldwide, the smaller the risk of dangerous inflationary pressures. Unfortunately, as discussed previously in this chapter, the prospects of such a global rebalancing occurring quickly and smoothly do not seem bright. Protectionism and deglobalization therefore could create the conditions for stagflation to return.

Big Government

From the mid-1960s until the late 1970s, the world experienced a large upsurge of government spending and employment. This was clearly one of the major causes of stagflation. Whatever one's political outlook about the virtues or vices of public spending, there can be no denying that government-administered activities are generally insensitive to competition. The growth of public-sector activities, therefore, inevitably and automatically makes an economy more prone to inflation since public-sector prices are almost completely insulated from competition and public-sector jobs are almost entirely unionized. And public-sector inflation can easily turn into stagflation, because wages and prices can keep on rising regardless of economic stagnation and mass unemployment.

This growth of the government's share in total economic activity was arrested and then reversed in America and Britain with the arrival of Ronald Reagan and Margaret Thatcher, respectively. Even in France under President Mitterrand, the relative growth of the public sector temporarily slowed.

In the years leading up to the crisis, however, this reduction in the size of government was abruptly reversed. Government employment and spending began to grow rapidly again from 2002 onward, not only in Britain under Labour, but also, much more surprisingly, in America under the apparently conservative administration of George W. Bush. The continuing expansion of the public sector, whatever the politics behind it, does increase the danger of inflation, and this will remain true whether or not the world emerges rapidly from recession. Big government is the only force in society that is capable of generating serious inflation even in conditions of mass unemployment and industrial overcapacity—in other words, of bringing back the nightmare of stagflation.

Stagflation, in turn, is a phenomenon so pathological and dangerous that it would almost certainly trigger another conservative counterrevolution, reversing all the recent progress toward an understanding of the constructive role of government in a modern capitalist economy. The supreme irony of Capitalism 4.0—and the greatest risk to its future—is that, in the process of recognizing the *importance* of government, the new political philosophy will try to expand the *size* of government. Attempting to expand the size of government, especially in the strained budgetary conditions created by the deep recession and financial crisis, would quickly lead to the self-destruction of the new model of capitalism. This is the paradox investigated in the next chapter, on the politics of Capitalism 4.0.

CHAPTER SEVENTEEN

Politics in Capitalism 4.0

The forms of government let fools contest
Whate'er is best administered is best.

—Alexander Pope

POLITICS WAS TRANSFORMED by the financial crisis in ways that seem contradictory but in fact are mutually reinforcing. After the bank bailouts and the U.S. government's takeover of General Motors, conservative ideologues could no longer present freer markets and less government as plausible answers to every challenge facing a capitalist society. Longer and deeper reflection on the crisis pointed to another even more disturbing conclusion for advocates of unrestricted private enterprise. Not only had the rigorously free-market model of capitalism introduced in the 1980s by Margaret Thatcher and Ronald Reagan proved unmanageable and unstable, it also had failed to produce the great leap forward in living standards and productivity claimed by the proponents of deregulation and minimal government.

The excuse offered by many conservatives after the crisis was that a truly free-market approach had never been properly tried and that all financial problems and international imbalances resulted from too much government interference and regulation, not too little. But such claims are too far-fetched to gain any political traction outside the Tea Party in the United States. It is hardly conceivable that democratic societies will try even more deregulation and even less government control after a thirty-year program of ambitious deregulation has so spectacularly failed. That leaves two possible political responses to the crisis.

The first possibility is to treat the financially led global capitalism introduced in the 1980s as basically a sound system, but one that needs to evolve in response to changing conditions—essentially the argument presented in this book. The Thatcher-Reagan age of capitalism, described here as Capitalism 3, produced tremendous economic progress and social benefits for about twenty-five years. Capitalism 3 finally succumbed, however, to an overzealous application of its own free-market ideology by an incompetent U.S. government and a misguided economic establishment. This interpretation of the crisis implies that economic liberalization and globalization should be preserved as far as possible and used as the foundation for a new adaptive, mixed-economy version of the capitalist system, which should prove even more productive and successful.

The second plausible response to the crisis is to argue that Thatcher-Reagan capitalism has been a fraud and a failure. The economic growth supposedly unleashed by the reforms of the 1980s was just an illusion, conjured up by a gigantic Madoff-style Ponzi scheme. After all the speculative bubbles and phony financial froth were blown away, the true wealth created from the 1980s onward turned out to be much smaller than the wealth created in the era of government-led, strictly regulated, high-tax capitalism from 1945 until the 1970s.

On this reading of history, even the apparent resolution of class conflicts that was arguably the greatest achievement of the 1980s was a mirage. The living standards of working people had actually fallen and this pauperization had simply been disguised by the ultimately ruinous build-up of mortgage debt. As this illusion vanished, the middle class and the poor should have realize that they gained nothing from the reforms of the free-market period. Their prospects in an austere postcrisis New Normal would be even worse than they were in the 1980s and 1990s and, therefore, far worse than in the Keynesian Golden Age of the postwar decades. If this view of the world turns out to be right and the post-crisis decades turn out to be even tougher for working people than the 1980s and 1990s, free-market capitalism would seem to be doomed, the Thatcher-Reagan reforms would be seen as a failure, and a return to the big government approach would seem inevitable. Yet oddly enough, this interpretation of the crisis has been embraced by almost all conservative economists and politicians. They continue to extol the virtues of the Thatcher-Reagan era, while simultaneously deriding as a cruel deception its claims to have raised living standards and accelerated genuine economic growth.

Either way, the events of 2007–09 thus marked a historic setback for free-market conservatism and seemed certain to usher in a period of more progressive politics worldwide. The only question seemed to be whether this new era would be led by centrist reformers or by a more radical left-wing politics that explicitly rejected many aspects of financial capitalism and globalization.

There was, however, another possibility: that moderate conservatives would seize the chance to modernize and improve the management of capitalism along the lines this book has suggested. Immediately after the crisis, the possibility that conservative politics would benefit from the near-collapse of capitalism, while progressive parties suffered, seemed out of the question. Yet this is exactly what happened in much of the world. How can we explain this paradox and what might it imply for the future?

The crisis revealed that the choice between free-enterprise capitalism and government-led socialism, sometimes parodied as America versus Europe, was a false dichotomy. American business could not survive without competent government, any more than European governments could survive without the tax revenues they raised from profitable private enterprise. At the same time, however, the huge financial costs of the recession and crisis created powerful pressures to reduce the size of government and brought forward by several decades the point when the costs of supporting the aging baby boom generation would become unsupportable, a fiscal crunch that governments had hoped to delay until around 2030.

The crisis convinced voters everywhere of the need for competent political leadership and active government. Politicians on the Right had no compunctions about suddenly demanding that the U.S. government "do something" about unemployment after the crisis and accusing the Obama administration of failing to act with sufficient boldness to overcome the recession. Traditional progressives, on the other hand, were thwarted and confused. Reverting to the New Deal Keynesian approach of Capitalism 2, as proposed by radicals such as Paul Krugman in America and Ed Balls in Britain, was not a serious option because governments had reached the political limits of their ability to borrow—and, in any case, voters distrusted politicians and public institutions almost as much as they hated banks.

To make matters worse for the Left, the crisis seemed to conform to a long-standing pattern of democracy, whereby conservative parties tend to do better when societies are under stress. As voters see their incomes and wealth eroding and find their traditional lifestyles under threat, the generalized demands for change escalate but the willingness to embrace any specific changes tends to disappear.

How, then, might all these conflicting trends in politics be reconciled? Not through a left-wing return to the bureaucratic expansionism of the 1960s and 1970s. And not by a right-wing reversion to the market fundamentalism of Capitalism 3. The only plausible way for politics to move forward in this environment will be by recognizing that government must expand and contract at the same time—a paradox very much in the spirit of Capitalism 4.0.

When capitalist society is seen as an evolving and adaptive system, the paradox of simultaneous government shrinkage and expansion should be neither intellectually surprising nor politically controversial. In the postcrisis phase of capitalism, the boundary between government and market will not be fixed or moved monotonically in one direction—always toward more government or always toward more market. The balance of responsibilities will keep shifting—with a bigger role for politics in some areas in certain periods and more reliance on markets in others. A larger role for government in managing the economy and in regulating finance would accompany the government's withdrawal from other areas of activity, to maintain a balance between government and private enterprise that is acceptable to distrustful voters.

A look around the world at how economic and social activities are organized suggests that many public services now provided by government, both in America and Europe, are not, in reality, public goods. The United States, for example, is generally viewed as an essentially private enterprise economy that confines its government to a much smaller role than most countries in Europe. Yet postal services, roads, bridges, airports, and public transport, which are often owned and managed by private enterprise in Europe, are almost entirely government-controlled in the United States. In

Europe, by contrast, private universities are almost unheard-of, despite the overwhelming evidence that higher education in Europe and Britain has fallen dangerously far behind America's largely private system.

Other activities have achieved the best results when operated by private business but regulated closely by governments. Banking is an obvious example, but another that will ultimately prove even more important, from both a political and an economic standpoint, is medical care. For politicians, health care, pensions, and education will ultimately raise much more difficult and politically controversial issues than banking.

It is far from clear that governments should dominate the provision of health care, pensions, and education, especially as societies become more affluent and complex and citizens demand greater control over their lives. It is equally unclear how governments that want to maintain or expand their citizens' entitlements to health, education, pensions, and social welfare will be able to raise the taxes required.

The earlier versions of capitalism offered fairly simple answers to such questions, but these no longer work. In Capitalism 1, there were almost no government responsibilities for social services and hence no serious revenue problems. Capitalism 2 saw a rapid expansion of social entitlements, leading to unacceptably high taxes. Capitalism 3, from the 1980s onward, believed it could square the circle by slashing all government programs except those related to health and pensions. But this approach, too, was reaching the limits of political and fiscal tolerance as the crisis struck and demolished the Capitalism 3 model. Now the shocks of recession and financial crisis have made financing of health and pensions unsustainable in almost all countries and will require far-reaching reforms. In considering these reforms, politicians and voters will have to ask themselves two related questions.

First, to what extent should governments dominate the provision of health care, pensions, and education in affluent, advanced economies with sophisticated consumers? After all, in many developing countries such as China and India, where educational standards and life expectancies are rising most rapidly, these responsibilities are left largely to the private sector and to market forces, despite the fact that populations are much poorer and less well-informed.

Second, what kind of tax structure will be able to pay for the government services that citizens demand? One of the little-noticed consequences of the 2007–09 crisis is that the U.S. and British fiscal systems, which rely heavily on income and capital taxes from their wealthiest citizens, have produced much bigger deficits than the tax systems of continental Europe, which raise most of their revenues from consumption, energy, and payroll taxes on the middle classes.

The implication is that left-wing politicians in America and Britain who want to expand or even maintain government spending now face an unexpected dilemma: Either they must allow the rich to keep getting richer to raise the necessary revenues from highly progressive taxes, or they must redesign the U.S. and British tax structures to bear more heavily on the middle-class and the poor.

The rest of this chapter will shed some light on such questions by considering ten surprising changes in politics that are likely to happen under Capitalism 4.0.

Conservatives Will Keep Winning Until Progressives Find a Narrative

Left-of-center parties around the world have failed to benefit from a catastrophic crisis of laissez-faire capitalism and an unprecedented public revulsion against wealth and finance. This failure points to an asymmetry between progressive and conservative politics that is particularly damaging to the Left in periods of dramatic economic change.

In times of social upheaval, conservatives always know what they are fighting for: to preserve, as far as possible, the status quo of wealth, income, and effective political power. To achieve their central objective of preserving as much as possible of the status quo, conservative politicians and voters are willing to bury minor ideological differences and unite. Progressives, by contrast, know only what they are against: the status quo, which they consider unjust. But if and when they are in power, progressives are riven by disagreements about what exactly is wrong with existing social and economic arrangements and how they should be replaced. Choosing from an infinite range of possible reforms, progressives find it difficult to unite around a single political program or even a single analysis of what they are trying to achieve and why. In periods of great insecurity and economic uncertainty, this asymmetry between defending the familiar and leaping into the unknown can become a fatal handicap. The only way progressive politicians can overcome it is with a convincing narrative about what they are trying to achieve and what has gone wrong with the status quo.

The United States Democrats could have argued, quite justly, that a relatively normal boom-bust cycle was turned into the greatest financial disaster in history by the Bush administration's ideological refusal to intervene in the mortgage markets and the banking system at a much earlier stage. Instead, the Democrats directed most of their political fire against bankers and Wall Street and President Obama accepted personal responsibility for the crisis. As a result, American voters started to blame the Democrats for unemployment and the recession and quickly lost sight of the Bush administration's role in bringing about the crisis.

The Left's failure to offer a convincing narrative about the crisis contrasts with the way conservatives handled the crises that confronted Ronald Reagan and Margaret Thatcher when they came to power. Reagan and Thatcher refused to take any blame for the economic hardships. Instead, they devoted the early years of their governments to convincing voters that economic disaster was entirely the responsibility of previous left-wing governments, militant unions, and liberal progressive elites. By the time economic conditions started improving, voters were so convinced of this narrative that the credit for recovery went entirely to Reaganomics and Thatcherism.

The economic pattern of the early 1980s may well be repeated, with the U.S. economy recovering strongly after the crisis. But progressive politicians are unlikely to get the credit for saving the economy, unless they can agree on a convincing narrative to explain the transition from the failed business and financial system to a new model of capitalism.

The one narrative that *cannot* work is to blame an enormously complex story on a single populist scapegoat: the greedy banker. With banks recovering from the crisis more profitably and quickly than voters had been led to expect, politicians of all parties have been branded by public sentiment as stooges of the very bankers they tried to blame. A proper debate about the role of government will become possible only when the public understands that a normal financial cycle was turned into a disaster by the polarized and oversimplified philosophy of market fundamentalism, not by bankers' or regulators' personality flaws. By offering such a systemic account of the crisis, politicians could capture the public imagination with a postcrisis narrative that is more constructive than the lynching of greedy bankers—and ultimately more dramatic. Political leaders could explain that with the demise of the old capitalist system, the world must now embark on the most exciting political project in a generation: the design of a new model of capitalism.

More Government Means Smaller Government

The central political paradox of Capitalism 4.0 is that a bigger role for government in macroeconomic management and financial regulation will have to be combined with a generally smaller and less costly government. This paradox follows inexorably from the laws of arithmetic. The Lehman crisis proved that a modern capitalist system cannot survive with a minimalist, do-nothing government; but the subsequent recession slashed tax revenues to the point where all government activities have to be drastically cut. Choices are thus inevitable between higher taxes and cutbacks in social entitlements or big reductions in all other discretionary public activities, including the core responsibilities of government, ranging from defense and law enforcement to support for scientific research and national culture. The simultaneous need for more government and for smaller government will demand a reassessment of political priorities on a scale not seen since the 1980s. In comparison with these existential choices, the rows over bankers' bonuses and financial regulation will appear inconsequential.

The only rational way of making such choices is through an open-minded and nonideological debate about the balance of responsibilities between government and private enterprise. In the short term, such debate has become more difficult than ever because the crisis has destroyed public trust in politicians as much as in bankers. To restore some faith in politics and trust in politicians, significant political groups will have to start explaining that the true origins of the crisis lay in the exaggeration of market fundamentalist ideology, not just in financial chicanery and regulatory incompetence. Progressives have a clear incentive to do this but may be unable to unite on any coherent narrative.

The incentive for conservatives is less obvious but ultimately more powerful: the raison d'etre of conservative politics is to preserve the capitalist system and to ensure that it creates ever greater wealth. To do this, conservatives must be ready to reform capitalism and to draw the appropriate lessons from systemic crises. Over time, conservative political movements, and their business supporters, whose main concern is to create economic conditions for faster growth and higher profits, will understand that simply reverting to the flawed market fundamentalist system that crashed in 2007–09 is far too risky. A new version of capitalism will emerge one way or another, but unless progressives can unite around a coherent vision, the task of creating the next generation of capitalism will fall to conservatives by default.

Democracy Means Less Power for Public Opinion

Continuous and ubiquitous opinion polling is transforming America and Britain from representative to direct democracies. Modern technology has made opinion polling so cheap and rapid that government by plebiscite, citizens' initiative, or Tea Party is becoming a possibility. The logical conclusion of this trend could be seen in the political stalemate in California during the crisis. The California constitution was changed by citizens' initiatives to require a supermajority in the legislature to raise taxes or to make major spending cuts. Because these supermajorities were almost always unattainable, California ran into continuous deficits, which in turn were also prohibited by the constitution. Similar gridlock has spread to Washington through the Senate's supermajority voting rules.

Such political chaos might have seemed acceptable and even welcome to the market fundamentalist worldview, which saw government activity as either frivolous or destructive. But maintaining the principle of constitutional representation is incompatible with an electronic version of the

Athenian agora (denounced as mob rule by both Aristotle and Plato). To make matters worse, the media and elected politicians themselves are starting to treat as politically illegitimate any government actions that defy public opinion. Whether elected officials are voting to send troops to foreign wars, to raise taxes, or reform health care, not only are they tempted to follow opinion polls to maximize their reelection chances, but the political culture regards it as their democratic duty to do so.

This trend toward direct democracy is a dangerous development for any complex society, especially ones where governments will have to play an increasing role in economic regulation and make difficult decisions about priorities and tradeoffs. Because opinion polls and referenda make no connection between higher spending and higher taxes while voters reflexively blame the government for anything that goes wrong, direct democracy will always demand more government without agreeing to bear the cost. It will be ever more tempting for oppositions, both on the Left and the populist Right, to mimic public opinion by complaining of government inertia and ineffectiveness—on jobs, health, housing, and so on—while refusing to acknowledge any connection with the necessary taxes. Looking back at the 1930s, the 1970s, and indeed the 1980s, a period of such Latin American–style populism may be inevitable during the sometimes chaotic transition from one version of capitalism to the next. The alternative course of synthesis and rational compromise will be achieved only when public belief in the importance of government is restored.

Either through deeper political reflection or through a series of further crises, the politics of rational choice among conflicting priorities will eventually prevail over California-style gridlock and rule by opinion polls. One way or another, the capitalist system's instinct for self-preservation will have to reverse the shift from representative to direct democracy.

Bigger Deficits Are Necessary but Impossible

Because of the recession and financial crisis, government deficits, public spending policies, and tax structures have all become unsustainable. Effectively, they have all coalesced into a single issue. Although pension and health entitlements were always going to become unaffordable as the baby boom generation retired, the recession has brought forward the fiscal day of reckoning by at least a decade. Had it not been for the crisis, tough fiscal choices might have been delayed until the 2020s or even the 2030s, but now every advanced economy must act before the middle of the present decade. To make sensible decisions on taxes and spending, it is essential for politicians and voters to understand that the main threat to government finances comes not from the large, but temporary, deficits caused by the credit crunch, but from pension and health care entitlements.

The fiscal costs of aging to the U.S. government, even assuming some moderation in the relentless rise of health care prices and no further expansions of health or pension entitlements, are calculated by the IMF as 495 percent of U.S. GDP.[1] That figure is thirteen times the accumulated cost of the deficits created by the recession and financial crisis, and is equivalent to roughly $70 trillion in today's money, or $400,000 of negative wealth for every American household. In comparison with such figures, public worries about $800-billion bank bailouts and fiscal stimulus plans should pale into insignificance.[2] The situation is broadly similar in Britain, Europe, and Japan.[3]

Large government deficits were necessary in the years after the crisis to support economic activity through the recession. In this sense, Keynesian economics was fully vindicated by the experience of 2009–10. But Keynesian economics also implies that public debts created in recessions must be brought under control as economic growth returns—and the only way to do this will be to recognize the enormous gap opening up between tax revenues and government promises about health and pensions. Facing up to the inevitable choice between significantly higher taxes and major reductions in health and pensions entitlements will be the greatest political challenge of the postcrisis years.

Priorities: Less Spending and More Taxes

Aneurin Bevan, the Labour politician remembered as the founding father of Britain's National Health Service, used to say that "the language of priorities is the religion of Socialism."[4] In the postcrisis period, priorities will have to become the religion of all governments, whatever their political ideology. For government debts to be stabilized at manageable levels, taxes, entitlements, and government services will have to be reformed in every advanced economy. But how can this be achieved in a political environment in which higher taxes and reduced entitlements are off the agenda?

The answer is that in the postcrisis environment, both conservative and progressive politicians will eventually be forced to engage in an honest debate about priorities or sacrifice their most cherished objectives: a robust economy and financial system, in the case of conservatives, and a viable welfare state, in the case of the Left. As a result, the public will in turn be forced to understand that government revenues are simply not sufficient to pay for the entitlements for which they have voted—and that cutting back the size and cost of nonentitlement services provided by government will never be remotely enough to bridge the gap. This is especially clear in the United States.

Even if the U.S. government's entire discretionary non-defense spending—everything government does in homeland security, education, science, transport, and so on—were reduced to zero, the federal budget would still be deep in deficit and the long-term outlook for public debt would still be unsustainable, given the present structure of entitlements and taxes.[5]

If the American public and politicians decide simply to ignore the budgetary arithmetic and run down all the functions of government apart from the issuance of checks for Medicare and Social Security, the United States, despite all its technological advantages, will eventually lose its position of global leadership and power. In the early 1990s, as Russia descended into ungovernable bankruptcy after the breakup of the Soviet Union, Russians derisively described their own country as "Upper Volta with rockets." Fiscal ungovernability could turn the United States into an Italy with Harvard and Microsoft. Something will have to give. Either voters and politicians will overcome the taboos introduced in bygone political eras against middle-class tax hikes, cuts in entitlements, and government regulation of medical costs, or the United States will cease to exist as a fully functioning sovereign nation. Given America's two-hundred-fifty-year history of overcoming existential crises, it is not hard to guess which outcome is the more likely. It may, however, take another financial crisis to force the decision.

In Britain and most of Europe, a similar debate about public finances has already been largely resolved. Cutbacks in public spending and increases in taxation have been accepted as inevitable. The debate is only about the nature of the tax increases and the spending cuts. Conservatives will want to reduce the role of the state by abolishing public services that could be provided by the private sector or left to individuals. Progressives will have to accept the fiscal arithmetic, but then offer a different response: to maintain or even improve the quality of public services while simultaneously reducing their cost.

Parties of the Left tend to believe this combination is logically impossible—in their worldview, any reductions in public spending are equivalent ipso facto to cuts in the services that the government provides. This idea, that the standard of public services is equivalent to the level of public spending, might have been defensible in the precomputer economy, when service industries were believed to be incapable of productivity growth. But in the modern economy, equating the quality of government with its cost is absurd. In Britain, for example, a budget reduction of 10 percent, spread over three years, is always described as a "savage cut." If the directors of any private company sent their line managers instructions to cut costs by 3 percent a year, this would not be considered an insuperable challenge, still less a sadistic abuse.

The political challenge for the Left in the coming decades will be to find ways to deliver the high standards of public service demanded by voters at a cost that taxpayers are willing to accept and the private economy is able to support. In Capitalism 4.0, politicians who equate all economies in public spending with the reactionary destruction of public services will find themselves increasingly marginalized.

International Experience: Learning from Others' Mistakes

In debating the balance between government and private enterprise, politicians who appeal to a priori ideologies of more government or more market will be gradually displaced by pragmatists who follow Franklin Roosevelt's call for "bold, persistent experimentation."[6] But even better than conducting experiments on the citizens and institutions of one's own country is to observe the experience of others. The United States, Europe, Japan, and

Australasia, instead of boasting of their own superior socio-economic models and rubbishing those of other countries, would do well to study one another's successes and failures. As Bismarck once remarked, "Fools learn from their mistakes; I prefer to learn from the mistakes of others."

In a period when all nations are making difficult decisions on priorities for public spending and the provision of public goods, an exchange of ideas and experience between countries at comparable levels of economic and social development will be valuable.

International experience suggests, for example, that transport systems, highways, and energy utilities generally work better under private management and ownership than under state control, even though strategic direction from government is necessary to achieve social objectives, for example, through taxes on pollution, subsidies for the social benefits of public transport, research on new technologies, insurance for nuclear installations, and premium tariffs for renewable power. Yet many services that have long been privatized in Europe are still provided by government entities in the supposedly free-market United States. For example, 89 percent of American households are served by public-sector water utilities, whereas in Britain and France the proportion is less than 10 percent.[7]

International comparisons would therefore suggest that many utility, transport, and land assets owned by various levels of American government could be readily privatized to reduce U.S. public debts. Such privatization would also help to reverse the chronic underinvestment in infrastructure that sometimes makes America look like a Third World country to visitors from Europe and Japan. An example of privatization where the benefits of experience could flow from America to Europe is higher education, which is completely state controlled and rapidly decaying in Europe and Britain but largely private and thriving in the United States.

All these are minor matters, however, in comparison with the really daunting public spending challenge facing all governments: how to deal with the core social entitlements to health, pensions, and basic education that consume roughly 70 percent of tax revenues[8] in all advanced nations. In dealing with these enormous and relentlessly growing burdens, the United States, Britain, and Europe have much to learn from each other's experiences and mistakes.

Commanding Heights:
As Socialism Has Retreated, It Has Won

In the 1950s and 1960s, the dream of the Labour Party in Britain was to "seize the Commanding Heights of the economy," leaving the unimportant foothills of economic activity to the private enterprise. In those days, the Commanding Heights were seen as the coal, steel, and railway industries—a perception that in itself reveals the absurdity of socialist central planning. Today, coal, steel, and railways have been privatized and have shrunk into insignificance, but the old socialist dream has been unexpectedly accomplished through the government dominance of health care, pensions, and education.

Health, education, and retirement savings already account for 20 percent to 30 percent of GDP and employment in all advanced economies—far more than the heavy industries coveted by socialists ever did. In the coming decades, they will continue to rapidly expand, as populations get older and economic activity becomes increasingly dependent on knowledge, advanced technology, and culture. Health, education, and pensions are the new economy's Commanding Heights. In postcrisis capitalism, with the government destined to play a much bigger role in the economy through demand management and financial regulation, maintaining a reasonable balance of power between the private and public sectors will require the government to retreat from some or all of these social fronts.

Education is the area where private provision is likely to grow most quickly and government to retreat. In higher education, this process is being driven by the overwhelming dominance of American universities in all branches of scholarship and knowledge. If other countries want to keep up with knowledge-based industries, they will have no choice but to reform higher education systems to make them more comparable to the United States. For school education, the prospects are less clear. Primary and secondary education requires government compulsion and subsidies as well as social consensus on broad educational standards. It is far from clear, however, whether schools are best run by public or private enterprise.

Educating children, perhaps more than any other human activity, raises endless questions to which no one can claim to have found all the answers.

Indeed, almost every country in the world believes itself today to be facing some kind of educational crisis. Under these circumstances, the best hopes for improvement must surely come from various market mechanisms and experiments, with different schools trying out many different approaches and with successes distinguished from failures through the trial and error of consumer choice. The standard objection to such choice is that some children will end up with a worse education than others, either because their parents make the wrong decisions or because the most popular schools will not admit everyone who applies. But after fifty years of claiming to deliver uniform educational standards for all children, centralized systems have manifestly failed in this objective, as in so many others. This is hardly surprising, because parents can never be prevented from promoting their own children's interests in a free society (or indeed in an unfree one, as evidenced by the revival of the hereditary principle in the government of North Korea).

It seems likely that as Capitalism 4.0 redraws boundaries between the state and the market, education will experience more competition and private provision—a gradual retreat by the government from this section, at least, of the Commanding Heights.

Health Reform: More Government and More Market

America's traditional insistence that private citizens should take responsibility for their own health care can be seen as evidence of proud self-reliance or shameful inhumanity. Choosing between these interpretations is a matter of ideological taste. So too is the British belief that medical attention should always be available to everyone on equal terms without any payment, at least at the time of need.

It is far from obvious whether the British are right to view medicine as a public good, to be provided equally to all citizens by the government, in the same way as law enforcement, or whether it should be treated as it is in America—as a private purchase, not very different in principle from the consumption of food, clothes, or housing, all of which are left entirely to private enterprise and free markets, even though they are essential human needs. But such theoretical and moral issues will no longer be the driving forces of health reform as governments are forced to clear up the fiscal debris of the crisis.

Whether or not voters experience a Damascene conversion in their attitudes to sickness and health, both America and Britain are becoming increasingly aware that their present health care systems are economically unaffordable, albeit in opposite ways. The only plausible solutions in both countries will involve a redrawing of the boundaries between the market and the State.

U.S. health-care costs have long been completely out of line with costs in other countries. The United States spends $2.5 trillion ($8,100 per head) on health care, or 18 percent of its GDP. This is half as much again as the 11 percent of GDP spent in France and Germany and almost double the 9 percent in Britain and the OECD as a whole. The world's next highest spender is Switzerland at only 12 percent of GDP. Yet in the United States, medical outcomes such as cancer and cardiac survival rates are generally no better than the OECD average and substantially worse than in France, Switzerland, and Japan.[9]

Until recently, however, the vast disparities between United States and international health costs made no impression on U.S. public opinion. Americans have simply assumed that the rest of the world was out of step. Americans believed that their system might be more expensive, but delivered more innovation and greater patient satisfaction than socialized medicine in other countries, often using the rationed and underfunded British National Health Service (NHS) as their counterexample.

In a mirror image of the false dichotomies distorting the U.S. health care debate, Britons have been told that American-style privatization, which would more than double costs and simultaneously reduce the scope of their health care, was the only alternative to a state-run NHS. It is often pointed out in Britain, for example, that the U.S. government spends as much in relation to national income on Medicare and Medicaid, which only offer partial coverage to 30 percent of Americans, as the British government does on the entire NHS, which provides unlimited coverage to the entire population.

In clinging to these ideological false dichotomies, so characteristic of the Capitalism 3 mindset, both the United States and Britain have studiously ignored the multitude of other countries, such as France, Germany, Switzerland, Canada, Australia, and Japan, which have combined public and private provisions in ways that deliver far better medical outcomes and greater customer satisfaction than the British system, at far lower cost than the United States. But why should anything change in the years ahead? The answer is that the financial crisis will focus attention on economic priorities as never before.

In the United States, the escalating costs of Medicare and Medicaid, especially with the addition of the Bush administration's unfunded prescription-drug benefit, account for most of the long-term costs of aging that are driving the government toward insolvency.[10] More importantly, the pressure of medical costs on private businesses and households is changing many political calculations in the postcrisis environment.

In Britain, political thinking will at some point undergo a comparable conversion, but in the opposite direction. The dark, almost unmentionable secret that will haunt British politics for the next decade is that the National Health Service has become an incubus, sucking the life out of all other public services, which have to be starved of funds to meet the insatiable demands of the NHS. Spending by the NHS has risen from 6.6 percent of GDP in 2001 to almost 10 percent of GDP in 2010, accounting for two-thirds of the increase in the share of public spending in national income. After the crisis, the public sector as a whole will have to shrink substantially, but health spending will, according to present plans, continue to grow rapidly, as the population ages and medical costs continue to escalate. The logical implication is that all nonmedical public services will continue to deteriorate and public-sector workers will continue to lose their jobs as long as the NHS continues to expand.

At some point in the postcrisis fiscal adjustment, therefore, Britain's progressive politicians will be forced to make a choice: If they want to preserve the rest of the welfare safety net and also represent the interests of public-sector workers outside health care, they must accept the inevitability of NHS reform. They must start campaigning actively for the costs of health care to be partially privatized. Because the NHS was declared sacrosanct in the manifestos of all political parties for the 2010 election, this will be an issue for the next parliament. By that time, however, proponents of active government may call for health reform and privatization, while conservatives view the NHS as a useful mechanism for starving the rest of the public sector.

Health Care Reform Will Become a Conservative Issue

As the recession gives way to global economic recovery and many American companies refocus their business strategies toward exports from a relatively sluggish domestic consumer market, corporate leaders will increasingly recognize the huge competitive disadvantage they suffer by paying almost twice as much for their employees' health insurance as their competitors in Europe and Japan. As long as the dollar remained extremely undervalued in the wake of the subprime crisis, this may not have mattered much. But if, as is likely, the dollar strengthens alongside a U.S. economic recovery, the competitive handicap imposed by U.S. health costs will become a high priority for all major American companies, their lobbyists, and the generally conservative politicians they support.

Following the collapse of General Motors and Chrysler, businesses across America have become aware that both companies were not just hobbled in global competition but ultimately forced into bankruptcy by the ruinous costs of health insurance. This should be a cautionary tale for all American businesses and their shareholders. Employers' responsibility for health insurance means not only a big cost disadvantage against international rivals whose workers are covered by government-financed health plan. In extreme cases, such as automobile manufacturing, the exposure to health costs can result in ownership of the entire company being handed over to its unions and employees.

Meanwhile, individual Americans, their borrowing power eliminated by the credit crunch, are finding extravagant medical costs a luxury they can no longer afford. As President Obama noted in his early efforts to promote health reform, average U.S. health insurance premiums increased by 58 percent during the eight years of the Bush administration, while average wages rose by only 3 percent. The long-term erosion of American living standards by health costs is strikingly illustrated in Figure 17.1.

FIGURE 17.1 U.S. CONSUMER SPENDING WITH AND WITHOUT HEALTH CARE
AS A PERCENT OF GDP

———— Total Consumer Spending   ———— Consumer Spending
          with Health Care   Excluding Health Care

Source: Reuters EcoWin.

This chart illustrates the role of health care costs in driving the "excessive" U.S. consumption widely regarded as the most fundamental cause of the instability in the world economy and of America's transformation from the world's biggest creditor to its biggest borrower. One of the hoariest clichés about the global economy is that America is a greedy and self-indulgent nation, spending more than 70 percent of GDP on private consumption. This compares with figures in the range of 55 percent to 65 percent in other advanced economies and is often cited as evidence of some fundamental malignancy in the structure of America's economy and even its society. But with health care spending excluded, the United States spends just 57 percent of GDP on private consumption, in line with the spending, excluding health care, in other advanced economies such as Germany, Britain, and France.[11] In short, the growth of America's consumption in relation to its income has been due entirely to the cost of health care—and the gap has been steadily increasing for thirty years. It could be argued from these figures that U.S. health spending, even more than Chinese currency manipulation, Alan Greenspan's monetary policy, lax regulation, or bankers' greed, was the true cause of the credit crunch, the subprime crisis, and the collapse of Capitalism 3.3.

Had President Obama focused more attention in the health care debate on costs and less on coverage of the uninsured, he might have managed to convince Americans that their present health care system was unsustainable and threatened bankruptcy not only for the government and individual businesses but for the entire nation. Why he chose not to do this will fasci nate historians, but the relevant question in the present context is whether the emergence of Capitalism 4.0 could create a more conducive environment for future reforms. The answer is Yes—with the main demands for action coming from the business community and the conservative politicians who represent its interests.

Progressives Will Fight for Less Progressive Taxes

Another unexpected by-product of the crisis, especially unsettling to political progressives, will be its effect on the politics of taxation, at least in the United States and Britain. Since the transition from the first era of capitalism to the second in the 1930s, taxes in all advanced economies have served two distinct purposes: to raise revenues for the running of government and to redistribute income from the rich to the poor. For most of the twentieth century, the two functions of financing government and redistributing income appeared to run in parallel, and this simplified the political debate about taxation. Advocates of higher taxes on the Left generally advocated more government activity and more redistribution. Right-wing tax opponents generally objected both to egalitarianism and the expansion of the state. In Capitalism 4.0, however, sharper distinctions will have to be made between the two goals of taxation—revenue raising and redistribution—especially by politicians on the Left because the crisis has revealed an internal contradiction in American and British progressive politics that no one noticed before.

Left-wing parties in Britain and America have fought for generations for more redistributive, or "progressive," tax systems, meaning that the highest possible proportion of revenues should come from the richest people. And, despite big cuts in the top rates of income tax from the 1980s onward, these campaigns have been generally successful—so much so that the United States, despite its image as a fervently antisocialist nation, has probably the world's most progressive tax system, according to OECD figures. Britain, even after Margaret Thatcher, was only slightly behind. This progressivity can be measured in many ways, but the easiest to understand is the share of total household taxes paid by the richest 10 percent of the population. This share is 48 percent in the United States and 39 percent in Britain, compared with an average of 32 percent among the twenty-four countries in the latest OECD study. In supposedly socialist France and Sweden, the corresponding figures are 28 percent and 27 percent.[12]

The reason for this surprising difference in tax structures is that the United States and Britain raise most of their government revenues through taxes on incomes, capital, and corporate profits, which bear mostly on people at the top of the income scale. European countries, by contrast, rely mainly on consumption and energy taxes, which are less redistributive and raise far more money from middle-class taxpayers and even from the moderately poor. Left-leaning politicians in the United States, and also to some extent in Britain, vehemently oppose reforms, such as consumption and energy taxes, that would move their fiscal systems toward the European model, on the grounds that such taxes would bear more on the middle class and the poor than the rich.

The eagerness to preserve a redistributive tax structure, however, results in an ironic consequence, which the crisis has brought to light. If progressive politicians want to finance a bigger government or a more generous welfare state, they have to make sure that the rich keep getting richer. To put it the other way round, if U.S. corporate profits, stock market gains, and high earnings are capped or restrained, either by government fiat or by economic conditions, the only way to finance a generous European-style welfare state is to move toward a less redistributive European-style tax system.

The evidence for these paradoxical conclusions comes from the effect of the crisis on public spending and taxes in the United States, Britain, and

Germany. Consider a question that baffled many economists and government officials during the 2008–09 recession. Why did the U.S. and British governments experience deficit blowouts of unprecedented proportions, while Germany and many other advanced economies that suffered equal or bigger output losses saw their deficits expand much less?

The answer is suggested by looking separately at public spending and taxes. The United States, despite the $800 billion Obama stimulus plan, actually had the smallest increase in public spending of the three countries, partly because of drastic cutbacks by the state governments. U.S. public spending increased by 3.2 percent of GDP during its two years of recession, compared with 3.4 percent in Germany and 4.7 percent in Britain over the corresponding period.[13] The real difference between the three countries' performance came on the tax side. The U.S. and British governments both suffered big drops in revenues: 2.2 percent of GDP in Britain and 3.2 percent in the United States. In Germany, meanwhile, the revenue-to-GDP ratio increased by 0.9 percent of GDP.[14] Translating these percentages into dollar figures, if the United States had a tax structure similar to Germany's, the Federal deficit would have been $600 billion smaller each year.

The highly redistributive Anglo-Saxon tax structures may seem morally fairer, because the rich can more easily afford to pay tax. They may also be politically more attractive because the rich are not very numerous, while the middle classes generally decide elections. Yet a comparison of socio-political conditions in Europe and America shows the flaw in this conventional wisdom in at least three separate ways.

First, the Left's attachment to tax progressivity ignores the incentive effects of high tax rates on the rich—not just on their work ethic but on their political actions. High tax rates create incentives for rich people to work less and exploit fiscal loopholes, but their political effect is much more important. When rich individuals, and the businesses they control, feel overtaxed, they use their wealth and influence on politics and public opinion to promote aggressively the ideology of minimal government—a pattern much more evident in the United States and Britain than in Europe.

Second, a highly progressive tax system makes public finances more unstable, as revealed in the crisis by the statistics just quoted. Because top salaries and business profits fluctuate much more with the economic cycle than middle-class incomes and household spending, the U.S. and British tax systems produce much bigger deficits in recessions. Meanwhile, in booms, they create temporary surpluses that tempt politicians into unjustified tax cuts that then force drastic cutbacks in public spending during the bust. This was the strategy for reducing the size of government described by President Reagan as "cutting government off at the pockets."

Finally, overreliance on progressive taxes means that the government's ability to provide new services to society becomes extremely dependent on the business and personal success of its richest citizens. This may create a perverse incentive for governments to promote greater income inequality. If the solvency of the state and the ability to fund basic services for the poorest people in society depends on the rich getting ever richer, it is tempting for even the most progressive politicians to support widening inequalities.

The implication of these arguments is that politicians who want to expand—or even just maintain—the role of government in the new economic conditions after the crisis will have to rethink their attitudes about taxation. In the previous fifty years before Capitalism 4.0, the debate about taxes was clearly polarized between the Left and the Right. Not only did the Left want generally to raise taxes, while the Right wanted to cut them, but their ideas about the tax structure were equally distinct. The Left pushed for progressive taxes and tried to put the maximum burden on high-end income taxes and corporate and capital taxes, seeing these as the fairest way to redistribute income from rich to poor. The Right, at least in Europe and Britain, generally preferred regressive taxes on retail sales, energy, and other mass-market activities, to spread the burden as widely as possible and achieve the lowest possible marginal rates.

In the years ahead, however, these priorities will have to be reconsidered, especially on the Left. Progressive politicians will have to realize that the fiscal politics of income redistribution is much more subtle than generally imagined before the ambiguous politics of Capitalism 4.0.

CHAPTER EIGHTEEN

Finance and Banking in Capitalism 4.0

The best is the enemy of the good.

—Voltaire

CAPITALISM 4.0 will demand new financial systems that will improve economic stability without sacrificing the main benefits of financial freedom and innovation. To achieve this will certainly mean dismantling some of the totems of market fundamentalism, but it will also mean challenging the new conventional wisdom that finance is an unproductive, parasitic activity and that driving bankers out of town, out of the country, or out of business is a desirable objective in its own right.

In this chapter I describe ten principles that reforms will have to satisfy to succeed with the complex trade-offs that Capitalism 4.0 will require.

Finance Is Indispensable

Allocating savings and investment is probably the single most important and productive task in any advanced economy. Banks and financial markets are imperfect mechanisms for carrying out this all-important task, but they are far better than any other system yet devised—or likely to be devised anytime soon. Regulations must therefore try to preserve financial flexibility and innovation, at the same time as improving economic stability. Capitalism 4 will differ from Capitalism 3 by recognizing that these two desirable objectives are in conflict, but it cannot resolve this tension by sacrificing all financial innovation and creating a static financial system or by resorting to the overweening government intervention of Capitalism 2.

Advanced capitalist countries, especially those with large and dynamic financial sectors such as the United States, Britain, and Switzerland, must resist populist demands to strangle nonbank financial institutions with punitive regulations inspired by the banking crisis. These countries have a clear comparative advantage in international finance. In a world of free trade, where prosperity generally progresses when nations specialize in their areas of comparative advantage, it is natural for Anglo-Saxon countries to have larger financial sectors and smaller manufacturing sectors than other countries. The Anglo-Saxon governments are therefore sensible to oppose regulations that damage financial institutions. Britain, for example, would be justified in using the same tough negotiating tactics in EU councils on behalf of finance that France employs to protect its farmers from agricultural reforms.

Freedom of finance will also prove to be a surprising political imperative in most advanced capitalist nations, despite the populist clamor against bankers after the crisis. Public opinion in the twenty-first century will simply not accept a return to the paternalistic financial regulations that existed from the 1930s to the 1970s. Voters would not tolerate the credit rationing, exchange controls, and restrictions on international travel that were taken for granted even in most free-market economies during the bureaucratic heyday of Capitalism 2. Britain, for example, effectively banned most foreign travel from 1966 until 1979 by imposing a limit of £50 on the cash, travelers' checks, and other monetary instruments that British citizens could legally take out of the country when they went on holiday abroad, an interference with personal freedoms almost impossible to imagine for anyone brought up since the 1980s. Equally inconceivable would be a return to the waiting lists for mortgages and auto loans or the rationing of credit for domestic appliances that were taken for granted in most of the world until the mid-1980s.

Populist enthusiasm for "driving the money changers out of the temple" has been legitimized and reinforced by the understandable, but nonetheless misguided, frustration expressed by two of the world's most respected policymakers in the immediate aftermath of the crisis: Paul Volcker's remark that the ATM was the only financial innovation that "had ever improved society"[1] and Adair Turner's comment that finance was a "socially useless" activity that rarely brought economic benefits to anyone except financiers.[2] Deeper thinking about the causes and consequences of the crisis will surely produce more constructive conclusions about the proper role of finance in modern societies.

Government Guarantees Are Unavoidable

The products banks sell are impossible to value accurately because they relate to unpredictable future events, most notably whether borrowers will repay their debts. This applies also to several other businesses, such as insurance, but banks have another unique characteristic. A bank's survival depends on the confidence of its depositors, who can withdraw their money at any time—and if confidence in one major bank collapses, a chain reaction of financial failures can easily follow, with catastrophic results for the economy as a whole.

Because finance is so inherently unpredictable, yet so indispensable to any modern economy, the financial system will always require implicit government guarantees. These guarantees cannot be replaced by regulations that force banks to divest of trading activities or reduce their size. The idea that a purely private financial system can exist without government backing of some kind is a market fundamentalist illusion. Far from representing a tough response to the banking crisis, attempts to reduce government support for financial systems will merely allow banks to enjoy implicit guarantees without having to pay for them.

Many regulators, especially central bankers, still believe that making bank guarantees explicit will create moral hazard. They also claim that governments keep investors on their toes with constructive ambiguity about which bank liabilities might enjoy taxpayer support. These views have been discredited by the financial crisis. When governments left any doubt about which bank liabilities were protected, they usually ended up offering guarantees to all creditors, no matter how junior, in all banks, no matter how small. Constructive ambiguity, far from saving taxpayer money, has turned out to be the greatest source of moral hazard.

This experience also refutes suggestions that moral hazard can be overcome by breaking up banks that are too big to fail. Breaking up some banking dinosaurs may well be sensible, for reasons of competition and managerial efficiency. But it is misleading to believe that any bank, however small, will be allowed to renege on its depositors or senior creditors in a period of systemic financial turmoil. Situations are bound to arise from time to time—perhaps only once every generation—when governments simply cannot allow any bank to fail. The collapse of a bank such as Lehman, with no consumer deposits, might have done no great harm had it happened a few years earlier. But against the background of a broader financial crisis, Lehman's failure was catastrophic and imposed costs on society hundreds of times greater than the modest (or zero) cost of providing temporary government guarantees.

Thus, even banks that are not "too big too fail" will sometimes be too important to fail. Public policy should recognize this explicitly, instead of pretending that there will be no bail-outs and then being forced to stitch together ad hoc public safety nets in the midst of extreme crises, at huge expense to the public and none at all to the banks. It is far better to recognize from the outset that, under certain conditions, all financial institutions will be supported by the government and then make sure that banks pay for this taxpayer support. There must be a financial quid pro quo for taxpayer guarantees that governments implicitly or explicitly provide to banks, through various insurance and contingent capital arrangements, such as those suggested by MIT's Ricardo Caballero, special tax regimes, or a host of other ideas.

Regulation Is Not Just About Market Failure

In the postcrisis Capitalism 4.0 worldview, policymakers must recognize that the markets are often wrong. They must be willing to regulate financial institutions, even without any evidence of particular market failures such as imperfect competition, information bottlenecks, or managerial incompetence.

Increasing bank capital will be necessary but not sufficient. Equally important is the reform of liquidity management. The first line of defense against future liquidity crises such as Lehman or Northern Rock will be for banks to hold much higher proportions of their assets in cash, central bank deposits, or short-term Treasury bonds. In the past, cash requirements, deposit requirements, and supplementary special deposits (known as *corsets* in Britain) were major tools for managing bank behavior and regulating credit cycles. But most of these liquidity requirements were gradually abandoned, at least in the United States and Britain, under pressure from market fundamentalist philosophy and from bankers, who naturally preferred to invest their depositors' money in riskier and higher-yielding assets.

As a result, British and American banks have kept far less money in safe and liquid assets than banks elsewhere. After the crisis, however, this situation has changed. In 2006, for example, the sum of circulating cash plus reserve deposits was 6.5 percent of GDP in the United States and only 5 percent in Britain. This compared with 9 percent in the eurozone and 17 percent in Japan. As a result of the money printed under the Fed and Bank of England quantitative easing program, the U.S. and British liquidity levels shot up to around 13 percent of GDP in early 2010, similar to the newly increased level in the eurozone. If this level of liquidity were permanently mandated by regulation, future financial crises would become much less likely. On top of that, the U.S. and British governments would gain seignorage revenue (the profit governments make from issuing money without paying interest) equivalent to between 0.25 percent and 0.5 percent of GDP—up to $70 billion a year in the case of the United States.[3] This money would effectively be a stealth tax on the banks, with the burden ultimately shared between their shareholders, borrowers, and employees. In the postcrisis political climate, that potential revenue would be an argument in favor of such stringent liquidity rules.

Capital Structures Must Be Refined

Once it is recognized, in defiance of market fundamentalist principles, that banks and governments everywhere are inextricably entwined, another important feature of bank reform becomes immediately apparent. Banks should be forced to define clearly and in advance which of their obligations represent a risk to their creditors and investors and which are 100 percent safe, guaranteed firstly by the bank's own capital and liquidity and ultimately backed by the government. If governments offer clear guarantees for *some* bank obligations and cast this safety net wide enough to cover all deposits and senior credits, regulators will be far more credible when they deny any support for other bank liabilities—equities, preferred shares, unsecured bonds, and so on.

The binary risks of bank liabilities—either totally guaranteed or not guaranteed at all—should be made even clearer by a drastic simplification of balance sheets. Ideally, banks should have just two kinds of liabilities: deposits or senior bonds of various maturities, which are totally safe, and pure equity, which can bear the entire risk of credit losses and liquidity mismatches. By draining the alphabet soup of hybrid capital structures that exploit ambiguities about the true risks of bank liabilities, regulators could remove one of the main causes of the 2007–09 crash.

Banking lobbies will resist any drastic simplification of capital structures because such a simplification would also diminish the opportunities for banks to minimize or avoid taxes. But, as in the case of the bank liquidity stealth tax, the public may conclude that any measures opposed by bank lobbies have ipso facto much to commend them.

Abolish Mark-to-Market Fundamentalist Accounting

The main function of banks and other financial institutions is to allow savers, borrowers, and investors to make economic provision for future events that are inherently unpredictable. It is by trading and reconciling conflicting bets about the future that financial markets redirect savings from extremely cautious bank depositors to risk-seeking entrepreneurs. To do this successfully, banks and financial institutions must enjoy far greater leeway in their accounting rules and disclosure requirements than other businesses.

Once it is recognized that the prices set in financial markets are always systematically misleading, accountants must abandon the quixotic idea of forcing banks to value all their assets according to the same rules as other companies. Because banks are in the business of maturity transformation, their assets will always be much longer-term and much less liquid than the deposits and other money they borrow. Banks must therefore be allowed to exercise their judgment, under the supervision of regulators, in assessing the long-term value of their loans, mortgages, and other assets and they must be allowed to smooth out their profits over long periods.

Forcing banks to adopt mark-to-market accounting was a catastrophic experiment, whose introduction coincided precisely with the beginning of the subprime crisis and whose suspension coincided with the end of the crisis. Regulators and politicians must overrule the vested interests of bankers and accountants, as well as the intellectual prejudices of market fundamentalist economists, and abolish mark-to-market accounting for good.

Credit Ratings Are Too Important for Credit Raters

The risk management of banks is too important to be outsourced to private credit rating agencies, accountancy firms, or the banks' own managements. Regulators and politicians, released from their obeisance to financial markets, must make their own judgments about the quality of bank assets and lending. Specifically, they cannot rely on private credit-rating agencies, with no special skills in economic forecasting and serious conflicts of interest, to determine the macroeconomic risks faced by the bank. Instead, regulators must impose their own macroeconomic models and assumptions about variables such as house prices, unemployment, and default risks when they assess bank solvency and capital requirements. Private credit-rating agencies failed to do this job in the past—and no conceivable reforms will endow them with the skills, credibility, or independence to do it in the future.

Mortgages Do Not Need Government

A new division of labor is essential between private and public mortgage operations. Although more government support for banks and depositary institutions in times of crisis is politically and economically necessary, government involvement in many parts of the financial markets has gone too far. What is required is a willingness to learn from international experience and to redraw boundaries between private and public enterprise. Most importantly, there is no need in the long run for huge government involvement in U.S. mortgage markets, German and Spanish regional banking, Japanese postal savings, or most recently, the nationalized British banks. Fannie Mae and Freddie Mac, the Government Sponsored Enterprises, which now provide over 90 percent of U.S. home mortgages, are by far the most important such anomaly. Although Henry Paulson was wildly irresponsible in trying to dismantle the GSEs in the midst of the greatest mortgage crisis in history, their future should be urgently resolved when the economy recovers and financial markets return to normal.

U.S. regulators and homeowners must be willing to learn from international experience. They should realize that purely private adjustable-rate mortgage markets in Britain, France, Sweden, Italy, and many other European countries proved much more robust in the crisis, as well as more responsive to consumer interests and more attractive for both borrowers and lenders, than the bureaucratic conforming thirty-year loans that dominate the mortgage market in the United States. In this respect, the U.S. financial markets have proved to be more vulnerable to the errors of bureaucratic paternalism and central planning than the markets in Britain and most of continental Europe.

Fiduciary Duty and Government as a Silent Partner

The idea that banks can be managed by their directors solely in the interests of shareholders is no longer acceptable after the crisis. Given the explicit or implied guarantees that all banks required in the crisis, public and fiscal authorities representing taxpayers will have to be permanently recognized as stakeholders in all banks. Moreover, the shareholders of banks, and the directors who were supposed to represent them, proved grossly incompetent in protecting their own interests, never mind their implied duties to the taxpayers whose support they required.

The free-market ideal of shareholder control was buried a year after the crisis in Alan Greenspan's famous recantation of his free-market philosophy under the Inquisitorial thumbscrews of the U.S. Congress:[4] "Those of us who have looked to the self-interest of lending institutions to protect share-holder's equity—myself especially—are in a state of shocked disbelief."

The media and Greenspan's many detractors after the crisis were shocked by this public admission of personal error by "the Master." The real shock, however, was the repudiation by the world's most celebrated free-marketeer of the key tenet of modern financial ideology: the idea that corporate man-agements' focus on shareholder value is the most reliable and efficient way of achieving economic progress. Following this repudiation, it is clear that the directors of any institution with a banking license and any possibility of ever requiring financial guarantees must accept a fiduciary duty of care to the government and the public. The taxpayer is effectively a silent partner in every banking business whether it is openly nationalized, like Royal Bank of Scotland, or purely private, such as Goldman Sachs or HSBC.

But if taxpayers are effectively partners in the banks, their interests must be represented alongside the interests of shareholders. How is this represen-tation to be achieved? One approach is to give taxpayers a permanent share of all bank revenues, either through special taxes or by forcing banks to keep a substantial portion of their deposits in zero-interest government bonds. Another is to ensure that management practices minimize the risk of im-plicit taxpayer guarantees ever being called, as the next section describes.

Politicians and Bank Shareholders Have the Same Interest

The need to protect taxpayers as the silent partners in every banking busi-ness will be a legitimate reason for regulators to continue to take an interest in bankers' bonuses and earnings even after the populist outcries die down. The surest way of protecting the interests of taxpayers as effective share-holders in the banks is to ensure that these companies make big profits—and then retain these profits as a cushion against future losses. The objective of bank profitability was spectacularly achieved after the crisis, partly as a result of government monetary policies—and given the likelihood of extremely low interest rates for many years ahead, banks will continue to be very profitable for many years. The next question is how bank directors can be made to retain these profits to stabilize their businesses, instead of paying them out as salaries and bonuses to employees.

Part of the answer is for governments to understand that the taxpayer's interest, as a silent partner in every banking business, is generally aligned with the bank's shareholders but at odds with the interests of bank employees. In a bank, as in any other private business, income must be shared between shareholders and employees. The peculiarity of the banking business, however, is that boards of directors, instead of representing the interests of shareholders, have considered it their duty to maximize the earnings of the employees. Banks, perhaps because of the partnership culture in the hedge funds with which they must coexist, have been managed as workers cooperatives, in which the interests of the workers come first and those of capital providers are treated as an afterthought. This must change.

Talent or Plunder?

What about the famous competition for talent in the banking business? If banks want to make big profits, don't they need to recruit financial geniuses whose talents amply justify their telephone-number rewards?

The answer is no. "Talent" is a word applicable to rock stars and Hollywood actors, not a concept relevant to bank employees. Most rich financiers are clever and hard working, but the same is true of many other people who are far less highly remunerated in other walks of life.[5] What makes bankers rich is not their personality, their intellect, or their talent but the capital and reputation of the institutions for which they work. Why and how do bankers secure for themselves much more of the value they generate for their companies than employees of other, even better capitalized and more reputable businesses such as IBM, Microsoft, or GE?

Pinning down the exact reasons for this is surprisingly hard, at least under the competitive efficient market assumptions of Capitalism 3.3. Stepping away from these theoretical abstractions, on the other hand, produces a straightforward explanation for the extraordinary rewards and the extraordinary losses in banking.

Readers old enough to remember the former Yugoslavia may recall a fashion among economists in the 1960s to extol the virtues of Yugoslav workers' cooperatives, which supposedly combined the benefits of free enterprise with social justice toward workers. This is what many banks became, especially after 1999, when Goldman Sachs became the last major investment banking partnership to convert itself into a listed company owned by outside shareholders. Banks became private enterprises, owned and capitalized by their shareholders but controlled and managed on behalf of the employees. The problem with idealistic theories about workers' control became apparent after the breakup of Yugoslavia and again after the crisis. Managers who saw themselves as responsible to their workers, rather than to providers of capital, paid out far too much of their revenues as wages, instead of building up the capital of the business. Over time, they allowed the wealth originally invested in the business to disappear. In effect, the workers plundered the businesses for which they worked, and eventually these businesses decapitalized and collapsed.

This kind of looting by the employees, more often inadvertent than deliberate, occurs almost inevitably in workers' cooperatives—and it happened to many banks. For years, banks were systematically undercapitalized in relation to the risks they were taking. To be properly capitalized for the amount of business they were doing, banks would have had to sell far more shares—probably two or three times as many as they issued. To raise so much extra capital would have required a corresponding twofold or threefold increase in profits. Generating such profits would have been feasible before the crisis, given the enormous revenues collected by most banks. But instead of using these revenues to increase their share capital and reward shareholders, the banks seemed intent on maximizing the bonuses they paid to their employees. In effect, bank employees were looting their companies at the expense of the shareholders. As a result, when the crisis struck, banks did not have remotely the capital they needed to withstand big losses. They came to the brink of collapse and their shareholders were largely wiped out.

The 1980s and 1990s witnessed the victory of capital over labor in almost every country and every business, with one supremely ironic exception. In finance, the workers triumphed over the owners of capital, making Wall Street and the City of London the last bastions of Marxist workers' control. In creating a new financial system after the crisis, politicians and regulators must reject market fundamentalism and simultaneously overcome this last vestige of Marxist thinking.

CHAPTER NINETEEN

The World of Capitalism 4.0

The G20 foreshadows the planetary governance of the twenty-first century.

—President Nicolas Sarkozy of France

CONVENTIONAL WISDOM maintained that the crisis of 2007–09 would mark the end of America's global dominance—not only as an economic model but probably also as a hegemonic military and geopolitical power. This could still turn out to be true. The U.S. economy could succumb to a double-dip recession if fiscal stimulus is withdrawn too quickly or if the Federal Reserve fails to keep interest rates low enough for long enough to ensure sustained growth. Fierce partisanship, aggravated by the unsustainability of the old politico-economic model, could make the country increasingly ungovernable. The government's debt could spiral out of control, not just for a few more years but for the indefinite future, damaging the domestic economy and paralyzing America's defense forces and its ability to project power. In short, the United States could succumb to the same fate as the Soviet Union after its economic model imploded in the 1970s.

This sequence of events is highly improbable because America, more than any other society in history, has shown a remarkable capacity for pragmatic adaptation. Nevertheless, in the spirit that nothing in human behavior is certain and therefore that nothing is impossible, it is worth thinking briefly about how a total breakdown of American leadership would affect the global balance of power. In the event of a further deterioration in America's political and economic conditions, it would be unrealistic to imagine the mantle of global leadership passing neatly to China or maybe to Europe, as suggested by some of the triumphalist rhetoric in Beijing and Paris, respectively, at the height of the crisis about the death of the Anglo-Saxon model.

A prolonged U.S. recession, combined with a descent into political ungovernability, would lead to chaos around the world. China might manage to protect its domestic economy against a second and much deeper global recession and financial crisis, as it did against the first one, but it is far too poor, too technologically backward, and too inward-looking to become a credible model for the rest of the world. Its socio-political institutions, while appealing to many developing countries, could never be a model for the affluent, democratic world. As for Europe, it would suffer even more economic and political damage than America from a prolonged depression, just as it did in the 1930s. A relapse into economic depression would produce a state of global anarchy in which the only things worth owning would be farmland and oil wells—and the guns, ammunition, and armed militias to protect them.

Much more probable is the opposite scenario: American and global capitalism will adapt, the policies of government stimulus will be continued until they have proved unequivocally effective, and the world will return to robust growth, with falling unemployment and normalizing financial conditions, after a year or two. The rest of this chapter will be based on this premise.

Let us suppose that American business continues to recover fairly quickly, as it has after previous deep recessions, and that a political consensus converges around a new model of capitalism. Quite possibly, as suggested in Chapter 17, this consensus will be led by conservative political and business interests motivated by the capitalist instinct of self-preservation, rather than by progressive reformers seeking idealistic solutions. Even in this benign scenario, the transition to Capitalism 4.0 will produce profound changes in the structure of global power.

Even on the assumptions that the global recession is followed by a normal recovery, that political gridlock can be overcome in Washington, and that stability can be maintained in the geopolitical system, some big and unsettling changes to the shape of the world lie ahead. This chapter considers ten global consequences of a successful transition to Capitalism 4.0.

Global Competition between the United States and China

Will the dominant new model of capitalism that emerges from this period of change be a new version of the democratic Western system? Or will it be some variant of the authoritarian state-led capitalism favored in China?

For many developing nations that will account for two-thirds or more of the growth in global economic activity over the coming decades,[1] the answer is unclear. In the twenty years since the demolition of the Berlin Wall, almost every nation has appeared to accept, at least in theory, the conventional wisdom known as the Washington Consensus: The only credible formula for long-term prosperity and development is "free markets and free people," however unwelcome both these liberal concepts might be to incumbent oligarchies and ruling elites. Now, after watching the near-collapse of global capitalism and the damage done to Western democracies by the crisis, citizens, as well as political leaders, of many developing countries are having second thoughts.

The apparent failure of Western capitalism has discredited liberalism in the eyes of many developing countries, as even the principle promoters of the Washington Consensus, the IMF and World Bank, have acknowledged in a series of confessional reports.[2] As a senior U.S. diplomat remarked a few months after the crisis: "Developing countries have lost interest in the old Washington Consensus that promoted democracy and liberal economics. Wherever I go in the world, governments and business leaders talk about the new Beijing Consensus—the Chinese route to prosperity and power. The West must come up with a new model of capitalism to produce dynamic growth that's consistent with our political values. Either we reinvent ourselves or we lose."[3]

From the opposite perspective, China's self-confidence and assertiveness has burgeoned after the crisis. Consider this editorial, published in July

2009 by the *People's Daily*, entitled "China's Spirit: A Great Wall of the Heart, built to ward off global crisis":

> In [the] face of China's upbeat economic recovery, the international community has enunciated from a variety of angles the boundless vitality of the Chinese economy and proceeded to explain and analyze the "China Road" and "China Model." Nevertheless, no adequate heed has been given to the motive force for the vigorous growth of Chinese economy or to *China's Spirit*, namely, the *spiritual* connotation of the China Road and China Model:
>
> "*China's Spirit* means precisely a historical initiative with a great foresight;
>
> "*China's Spirit* means precisely a united, cohesive great power to tide over the hard times;
>
> "*China's Spirit* means precisely the heroism to forge ahead in the face of difficulty or hardship;
>
> "*China's Spirit* means precisely the constancy of purpose to take the helm of the future.[4]

There are several ways of dealing with, or trying to dodge, the existential challenge to democratic capitalism presented by the widening appeal of the Chinese Model. The easiest approach is blank denial. Instead of thinking about how the collapse of the old model will change the future of capitalism, it is easier to focus on the past—to quibble about financial regulations, denounce bankers' bonuses, and argue about whether to blame Alan Greenspan or Goldman Sachs. Another form of denial is to pretend that the Chinese and Western models of capitalism are not really very different. Everyone, after all, is in business to make money, so on the issues that matter, no great rift exists between Chinese and Western values or even their politico-economic approach.

The view that the two models of society can prosper side by side, in peaceful coexistence and mutual respect, is standard in companies with big investments in China and is also the official line of both Chinese and Western governments. It is not entirely without foundation.

The idea of a natural convergence, Panglossian though it may seem at present, will become more plausible as Capitalism 4.0 evolves because the Chinese Model is in many ways dynamic and adaptive. In the 2004 article that first proposed the concept of a Beijing Consensus, the scholar Joshua Ramo, of Kissinger Associates, suggested that one of the main advantages of the Chinese-inspired approach over the then-existing Western model was Beijing's commitment to innovation and constant experimentation. The Washington Consensus, Ramo argued, would eventually be undermined by its dogmatism, complacency, and unrealistic theoretical assumptions. The Beijing Consensus, by contrast, would be based on the understanding that there can be no perfect solutions and no permanent ideologies because modern economic life has created a "Heisenberg society" in which the only certainty is uncertainty and constant change. Successful development strategies will therefore require dynamic and adaptive planning, with policies continually adjusted to a rapidly changing social and economic environment.[5] Anyone who has read this far will be struck by the resemblances to Capitalism 4.0.

Despite such resemblances at the pragmatic level of economic policy, however, the hopes for a durable convergence between the Chinese and Western models are probably an illusion. Whether we look at business practices, trade policies, political and human rights, or geopolitical interests, it appears more likely that China and the West will find themselves on a collision course. Serious conflict may not occur for years or even decades, but the two models of politico-economic development will eventually prove economically incompatible, even if they are capable of peaceful coexistence in the military and diplomatic sense.

To examine the Chinese side of its long-term rivalry with the democratic model is beyond the scope of this book, but many excellent studies have been written recently on this subject, most of which come to the conclusion that democratic capitalism will probably prevail, in the end.[6] To flesh out this sketch of the international implications of the new capitalist model, it is enough to summarize some of the main reasons for this view.

First, China's remarkably successful development as a capitalist country since the 1980s should not disguise the fact that an inherent contradiction exists between the freedom to innovate and compete, which is at the heart of the capitalist system, and the regimented obedience demanded by an authoritarian political system. This contradiction may not matter much in the early phases of capitalist development, when growth is driven mainly by massive infrastructure investment and the adoption of ideas and technologies developed by more advanced nations. But as China's living standards start to approach Western levels, which even at the present rate of growth will not happen until around 2030 or 2040,[7] the contradictions between authoritarian politics and liberal economics will become more acute.[8]

Second, China's reliance on exports, especially to the U.S. consumer market, will be much more problematic in the future as U.S. economic policy is directed to reducing foreign borrowing and the concomitant trade deficits. China's leaders have acknowledged the dangers of overdependence on exports and are trying to shift the emphasis of their development plans toward domestic growth. But this process will be difficult and will result in slower productivity and economic development, because most of the technological and managerial improvements in Chinese economy came from the export sector. Moreover, China's authoritarian politics will find it difficult to adapt to a society that emphasizes consumption over production. Even democratic Asian societies, such as Japan and South Korea, which pride themselves on counterbalancing Western materialism with Asian or Confucian values, have been unable to maintain their remarkable growth rates once the export-led phase of their development runs out of steam.[9]

Third, the next stage of China's development—from a cheap-labor economy based on imitation to an affluent economy based on innovation—will require it to create what Will Hutton has called the "soft infrastructure of capitalism": secure property rights, representative government, an independent judiciary, and a business culture that is not solely driven by the desire for instant personal enrichment. Many Western commentators and politicians believe that such conditions for the long-term success of a capitalist economy are features of the liberal mentality created by the Western Enlightenment and that capitalism's need to foster this liberal mentality will ultimately threaten the Communist Party's control of independent thinking and thus its monopoly of power.

Fourth, China is too poor, too technologically backward, and too culturally specific to be a credible model for other emerging nations and thus to become a genuine global leader. China's influence in the world economy has less to do with its economic success than with the sheer size of its population. Within a year or two after the crisis, China will certainly become the world's second largest economy. In terms of income per head, however it will scarcely figure among the top one hundred nations. According to the 2009 rankings calculated by the IMF, and even allowing for the relatively low cost of consumer products in China,[10] its national income per head of $6,500 places it ninety-seventh in the world—far below Russia's per capita income of $15,000, Brazil's $10,500, South Africa's $10,000, or even Thailand's $8,000. By way of comparison, U.S. per capita income, using the same methodology, was $46,000 and income in Portugal, the poorest western European country, was $22,000.

Finally, China's political arrangements, which combine strict authoritarian control with remarkable political stability, are unique and depend on its long history of strong centralized rule, its ethnic homogeneity, and its Confucian culture. These conditions are unlikely to be successfully replicated in any other nation. Even if other developing countries are inspired by China's example, they may not have the option of following the Chinese Road.

Convergence between the United States and Europe

Even if liberal democracy remains the most plausible and attractive model for long-term political and economic development, surely the collapse of financially oriented capitalism has surely discredited the Anglo-Saxon model in comparison with the more consensual European approach? This view was certainly widespread in the immediate aftermath of the crisis, but the opposite is true.

Assuming that the United States recovers from the recession much faster than continental Europe and that Britain also emerges from the recession with less permanent damage than many of the countries in the eurozone—both of which are likely events—the crisis will reaffirm the relative resilience of Anglo-Saxon financial capitalism, provided Anglo-Saxon capitalism is not confused with the exaggerated market fundamentalism of Capitalism 3.3.

Many vestiges of Capitalism 2's bureaucratic state-led system survived in continental Europe (as well as in Japan) well after they were swept away in Britain and America by the Thatcher-Reagan revolutions. In the twenty years before the crisis, continental Europe was able to mask some of the consequences of its refusal to accept the social dislocations of the Thatcher-Reagan period, albeit at the cost of slow growth and relative decline. For Europe to stay on this trajectory of relatively comfortable decline will be more difficult after the 2007–09 crisis.

As global capitalism converges toward a new model, in which governments are smaller but more active, and national economies are more balanced and less leveraged, Europe will experience even more wrenching changes than Britain and the United States.

Although European leaders, businesses, and investors were at first complacent about the financial upheavals of 2007–09, believing them to be a purely Anglo-Saxon phenomenon, it soon became apparent that the crisis would exacerbate at least three profound structural problems which had been easy to cover up during the financial boom.

First, the falling demand for manufactured goods caused by the consumption slowdown in America, Britain, Spain, Ireland, Greece, and other highly indebted countries had an even bigger effect on Germany and other exporting economies than it did on the United States. Second, southern and central Europe faced potentially catastrophic financial crises because their consumers and governments had become even more addicted to cheap and seemingly unlimited credit than the subprime borrowers of California and Nevada. Third, the euro was transformed into a source of vulnerability, rather than strength, because of the market fundamentalist theories on which the European Monetary Union was designed, back in the heyday of monetarism in 1989. The result has been a perfect storm of converging economic and financial pressures that has made Europe weaker economically and more inward-looking politically, at least in the first few years of the postcrisis period.

The U.S. economy, by contrast, is being structurally strengthened, at least in relation to Europe, by the rebalancing of industry and trade in the postcrisis recovery. The slowdown in U.S. consumption, along with the ultracompetitive valuation of the dollar against the euro and the yen, is redirecting economic activity from relatively low-productivity industries such as house building, retailing, and consumer finance to the production of capital equipment, export-oriented manufactured goods, and new energy technologies. The growth of these industries will also play to the U.S.

economy's natural competitive advantage in technology and research. And if U.S. health care reform gains further political traction as a result of financial pressures created by the crisis, the international competitiveness of American business will enjoy another tremendous boost.

Over time, European capitalism will doubtless adapt to the new global environment and evolve its own reasonably successful version of the capitalist model, because Europe's political and economic institutions are fundamentally as strong as those in the United States and Britain. But Europe's variant of Capitalism 4.0 will require some big institutional changes. In macroeconomic policy, Europe will have to undergo a philosophical revolution against market fundamentalist orthodoxy, which during the 1990s became more entrenched in the European Central Bank and the German finance ministry than in American and British macroeconomic institutions. Industrial and labor policies will have to move just as radically in the opposite direction—away from the paternalistic bureaucratic traditions left over from the era of Capitalism 2 and toward a much greater acceptance of market forces, even when they cause social dislocation.

As Europe adopts more Keynesian macroeconomic policies and more market-oriented approaches to industry and labor, greater convergence between the Anglo-Saxon and European models is likely. As a result of this convergence, the philosophical rivalry and occasional friction between the United States, Britain, and Europe is likely to diminish.

On the other hand, the commercial competition between businesses in Europe and the United States will continue to intensify as both economies concentrate increasingly on the same high-value industries and apply broadly similar philosophies of economic management. But the ideological convergence, juxtaposed against the rivalry with China, will bring Europe and America politically closer together. As a result, the contrast between Western democratic capitalism and China's authoritarian model will be highlighted more starkly than ever.

The Rivalry of Western and Asian Values

The crisis convinced many politicians and opinion leaders in emerging countries that democracy was a flawed concept. Assuming, however, that the economic recovery and the new model of Western capitalism evolve roughly as expected, this global disillusionment with democracy is unlikely to continue for long.

Instead, a closer convergence between the American and European models will make a reformed version of democratic capitalism more ideologically attractive to most emerging countries—especially Asian countries with traditions of social cohesion and respect for state power. This is essentially the view of democratic Asian scholars such as Kishore Mahbubani, whose widely discussed book, *The New Asian Hemisphere*, maintains that Asia wants to replicate, not dominate, the West and will increasingly attempt to do so by absorbing and implementing best practices in areas such as economics, science, and the rule of law.[11] In a similarly optimistic vein, Anne-Marie Slaughter, a leading liberal scholar in the U.S. foreign-policy establishment and appointed by President Obama as the U.S. State Department's Director of Policy Planning, argues that America's newfound ideological open-mindedness and recognition of its own imperfections will make the U.S. model more attractive to developing countries. Her eloquent book on the future of U.S. foreign policy, *The Idea That Is America*, could almost be a manifesto for the intellectual changes demanded as capitalism moves toward a new politico-economic model.

Beyond such philosophical issues, there are several concrete reasons why a convergence of American and European thinking will favor the dissemination of Western democratic values, as opposed to China's authoritarian approach.

First, the economic recovery, if it continues along the lines suggested in this book, will emphasize again the resilience of democratic capitalism. This extraordinary capacity for survival, in stark contrast to the brittleness of the authoritarian regimes blown away in Latin America, Asia, and eastern Europe by previous financial crises, will increasingly commend the Western democratic model to the politicians and citizens in developing countries trying to keep their nations together after decades of chaos and war.

Second, the United States will move closer to the center of gravity of international thinking if it becomes an adaptive mixed-economy of the kind described in this book, with more constructive and flexible interactions between government and the market. This movement toward global standards will in itself make America more attractive as a model and should, over time, increase U.S. influence in international institutions. The reversal or modification of many of the Bush administration's unilateral foreign, social, and environmental policies will send the signal that Americans no longer live in a different mental universe from the rest of the world.

Third, for Europe, an intellectual convergence with America will require policymakers and electorates to acknowledge some of the dysfunctional features of the European socio-economic system that have allowed special interests, such as agricultural lobbies and trade unions, to disguise what is essentially exploitative rent-seeking economic behavior, as culturally unique characteristics of the European model. The aftermath of the financial crisis is forcing Europe to adopt more market-oriented policies for trade, labor, and agriculture, and these policies will make its economic interactions with emerging economies more mutually beneficial and economically constructive. The EU should thus become an even more effective motor for the expansion of democratic capitalism, especially in Africa and the Middle East.

A fourth reason for the dissemination of Western values is that the crisis has shown extreme imbalances in trade to be unsustainable in the long term. As a result, China's export-driven economic model will look riskier and less attractive to other developing countries. Moreover, because China's comparative advantage comes mainly from low labor costs, its continuing export growth is mainly occurring at the expense of other low-wage developing countries. Thus, unless China redirects its economic growth from exports to domestic consumption much faster than anyone is expecting, China's future trade frictions will be mostly with other developing nations, especially if U.S. imports slow down. These tensions will be aggravated by China's large investments in commodity-producing countries such as Brazil and South Africa. China will be seen as pushing these countries toward even greater dependence on raw materials, at a time when they are trying to rebalance their economies in favor of manufacturing and export-led growth.

Finally, if the rivalries with China over trade, finance, and democratic principles intensify, the United States, Europe, and Japan will devote more attention to developing nations whose political and economic traditions are closer to the norms of advanced capitalist countries. The rise of India could be particularly significant because India is a potential economic giant with a political and business culture much closer to the West's. The Indian development model, with its emphasis on domestic consumption growth rather than exports, will also make it more complementary with the restructuring of Western economies, especially the U.S. economy, that lies ahead. As U.S. economic growth becomes more dependent on exports, instead of housing, finance, and consumption, America will need closer ties with other large economies that are willing and able to become major importers. From this point of view, India, along with Brazil, South Africa, and maybe even Russia, could emerge in the decade ahead as more complementary trading partners for the United States than China. If so, the focus of Western economic, as well as geopolitical, thinking should shift in the next decade toward India and other large developing countries and away from the Sino-centric approach of the precrisis years.

Business Interests Will Embrace the New Model

As Capitalism 4.0 begins to evolve, the reflex reaction of business leaders, especially in America and Britain, is to oppose the increased interaction of government implied by the new model. In time, however, this attitude is likely to change to one of acquiescence and ultimately even enthusiasm, for cooperation between business and government of the kind seen in many Asian and European countries and also in America during the heyday of the Eisenhower administration's military-industrial complex.[12] Businesses will recognize that proactive macroeconomic management and financial regulation are essential for the survival of the capitalist system. Many will also decide that, from their narrow corporate standpoints, cooperation with government is usually more profitable than opposition.

For the thirty years following the Thatcher-Reagan revolutions, business leaders took it as axiomatic that virtually all regulation and government intervention was damaging to their interests and that companies should devote substantial resources to campaigning for a minimalist state. The closure of manufacturing industries was justified as a natural and unavoidable consequence of market economics. Ruthless industrial restructuring and the single-minded pursuit of shareholder value were not only presented as inevitable but also seen as desirable, or at least rational and efficient.

What will happen now that these economic concepts of rationality and efficiency have been discredited? As the dust settles after the recession and financial crisis, a deep reconsideration of the relationships between corporate managements, shareholders, and governments must begin. Businesses will have to acknowledge wider definitions of their objectives than maximizing their company's share price, especially in the short term. Governments will have to take more seriously all sorts of proposals for subsidies and taxes directed at specific industries or sectors, of a kind that were ruled out of order by Capitalism 3. And as businesses find themselves interacting more and more with government, they will stop fighting ideological battles against the principle of active government. After businesses realize that greater government intervention is inevitable, they will try to turn inevitable into profitable.

As Capitalism 4.0 evolves, this pragmatism in business attitudes will gradually mutate into a broader ideological change. Corporate managements will be forced to recognize that much of the political lobbying on which they spent billions during the market fundamentalist era was against the interests of their own shareholders, catastrophically so in some cases. The most extreme examples were the U.S. auto manufacturers, which lobbied themselves into bankruptcy with their campaigns against government fuel-economy standards and health care reforms. The banking industry did the same by opposing mortgage regulation and compulsory clearing of derivative contracts. Most utilities acted against their shareholders' long-term interests by fighting pollution and climate-change policies that would ultimately make their companies more valuable, at the expense of oil and coal producers. And many U.S. labor-intensive industries put ideology before the interests of their shareholders by lobbying against health reforms.

Defense has long been an exception to the business community's general preference for small government, but in the future, business lobbying on defense contracts will be overshadowed by an interest in health care—with business interests lobbying *in favor* of more government regulation of medical costs and a shift of health care responsibilities from employers to the state. As the taboos against government involvement in the private economy break down, business interests will also press for more subsidies in science, higher education, and technology and more government strategic planning in energy policy, transport infrastructure, and trade development. However, a return to the outright protectionism and subsidization of sunset industries of the 1960s and 1970s is unlikely. The integration of the world economy and globalization of industrial supply chains is irreversible and the costs of protectionist policies would be too high. The upshot is that businesses will be forced to respond more pragmatically both to politics and market forces if they are to find ways simultaneously to maximize profits and achieve political and social ends.

Under Capitalism 3.3, such mixing of government and business, even if it could not always be avoided for practical reasons, was assumed to be intrinsically damaging to the economy and politically corrupting. In Capitalism 4.0, this adversarial thinking no longer makes sense. Managements and investors will need to discover new ways to reconcile financial and political targets. Those who refuse to do so will be driven out of business.

Trade and Industrial Structures

During the two extraordinary decades between the demolition of the Berlin Wall and the financial crisis, a Circle of Manipulation[13] in global finance and trade allowed China and the United States to grow in mutual dependence. China provided cheap labor and excess savings, while the United States created new products and technologies as well as the consumer demand to absorb them.

A similar Circle of Manipulation was spinning in Europe, where German capital provided vendor financing to Spanish, Greek, and French consumers, enabling them to buy more and more German luxury cars and expensive washing machines. Until the 2010 financial crisis in the eurozone, Europe's dependence on this circular flow of international finance was less remarked than the imbalance of trade and finance between the United States and China. But as the Greek crisis revealed, the recycling of capital inside Europe was even larger relative to the economies involved and potentially more unstable than the interdependence, sometimes described as mutually assured financial destruction, between the United States and China.[14]

In the decade ahead, both of these circular flows of finance and trade are bound to slow and even perhaps go into reverse. A rebalancing of global trade is inevitable in the postcrisis era, partly because the financial flows implied by enormous trade deficits have proved unsustainable, but also for a deeper political reason related to the change in economic thinking as the world transitions to a new capitalist model.

As the world loses faith in pure free-market thinking, political pressure is bound to intensify against the continuing displacement of manufacturing jobs implied by an absolutist application of international trade theory. The strict logic of free trade implies that all nations should specialize in economic activities in which they have comparative advantage, while allowing declining industries to die. Taking this theory to its logical conclusion, Britain would sell nothing to the rest of the world except financial services, the United States would concentrate entirely on high-tech electronics and Hollywood film production, all Germans would be employed in making cars and machine tools, and China would manufacture all the labor-intensive mass-production goods in the world.

In reality, the extreme specialization described in high-school economics textbooks was never realistic. Even the smallest countries, such as Luxembourg, Singapore, or Abu Dhabi, want to support a variety of industries to preserve a range of skills among their workers and to avoid the dangers of overdependence on one industry, however prosperous or promising it may appear. The relentless free-market thinking of Capitalism 3.3 dictated increasing specialization. However, the near-death experiences of the 2007–09 crisis, not only in U.S. and British finance but also in the export industries of Germany, China, and Japan, have made policymakers increasingly wary of this approach.

At the same time, the financial imperative of global rebalancing implies macroeconomic policies in the major importing countries that promote manufacturing industry and exports, rather than consumption, housing, and finance. Slower consumption growth in America, Britain, Spain, and France is forcing China, Japan, and Germany to reconsider their industrial specialization as well. Accelerating these trends will be the new philosophical acceptance of greater government intervention in finance, industry, and international commerce, which will expose businesses and investors to new incentives, subsidies, and possible trade restraints.

The next phase of capitalism will therefore be marked by a massive amount of industrial restructuring in every country, as businesses worldwide have to shift their corporate strategies in a scramble to keep up with the changing flows of global trade. Many of the consequences of this wide-ranging industrial restructuring have already been discussed in this book, but three particular points are worth repeating in this concluding chapter, because of their global effect in Capitalism 4.0.

First, the redirection of global trade just described implies that the growth of the world economy in the next decade could involve much more investment than is conventionally predicted, because so much of the world's industrial capacity is in the wrong businesses, located in the wrong places. Second, the priority accorded to free trade principles by all nations, at least in their rhetoric, will become more conditional. The theoretical benefits of free trade and comparative advantage will be counterbalanced explicitly by other economic objectives—initially the imperative of job creation after the recession and later the desirability of preserving a diversified industrial structure. Third, the pressure to coordinate macroeconomic and currency policies among the major trading economies—America, Europe, China, and Japan—will become irresistible. Such coordination will have major implications for the post-Bretton Woods system of floating exchange rates and for the governance of global political and economic institutions—two issues discussed at the end of this chapter.

Limits to Growth and Physical Resources

The market-knows-best philosophy of Capitalism 3.3 assumed that there could be no constraints on the growth of the world economy. If any physical or environmental limits to growth did appear, the market would soon send the right price signals to ensure that these obstacles were automatically avoided. Following the financial crisis, this reassuring belief, based on the oversimplified assumption that efficient markets always discover and transmit long-term social preferences, is no longer credible. The emergence of Capitalism 4.0 is therefore encouraging serious thinking about the physical and environmental constraints on economic growth.

Will this mean abandoning the expectation of continuously rising material living standards, as demanded by the antiglobalization and anticapitalist movements? If it did, the chances of the Western democratic model prevailing in its long-run competition against China's authoritarian capitalism would be greatly diminished. The likelier alternative is that Capitalism 4.0 will use new combinations of public policy and market incentives to overcome the constraints on economic growth.

Whether this effort will succeed is impossible to predict, but the history of technical progress and social change in adaptive capitalist systems suggests that success is much more likely than failure. The "bold persistent experimentation" recommended in the 1930s by Roosevelt will be a prominent feature of energy and environmental politics at both national and global levels in the decades ahead.

The physical constraints on the future growth of the world economy can be divided into two broad categories. On one hand are concerns that the world is running out of raw materials, most obviously oil, but also other minerals and the vast quantities of fresh water required to feed and urbanize a global population of nine billion. On the other hand, even more anxiety exists about the catastrophic environmental effect if carbon-based fossil fuels do *not* run out.[15] Like several of the other issues raised in this chapter, the debate about the limits to growth is vast, inspiring libraries of books and studies.[16] This section merely suggests how this debate could be affected by the transition to a new politico-economic model.

Energy supply offers a striking example of the way that both geopolitical and economic conditions could be transformed by a change in thinking about economics and the relationships between politics and markets.

When oil prices hit $150 a barrel[17] shortly before the Lehman crisis, the financial markets debated the theory of peak oil, which stated that global oil production at the end of the twentieth century had reached its physically sustainable limits in the 1990s and was about to enter an inexorable decline. Some investors and policymakers combined the peak oil theory with the assumption of efficient markets to conclude that oil prices would rise dramatically—that the $150 per barrel oil price was only the beginning of a supercycle upswing. The good news, according to market fundamentalists, was that much higher oil prices would automatically create a long-term equilibrium between supply and demand in the energy markets, albeit at the cost of permanently weaker world economic activity and a huge transfer of resources from energy consumers to oil-producing countries such as Saudi Arabia.

Suppose, however, that the prices set by financial markets are often sending the wrong signals about long-term energy needs, especially from the standpoint of society as a whole, which experiences pollution, geopolitical instability, and other external effects from oil production and consumption.[18] In that case, market prices are not necessarily the best instruments for shaping the long-term energy balance and the debate about a peak in oil *production* becomes a distraction from a more important question: Does a public policy exist that could reduce long-term oil *demand* and make sure this demand keeps falling faster than oil supply? This type of question about active government policy could scarcely be asked in the market fundamentalist period but will be crucial to evolving energy and environmental policy in Capitalism 4.0.

In the years ahead, the purpose of public policies will not be to keep the supply and demand of oil in equilibrium, as assumed by conventional economics. Financial markets could achieve this equilibrium with no help from the government by simply pushing oil prices back to $150 or more. The point of political intervention will be to bring about a different kind of equilibrium in the oil market to achieve three different objectives that financial markets, acting on their own, could not even be expected to recognize.

The first objective will be to balance oil supply and demand in a way that does not inflict unnecessary damage on economic activity and living standards in oil-consuming countries. The second objective will be to avoid the geopolitical risks to Western democracy of allowing a return to the $150 free-market oil price, which resulted in a windfall of some $1 trillion annually to some of the world's most unstable, undemocratic, and politically hostile regimes.[19] The third will be to combine the rebalancing of supply and demand with environmental imperatives.

How could all these goals be attained? After it is acknowledged that public policy should shape the incentives created in financial markets, rather than merely accepting and following them, the answer is obvious—and has been advocated by many energy economists for years.

Governments of energy-consuming nations can curb demand for oil by raising its price *within* their own economies, while ensuring that little of the extra money spent by Western energy consumers flows to oil producers. The objective of Western governments, should be to deny energy producers as much as possible of the unearned rent they receive because they live on top of oil fields. This unearned "rent" is simply the difference between the selling price of a barrel of oil in the world market and what it costs to produce, taking into account the costs of technology, transport, financing, and so on. The production cost in a typical Middle Eastern country such as Saudi Arabia or Abu Dhabi is around $10 a barrel. So if the selling price is $150, the rent component is $140. Thus, if oil prices returned to $150, the pure rent on ten billion barrels annually of OPEC oil production would come to around $1.4 trillion.

A key objective of energy policy in the next decade will be to redirect as much of this rent as possible from the rulers of oil-producing countries to the governments and taxpayers of the energy-consuming world. Four major steps in this direction are likely after politicians, voters, and business lobbyists recognize the new political and economic possibilities created by the transition from market fundamentalism to Capitalism 4.0.

The first and most important step would be for the U.S. government to reduce America's ruinous and politically self-destructive dependence on imported oil. This could be accomplished quickly by introducing European-style energy taxes in America. These energy taxes could be offset by cuts in taxes on income and employment, or used to reduce government deficits, or even redirected into cash payments for drivers in rural areas. In any of these cases, the unearned rents received under the present free-market system by oil producers would remain within the United States instead of flowing into the coffers of potentially hostile regimes in Russia, Venezuela, or the Middle East. Such a shift in the U.S. tax system would have an enormous effect on global oil demand. If U.S. oil consumption were reduced to today's European level, which would be plausible given the comparable populations, climatic conditions, and levels of development of these two continental economies, the reduction in global oil demand would be roughly equivalent to China's entire oil consumption.[20]

The second step would be for governments around the world to introduce a system of steadily escalating energy taxes or tradable carbon permits. Escalating taxes and carbon costs would send an unmistakable market signal to businesses and consumers worldwide that the price of burning fossil fuels will continue inexorably rising to the point where alternative energy sources become far cheaper not only than oil and natural gas but even coal. The result would be an upsurge in alternative energy investment and scientific research that would produce dramatic reductions in the cost of noncarbon energy in a few decades.

The third step would be for developing countries, which are now responsible for all the growth in world oil demand,[21] to eliminate their energy subsidies and ultimately replace their other domestic taxes with a global energy tax and carbon trading regime. As in the case of proposals for the United States to adopt European-style energy taxes, the revenues raised from energy users could be immediately returned to consumers or workers through corresponding cuts in other taxes. If consumers in developing countries faced much higher energy prices, they would change their behavior—for example, by buying smaller, more fuel-efficient vehicles—faster than European and American consumers. A $5 gallon is a far greater burden relative to total income for Chinese, Brazilians, or Indonesians than it is for Americans or Europeans.

The fourth step would be for all energy-consuming countries, especially the most advanced economies such as the United States, Europe, and Japan, to defy the principles of market fundamentalism twice over, by matching the taxes on oil consumption with big subsidies for research and investment in renewable and nuclear energy.

The objective of all these programs should be nothing less than the transformation of all industries from carbon-based to electricity-based technologies—and to create a global energy system that favors technological solutions in which advanced capitalist economies enjoy comparative advantage, rather than extractive industries in politically unstable countries.

If measures such as these were adopted by all energy-consuming governments—or even by the U.S. or European governments acting on their own—the market mechanism would become an extraordinarily effective tool for reducing long-term oil demand. Such measures would also shift the balance of geopolitical power from nondemocratic commodity countries that rely for their wealth and power on unproductive and environmentally damaging resource extraction to democratic nations whose wealth and power depends on innovation and technological progress.

If this process were activated, the limits to growth and peak oil theories would never need to be tested. Instead, a large part of the world's oil supplies would eventually be abandoned, almost worthless, in the ground, like the vast reserves of coal that remain underneath the soil of Britain, which were once believed to be the nation's greatest treasure.

The potential effect on energy production of drastically raising prices to oil consumers was famously summarized at the time of the 1974 energy shock by Shaikh Yamani, then the Saudi oil minister, who reminded his OPEC colleagues that if they got too greedy, the world would replace oil with other energy sources. "Remember," he warned, "the Stone Age did not end because the cavemen ran out of stones."[22] If some political wisdom can be combined with the power of market forces, the Oil Age will end long before the world runs out of oil.

The Environment Can Become a Positive Economic Story

The evolution of Capitalism 4.0 should encourage much clearer and more constructive thinking about the new incentives required for changes in technology and behavior to reduce pollution. Public subsidies, taxpayer guarantees, and regulatory interventions that were taboo to market fundamentalist thinking will increasingly be taken for granted in public debate. The scale of the potential change can be gauged by a few figures that show how drastically both governments and private businesses have been reducing their investment in energy research for the past thirty years, despite all the hand-wringing about global warming.

The U.S. federal government, for example, has halved its energy research spending since the 1980s and in 2008 spent just $5 billion a year on all energy R&D. The rest of the world's governments between them spent about the same amount. This is one-fourteenth of the U.S. government's military research spending and one-sixth of its spending on medical R&D. The disparity is even greater in the private sector. Power generation companies on average spend just 0.5 percent of turnover on R&D. This compares with 3 percent in the motor industry, 8 percent in electronics, and 15 percent in pharmaceuticals. The entire global research effort in all forms of noncarbon energy, including nuclear power, in 2008 was about double Microsoft's spending on an upgraded version of Windows and Office and far smaller than the resources devoted to new weapons systems or cancer research. By contrast to the $10 billion spent globally on alternative and nuclear energy research, an estimated $250 billion is spent annually on subsidizing the extraction and burning of fossil fuels.[23]

Such disparities suggest that markets are not sending remotely appropriate price signals to motivate investment and innovation in energy technology on the scale required. The reaction in Capitalism 3.3 to such findings was to seek evidence of market failures that might explain this absence of investment: lack of competition, gaps in insurance coverage, information lapses, and so on. Usually, no one could discover such evidence of market failures. And when market failures such as lack of competition were discovered, the solutions were elaborate and cumbersome, such as auctioning new capacity and introducing financial derivatives into electricity markets. In practice, these efforts to correct textbook market failures have often made things worse—for example, investment in research and technology has fallen even further where electricity markets have been liberalized.

This approach will change radically in the coming years. The inference will be that research, development, and the deployment of new nonpolluting energy sources may require far greater levels of public support. Under these circumstances, the environmental movement, if it is serious about achieving its objectives, should present clean energy as an opportunity for governments to create more economic activity and employment, rather than limit economic growth. Environmentalists and politicians should also emphasize that large sections of the business community will profit, rather than lose, from government initiatives on energy, carbon emissions, and other environmental issues.

Political incentives designed to promote investment in a new global energy infrastructure should be particularly attractive to American business.

The United States (and, to a lesser extent, Britain) has clear comparative advantages in innovative science-based industries and also in finance—the two sectors of the world economy that will prosper most as the world invests the trillions of dollars required to replace fossil fuels. Thus, a shift in the global economy that placed a much higher price on carbon and other forms of pollution—and hence on the technological progress required to avoid them—would benefit the U.S. and British economies, even if it was costly to the world as a whole.[24] Just one of the mechanisms behind this shift—an increase in carbon trading estimated at $5 trillion annually by the British government's Stern Report—could easily bring economic benefits to the United States and Britain comparable to the losses they have suffered from the collapse of the international market in mortgage bonds.

Before the financial crisis, such arguments about the potential profitability of environmental investment and carbon trading were understandably unpopular with hair shirt environmentalists. During the reign of market fundamentalism, large-scale investments of public money in energy research and carbon trading were never going to happen. Appeals to the profit motive achieved nothing and only distracted from the Green Movement's moral message. Greens, therefore, often gave the impression that their true objective was not so much to protect the environment and prevent climate change as to weaken capitalism and lower material living standards. This emphasis on austerity was always political risky but will become suicidal for the environmental movement in the years after the crisis, because boosting economic growth and employment will be the top priorities of public policy in all nations.

Once Capitalism 4.0 lays to rest the market fundamentalist assumption that all forms of energy must be commercially competitive with fossil fuels, environmentalists should refocus their campaigning on large-scale public investment and subsidies in new technologies. These will create economic gainers who can become business allies for the Green Movement.

Prosperity Without Growth Is an Illusion

Progressive social and environmental policies will be accepted by most societies only if a convincing case can be made that these policies will, on balance, improve living standards, raise wages, and give people more freedom and choice. If progressive policies demand severe sacrifice from consumers and voters, they will never be adopted.

A statement like this may sound cynical in prosperous countries such as America and Britain. But it is in relatively poor developing economies that most of the action will be needed to safeguard the world from serious systemic threats—and poor countries will always give priority to economic growth. China is commissioning as many coal-fired power stations every two years as Britain has built in its entire history.[25] And from the vantage point of a Chinese laborer in a sweatshop, a landless Indian peasant, or a migrant fruit picker in Brazil or Kenya, there is nothing hypocritical about refusing to make material sacrifices on behalf of unborn generations who may be enjoying Western levels of comfort in 2050 and beyond. The ruling elites who run countries such as China, Nigeria, Iran, and Russia and who dominate politics even in such genuine democracies as India and Brazil will be even less likely than their citizens to agree to actions that might damage their own material interests or risk destabilizing their power.

How, then, will the apparently conflicting goals of social responsibility and economic growth be reconciled? Part of the answer lies in reshaping market incentives to channel more resources into new technologies and related industries and jobs. Another partial answer, as described in the preceding section, will be for governments to recapture through taxation or emissions trading, some of the economic rents that oil producers currently extract from the energy-consuming world. There is, however, a deeper way of looking at the question of how growth and social sacrifice can be reconciled: The world can think more carefully about what exactly is meant by growth and sacrifice.

To take an extreme example, the mining and sale of asbestos created many jobs and expanded GDP, until asbestos was banned in most of the world around 1990. Tens of billions of dollars were then spent on treating the victims of asbestosis and compensating their grieving dependents, and this health spending created even more employment and economic growth. Does this mean that banning asbestos resulted in a major sacrifice for society? The answer is clearly no. But the banning of asbestos did, in fact, reduce GDP growth, at least until new materials were introduced to take its place. On conventional measures of economic performance, therefore, creating an asbestos-free economy did impose big economic losses—and mining companies that were put out of business argued that these losses represented a substantial sacrifice for society as a whole.

Asbestos may seem an anomalous and contrived example, but there are many others, most strikingly the CFC refrigerants, whose elimination from the atmosphere under the 1989 Montreal Convention restored the earth's ozone layer in just twelve years.[26] As in the case of asbestos, manufacturers and users of CFCs initially opposed the ban, on the grounds that it would inflict intolerable costs on the refrigeration business and result in a loss of output and jobs. Yet once the decision was taken, these supposed economic sacrifices were recognized as social gains. Not only was the hole in the earth's ozone layer corrected, but the refrigeration business suffered no damage, because all competitors were identically affected and were easily able to pass on to consumers the modest costs of the necessary technological changes. Meanwhile, a new industry was created manufacturing alternatives to CFCs. Who knows if a similar case study will one day be presented to twenty-second-century readers, baffled by the public opposition in the middle of the twenty-first century to a global ban on coal mining, oil production, or surface irrigation.

The point of these examples is not to suggest that bans on coal mining or oil production are necessary or likely. Instead, these examples illustrate that economic statistics often describe social reality in ways that are not just marginally inaccurate but profoundly misleading. One of the most interesting long-term results of capitalism's reinvention after the crisis will be a more serious debate about how the concepts of social welfare and economic growth can be statistically measured and intellectually reconciled.

Inventing a convincing measure of true social values created (or sometimes destroyed) by economic activity has been the Holy Grail of normative, or welfare, economics since Adam Smith, who devoted a large part of *The Wealth of Nations* to this subject. The relationship between market prices and social values was a puzzle that has obsessed economists since Smith, including Marx, Mill, Hayek, and Keynes. But the efforts to relate prices to social values were largely abandoned in the 1960s. The intellectual dominance of market fundamentalism at first encouraged and then essentially required serious economists simply to assume that social values and market prices were one and the same. The autumn of 2009, however, saw a potentially historic breakthrough in the consideration of economic and social values.

In September 2009, the International Commission on Measurement of Economic Performance and Social Progress, headed by three of the world's most distinguished economists—Joseph Stiglitz, Amartya Sen, and Jean-Paul Fitoussi—and commissioned by President Sarkozy of France, produced a report on more comprehensive measures of economic performance, accounting for such factors as environmental degradation, income distribution, and measures of the quality of life. The significance of this report was not in its detailed recommendations, which will take years of further discussion to transform into a usable consensus, but in the questions it raised about the relationship between politics and economics.

As Stiglitz said, "In our performance-oriented world, what we measure affects what we do. If we have poor measures, what we strive to do (say, increase GDP) may actually contribute to a worsening of living standards. We may also be confronted with false choices, seeing trade-offs between output and environmental protection that don't exist. By contrast, a better measure of economic performance might show that steps taken to improve the environment are good for the economy."[27] Sarkozy expressed the same sentiment from a politician's standpoint: "To ask ourselves questions about how we measure [economic performance and social progress] is to ask ourselves what our goals truly are. We will not be able to change our set ways if we do not change the way we measure and represent these things."[28] This sentiment will resonate strongly in the new thinking of Capitalism 4.0.

However, one major political problem, apart from the intellectual puzzles of defining social welfare, will need to be overcome. The problem is that many of the most enthusiastic advocates of this approach, because of their links to the labor, green, and antiglobalization movements, have a natural bias against the capitalist system. They therefore see the redefinition of economic objectives as a way to reduce growth and the reform of economic statistics as a way to emphasize the harm that capitalism does. This may be a valid argument in the case of clearly dangerous products, such as asbestos, CFCs, or fraudulent mortgages, but the opposite way of looking at the same measurement problem would be politically much more promising, as well as more truthful.

Rather than concentrating on the unmeasured harms inflicted by capitalism, a more constructive approach is to focus on the many unmeasured public goods, ranging from clean air to law and order, which the market system values at zero because they are available for free.

The zero value attached to public goods such as air is merely a matter of social convention. The copyright to Windows, for example, is regarded as private property, and Microsoft is paid a substantial sum every time its software is bought. As a result, Microsoft has strong incentives to continue producing new software, and if it raises the price of Windows, this is legitimately counted as a contribution to economic growth. Air, on the other hand, is a public good and many businesses consider it outrageous that the U.S. government should even think of charging for its use through tradable carbon permits. Yet the same businesspeople who denounce carbon trading, insist that the U.S. government should go to enormous lengths to protect the Windows copyright, even though copies of Windows can be reproduced much more cheaply than clean air.

Water, like air, was seen as a free good, a gift of nature, in many parts of the world until the late twentieth century—and still is in some countries. As a result, huge amounts of water were wasted. But after a price was placed on water, whether by privatized water companies or by governments forced to respond to shortages, the use of water became far more efficient. As a result of this experience, it is now almost universally acknowledged that the best answer to the impending water crisis in many parts of the world is to raise the price of water substantially, to reflect its true economic value. Such a reform would be painful to farmers and unpopular among urban consumers, but it would almost certainly raise overall GDP by putting a high market value on a resource that society produces and consumes in enormous quantities. And this increase in GDP would accurately reflect the true social effects of raising the price of water, because society would now be valuing the enormous benefits of reliable access to fresh water, which had previously been underestimated or simply ignored.

By correcting such anomalies and attaching properly high prices to previously free or undervalued resources—from clean air to good education and even social equality—a reinvented model of capitalism could create powerful incentives for markets to preserve the global environment and improve society. Such an effort to reconcile market prices with social values could surprise politicians with its economic effects: On any reasonable measure of economic performance, putting high prices on public goods and environmental resources would lead to higher, not lower, economic growth.

Currencies and Financial Relations: Will There Be a New Bretton Woods?

A comprehensive reform of the global currency system has been widely demanded in the aftermath of the crisis. The French, Chinese, and many other governments have called for a new Bretton Woods and for a new international reserve currency to replace the dollar. These calls have sometimes been endorsed by such prominent U.S. and British policymakers as Paul Volcker and Gordon Brown. Yet the frequently demanded diminution in the international role of the dollar and return to the Bretton Woods system of fixed exchange rates has not happened and is very unlikely to happen in the decades ahead.

One thing the crisis proved beyond doubt was the value of floating currencies. Exchange rate flexibility gave governments around the world the freedom to cut interest rates and to support their economies with fiscal stimulus that could never have been imagined in the days of Bretton Woods. Conversely, the financial turmoil that engulfed the eurozone after the worst of the banking crisis was over in other countries reminded the world of the dangers of long-term commitments to fixed exchange rates and of the immense costs of defending currencies in a system disturbingly reminiscent of the gold standard of the 1930s. Any reversion to fixed exchange rates, still less to a gold-based system such as Bretton Woods, therefore seems out of the question. Since 1971, the world has lived without any monetary standard for the first time in history, and this is not about to change. Pure paper money is simply too powerful and too useful to be uninvented—like nuclear weapons, penicillin, or the pill.

An international financial reform that *is* likely under Capitalism 4.0, however, is a resumption of the managed, but flexible, currency policies of the 1980s. As governments and central banks move beyond the monetarist period's sole preoccupation with price stability and accept broader responsibilities for managing employment and real economic growth, exchange rates and trade imbalances are again becoming a major feature in international economic relations. The end of market fundamentalism has eroded the strict precrisis doctrine that currency relationships must be left to market forces. Instead, the years ahead are likely to see increasingly explicit negotiations over trade imbalances and concerted currency interventions.

There will be no return, however, to the government's futile efforts in the 1960s and 1970s to take full control over international financial flows. Instead, currency interventions and global macroeconomic coordination in the future are likely to represent a pragmatic compromise between the precrisis period's exaggerated faith in efficient markets and the overly prescriptive policies of the Keynesian Golden Age. Given that the U.S. and British governments were willing to engage in the massive currency interventions of the Plaza Agreement and the Louvre Accord in the mid-1980s, during the heyday of Thatcherism and Reaganomics, it is hard to see why governments of the future should consider any interference with market forces in foreign exchanges to be ideologically out of bounds. Instead of either a government-controlled fixed-rate system or the purely market-based clean floating of the precrisis period, the currency relations of the future will probably be closer to the 1980s model of a managed float.

Within this system of floating but partially managed exchange rates, the dollar shows every sign of retaining its pivotal global role. A serious challenge to the dollar's reserve currency status is hard to imagine because there is no alternative reserve currency and no reason to expect one to emerge. Those who believe that U.S. budget deficits and monetary expansion will destroy the dollar's international status must point to another currency that is underpinned by stronger fiscal and monetary foundations. At present, the only possible contender might be the Chinese yuan—and that cannot be considered a serious international currency because it cannot even be legally owned outside China. For the yuan even to begin the long journey toward reserve currency status, China must make its currency fully convertible and open its capital markets to foreign investors. Significant reform in this direction is unlikely for at least another decade, because currency convertibility and open capital markets would substantially weaken the Communist Party's capacity for economic and social control.

The only possible alternative to the dollar as the key currency of global trade and finance would be some kind of artificial international money created and managed by an international institution such as the IMF. The dollar could in principle be replaced by the IMF's special drawing rights (SDR), but for this to happen, the United States, China, and Europe would have to give up a significant part of their economic sovereignty and accept the superior legitimacy of the IMF, and of the UN system to which it ultimately belongs. This would indeed be a big step forward in global cooperation. But it is a step the world shows no sign of taking, even on the thirty- to forty-year timescale during which the new version of capitalism can be expected to survive.

Will Global Governance Be Strengthened to Resolve Global Problems?

The financial crisis profoundly altered politics around the world. It convinced voters of the need for competent administration and regulation but also spread terror about the costs of governments and their debts, and created tremendous confusion about the culpability of financiers, regulators, and politicians, past and present. With the election of a new U.S. administration dedicated to effective government, America moved closer to the center of world opinion on many issues where it had previously been in a minority of one. As a result, the crisis paradoxically made the United States more attractive as a political model and leader for other democracies. The hopes of a great leap forward in global governance were further encouraged during the crisis by the sudden emergence of the G20 (Group of Twenty) as an effective forum for taking urgent economic decisions—a forum that was both more representative and more powerful than the increasingly irrelevant G7 and G8 advanced economies (with Russia sometimes included and sometimes kept out).

But as the crisis subsided, so did the international willingness to cooperate. The unwieldy UN system of decision-making by unanimity was again discredited by the failure of the Copenhagen Summit on climate change and the continuing deadlock in the World Trade Organization over the Doha trade round. No great progress can be expected in either of these institutions, despite the many reforms occurring in the global capitalist system as a whole. Efforts to expand the UN Security Council have come to nothing, because middle-sized powers such as Britain and France will never agree to give up their powers of veto or consolidate themselves into a single European vote. Even the modest hopes of reforming the IMF and World Bank to increase the representation of China have been thwarted by small countries such as Belgium and Italy refusing to accept a dilution of their largely illusory prestige and power.

There is a clear contradiction between this paradoxically chaotic paralysis in global political institutions and the urgent need for a new model of capitalism in which governments and markets interact in new and complex ways. The most critical challenges facing the world in the coming decades—financial instability, trade imbalances, fiscal and monetary policy, carbon emissions, nuclear proliferation, terrorism, and even the tension between the Chinese and Western models—must all be tackled in a global context. It is surely then inevitable that the closer coordination between markets and government described in this book will have to move from the national to the global level.

In January 2010, President Sarkozy of France delivered a speech to the World Economic Forum in Davos that took many of the arguments presented in this book to their logical conclusion—and then sometimes beyond. With Sarkozy taking over in 2011 as head of the G20, his comments, culminating in a call for an unprecedented leap forward toward global government, therefore seem a fitting epilogue for this book:

> We are not asking ourselves what will replace capitalism, but what kind of capitalism we want . . . From the moment we accepted the idea that the market was always right and that no other opposing factors need be taken into account, globalization skidded out of control . . . This was not a crisis in globalization. This was a crisis of globalization . . . What remains to be done

is to bring into being a new growth model, invent a new linkage between public action and private initiative . . . The G20 foreshadows the planetary governance of the twenty-first century. It symbolizes the return of politics whose legitimacy was denied by unregulated globalization. In just one year, we have seen a genuine revolution in mentalities. For the first time in history, the heads of state and government of the world's twenty largest economic powers decided together on the measures that must be taken to combat a world crisis. They committed themselves, together, to adopting common rules that will radically change the way the world economy operates.

President Sarkozy rightly observed that the crisis focused attention on the inescapably global dimension of the serious, even existential, challenges facing mankind. Moreover, the crisis proved that the world could not rely blindly on market solutions.

In the national context, the response to the failure of market fundamentalist thinking has been clear, at least in principle: Democratically elected governments and publicly accountable regulators have gained more power. But at the international level, effective public institutions do not exist—and such institutions probably cannot exist, because there is no true legitimacy in the transfer of sovereignty from the nation state to global institutions.

How then will the world behave in the next phase of capitalism, when the necessity of more effective government is fully recognized, but no instruments or institutions exist for carrying out the functions of government at the global level, where so many of the greatest challenges have to be faced? The incipient thinking of Capitalism 4.0 has not begun to offer any answers. Yet this question will have to be answered as newly empowered governments and newly expectant electorates find their efforts to create more constructive partnerships between politics and economics continually thwarted by international clashes of interest.

An ever-widening gulf between global challenges and national institutions may turn out to be the fatal inner contradiction that precipitates the downfall of Capitalism 4.0—and its replacement by Capitalism 4.1, Capitalism 4.2, and ultimately Capitalism 5.

All we can say for certain is that global politics in the years ahead will be messy, confusing, and full of conflicts; that there will be more international imbalances and confrontations and more financial bubbles and crashes, with origins we cannot imagine; and that the progress of democratic capitalism, when and where it happens, will proceed by fits and starts. We can be certain also that the new model of the capitalist system now emerging will leave many questions unanswered and will contain some fatal contradictions.

Nothing about this new version of the capitalist system will be rational or perfectly efficient or eternally balanced. The future will always be unpredictable and ambiguous and inconsistent—just like human life. For that is what Capitalism 4.0 is about.

Epilogue

I N THE PERIOD SINCE this book was first published, many of the events and policies anticipated have become undeniable facts. When it comes to interpreting these facts, however, opinions can genuinely differ, and intense debates will continue for many years about the meaning of the events that followed the 2008 financial crisis. Fortunately, most of the analysis in this book has gained in plausibility after an extra year of hindsight.

Plausibility may, of course, seem a very weak standard—especially when set against the certain knowledge claimed by true economic prophets. But outside the fantasy world of sensationalized media headlines and paranoid TV propagandists, honest economists (and, for that matter, honest politicians or business leaders) can rarely claim anything more conclusive than plausibility for their ideas.

If art is the search for beauty and science is the search for truth, then economics is the search for plausibility. Economic theories can almost never be described as either right or wrong. Because economics seeks to understand human interactions that are far too complex to be modeled or analyzed in any precise scientific manner, it will always be essentially a speculative subject, more akin to history or psychology than to physics or biology in its claims of veracity and explanatory power.

Economists sometimes assume a posture of humility and appear to acknowledge the uncertainties inherent in their subject by using probabilities and statistics to describe the world. But even when they confine themselves to probabilities and statistics, economists face an insuperable obstacle in trying to interpret the world—especially in studying large-scale trends and cycles in financial markets and macroeconomics: there have not been remotely enough macroeconomic cycles or truly systemic structural transformations since the dawn of modern history for any scientifically meaningful conclusions to be drawn by methods of statistical inference. Since World War II, for example, there have been only five or six global recessions (depending on definitions), and only two of these occurred since the structural changes of the 1980s that completely transformed the behavior of the world economy. As for genuine changes in structural trends—the kind discussed in Part II of this book—there have been only two or three industrial revolutions in history comparable to the one now unfolding, and the capitalist system has gone through only three distinct versions.

Thus, statements like "this recession is deeper and longer than normal" have no genuine scientific meaning. Neither does this book's contention that fundamental transformations of the capitalist system are normally accompanied by a new understanding of economics. It would take dozens or, strictly speaking, hundreds of global recessions or systemic crises before we could give any meaning to the word *normal*—or to establish whether my sweeping statement about capitalist transformations is true.

Most of the time, therefore, intellectually honest economists must be content with hand-waving generalizations that can make no greater claim to objective truth than statements made by historians, financiers, or even politicians. Yet despite the impossibility of ever achieving scientific rigor, economists can and must link their ideas to facts in the real world. While economic ideas cannot be held up to scientific standards of truth, they can be judged for their plausibility and usefulness. Do they structure our understanding of events in the real world and help us reach decisions that turn out to be socially useful? Or do they merely reinforce prejudices, entrench vested interests, and encourage bigger policy mistakes?

A year after *Capitalism 4.0* was first published, how does it stand up to such tests of plausibility on the main issues it raised?

1. Did the Great Recession Turn into a
Great Transition or a Great Stagnation?

Conditions in the world economy improved dramatically in 2010, as did the outlook for all major national economies and regions with the significant exceptions of Britain and the periphery of Europe. These improvements defied the consensus expectations that existed at the time this book was written and strongly reinforced the message that the irresistible force of monetary and fiscal stimulus had overwhelmed the immoveable object of overindebted consumers and de-leveraging banks.

The economic recovery was not recognized by the mainstream media and the general public until late 2010 because the indicators that affect ordinary workers and small businesses were, as usual, the last to improve: unemployment started falling, but very slowly; house prices stabilized, but at low levels; and bank credit for small businesses and consumers was cheaper, but still very hard to obtain. Forward-looking financial indicators, by contrast, improved dramatically in 2010: stock markets recovered to within a few percentage points of their records; currencies stabilized; and corporate profits soared to all-time highs.

In Europe, economic recovery was slower than in America, but it had also become undeniable by early 2011, even taking into account the troubles of the semibankrupt peripheral nations that came to be known ungraciously as the PIGS (Portugal, Italy, Greece, and Spain). Meanwhile, China, India, Korea, Russia, Brazil, and other emerging economies went from strength to strength, powered by the global megatrends described in Part II. In aggregate, the developing nations increased their output by almost half in the five years from 2005 to 2010—a continuous record of growth they had never achieved before.

The upshot was that the world economy, instead of sinking into long-term stagnation or double-dip recession, rebounded to a growth rate of 5 percent in 2010. This was about as strong as global growth had ever been before the crisis and was well above the average growth of 3.5 percent in the previous two decades. On a long-run chart of economic performance in emerging markets, the so-called Great Recession was already looking like a minor blip. It may well look that way eventually for the United States,

Germany, and Scandinavia too—but probably not for Britain and southern Europe.

The prospects for Britain, in particular, turned suddenly bleaker as 2010 progressed, mainly because the government adopted a surprisingly fundamentalist and backward-looking approach to economic policy at odds with its centrist political image. Even though many of the reforms undertaken by the government were likely to benefit the British economy in the long run, the loss of wealth and income, and the weakness of demand caused by the crisis, was needlessly exacerbated by panic measures to reduce the budget deficit. Cuts in welfare benefits and reductions in public sector wages, pensions, and jobs may well have been justified in terms of economic efficiency and, in some cases, even of social justice. But in contrast to U.S., French, and even German policymakers, the new British government willfully ignored the Keynesian effects on the economy of depressing consumer incomes and spending power.

In effect, the British government had decided to rerun Margaret Thatcher's experiments with the fundamentalist economics of the precrisis era—just when these ideas were quietly abandoned in America and other leading economies, including China, Germany, and Japan. The risks to Britain were disguised for a while by its economy's strength in early 2010. But this was deceptive, a consequence largely of the fiscal and monetary stimuli introduced by the Labour Government in early 2009, which continued to work their way through the economy for another year or so. Because of the lags between policy changes and their economic effects, Britain in 2010 was still living under the Gordon Brown's policies. The economic performance of David Cameron's Britain would not become apparent until 2011.

The contrast between Britain's severe fiscal austerity from mid-2010 onward and the continuing budgetary laxity of the Obama administration set up a fascinating controlled experiment of a kind rarely seen in economics. Britain and the United States are two economies with similar economic structures facing similar challenges: big falls in house prices, high levels of consumer debt, huge budget deficits, structural dependence on high-income wholesale finance, relatively small manufacturing sectors, and a need to rebalance their economies toward export-led growth. They were both hit hard by the crisis, and they reacted with similar policies in the initial phase from

2007 to 2009, rescuing and then guaranteeing their banks, undertaking substantial fiscal stimulus (though not quite as big as China and Germany, relative to the size of their economies), and vastly expanding the money printed by their central banks.

The initial results of these policies were broadly similar, since both the British and U.S. economies rebounded strongly from late 2009 onward. But from mid-2010 onward the two countries' policies diametrically diverged. Britain began the fastest and deepest program of government deficit reductions ever attempted by an economy of its size in the postwar period. Meanwhile, the political gridlock in Washington ensured that a policy of fiscal laxity would continue at least until the presidential election of 2012.

Similar experiments, though less precisely controlled, were being conducted in Europe, with Greece, Ireland, and Spain attempting huge budget reductions after the crisis while fiscal policy in Germany, France, and Scandinavia stayed on a fairly steady course.

If economics were truly a scientific study, these controlled experiments—similar economies with similar initial conditions pursuing very different policies—might settle once and for all the debate between Keynesians, who believed that premature fiscal contraction would stifle economic recovery, and monetarists and supply-side economists, who argue that reducing public spending and deficits is always and everywhere good for economic growth. But economics is not a science and the inconclusive arguments will doubtless go on.

2. If Economic Recovery Is So Strong, Why Does Nobody Believe This?

There are three plausible reasons why the radical improvement in global economic conditions was met with almost universal skepticism, at least until the end of 2010. First, the simplest explanation of widespread skepticism about recovery is that disbelief is normal at this stage of the economic cycle. Near the bottom of previous recessions, public and media opinion has often confused cycles with trends. An article that came to my attention after this book's original publication perfectly illustrates this syndrome.

If America's economic landscape seems suddenly alien and hostile to many citizens, there is good reason: they have never seen anything like it. Nothing in memory has prepared consumers for such turbulent, epochal change, the sort of upheaval that happens once in 50 years. The outward sign of the change is an economy that stubbornly refuses to recover from the recession. In a normal rebound, Americans would be witnessing a flurry of hiring, new investment and lending, and buoyant growth. But the U.S. economy remains almost comatose a full year and a half after the recession officially ended. Unemployment is still high; real wages are declining.

The Great Depression was the last time the economy staggered under as many "structural" burdens, as opposed to the familiar "cyclical" problems that create temporary recessions once or twice a decade. The structural faults, many of them legacies of the 1980s, represent once-in-a-lifetime dislocations that will take years to work out. Among them: the job drought, the debt hangover, the defense-industry contraction, the savings and loan collapse, the real estate depression, the health-care cost explosion and the runaway federal deficit.[1]

This article was published, like the other purple passages quoted in Chapter 8, in 1992. With hindsight it turned out that the "comatose" period this article lamented was already over by the time it was written. In fact the U.S. economy had just embarked on the longest period of sustained economic expansion and job growth in recorded history. But none of this was apparent at the time. There are good reasons to believe that something similar may happen in 2011 and beyond, as the cyclical dynamics of financial boom and bust give way to the slower-moving but more powerful megatrends in technology, economic thinking, and politics described in Part II of this book.

Political change was, in fact, a second reason for the skepticism about postcrisis recovery, especially in the United States. American politics by the end of the crisis had become more polarized than at any time since the Civil War, as evidenced by the studies quoted in Chapter 17. But in the run-up to the November 2010 congressional elections, the country's most influential media and business voices, from the *Wall Street Journal* and Fox News on the Right, to the *New York Times* and MSNBC on the Left, were united on one issue. They all loathed the Obama administration, albeit for very different reasons. The result was an inadvertent conspiracy by the two ends of the political spectrum to sensationalize the country's economic problems and to belittle the improvements that were already appearing in the statistics, in the stock market, and so on.

Once the elections were over, American politics began to move back toward some degree of comity, if not consensus: Businesses refocused their attention on profits and investment instead of opinion polls. The public and the media began to notice the improving economic conditions disguised by the political antagonisms leading up to November 2010. And this change in perceptions rapidly affected the economic fundamentals, boosting both consumption and employment. The improving real economy then validated and reinforced the changing perceptions, in a classic case of George Soros's reflexivity.

In Britain, unfortunately, the reflexivity of politics and economics worked the opposite way. The general election of May 2010 inspired optimism about the country's economic prospects and about the possibility of creating a new political consensus along the lines described in this book. But the new coalition government decided to take advantage of this newfound economic confidence and political consensus to intensify the substantial budget reductions already planned under Labour, creating a deflationary environment of unprecedented severity. Despite the fact that Britain was almost immune to currency and bond market pressures for the reasons explained in Chapter 15, the new coalition government behaved as if the country were facing an existential financial challenge comparable to the market attacks on Greece, Ireland, and Spain. The government hoped that by taking exceptionally aggressive action against budget deficits it would instill confidence in businesses and consumers, creating a virtuous circle of investment, job creation, and rising tax revenues.

But by early 2011 the circle of reflexivity appeared to be turning in the opposite direction. The squeeze on personal incomes was forcing consumers to cut back their spending, and that in turn was likely to discourage businesses from investment and employment. Britain, therefore, was the one major economy in which economic growth and political confidence seemed likely to deteriorate instead of improve in 2011 and beyond.

A third explanation for the continuing skepticism about recovery was the alarming level of unemployment in America even after the recession theoretically ended in June 2009. Most Americans believed, much like the authors of the 1992 article quoted above, that their country was suffering a jobless recovery and sinking into permanent stagnation, similar to Japan's "lost decade" after the bursting of its bubble economy in 1989.

But the widespread belief that America's recovery was jobless was factually false. The U.S. economy created a net 1.4 million jobs in the twelve months before December 2010. This was slightly more than the 1 million jobs created in the corresponding twelve months of the 1991–92 expansion and a much better performance than the truly jobless recovery of 2002–03, when the United States continued losing jobs for two years after the recession theoretically ended.

Moreover, the high level of U.S. unemployment after the recession was not really attributable to the financial crisis. This could be seen from the experience of other countries, especially the other wealthy and advanced economies in Europe. American policymakers and commentators rarely bother with such international comparisons, but if they did they would notice that Europe—especially Germany, France, and Scandinavia—experienced far smaller job losses in the recession, despite the fact that their economic activity fell even farther and faster than America's.

The United States suffered a smaller fall in GDP than any of these European countries and by late 2010 had become the first major advanced economy to recover to its prerecession level of output, leaving Germany, France, and Sweden well behind. Yet despite the relatively strong U.S. growth performance, American unemployment in late 2010 was almost twice its 2008 level (9.4 percent in December 2010 compared with 5.0 percent in January 2008), whereas French and Swedish jobless numbers increased only slightly during the crisis and Germany actually reduced its unemployment from 7.9 percent to 6.7 percent. Taking the unemployment statistics at face value, it was easier by the end of 2010 to find a job in the ex-Communist industrial rustbelt of eastern Germany than it was in high-tech California.

What was the cause of this divergence between European and U.S. unemployment? As noted, it was certainly not any difference in economic growth. Neither was it greater financial stability in Europe, since the euro-zone had by 2010 become the cockpit of the global financial crisis. The key to Europe's better job record appeared to be business attitudes and government policies very much at odds with American free-market thinking.

In Germany and Sweden, governments offered generous subsidies for companies that kept idle workers on their payrolls through the recession, while stringent employment laws imposed large costs for letting workers go. In America, by contrast, companies hired and fired their workers at will and business received no public subsidies for maintaining their payrolls when their business declined. Productivity growth and profitability thus remained unusually high in America throughout the recession, whereas in Europe businesses preserved jobs, albeit at the cost of temporary reductions in productivity and profits.

According to precrisis economic orthodoxy , based on the theories of efficient markets and rational expectations, America's free-market approach to labor was unambiguously superior to Europe's more regulated system, not only for profits but also for job creation. And this theory was surely right when applied to extreme cases of sclerotic labor markets such as Greece and Spain, where rigid labor regulations had locked in appallingly high unemployment for many years. But like so many other free-market doctrines, labor deregulation may have been taken beyond its logical conclusions in the economic thinking of Capitalism 3.3.

One of the most intriguing lessons from the postcrisis recession is that America may have lessons on employment policy to learn from Europe, and not just the other way round. If the intolerable level of U.S. unemployment persists for many years after the crisis, then this should be seen as evidence that the single most important claim of market fundamentalist economics is simply wrong. According to this precrisis economic theory, a deregulated economy automatically produces full employment, while government interference destroys private-sector jobs. But what if the highly regulated German and Swedish labor markets achieve and maintain permanently lower unemployment? If this happens, then the central theorem of orthodox economics will have been falsified. It will then become even clearer that Capitalism 3.3, the model of political economy built on this theory, has come to the end of its useful life.

3. Was the Financial Crisis Really
Just an Avoidable Liquidity Problem?

Banks all over the world have repaid their government loans ahead of schedule, and the U.S. and British governments are likely to make handsome profits on the financial rescues of 2008–09. Even the rescue of AIG, initially estimated to cost over $200 billion has turned out to be highly profitable after mark-to-market accounting was replaced by traditional methods of valuing the financial risks that it had insured.

The post-Lehman performance of banks and financial markets has thus strongly reinforced the core arguments of Chapter 10—that the credit crunch really was a temporary liquidity crisis and that it did not reflect the structural insolvency of the entire world financial system. From this, it follows that the terrible economic and social consequences that followed the Lehman failure could largely have been avoided with earlier and more comprehensive government intervention, especially if this had been backed by sensible regulatory reforms and a return to traditional accounting, instead of the mark-to-market accounting introduced into banking shortly before the crisis.

Mark-to-market accounting is a classic case of an ideologically convenient theory invented under Capitalism 3.3 to entrench belief in efficient markets and at the same time to serve vested interests by inflating bank bonuses and allowing companies such as Enron and WorldCom to conjure up phantom profits. Strangely enough, however, the low-cost regulatory and political measures that could possibly have averted the crisis—and could certainly have reduced its collateral damage—have continued to be downplayed in the postcrisis response. It seems that politicians and regulators preferred writing checks for trillions of taxpayer dollars over acknowledging that their decisions were based on a false and simplistic economic ideology.

Other failures of bank regulation, especially in the United States and Britain, could be attributed to a similar cause—the refusal of political leaders to question market fundamentalist economic thinking. Banks were able to lobby successfully against foreclosure reforms, restrictions on commodity speculation, and close supervision of credit default swaps on the grounds that such regulations could not be legitimized by any demonstrated evidence of market failure.

Such lobbying by banks was often against the interests of their own shareholders. For example, foreclosure reforms in the United States could have protected bank profits by helping defaulting borrowers to stay in their homes, as they generally do in Britain. House prices in Britain fell as steeply as they did in the United States in 2008–09, and loans with zero down-payments were even more widespread, but British banks suffered only minimal losses on their home mortgage books partly because lending terms were quickly renegotiated and eased. U.S. banks, by contrast, continued to oppose radical foreclosure reforms that could have protected their shareholders from tens of billions of dollars in losses on the grounds that such reforms would interfere with free-market forces.

Similarly, global agreements on restructuring bank compensation could have prevented a re-escalation of bank labor costs worth many billions to shareholders. But bankers, fervent in their support for labor reforms designed to cut wages in industries such as steel, coal, and autos, were unable to see any benefit in political measures to reduce labor costs in their own business.

In finance, therefore, politicians and regulators continued to resisted the main arguments of this book: that banking is a structurally unique business that by its nature must always and everywhere rely on government support, and that as a consequence, banks, their employees, and their customers should be forced to pay for this government insurance in advance. Instead, market fundamentalist thinking allowed the banks to sidetrack the postcrisis policy response into pointless debates about market failures and breaking up the banks that are too big to fail. These irrelevant arguments allowed the bankers themselves to get off scot-free—unrepentant, and richer than ever.

4. Is It Fair to Blame the Crisis on Henry Paulson?

In a broadly generous review of *Capitalism 4.0*, Lord Robert Skidelsky, one of the world's preeminent historians of economics, responded with the following caustic comment to the account of the financial crisis in Chapter 11:

That a three-week delay in applying the 'correct' remedial measures to a U.S. banking failure caused the world economy to collapse is wildly implausible. Kaletsky's assertion recalls Keynes's remark that, starting from a false premise, a relentless logician can end up in Bedlam.[2]

The *Economist*, in another generally flattering article, described my attribution of personal responsibility for the crisis to Henry Paulson as "unseemly as well as unconvincing."[3]

Yet the rapid recovery of the banks and the successful management of what was potentially a far bigger financial crisis in Europe suggests the conclusion about Mr. Paulson was exactly right. The U.S. Treasury's decisions to bankrupt Lehman and not to put in place any remedial measures until a month later really were fatal. In fact, with every month that passes, it becomes more plausible that most of the immense economic losses caused by the crisis could have been avoided if governments had acted just a few weeks earlier in implementing the guarantees and bank recapitalizations announced by Britain on October 8, 2008, and imitated by the U.S. and other leading economies the following week. Lehman might still have gone bankrupt, and Fannie and Freddie might still have required nationalization, but if a strong safety net had been put in place before Paulson made these fateful decisions, the damage to other, perfectly healthy financial institutions would probably have been averted.

In that case, the collapse of world trade and industrial activity resulting from the disappearance of bank credit in the fourth quarter of 2008 would never have happened, and the Great Recession might well have been nothing worse than a mild slowdown caused by the loss of a few hundred thousand banking and construction jobs.

The rapid recovery of wholesale banking after the safety nets were put in place also suggests that the crisis was *not* an inevitable result of what European policymakers described after the crisis as the "hypertrophy" of the financial sector—meaning that global financial activity grew far too rapidly, like a cancer, in relation to the world economy it was meant to serve. Two years after the crisis the scale of global financial activity and the size of the banking system was again nearing its precrisis level and was still rapidly growing. Banks and bankers were becoming as rich as before. It seemed, therefore, that most of the growth of finance in the precrisis decades reflected the genuine demand created by the explosive growth of global investment and trade.

The conventional view about the rapid recovery of finance is that the bankers have, as usual, taken governments and taxpayers for a ride. But while it is true that banks have been scandalously effective in lobbying against desirable new regulations, it is not true that bank profits have been restored at taxpayers' expense. Despite a few spectacular exceptions such as Ireland and Iceland, most governments had by late 2010 begun to extract far more money from the banks than they put in, and they could look forward to large profits once they returned nationalized banks to private ownership. What about the huge deficits run up by the British and U.S. governments? In most cases, with Iceland and Ireland again standing as tragic exceptions, postcrisis public deficits had nothing to do with the direct costs of the bank rescues but were due, as explained in Chapter 16, to the loss of tax revenues caused by the post-Lehman collapse in economic activity. Moreover, the countries whose governments and taxpayers did suffer genuine banking losses mostly had highly regulated financial systems with very little exposure to the international wholesale banking and speculative "casino banking" that was growing fastest before the crash.

It seems, therefore, that the main problem with the Anglo-Saxon banking system was neither its scale nor even the nature of its business models but the way these business models were implemented. Flawed risk-management models based on false economic theories about so-called efficient markets led to excess leverage and perversely pro-cyclical regulatory reforms that encouraged banks to increase their risk exposures as profits expanded, instead of taking advantage of booming profits to reinforce their financial stability. Politicians assumed—and most again assume—that the market knows best. Therefore, they concluded—and in most cases still conclude—that it is wrong and politically illegitimate for the state to intervene in the financial sector, either with intrusive regulation or with strong public safety nets or other convincing mechanisms for timely emergency support.

That a meltdown *can* be averted with judicious government intervention was demonstrated by the financial events in Europe that followed the near-default by Greece. Europe's financial fundamentals in 2010 were much worse than the underlying causes of the subprime fiasco. But European policymakers seemed to learn from the U.S. Treasury's dismal experience.

The Europeans stated clearly from an early stage in the crisis that they would do whatever it takes to protect the euro and to avoid both sovereign defaults and bank failures. They provided unlimited financing to all European banks, whether or not they were solvent. And they resisted market fundamentalist demands to impose losses on bank creditors.

It still remains to be seen whether Europe can avoid Paulson's mistake of trying to do just enough to avoid immediate catastrophe while putting off the huge shock-and-awe interventions required to restore financial stability and stop the crisis once and for all. Is it really conceivable that the eurozone, with its seventeen squabbling governments and central banks, will pull off this intricate balancing act, which the U.S. Treasury and Federal Reserve so spectacularly failed to manage? In practice, this seems almost impossible. But then so does a break-up of the euro. The euro crisis, therefore, seems to be another case like the ones discussed in Chapter 14—of an irresistible force meeting an immoveable object. Something will have to give.

In the case of Europe, what gives will probably have to be both the legacy of big-government socialism in Greece, Spain, Italy, and France and the last remnants of fundamentalist monetarism in the German government and the European Central Bank. Such ideological flexibility—which is moving both southern and northern Europe, from opposite directions, toward the philosophy of Capitalism 4.0—may well prove possible because European leaders enjoy a key advantage over the Bush administration in crafting a response to financial crisis: they are not bound by the fundamentalist doctrine that the market is always right. Even in Germany, the belief in monetarism and fiscal consolidation is more a pragmatic response to the economic conditions of the 1970s and 1980s than an article of ideological faith.

Market fundamentalist economic doctrine was what prevented the Bush administration from taking the necessary preventive measures to avert the Lehman disaster—or even to cope in a timely manner with the economic consequences of what they had unleashed. The true cause of the

Lehman crisis was not the hypertrophy of the global financial system but the false economic ideology of the precrisis period. This conclusion is becoming ever clearer as the passage of time offers more perspective on this avoidable disaster.

5. Is the Crisis Changing Economic Thinking?

When the post-Lehman recession ended in the summer of 2009, economists and financial commentators were almost unanimous in believing that a sustained recovery was impossible, although there was much disagreement about the reasons why the world economy, and the U.S. economy in particular, would succumb either to a second recession or a long period of Japanese-style stagnation. This conventional wisdom could broadly be divided into four schools of thought:

First, a group of ultra-Keynesians had as its most prominent public spokesmen Paul Krugman of the *New York Times*; Martin Wolf of the *Financial Times*; and Joseph Stiglitz, Nouriel Roubini, and George Soros, who were ubiquitous in influential publications and at conferences around the world. These Keynesian ultras insisted that there could be no proper economic recovery. In fact, they insisted that a double-dip recession was almost certain because governments had not spent nearly enough on fiscal stimulus to counterbalance the enormous reductions in private consumption and investment that would inevitably follow the financial crisis. This group directed its harshest criticisms against the U.S. government, arguing that President Obama would have had to boost public spending and borrowing another trillion dollars or so to revive normal growth and reduce unemployment.

The second group of skeptics attacked from the opposite direction. Based in the bastions of monetarist orthodoxy at the University of Chicago, the German Bundesbank, the British Conservative Party, and the *Wall Street Journal* editorial page, they argued that fiscal stimulus, far from supporting the economy, was damaging employment and growth. Deficits were undermining business and consumer confidence, and the best way to revive economic activity was to slash public spending.

Another, more extreme school of conservative commentators charged that stimulus policies would not just prove counterproductive but catastrophic, causing an inflationary disaster. Niall Ferguson, the Harvard economic historian, Rand Paul, the influential Tea Party candidate then congressman, and Marc Faber, a controversial Swiss financial pundit, were among the most widely quoted pundits who predicted that a Weimar-style hyperinflation would follow the so-called debasement of the dollar by the U.S. government and the Federal Reserve. They also predicted, to the delight of gold investors everywhere, that by discrediting government bonds and paper money, U.S. monetary policy would direct a flood of savings into the one reliable store of wealth remaining, namely gold.

Finally, there was a fourth group of skeptics who believed that a modest recovery from recession was likely, but predicted that a return to the precrisis normality of full employment and robust growth was inconceivable because the world economy would suffer for years, or even decades, from the damage caused by the financial crisis. The most prominent proponents of this viewpoint, which was also widely accepted in the business community and the financial markets, were Mohamed El-Erian, the head of the world's biggest bond investment group, Pimco, and Kenneth Rogoff, a former chief economist of the IMF. El-Erian coined the term *New Normal* to describe the many years of stagnation that lay ahead for the U.S. and world economies, and Rogoff's book *This Time Is Different: Eight Centuries of Financial Folly* acquired an almost scriptural authority among devotees of the New Normal, since it appeared to prove with statistical rigor that financial crises invariably result in long periods of very weak growth.

Eighteen months into the postcrisis period, it may be too early to claim that all these dangers have been averted, but it can be confidently asserted that none of the theoretical criticisms of the policy response have been supported by the evidence so far.

Printing money did not fuel inflation, and budget deficits did not trigger bond market panics. On the contrary, inflation fell to a postwar low in the United States, the country undertaking the most aggressive monetary expansion. Long-term interest rates all over the world plunged to the lowest levels on record. And investors, far from losing confidence in paper money, piled into cash and government bonds, while gold started falling, instead of rising, as the Fed printed more money and the U.S. economy recovered.

If economics were truly a scientific discipline, the simple-minded monetarism still popular among many politicians and business leaders would already have been refuted by the absence of inflation in the United States. In the future, the controlled experiment with opposite fiscal policies that started in Britain and America from 2011 onward would be observed carefully by economists everywhere in the hope of settling once and for all the arguments about the effects of Keynesian fiscal policy on economic growth and employment.

But economics is not a scientific discipline and such regard for reality is probably too much to hope for. Since the crisis, the right-wing devotees of efficient markets, rational expectations, Ricardian Equivalence, and the other fundamentalist theories described in Chapter 11 have become even less willing than in the past to submit their theories to empirical testing. Instead, they have relied more than ever on self-serving theoretical assumptions and the brute force of populist conservative rhetoric. Equally intransigent have been the Keynesian ultras, who ridiculed the postcrisis stimulus policies as doomed to failure and then simply changed the subject when their predictions turned out to be wrong.

The New Normal theories about permanently low growth and high unemployment also became less credible as 2010 wore on and the world seemed to make a successful transition from a recovery powered by government stimulus to a period of self-sustaining expansion, driven by consumer spending and private investment. Because of the strength of emerging markets, the global expansion was stronger than previous business cycles, and by late 2010 even the advanced economies seemed to be growing at roughly their typical rates of precrisis decades: a little over 3 percent in the United States and around 2 percent in Europe and Britain. While the levels of output and employment in the United States and Europe remained well below where they would have been if the financial crisis and recession had never happened, the experience from late 2010 onward suggested no great difference between the New Normal and the Old Normal. This did not, of course, prevent the economists who had predicted many years of postcrisis stagnation from claiming that they were still right.

6. Are New Economic Policies Emerging from the Crisis?

Although academic economists will doubtless continue to fight their rearguard actions for the reasons explained in Chapter 11, the crisis is encouraging a faster evolution in policy thinking. Since September 15, 2010, politicians and central bankers have paid almost no attention to academic economics and instead have improvised unorthodox policies in the adaptive spirit of Capitalism 4.0. The results have mostly proved successful, along the lines suggested in Chapters 14 to 16.

The huge fiscal and monetary stimuli introduced in 2009 worked more or less as predicted by Keynesian economics, triggering stronger than expected recoveries around the world.

Monetary theories were transformed by the crisis even more than fiscal policies. Single-minded inflation targeting—the key doctrine of the Thatcher-Reagan monetarism, designed to absolve governments of any responsibility for unemployment—was abandoned. This happened explicitly in the United States, where the Fed publicly emphasized its dual mandate, requiring it to control both unemployment and inflation, and acknowledged for the first time that unemployment could not be reduced simply by stabilizing inflation expectations, as the official monetarist doctrine had asserted since 1979.

The Bank of England and the European Central Bank also effectively abandoned their 2 percent inflation targets, but unlike the Fed they never openly admitted this, since market fundamentalism continued to determine the legal mandates of these central banks. Sadly, these central bankers continued to behave like obsessive compulsives, imagining that they could focus on only one objective instead of admitting openly, like the Fed, that their main challenge in the postcrisis period was to accelerate growth and reduce unemployment. Why was it considered dangerous for central bankers to balance many desirable but sometimes conflicting objectives, like sane human beings in any other walk of life? This is a question that could not be asked at all in the precrisis economic orthodoxy. And even in early 2011 it could be asked only within the Fed—and then sotto voce. But the fact that the world's most important economic institution had started to respond to this question was one of the clearest indications that the era of market fundamentalism was ending and the transition to the next model of capitalism was under way.

7. Is the New Capitalism Just a Return to Big Government and Capitalism 2?

The need for a new model of capitalism was widely acknowledged after the crisis, at least outside the United States. Chinese government leaders spoke more and more explicitly about their ambition to create a new model of capitalism after the failure the American and Western approach. Even in Britain, a new understanding of the interactions between politics and economics became a central theme of the Conservative-Liberal coalition's rhetoric, with the Big Society slogan implying all kinds of new partnerships between business, government, and civil society. On the Left, Gordon Brown echoed this book's analysis in his personal memoir of the crisis, *Beyond the Crash*: "The twentieth century was dominated by a sterile battle between markets and states, between the public and private sectors. The answer is not to reject markets, nor to reject government action. Instead, recognizing that both markets and the state can fail, the answer is to find a new way for individuals, markets and governments to work together."[4]

But are such calls for more collaboration between government and business simply a return to the big government ideology of Capitalism 2? That was a widespread view in the United States, especially before the November 2010 election. The Tea Party largely succeeded in branding any discussion of business-government relations as socialist treason.

On closer inspection, however, such claims were absurd—and even the U.S. Republican Party moved toward a more pragmatic posture, partly in response to pressure from the business community, once the election was out of the way. As they looked around the world, even conservative business leaders began to notice that governments were actually reducing their involvement in many areas previously regarded as impregnable bastions of the public sector—higher education and welfare in Britain, health care and pensions in continental Europe, charter schools in the United States. In America, public-private partnerships for the management of roads, water, and airports were coming belatedly onto the political agenda, and wide-spread privatization of such assets will probably follow, as state and local governments attempt to balance their books.

But whereas public spending began to decline in 2010 as stimulus funds were exhausted—a fall that will doubtless accelerate in 2011 and beyond—governments were also under pressure to take on new responsibilities, especially to regulate finance and "create jobs." Governments all over the world must now find ways of expanding and contracting at the same time, much as described in Chapter 17.

As a result of these contradictory pressures for less government and more government, the present model of capitalism has begun to look unsustainable both from the Left and the Right. The Tea Party's vision of a market economy with almost no role for government (to the point of abolishing the Federal Reserve Board) would involve a revolution much greater than the one proposed in *Capitalism 4.0*.

While Capitalism 4 can be derided—and has been—as an attempt to turn the clock back to a slightly improved version of Capitalism 2, which failed in the 1970s, the Tea Party is quite explicitly demanding a return to the unqualified free market idealism of Capitalism 1, including even a fundamentalist "strict construction" of the Constitution and the writings of America's founding fathers. As the ultra-conservative rhetoric begins to be translated into concrete policy proposals, American voters may recall the collapse of Capitalism 1 in the period between the Russian Revolution and the late 1930s. This dreadful precedent will probably deter America from following the logic of market fundamentalism to the final *reducio ad absurdum* represented by the Tea Party. But one last fling is possible with a market fundamentalism even more extreme than President Bush's version of Capitalism 3.3. Since such an experiment would probably result in a breakdown of some kind in the U.S. system of democratic government, this is perhaps the most serious systemic danger facing the world in the postcrisis years.

There is frightening evidence, in fact, that American voters have become almost childishly capricious and inconsistent in their attitudes toward politics, demanding balanced budgets, lower taxes, and higher spending on health and pensions entitlements all at the same time. In a poll published by Reuters/Ipsos in early 2011, for example, 71 percent of respondents wanted Congress to default on Treasury obligations rather than accept an administration request to increase the limit on national debt. But the poll also showed more than 75 percent opposed to any cutbacks in Social Security or Medicare, and clear majorities against tax increases of any kind.[5] The only fiscal program that most Americans seemed ready to support, therefore, was repealing the laws of arithmetic.

The people of Europe, by contrast, responded to the crisis with a surprising willingness to reconsider priorities, especially in pensions and health care, as discussed in Chapter 17. Such fundamental reassessments, which are ultimately unavoidable in all advanced economies because of population aging, were imposed on Greece, Spain, and Ireland by the financial markets, but they also began to be implemented without external pressure in Britain, Germany, Scandinavia, and France. It may be, therefore, that most of the innovative thinking on government budget limits that will be demanded by the new political economy will happen in Europe and not in the United States.

8. Will Conservative or Progressive Politics Gain from the Crisis?

One of the most intriguing questions of the postcrisis period is why progressive parties failed to benefit from the greatest crisis of capitalism in eighty years. The backlash against bankers and financiers has not translated into support for policies to narrow income inequalities through punitive or even mildly redistributive taxation. Instead, conservative movements all over the world have gained votes by running populist campaigns against bankers, while left-wing politicians such as Barack Obama and Gordon Brown have ended up bearing most of the blame for the crisis.

By ascribing the crisis primarily to the misdeeds of banks and bankers, the Left made two big mistakes. The first mistake was analytical and strategic. Laying the blame on bankers distracted public attention from the market fundamentalist thinking—of which bank deregulation was just one minor example—that caused the crisis. The Left failed to explain that it was right-wing ideology—and not just personal incompetence or greed—

that justified the recklessness of bankers, emasculated banking supervision, and prevented governments from intervening to preserve financial stability when required.

Having failed to explain the role of ideology in the crisis, the Left gave conservatives an opening to claim that the real problem was not excessive market freedom but excessive government. So efficient was the rewriting of history that David Cameron was able to proclaim shortly before he won the 2010 British election: "Labour say that to solve the country's problems we need more government. Don't they see? It was more government that got us into this mess."[6]

The Left's second mistake was tactical. If banks had been truly responsible for the crisis, they should have been ruthlessly nationalized and their creditors should have been expropriated, as demanded by many progressive economists and financiers such as Joseph Stiglitz, George Soros, and Robert Reich. But practical politicians, from Barack Obama and Gordon Brown downward, sensibly refused to do this, realizing that wholesale nationalization would have been catastrophically destabilizing at a time when the private sector was already in a state of panic—as well as politically impossible to implement. Because nationalizations and punitive measures never happened, the Left's response to the crisis seemed inconsistent, ineffectual, and weak; progressive leaders put all the blame on bankers and then did nothing much to punish them or even bring them to heel.

The Right, by contrast, provided voters with a narrative of the crisis that sounded coherent, even if it was false. This narrative was simply to identify Big Government as the root of all evil. In both the U.S. and British election campaigns of 2010, the suicidal recklessness of bankers in subprime lending was blamed routinely on some cautious regulatory guidance that had encouraged modest lending to low-income households. Even more bizarrely, voters soon started to blame the recession and unemployment not on the Lehman bankruptcy but on the fact that AIG, Citibank, and Royal Bank of Scotland were bailed out.

With conservative politics in the ascendant in the United States, Britain, and most of Europe, it is now even clearer than it was when Chapter

17 was written that by blaming the crisis on banks and bankers instead of on the economic ideology of Bush and Paulson, the Left made one of the biggest political miscalculations of modern times.

9. Where Will the New Model of Capitalism Be Invented?

Despite the counterintuitive success of right-wing politics after the crisis, the demise of Capitalism 3.3 as an economic model has been widely acknowledged, and the need for a new relationship between governments and markets has become a major subject for debate in Europe and Asia, but not yet in the United States. America's reluctance to acknowledge the need to reinvent its economic model may be symptomatic of the psychological denial to be expected in a declining hegemonic power. But while Republicans fought successful rearguard actions in 2010 to prevent the sort of government activism in finance, energy, and trade policies described in Part V of this book, it is unlikely that voters will, in the long run, support their efforts to preserve America's precrisis status quo.

Although the results of the 2010 congressional elections were widely described as a triumph for radical free-market ideas, the voting patterns did not really bear this out. Radical Tea Party candidates did well in congressional districts that were already Republican strongholds, but they notably failed in statewide Senate races where single-party gerrymandering could not happen and political centrists cast the decisive votes. Extremist Republicans were defeated in the Senate contests in Delaware, Nevada, and above all in Sarah Palin's home state of Alaska, where voters were so repelled by the radical candidate that a write-in candidate was elected for the first time. These events suggested that U.S. market fundamentalism was already waning by late 2010.

With U.S. progressive forces in disarray, however, it will be difficult for America to lead the restructuring of the world economy, at least until the Obama administration and the Democratic Party consciously recognize the need to reinvent the model of capitalism they inherited from Ronald Reagan and George W. Bush. Obama's 2011 State of the Union speech, with its call for national efforts to redefine America's economic ambitions and for new public-private partnerships to achieve the necessary results, may have signaled some such new thinking. But American progressives continued to resist atavistically the redefinition of government and broadening of the tax base that will be needed for any new model of capitalism to succeed.

In Britain, similarly, the early months of the coalition government saw encouraging signs of genuine innovation, with serious debates about priorities for government spending, new ideas on reforming health, education, and welfare, and more active industrial, environmental, and trade policies. By early 2011, however, most of these initiatives were running out of steam, as government departments found themselves paralyzed by drastic spending cuts in the absence of a coherent strategy for government reform.

Europe was also looking consciously for new ideas on the relationship between economics and politics, especially in areas such as environment and technology, as well as finance. The unexpected successes of interventionist industrial and employment policies in northern and central Europe are likely to give more impetus to such ideas. However, the near-breakdown of the euro is likely to monopolize the attention of European politicians and business thinkers in the two or three years ahead.

Thus, despite the progress in Europe and the clear opportunities for reform in the United States and Britain, the reinvention of capitalism could be left to China, as in the pessimistic scenario sketched in Chapter 19. As this becomes apparent, however, U.S. and European businesses are bound to react with alarm. Instead of watching passively from the sidelines as China starts to reinvent the capitalist model, Western businesses will put pressure on their governments—and particularly on conservative pro-business parties—to take control of the reform process.

To give one example, China has resolved to leapfrog Western technology by becoming the world's leading alternative investor in renewable power. By 2010, 40 percent of the world's entire investment in clean energy was undertaken by China, India, and Japan, and by 2020, China plans to install 100 gigawatts of wind power plus 20 gigawatts of solar power, an $800 billion investment program likely to be as big as the rest of the world's programs combined. India, meanwhile, is not only installing its own 20 gigawatts of solar power but also developing nuclear reactors based on thorium, an extremely abundant and low-radiation element that could potentially revolutionize nuclear power.

France and Germany are the only Western countries to have shown any interest in these technologies. The pay-off periods are far too long to justify private or even government investments if assessed on conventional economic measures of expected financial returns. So in other capitalist economies, which insist on allocating resources entirely through financial markets or market-based government proxies, technology investments with 30-, 40- or 50-year horizons may simply be impossible to undertake.

As a result of such calculations, businesses in America and Europe, particularly those involved in very long-term technologies and projects, could soon see the merits of engaging with moderate politicians on both the Left and Right to create a new business-government model. The alternative will be for Americans and Europeans to accept that their era of Western leadership is over and that the restructuring of the global economy—of energy and environmental technologies and even of financial markets—will increasingly reflect Chinese interests.

10. How Long Must We Wait for Capitalism 4.0?

Of all the debatable ideas in this book, perhaps the most overoptimistic was the suggestion that the new model of capitalism will evolve within a few years. The trouble with this claim is that the "muddling through" approach described and praised in the first three chapters is turning out to be even more successful than expected. As the gloom of the crisis starts to lift, business as usual, a risibly improbable outcome a year ago, is looking quite possible. The pace of the reforms described in this book may therefore be slower than suggested, even if their direction is clear.

Looking back at the previous transitions described in this book, it appears that the timescale suggested may be much too short. The last great transition, in the 1970s, took roughly seven years to accomplish, from 1974 to 1980. In the 1930s, the process took ten years, from 1932 to about 1942. In the first crisis of capitalism, the upheavals establishing the British-dominated free-trading system could be dated roughly from 1800 to the final defeat of Napoleon in 1815. A reasonable timescale for the transition to Capitalism 4.0 might therefore be more like ten years, rather than the four or five years implied in Part IV. But despite the length of the process, the evidence of systemic evolution is everywhere becoming clear. Reinventing capitalism will be a work in progress for years or even decades, but the great transition has begun.

Notes

Introduction

1. Edmund L. Andrews, "Greenspan Concedes Error on Regulation," *New York Times*, October 23, 2008.

2. Ayn Rand, "Introducing Objectivism" (August 1962), in *The Objectivist Newsletter: 1962–1965*, 35.

3. This point is made brilliantly by the British economist, John Kay, in his analysis of the interdependence of economics and politics in all capitalist societies, *Culture and Prosperity: The Truth About Markets—Why Some Nations Are Rich but Most Remain Poor*.

4. See most recently Angus Maddison's *Growth and Interaction in the World Economy: The Roots of Modernity* and Mancur Olson's *Rise and Decline of Nations: Economic Growth, Stagflation, and Social Rigidities*.

5. Ricardo Caballero of MIT, in what was probably the most penetrating analysis of the financial crisis by an academic economist, made the specific comparison between credit guarantees and the placement of defibrillators in public places: "The moral hazard perspective is the equivalent of discouraging the placement of defibrillators in public places because of the concern that, upon seeing them, people would have a sudden urge to consume cheeseburgers since they would realize that their chances of surviving a Sudden Cardiac Arrest had risen as a result of the ready access to defibrillators . . . People indeed consume more cheeseburgers than they should, but this is more or less independent of whether defibrillators are visible or not. Surely, there is a need for advocating healthy habits, but no one in their right mind would propose doing so by making all available defibrillators inaccessible. . . . By the same token, and with very few exceptions, financial institutions and investors in bullish mode make portfolio decisions which are driven by dreams of exorbitant returns, not by distant marginal subsidies built into financial defibrillators. Nothing is further from these investors' minds than the possibility of (financial) death, and hence they could not ascribe meaningful value to an aid which, in their mind, is meant for someone else." Ricardo J. Caballero, "Sudden Financial

Arrest," Mundell-Fleming Lecture, IMF, November 2009. Available from http:// www.imf.org/external/np/res/seminars/2009/arc/pdf/caballero.pdf.

6. Bernanke's testimony on September 23, 2008, suggesting that the government should use hold-to-maturity valuations instead of mark-to-market valuations for calculating asset prices and bank solvency, was ignored by Paulson, and therefore by Congress and the markets. Yet it offered an obvious way out of the crisis, which was ultimately adopted a month later. See Mark Landler and Steve Lee Myers, "Buyout Plan for Wall Street Is a Hard Sell on Capitol Hill," *New York Times*, September 23, 2008.

7. "Leaders must become systems thinkers who are comfortable with ambiguity. I am an applied math major and an MBA. In school, I loved science. My career has grown in a linear fashion. There wasn't much ambiguity in my education. I grew up in a simpler world, both economically and geopolitically." Jeff Immelt, "Renewing American Leadership," *Washington Post*, December 10, 2009.

8. "What we don't know yet is whether my administration and this next generation of leadership is going to be able to hew to a new, more pragmatic approach that is less interested in whether we have big government or small government; they're more interested in whether we have a smart, effective government." Barack Obama in a December 2008 speech quoted in Dan Balz, "One Year Later Assessing Obama: Testing the Promise of Pragmatism," *Washington Post*, January 17, 2010.

9. Lawrence Summers, remarks at the 40th World Economic Forum, Davos, Switzerland, January 29, 2010.

Chapter One

1. There are a few notable exceptions. Niall Ferguson, the Harvard economic historian, ends *Ascent of Money*, his world tour of economic history in just two hundred pages, with an appeal for economists and historians to learn from evolutionary biology. Another brilliant book that draws these disciplines together is Paul Seabright's *Company of Strangers*, but this book focuses more on microeconomics than on the relationship between capitalism and politics.

2. "Market economies work to produce growth and efficiency, but only when private rewards and social returns are aligned." Joseph Stiglitz, "Incentives and the Performance of America's Financial Sector," testimony at Hearing on Compensation in the Financial Industry, House Committee on Financial Services, January 22, 2010, 3. Available at www.house.gov/apps/list/hearing/financialsvcs_dem/ stiglitz.pdf. For a detailed nontechnical summary of Stiglitz's pioneering work on the misalignment of private incentives and social returns, see Joseph E. Stiglitz, Jaime Jaramillo-Vallejo, and Yung Chal Park, "The Role of the State in Financial

Markets, *World Bank Research Observer*, Annual Conference on Development Economics Supplement (1993): 19–61.

3. In response to scientific evidence that chlorofluorocarbons (CFCs) were depleting the ozone layer, forty-three nations signed the 1987 Montreal Protocol to restrict CFC production to 1986 levels and cut production by 50 percent by 1999. At a 1992 meeting in Copenhagen, these nations further bolstered the protocol, agreeing to ban CFCs by 1996. In an immediate response to this series of accords, manufacturers began to develop alternatives to CFCs. The ban has lead to a surprisingly rapid decline in atmospheric CFC levels, which has allowed the ozone to begin to recover. Scientists project that the 25 million km^2 hole in the ozone over Antarctica will have decreased by 1 million km^2 by 2015 and that a full return to 1980 ozone levels can by expected by 2068. See Richard Benedick, *Ozone Diplomacy: New Directions in Safeguarding the Planet* and Paul A. Newman et al, "When Will the Antarctic Ozone Hole Recover?" *Geophysical Research Letters* 33 (2006).

4. Andrew Mellon quotation from Herbert Hoover's autobiography, *The Memoirs of Herbert Hoover: Vol. 3, The Great Depression*, 31–32.

5. In 1934, Joseph Schumpeter wrote, "depressions are not simply evils, which we might attempt to suppress, but . . . forms of something which has to be done." Joseph Schumpeter, "Depressions," in Douglass Brown et al., *The Economics of the Recovery Program*, 16.

6. This statement is itself an instance of the "paradox of the liar," which is related to the impossibility of devising a logical system that is both internally consistent and complete, demonstrated by Russell and Goedel. This, in turn, relates to the fundamentally fallacious structure of the modern economics of rational expectations and efficient markets discussed in Chapter 14. The failure of the policies built on these logically incoherent assumptions complete a satisfying intellectual circle by linking back to the crisis of 2007-09.

7. See George Soros, *The New Paradigm for Financial Markets: The Credit Crisis of 2008 and What It Means*, particularly Chapter 3, "The Theory of Reflexivity," and Chapter 4, "Reflexivity in Financial Markets."

8. Thomas Hobbes, *On the Citizen (De Cive)*, Chapter 1, Section XIII, 30.

9. Blaise Pascal, *Pensées*, 121–126.

Chapter Two

1. This phrase was coined in 1989 by John Williamson to described the free-market policies imposed on post-communist and developing countries by the U.S. government, along with the IMF, the World Bank, the World Trade Organization, and other international institutions. See John Williamson, "What Washington

Means by Policy Reform," in John Williamson, ed., *Latin American Readjustment: How Much Has Happened*.

2. See Alain Gresh, "Understanding the Beijing Consensus," trans. Stephanie Irvine, *Le Monde Diplomatique English Edition* (November 2008). The Beijing Consensus is described more extensively in Chapter 24.

3. Joseph Schumpeter, *Capitalism, Socialism and Democracy*.

4. "When they faced a graduated income tax in 1913, businessmen everywhere judged it the most destructive legislation in the nation's history." Robert Wiebe, *Business Men and Reform: A Study of the Progressive Movement,* 196.

5. David Lloyd George, chancellor of the exchequer, described his "People's Budget" of 1909 as "a war budget. It is for raising money to wage implacable warfare against poverty and squalidness" (April 29, 1909). The solid Conservative majority in the House of Lords, however, answered this rallying cry with an outright rejection of a progressive tax, in spite of an unwritten but well-established tradition that prevented the House of Lords from vetoing any financial bill passed by the elected chamber. In response to this breach, the Liberal leadership of the House of Commons dissolved parliament and called for a new election. Parliament reconvened with a slightly smaller Liberal majority than before but a strong coalition in favor of tax, which the House of Lords could not deny a second time. With the budget now passed, the Liberal ministers proposed legislation that would limit the House of Lords to a suspensive veto of two years for nonbudget items and of one month for all money bills. The House of Lords passed the Parliament Act of 1911 after the king threatened to expand the number of Liberal peers, thus guaranteeing its passage, if they vetoed it. See Edward Potts Cheyney, *A Short History of England*, 691–95, and Eric J. Evans, *Parliamentary Reform, c. 1770–1918*, 86.

6. In 1932, the U.S. government raised the top marginal income tax rate from 25 percent to 63 percent on incomes greater than $1 million. The top marginal rate stayed high for decades, peaking at 94 percent 1944 and 1945, remaining above 90 percent from 1950 to 1063 and not dipping below 70 percent until 1979. Statistics from Joint Committee on Taxation, "Overview of Present Law and Economic Analysis Relating to Marginal Tax Rates and the President's Individual Income Tax Rate Proposals," public hearing before the Senate Committee on Finance, March 7, 2001, and Maxim Shvedov, Congressional Research Service, "Statutory Individual Income Tax Rates and Other Elements of the Tax System: 1988 through 2008," May 21, 2008.

7. Andrew Gamble, *The Spectre at the Feast: Capitalist Crisis and the Politics of Recession*, 7.

8. Ibid.

9. The Whig view of history, as pioneered by Thomas Babington Macaulay in his five-volume *History of England from the Accession of James the Second* and other

liberal historians, cast the history of England as a heroic teleological progression toward a promise land of democratic prosperity. See Herbert Butterfield, *The Whig Interpretation of History*, and Keith Sewell, *Herbert Butterfield and the Interpretation of History*.

10. This is an oversimplification because social reformers from the early nineteenth century onward campaigned for action on child and female labor, working hours, working conditions, and many other issues. These campaigns, however, were generally directed toward making capitalism more socially tolerable, rather than economically more effective.

Chapter Three

1. Robert Heilbroner, *The Worldly Philosophers*, Chapters 1–2.

2. Max Weber, *The Protestant Ethic and the Spirit of Capitalism*.

3. Adam Smith, *The Wealth of Nations, Books 1–III*, 119.

4. Seabright, *The Company of Strangers*, 14–15.

5. The first edition of Smith's *The Wealth of Nations* was published on March 9, 1776 by W. Strahan and T. Cadell in London. Andrew Skinner notes the coincidence of its publication on the eve of the Declaration of Independence in his introduction to Smith's work. Andrew Skinner, introduction to *The Wealth of Nations, Books I–III*, by Adam Smith, 6.

6. Keynes and others have traced the first recorded use of the phrase "laissez-faire"—which literally means "let do" or "let make"—to a speech by French minister Rene de Voyer, Marquis d'Argenson, in 1751 in which he declared, "*Laissez faire, telle devrait être la devise de toute puissance publique, depuis que le monde est civilisé.*" (Let it be, such should be the motto of every public power, ever since the world is civilized.) Keynes notes as well the absence of the term from the writings of classical economists Smith, Ricardo, and Malthus. It first appeared in English in 1774 in George Whatley's *Principles of Trade*, coauthored by Ben Franklin. See John Maynard Keynes, "The End of Laissez-Faire."

7. This is another oversimplification. The rivalry between protectionism and free trade dominated most politics of the nineteenth century in both America and Britain and was arguably a major force behind the U.S. Civil War. There was not, however, any serious contest to free enterprise ideology at the level of economic analysis.

8. Charles Loyseau outlined the six rights of the king in his *Des Seigneuries* (1610): to write law, to select government officials, to wage war and orchestrate its peace, to serve as the final arbiter of justice, to coin currency, and to tax. The rights and responsibilities of government were traditionally believed to include but also to

be limited to this list for several centuries after its publication. See Mildred Pope, *Studies in French Language and Medieval Literature,* 33.

9. John Maynard Keynes, *The Economic Consequences of the Peace,* 15–16.

10. Ibid., 16–17.

11. Between 1880 and 1914, anarchist terrorists and communist revolutionaries killed at least ten reigning monarchs or heads of state and arguably precipitated World War I by assassinating Archduke Franz Ferdinand. The list of victims from this period included Tsar Alexander II in 1881, French President Marie-Francois Sadi Carnot in 1894, and U.S. President William McKinley in 1901. See Rick Coolsaet, "The Business of Terror: Anarchist outrages," *Le Monde Diplomatique,* English Edition (September 2004).

12. Universal male suffrage was introduced in Britain in 1918 as a direct response to the shared sacrifice of the war. Women's voting was still subject to property and age restrictions until 1928.

13. Woodrow Wilson at Versailles was an honorable exception. For a detailed discussion of Wilson's attempt to prevent reparations for Germany and Clemenceau and Lloyd George's insistence that Germany pay for its "war guilt," see Paul Johnson, *A History of the American People,* 648–651.

14. John Maynard Keynes, *The General Theory of Employment, Interest, and Money.*

15. Hjalmar Schacht, the German Finance Minister from 1934–37, on the other hand, was an early convert to Keynesian economics and had several meetings with Keynes as a minister in the pre-Nazi German government. "Keynes had talks with Melchior [Germany's representative to the League of Nations Finance Committee] and Dr. Schacht on this subject [the deflationary influences in the world] and found that they agreed with his views." Roy Harrod, *The Life of John Maynard Keynes,* 394; see also 513–525. Hitler demoted Dr. Schacht in 1937 after disagreements with Goering over economic policy and speeches he had given denouncing "unlawful activities" against the Jews. In 1944, he was arrested on suspicion of involvement in the assassination attempt against Hitler and ended the war in the Dachau concentration camp.

16. The Bank of England was still technically a private company until 1946. Although it took its responsibilities for managing the City of London's financial markets seriously, it never relied on taxpayer funding. Before 1914, its operations were aimed almost exclusively at financial order, rather than macroeconomic stability. The classic description of the Bank of England's role in the global financial economy of the nineteenth century is Walter Bagehot's *Lombard Street: A Description of the Money Market.*

17. Gordon Brown speech at Imperial College, London, http://www.number10. gov.uk/Page17303.

Brown's version of the story is a slight exaggeration. In fact, in 1929, Keynes cowrote a pamphlet called *We Can Conquer Unemployment* with Lloyd George, Hubert Henderson, and Seebohm Rowntree. The Treasury library contains a copy with the words *Extravagance, Inflation,* and *Bankruptcy* scrawled over the cover by some unknown Treasury official. A facsimile of this pamphlet is reproduced in Peter Clarke, *Keynes: The Twentieth Century's Most Influential Economist.*

18. Some debate exists as to whether Sidney Webb or Tom Johnston, former parliamentary secretary for Scotland and Lord Privy Seal, uttered these words of surprise. See Barry Eichengreen and Peter Temin, "The Gold Standard and the Great Depression," *Contemporary European History,* 9:2 (2000): 202.

19. This was the arrangement whereby foreign governments were allowed to exchange their dollar reserves into gold at the fixed price of $35 an ounce, even though this facility was not available to private holders of dollars. Michael Bardo and Barry Eichengreen, eds. *A Retrospective on the Bretton Woods System: Lessons for International Monetary Reform,* 222–224 and 461–494.

20. Michal Kalecki, "Political Aspects of Full Employment," *Political Quarterly* 14 (1943), reprinted in Michal Kalecki, *Selected Essays on the Dynamics of the Capitalist Economy.*

Chapter Four

1. In conversation with the author in November 2003. De Klerk makes the same point less explicitly in his autobiography, *The Last Trek.* See also the interview in the *Financial Times,* January 23, 2010, with de Klerk about his decision to lift the ban on the ANC twenty years earlier: "Encouraged by the fall of the Berlin Wall, which took away the root *gevaar* [red danger] or fear of a communist takeover, de Klerk was emboldened to press ahead."

2. Interview with the author in November 2003. See "Asia Now Aspires to the Charms of a Bourgeois Life," *The Times,* London, January 8, 2004. The "Hindu rate of growth" was the sarcastic description of India's low growth rate of only 3.5 percent from 1960 to 1990, while other Asian countries were growing by 6 percent or more. After 1991, India's average growth rate accelerated to around 7 percent. See John Williamson and Roberto Zagha, "From the Hindu Rate of Growth to the Hindu Rate of Reform."

3. The *WEO* is a document produced twice yearly by the IMF that assesses conditions in the world economy and provides two-year forecasts for each of the 186 member nations. See http://www.imf.org/external/np/exr/facts/glance.htm.

4. Transcript of Press Conference on the World Economic Outlook Report, available from http://www.imf.org/external/np/tr/2006/tr060914.htm.

5. This, at least, was the conventional view. The phrase *dismal science* is widely thought to reflect the cynicism of market economics: its assumption of human selfishness, its obeisance to greed, and its obsession with scarcity—even of such obvious human birthrights as air, water, and health. However, the origin of the phrase *dismal science* was very different—liberal economists were accused by English conservatives of *dismal* thinking because they opposed the African slave trade, which the English upper classes believed to be essential for the preservation of their wealth, power, and culture. The phrase *dismal science* was first used by the conservative historian Thomas Carlyle in a diatribe against what Carlyle described as John Stuart Mill's *dismal* argument that landowners should be expected to pay normal wages on their West Indian plantations—and that if plantation economics did not allow such wages to be paid, the owners should be put out of business rather than allowed to enslave their fellow human beings. Yet the *dismal* adjective has stuck firmly to economics despite its paradoxical origin. Peter Groenewegen, "Thomas Carlyle, 'The Dismal Science,' and the Contemporary Political Economy of Slavery," *History of Economics Review* 34 (Summer 2001): 74–94.

6. Galbraith quoted in *The Observer*, London, April 3, 1977.

7. Deng Xiaoping, "Build Socialism with Chinese Characteristics," Speech to the Council of Sino-Japanese Non-Governmental Persons (June 30, 1984), printed in William De Bary and Richard Lufrano, eds., *Sources of Chinese Tradition: From 1600 Through the Twentieth Century*, vol. 2, 507–510.

8. The key events in computer technology were the introduction of the first standardized IBM personal computers and Intel microprocessors in 1983, the addition of a Graphical User Interface (GUI) to the Apple Macintosh in 1984, the Windows GUI by Microsoft in 1986, and the release in 1990 of Windows 3.0, a much improved GUI developed for the IBM 386 computer.

9. See, for example, Edward Glaeser and Janet Kohlhase, "Cities, Regions and the Decline of Transport Costs," and Nils-Gustav Lundgren, "Bulk Trade and Maritime Transport Costs: The Evolution of Global Markets," *Resources Policy* 22:1–2 (March–June 1996): 5-32.

10. Jeffrey Frankel, "The Japanese Cost of Finance: A Survey," *Financial Management* 20:1 (Spring 1991).

Chapter Five

1. Quoted in *New York Times*, October 8, 2006.

2. John Naisbitt, *Megatrends*.

3. Toffler elaborated and popularized the idea of a post-industrial society. Although this term was invented by the sociologist Daniel Bell in *The Coming of the*

Post-Industrial Society, its relationship to information technology was developed most convincingly by Toffler in his book *The Third Wave.* Ignored by "serious" academics, Toffler was the only modern Western economist or social scientist to appear in a list of "Fifty foreigners shaping China's modern development" published by *People's Daily* in 2006. http://english.people.com.cn/200608/03/eng20060803_289510.html.

4. Martin Wolf, *Why Globalization Works.*

Chapter Six

1. Known to philosophers as Petronius's Paradox, this statement is usually attributed to Gaius Petronius Arbiter, a Roman patrician believed to be the author of the *Satyricon.* Petronius's Paradox is considered a classic example of a self-referential statement that contradicts its own premise and is therefore logically meaningless.

2. Ben Bernanke, "The Great Moderation," remarks at the meetings of the Eastern Economic Association, Federal Reserve Board, Washington, DC, February 20, 2004.

3. Olivier Blanchard and John Simon, "The Long and Large Decline in U.S. Output Volatility," *Brookings Papers on Economic Activity* 1 (2001): 135–64.

4. Charles Gave, Anatole Kaletsky, and Louis-Vincent Gave, *Our Brave New World,* available from http://gavekal.com/eBooks/OurBraveNewWorld.pdf. See also Jonathan R. Laing, "Welcome to Sizzle Inc.: The 'platform economy'—a business model focused on knowledge while outsourcing production—heralds an age of unprecedented U.S. prosperity" (cover story), *Barron's,* December 25, 2006.

5. It has been estimated that at least 40 percent of world trade in manufactured goods consists of transactions within companies, not between them. See Jeffrey Frieden and David A. Lake, *International Political Economy: Perspectives on Global Power and Wealth,* 153, and Jose de la Torre, "U.S. Investment in Japan Is Key to Closing the Massive Trade Gap," *LA Times,* April 9, 1995.

6. Richard Fisher, president of the Federal Reserve Bank of Dallas, gives a similar example. Everyone knows that all mass-market toys these days are made in China. This gives many Americans the impression that all the money they spend in toy stores ends up in China. However, only "ten percent of the value of a Barbie Doll priced at retail comes from China. The rest of it is all added on through the distribution system, merchandising, and margin." Fisher interviewed in Steven Beckner, "Fed's Fisher: Depreciating Dollar Not Necessarily Inflat'ry," *Market News International,* November 19, 2009.

7. Milton Friedman, "Inflation and Unemployment," Nobel Memorial Lecture, Section 3, "The Natural Rate Hypothesis," December 13, 1976.

8. Samuel Brittan, *The Treasury Under the Tories, 1951–1964.*

9. Arthur Burns, "Economic Research and the Keynesian Thinking of Our Times," 1946, reprinted in Arthur Burns, ed., *The Frontiers of Economic Knowledge*, 4.

10. Arthur Burns, *Prosperity Without Inflation*, 30.

11. Norman Lamont, Chancellor of the Exchequer, HC Deb, May 16, 1991, vol. 191, c. 413.

12. C.A.E. Goodhart, "Monetary Relationships: A View from Threadneedle Street," *Papers in Monetary Economics*, vol. 1 (Sydney: Reserve Bank of Australia, 1975).

13. Technically, economists describe the period from December 1979 to November 1982 as two separate recessions, interrupted by a brief period of growth in late 1980. But this period was effectively one long ordeal in terms of mass unemployment, plunging asset prices, and general economic misery.

14. Anatole Kaletsky, *The Costs of Default.*

15. For the ideological reasons discussed in Chapter 6, this shift in U.S. economic management would not be publicly admitted until six or seven years later, after the recovery from the 1987 stock market crash, and it has not been fully acknowledged in Fed rhetoric even to the present day. The Fed's actions, however, make it clear that policy is guided by the dual mandate to balance inflation and unemployment.

Chapter Seven

1. The Banking Act of 1933 (Glass-Steagall), which created the FDIC, and the Banking Act of 1935 imposed an interest rate of zero on demand deposits and authorized the Federal Reserve to cap interest rates on savings deposits paid by commercial banks. These regulations remained in effect until the Monetary Control Act of 1980 created the Depository Institutions Deregulation Committee with the express purpose of gradually dismantling them. R. Alton Gilbert, "Requiem for Regulation Q: What It Did and Why It Passed Away," *Federal Reserve Bank of St. Louis Review* (February 1986): 22–37.

2. Britain imposed hire-purchase controls off and on from the late 1940s until 1982. Foreign exchange controls regulated foreign currency exchange, international trade and foreign investment in Britain from 1939 until 1979. See M. J. Artis and Mark P. Taylor, "Abolishing Exchange Control: The UK Experience," Discussion Paper No. 294, Centre for Economic Policy Research (February 1989).

3. The FNMA thirty-year mortgage rate declined from 8.1 percent in 1999 to 5.8 percent in 2004 and to 6.2 percent in 2005. It was down to 5 percent in early 2010.

4. Personal debts rose to 186 percent of disposable income in 2008.

5. Japan had an enormous property boom in the late 1980s and Germany a very large one in the early 1990s after reunification. These had left both countries with an excess supply of new houses far larger than the modest inventory of 250,000 units in the U.S. market in late 2009.

6. According to analysis by R. R. de Acuña, Spanish property consultants, the supply of property for sale in Spain at the beginning of 2009 was 1,623,042, of which approximately 1 million were newly built houses or houses under construction and nearing completion and 600,000 were resales of existing homes. Emma Ross-Thomas, "Spanish Home Prices Fall for Seventh Quarter as Slump Deepens," *Bloomberg News*, September 30, 2009.

7. The total inventory of new homes for sale in the U.S. was 231,000 in December 2009, according to the monthly construction statistics published by the U.S. Census Bureau. "New Residential Sales in December 2009," *U.S. Census Bureau News*, January 27, 2010.

8. This regional diversity also largely explains the difference between the national house price statistics used in this chapter and the more extreme numbers that often appear in media and Wall Street analysis. These analyses usually employ the Case-Shiller (CS) house price index, which is supposed to give a more accurate picture of price movements than the figures quoted above from the National Association of Realtors (NAR). Between 1996 and 2006, the NAR index increased. The Case-Shiller approach compares the selling prices of identical houses which have been sold repeatedly over a period of time, rather than averaging the prices of all the homes that happen to have sold in a particular month or quarter. The Case-Shiller approach has suggested more extreme movements in the latest cycle, possibly because it disregards the shift in market demand toward smaller and cheaper houses as prices rise. Thus the NAR and CS national indices moved together closely until the summer of 2005. At that point, the NAR index suggested that the U.S. housing market had peaked, and remained fairly flat for the next two years, before collapsing in mid-2007. The CS National index, by contrast, continued to rise for another year, peaking only in the summer of 2006. As a result, the CS National index showed a cumulative price increase of 92 percent since the beginning of the decade, while the NAR index suggested a more moderate appreciation of only 68 percent.

Even more important than the difference in methodology is the different geographic coverage. The most widely quoted Case-Shiller indices cover only twenty big cities, including Las Vegas, Miami, and Phoenix, which happen to have experienced the most extreme housing booms and busts. The NAR figures, by contrast, cover the entire country and show the cycle to have been less extreme. The Case-Shiller national figures are closer to the NAR national statistics and the official statistics published by the Federal Housing Finance Agency. But these broad national figures are published only quarterly rather than monthly, and with a considerable lag, and therefore receive less attention in the media and on Wall Street. Between January 2000 and the peak of the U.S. housing market in mid-2006, the NAR index increased by 68 percent, the CS National index by 92 percent, the CS 20 index by 106 percent, and the CS 10 index by 126 percent. By the middle of 2009, the Case-Shiller indices had fallen back and the CS National index showed a cumulative gain since 2000 only 2 percent higher than the NAR.

9. Professor Robert Shiller of Yale, probably the most famous and academically distinguished of these Cassandras, freely admitted in a talk he gave in January 2010 at the World Economic Forum in Davos that "many economists [presumably himself included] were predicting a housing crash for at least a decade before it occurred." He added that Nouriel Roubini (another celebrated prophet of doom) "was predicting calamity for the U.S. economy from the moment I first met him back in 2000."

10. Charles Prince quoted in Michiyo Nakamoto and David Wighton, "Citigroup Chief Stays Bullish on Buy-outs," *Financial Times,* July 9, 2007.

11. Herbert Stepic, CEO of Raiffeisen International Bank, the second biggest lender in central Europe, speaking at the EBRD Annual Meeting in Kiev on May 19, 2008. Stepic quoted in Simon Shuster, "Raiffeisen says forex loans 'sinful' but unavoidable," *Reuters Financial Newswire,* May 19, 2008.

12. John Maynard Keynes, "The Consequences to the Banks of the Collapse in Money Values" (1931), in *Essays in Persuasion,* 176.

13. Barney Frank in CNBC debate, "Back to the Future: The Next Global Crisis," January 27, 2010.

14. George Soros, *The New Paradigm for Financial Markets: The Credit Crisis of 2008 and What It Means.*

Chapter Eight

1. I quote Soros because, of all the prophets who supposedly saw every detail of the financial crisis long in advance, he was the only one with the intellectual integrity to admit that he had been "crying wolf" for the previous twenty years. Most of the others were far more consistent throughout the past two decades in wrongly predicting financial catastrophe, but unlike Soros, they never had the honesty and self-awareness to realize when they were wrong. What made Soros unique among the prophets of doom was this unusual flexibility and willingness to admit mistakes. These qualities have been justly rewarded with a stellar intellectual reputation—plus trading profits of $20 billion.

2. Britain's retail price index has risen 165-fold since the first half of the eighteenth century, according to the Bank of England. The conversion into dollars uses an exchange rate of $1.6 to the pound, and the relationship with wages assumes average annual growth of 1 percent. http://www.bankofengland.co.uk/education/inflation/calculator/.

3. Christopher Reed, "'The Damn'd *South Sea*': Britain's Greatest Financial Speculation and Its Unhappy Ending," *Harvard Magazine* (May–June 1999).

4. George Soros, *The New Paradigm for Financial Markets*.

5. Mohamed El-Erian, *When Markets Collide: Investment Strategies for the Age of Global Economic Change*.

6. *The Gartman Letter*, January 27, 2009. http://www.thegartmanletter.com.

Chapter Nine

1. This is one facet of Joseph Schumpeter's famous process of "creative destruction," though not the most important one, which is driven by technological innovation, rather than credit. Schumpeter, *Capitalism, Socialism and Democracy*.

2. The more extreme followers of the Austrian school even demand the repeal of "tyrannical" laws against drunk driving. See Llewellyn Rockwell Jr., "Legalize Drunk Driving," *Mises Daily*, Ludwig von Mises Institute, November 3, 2000. Available from http://mises.org/daily/2343.

3. Andrew Mellon, the U.S. treasury secretary from 1921 to 1932, was probably the last true believer in the Austrian view to hold a position of high authority. He famously advised President Hoover to allow the Great Depression to run its course, to "Liquidate labor, liquidate stocks, liquidate farmers, liquidate real estate . . . It will purge the rottenness out of the system." Mellon quotation from Herbert Hoover's autobiography, *The Memoirs of Herbert Hoover: Vol. 3, The Great Depression*, 31–32. For more details, see Chapter 11.

4. This accelerator-multiplier concept, first proposed by Sir Roy Harrod, was later refined by Paul Samuelson and Sir John Hicks and became the standard Keynesian business cycle model.

5. Justin Lahart, "In Time of Tumult, Obscure Economist Gains Currency," *Wall Street Journal*, August 18, 2007.

6. George Soros, *The Soros Lectures: At the Central European University*.

7. Alan Greenspan, "The Challenge of Central Banking," remarks at the Annual Dinner and Francis Boyer Lecture of the American Enterprise Institute for Public Policy Research, Washington, DC, December 5, 1996. Available from http://www.federalreserve.gov/boarddocs/speeches/1996/19961205.htm.

8. Robert Shiller, *Irrational Exuberance*.

9. Benoit Mandelbrot and Richard Hudson, *The (Mis)behavior of Markets: A Fractal View of Risk, Ruin and Reward,* 4.

10. Nassim Nicholas Taleb, *Fooled by Randomness: The Hidden Role of Chance in the Markets* and in *Life and the Black Swan: The Impact of the Highly Probable.*

11. The term *normal distribution* describes prices or any other form of data that cluster predictably and reliably around a mean value in a bell curve pattern.

12. Malcolm C. Sawyer, *The Economics of Michal Kalecki.* See also Robert Rowthorn, "The Political Economy of Full Employment in Modern Britain," Kalecki Memorial Lecture, Department of Economics, University of Oxford, October 19, 1999.

13. Robert Skidelsky, *Keynes: The Return of the Master,* 62.

14 The question is taken up on IBM's Web site: http://www-03.ibm.com/ibm/history/reference/faq_0000000047.html.

15. Gartner, Inc., "Press Release: Gartner Says Worldwide PC Shipments to Grow 2.8 Percent in 2009, but PC Revenue to Decline 11 Percent," November 23, 2009.

16. Nicolo Machiavelli, *The Prince,* 88.

Part III

1. John Maynard Keynes, *General Theory of Employment, Interest and Money,* 383.

Chapter Ten

1. Ricardo J. Caballero, "Sudden Financial Arrest," Mundell-Fleming Lecture, IMF, November 2009. Available from http://www.imf.org/external/np/res/seminars/2009/arc/pdf/caballero.pdf.

2. Interview with Oliver Blanchard, See *IMF Survey Magazine Online,* September 2, 2008. Available from http://www.imf.org/external/pubs/ft/survey/so/2008/int090208a.htm.

3. Tamora Vidaillet and Veronique Tison, "Letting Lehman go was big mistake: French finmin," *Reuters,* October 8, 2008. Available from http://www.reuters.com/article/idUSTRE49735Z20081008.

4. Reflecting the argument in the rest of this chapter, Blinder said: "After Lehman, no financial institution seemed safe. So lending froze, and the economy sank like a stone. It was a colossal error and many people said so at the time." See David Wessel, *In Fed We Trust,* 23. Tim Geithner reportedly shared this view: "Geithner thought that publicly drawing a 'line in the sand' during a financial crisis was lunacy." Geithner quoted in Wessel, 15–16.

5. Andrew Ross Sorkin, *Too Big to Fail,* and Wessel, *In Fed We Trust.*

6. Milton Friedman and Anna Jacobson Schwartz, *A Monetary History of the United States, 1867–1960.*

7. Mellon's role in the decision to liquidate the U.S. banking system was emphasized by Milton Friedman and also by President Hoover in his memoirs. Herbert Hoover, *The Memoirs of Herbert Hoover: Vol. 3, The Great Depression,* 28–30. R. G. Hawtrey of the British Treasury wrote in 1938 that Mellon and others who believed in 1930–1933 that excessive inflation posed the greatest threat were "crying 'Fire! Fire!' in Noah's Flood." R. G. Hawtrey, *A Century of Bank Rate,* 145.

8. Hoover, *Memoirs, Vol 3,* 30. Giving effect to this moral crusade, Mellon urged the Federal Reserve to "weed out" weak banks by limiting the money supply and reneging on its lender-of-last-resort obligations. He also demanded that government spending be cut to balance the Federal budget and bitterly opposed the fiscal stimulus proposed by Hoover even before the election of Franklin Roosevelt.

9. By the time of his appointment as treasury secretary, he was the third-highest income taxpayer in the country, behind John D. Rockefeller and Henry Ford. David Cannadine, *Mellon: An American Life,* 349.

10. In January 1932, Mellon faced impeachment proceedings in the Congress but averted a final vote by resigning to become U.S. ambassador in London.

11. This intellectual background is admirably presented in a paper by Bradford de Long, who explains that Mellon's "liquidationist" views were not just a personal whim but reflected a strong professional consensus among the leading pre-Keynesian economists of his period, including Friedrich Hayek, Joseph Schumpeter, and Lionel Robbins. J. Bradford De Long, "Liquidation Cycles and the Great Depression," NBER Working Paper, June 1991. Available from econ161.berkeley.edu/pdf_files/Liquidation_Cycles.pdf.

12. Paul Krugman, "How Did Economists Get It So Wrong?," *New York Times Magazine,* September 6, 2009.

13. Second quarter GDP was subsequently revised back down to 1.5 percent, but this still left U.S. economic activity up to the middle of 2008 well above recession levels.

14. The reduction of the U.S. trade deficit from its peak of 6.5 percent of GDP in 2006 to 4 percent of GDP just before September 15 accounted for roughly half the U.S. economy's total growth in 2007 and 2008.

15. For a long time, investors and economists ignored this critical distinction between financial and nonfinancial leverage. Policymakers began to draw attention to it after the collapse of Lehman. For example, following are two speeches from the top financial regulators in London, whose financial institutions were responsible for much of the global leveraging and securitisation.

"The fact that much of the increase in debt occurred within the financial sector means that the necessary unwinding of balance sheets could and should take place primarily within the financial sector . . . without restricting lending to the 'real' economy." Mervyn King, "Speech to the CBI Dinner," January 20, 2009. Available from www.bankofengland.co.uk/publications/speeches/2009/speech372.pdf.

"The huge growth of intrafinancial system leverage has a relevance to the urgent issue of short-term macro economic management. The more that we can ensure that bank deleveraging takes the form of the stripping out of intertrader complexity, and the less it takes the form of leveraging vis-á-vis the nonbank real economy, the better." Adair Turner, "The Financial Crisis and the Future of Financial Regulation," The Economist's Inaugural City Lecture, January 21, 2009. Available from www.fsa.gov.uk/pages/Library/Communication/Speeches/2009/0121_at.shtml. For a detailed discussion, see Anatole Kaletsky, "Not All Loans Are the Same," *The Times*, London, January 26, 2009.

16. Mervyn King quoted in Bank of England, *Quarterly Inflation Report*, February 11, 2009, 25. Available from http://www.bankofengland.co.uk/publications/inflationreport/conf090211.pdf.

17. "Lehman Bankruptcy Losses Pegged at $75 billion," *Bloomberg News*, December 30, 2008.

18. "The troops got to Fallujah in a couple of weeks and seized the radio towers, but there was no plan to run the country once the shooting stopped." Mudd quoted in Wessel, *In Fed We Trust*, 187.

19. Before the era of modern central banking, guarantees were offered by private institutions whose paper was universally acceptable as a form of money, such as the privately owned Bank of England, the Morgan Bank in the 1907 panic, or the Rothschild family in early nineteenth-century Europe. After J.P. Morgan gave his personal guarantees to stop the U.S. bank panic in 1907, "crowds cheered when he walked down Wall Street and world political leaders sent telegrams expressing their awe that one man had been able to do that." Howard Means, *Money & Power*, 142. See also Ron Chernow, *House of Morgan*.

20. Financial Accounting Standards Board, FAS Statement No. 157: Fair Value Measurements, September 2006. Financial Accounting Standards Board, FAS Statement 157–4: Determining Fair Value When the Volume and Level of Activity for the Asset or Liability Have Significantly Decreased and Identifying Transactions that Are Not Orderly, April 9, 2009.

21. Testimony of Michael W. Masters before the Senate Committee on Homeland Security and Governmental Affairs, May 20, 2008. Available from hsgac.senate.gov/public/_files/052008Masters.pdf.

22. The mechanism whereby financial investors inadvertently drove up oil prices, inflicting great damage on the world economy and their own long-term interests, was explained in the Congressional testimonies of Michael Masters and George Soros mentioned earlier and is discussed in greater detail in Chapter 15.

Any such linkage between financial investment and rising commodity prices is denied by investment banks, which have profited handsomely from creating financial derivatives linked to oil and other commodities.

23. See Anatole Kaletsky, "Relax. Our Economy Isn't Manic Depressive," *The Times*, London, January 24, 2008.

24. "The year-end results season offers stock markets a last chance to make plausible estimates of mortgage losses and recapitalize the banks. If the banks [and] their auditors and shareholders cannot quickly do this, then government intervention will become inevitable to underwrite the solvency, as well as the liquidity, of the banks." Anatole Kaletsky, "This Crisis Is No Longer a Simple Problem of Liquidity," *The Times*, London, December 17, 2007. The problem was that this intervention happened only nine months later than expected—which was nine months too late.

25. "It's my weakness and my strength: I have a focus. I have a one-track mind when I'm working on something. I've never tried to look ahead." Henry Paulson quoted in Todd Purdum, "Henry Paulson's Longest Night," *Vanity Fair*, October 2009.

26. Henry Paulson, *On the Brink*, 1.

27. See Sorkin, *Too Big to Fail*, 224. See also Paulson, *On the Brink*, 144, 170. "[The President] disliked everything the GSEs represented . . . We had within a few months managed to force massive change at these troubled but powerful institutions that had stymied reformers for years."

28. "I pressed Lockhart on the need for receivership but he repeatedly told me that this would be difficult because FHFA's most recent regulatory exams had not cited capital shortfalls. . . . [Two weeks before the GSE seizure FHFA] had sent the GSEs draft letters reviewing their second-quarter financial statements and concluding that the companies were at least adequately capitalized and in fact exceeded their regulatory capital requirements. . . . Only FHFA had the legal powers to put the GSEs under and I was worried about its backsliding." Paulson, *On the Brink*, 163–5.

29. Kaletsky, *The Costs of Default*.

30. See Paulson, *On the Brink*.

31. This was not just the wisdom of hindsight—see Anatole Kaletsky, "Hank Paulson Has Turned a Drama into a Crisis: By punishing shareholders, the U.S. Treasury Secretary had made the rescue of other trouble banks almost impossible," *The Times*, London, September 16, 2008.

32. This was the closing price on September 9, 2008. This price compared with a decline of just 1.5 percent for the S&P 500.

33. Jun Kwang Woo quoted in Bomi Lim and Seonjin Cha, "Korean Development Bank Ends Talks for Stake in Lehman," *Bloomberg News*, September 10, 2008.

34. Matt Turner, "Markets Wipe Almost 40% off Lehman as KDB Talks Collapse," *Financial News*, September 9, 2008. A week later, when Morgan Stanley had to be rescued by Japan's Mitsubishi Bank, Paulson changed his position. Mitsubishi made clear that without this indemnity from the U.S. Treasury it would not make the Morgan Stanley investment for exactly the reasons explained in the text. By this time, Paulson had begun to draw the lessons from the GSE, Lehman, and AIG debacles and agreed to provide the Japanese bank with private guarantees against expropriation. These guarantees were merely rumored at the time. For example, the *Washington Post* reported that "Treasury officials assuaged those concerns, pledging that if the government did make investments in banks, Mitsubishi wouldn't see its investment disappear." Zachary Goldfarb, "Morgan Stanley-Mitsubishi Deal Closes, *Washington Post*, October 14, 2008. But they were subsequently confirmed by Paulson himself: "Mitsubishi UFJ was worried that if it invested, the U.S. government might step in and wipe out its position. . . . [Treasury Undersecretary] Dave McCormick learned that the Japanese bank was worried that if the U.S. government bought equity in Morgan Stanley, we would dilute their investment. It was a reasonable concern and he had indicated that Treasury would structure any subsequent investment to avoid punishing existing shareholders. Dave suggested writing a note on Treasury letterhead to reassure the Japanese." Paulson, *On the Brink*, 347, 354.

35. Ibid., 18.

36. See Paulson, *On the Brink*, 264: "If they go, we're next."

37. See Wessel, *In Fed We Trust*, 199–200: "In every major banking crisis [Bernanke] had studied, the government had had to put capital into the banks . . . and guarantee the banks' debt. So far, Bernanke had deferred to Paulson on the timing of going to Congress, while Paulson had been reluctant to propose anything that Congress, in an election year, might reject. Bernanke and Giethner saw this as the inevitable and costly politics of responding to banking crises in a democracy. The most effective solution always calls for lots of taxpayers' money upfront— 'overwhelming force,' as Geithner called it. . . . Bernanke was usually soft-spoken and mild-mannered. He was not this time. 'We can't do this anymore, Hank. We have to go to Congress.' . . . The Fed was at its limit."

38. Ben Bernanke repeatedly spoke of using hold-to-maturity accounting instead of mark-to-market accounting during the Congressional testimony in which he and Paulson tried to explain the original version of the TARP scheme, but Paulson either ignored or failed to understand all the questions relating to such accounting changes. These reforms were implemented in March 2009, after Paulson had left office. Bank stocks began recovering within days and soon banks were able to raise private capital. Ben S. Bernanke, Statement before the Senate Committee on Banking, Housing, and Urban Affairs, September 23, 2008. Transcript available

from http://banking.senate.gov/public/index.cfm?FuseAction=Hearings.ByMonth&DisplayDate=09/23/08.

39. These UK government guarantees were only reluctantly offered after extreme pressure from the Bank of England, which quickly discovered that it could not reverse the run on Northern Rock's wholesale deposits with the limited support that it was able to provide as lender of last resort. Author's unattributable interviews with UK government officials.

40. Mervyn King, interviewed by Robert Peston, BBC Business, November 6, 2007. Transcript available from http://news.bbc.co.uk/2/shared/bsp/hi/pdfs/06_11_07_fo4_king.pdf.

41. Caballero, "Sudden Financial Arrest."

Chapter Eleven

1. Mill did not actually introduce the name *Homo Economicus*. Although he organized his economic theory in *Principles of Political Economy* (1848) around the idea of this hyperrational being, the term *Homo Economicus* originated in the writing of Mill's late nineteenth-century critics. See Joseph Persky, "Retrospectives: The Ethology of Homo Economicus," *The Journal of Economic Perspectives* 9:2 (Spring, 1995): 221–231.

2. Named after the Italian mathematician Vilfredo Pareto, who first explicitly formulated this definition. See John Cunningham Wood and Michael McLure, eds., *Vilfredo Pareto: Critical Assessments*, 331.

3. The period of phenomenal technological and economic progress based on the development of electrical, chemical, steel, and petroleum industries from 1865 to 1900 is often described as the Second Industrial Revolution. See David S. Landes, *Unbound Prometheus: Technological Change and Industrial Development in Western Europe from 1750 to the Present*, Chapters 4 and 5.

4. The three body problem has proven problematic to physicists since Newton. Although classical physics does a reasonable job of predicting the interactive movement of two mass bodies, it is much more difficult to predict the movement of three such bodies because their gravitational forces interact so complexly. Newton wrestled with this problem in his 1729 *Philosophiae Naturalis Principia Mathematica*, in which he attempted to analyze the movement of the earth, the sun, and the moon, and the problem continued to challenge classical physicists throughout the eighteenth and nineteenth centuries. Although relativity, quantum mechanics, and computers have helped scientists grasp the problem more effectively, three-body movement is still not completely understood. See, for example, Sverre J. Aarseth, *Gravitational N-Body Simulations*.

5. These were less familiar in the 1930s, but have since opened up rich seams of research in economics led by complexity theorists such as Brian Arthur, Duncan Foley, and Paul Ormerod, all building on the work of Benoit Mandelbrot and John Holland. See M. Mitchell Waldrup, *Complexity: The Emerging Science at the Edge of Order and Chaos*, and Paul Ormerod, *The Death of Economics*.

6. D. D. Raphael, Donald Winch, and Robert Skidelsky, *Three Great Economists: Smith, Malthus, Keynes*, 243.

7. See published speech: Gerard Debreu, "The Mathematization of Economic Theory," *American Economic Review* 81:1 (March 1991): 1–7.

8. Also known as Knightian uncertainty after the American economist Frank Knight. See Frank Knight, *Risk, Uncertainty, and Profit*.

9. David Ricardo, "Essay on the Funding System," in *The Works of David Ricardo*, 513–548.

10. David Viniar quoted in Emiko Terazono, "Bean in Barcelona," *Financial Times*, August 26, 2009.

11. When asked by John Cassidy of the *New Yorker* how the theory of efficient markets had held up in the crisis, Chicago economist Eugene Fama responded, "I think it did quite well in this episode. . . . [This] was exactly what you would expect if markets are efficient." He went on to suggest, "I don't know what a credit bubble means. . . . I don't even know what a bubble means. These words have become popular. I don't think they have any meaning." Eugene Fama quoted in John Cassidy, "After the Blowup: Laissez-faire Economists Do Some Soul-searching—and Finger-pointing," *New Yorker* (January 11, 2010): 30.

12. The Joint Hypothesis problem arises because any test of market efficiency is actually a simultaneous test of two hypotheses: One, that markets are efficient, and two, that our models of the market are accurate. Such a test of two hypotheses is necessarily inconclusive. See, for example, Joachim Zietz, "A Note on Tests of Efficient Market Hypotheses: The Case of the Forward Exchange Rate," *Atlantic Economic Journal* 23:4 (December 1995): 310–317.

Chapter Twelve

1. Benoit Mandelbrot and Richard Hudson, *The (Mis)behavior of Markets*.

2. This is also true of the three-body problem of classical physics. As mentioned, economists seem to believe that a million-body problem of economics can be solved precisely while physicists have to content themselves with approximate solutions to a problem involving just three bodies. Whether this arrogance reflects the hubristic attitude of theoretical economists or their ignorance of mathematics is left for the reader to judge.

Chapter Thirteen

1. Although Buffet referred to financial derivatives as financial weapons of mass destruction, his company Berkshire Hathaway was a leading player in these markets. Edward Jay Epstein, "Hidden Stake in Financial Weapons of Mass Destruction," *Vanity Fair,* February 2, 2009.

2. Steve Benen, "What Has Government-Run Health Care Ever Done for Us?" *Washington Monthly,* July 29, 2009. Economist Arthur Laffer was apparently similarly confused: "If you like the Post Office and the Department of Motor Vehicles and you think they're run well, just wait till you see Medicare, Medicaid, and health care done by the government." Arthur Laffer on CNN Newsroom, August 4, 2009. Clip available from Media Matters at http://mediamatters.org/mmtv/200908040014.

3. James Buchanan, *Public Choice: The Origins and Development of a Research Program.*

4. See, for example Kenneth Arrow, *Social Choice and Individual Values,* and Mancur Olson, *The Logic of Collective Action: Public Goods and the Theory of Groups.*

5. Buchanan, *Public Choice,* 8–9.

6. *Rent seeking* is the economic term used to describe behavior that extracts unearned value from other participants in the economy, without making any contribution to productivity, for example by gaining control of land and natural resources or by taking advantage of regulations that may affect consumers or businesses.

7. Such questions are prevalent throughout both Plato's *Republic* and Aristotle's *Politics.*

8. A sunset clause creates an expiration date, at which point a law will go off the books unless it is renewed. Sunset clauses have been present in U.S. legislation from the Alien and Sedition Acts of 1798 to the USA Patriot Act, portions of which have come up for renewal in 2010. Sunset clauses exist in a wide range of other countries, including Canada, Australia, Germany, New Zealand, and the United Kingdom, where the income tax must be renewed yearly by Parliament. See Steve Charnovitz, "Evaluating Sunset: What Would It Mean?" in Thomas Lynch, ed., *Contemporary Public Budgeting.*

9. *Acquis communautaire* is defined succinctly on EUROPA, the official Web site of the European Union, http://europa.eu/scadplus/glossary/community_acquis_en.htm.

10. Coal is cheaper and much more abundant than oil but not as usable because of its bulk.

11. See, for example, International Energy Agency, *Oil Market Report,* June 10, 2008 and British Petroleum, *BP Statistical Review of World Energy,* June 2008. For more details, see Ahmad Abdallah, *Peak Demand* (Hong Kong: GaveKal

Research, 2008). Available from http://gavekal.com/Publication.cfm?rT=1&fileto
open=3805.

Despite this overwhelming evidence, government regulators in the United
States and elsewhere insisted on the market fundamentalist view that the rise in
prices must ipso facto reflect a fundamental imbalance between supply and demand. CFTC Chief Economist Jeffrey Harris, for example, told a House Agriculture subcommittee, "the economic data shows that overall commodity price levels,
including agriculture commodity and energy futures prices, are being driven by
powerful fundamental economic forces and the laws of supply and demand." Harris quoted in Ianthe Jeanne Dugan and Alistair MacDonald, "Traders Blamed for
Oil Spike," *Wall Street Journal*, July 28, 2009.

12. Although this view is controversial on Wall Street, the best evidence for it
comes from the financial markets themselves—the detailed numerical analysis presented to Congress in 2008 by the leading commodity trader Michael Masters and
the fact that oil investment was used as a hedge against the weak dollar, with the
price of oil moving on a daily basis in inverse proportion to the dollar and with no
regard to any changes in physical supply or demand. See Testimony of Michael W.
Masters before the Senate Committee on Homeland Security and Governmental
Affairs, May 20, 2008. Available from hsgac.senate.gov/public/_files/052008
Masters.pdf. See also Mark Cooper's subcommittee statement: "The debate about
whether excessive speculation contributed to the run-up in commodity prices is
over. The reports of this committee on oil, natural gas, and most recently wheat . . .
leave no doubt that excessive speculation was an important cause of problems in
commodity markets. The only question on the table is what we should do to prevent excessive speculation from afflicting these markets in the future." Mark
Cooper, "Excessive Speculation in Commodity Markets and the Collapse of Market Fundamentalism," Statement before Senate Committee on Homeland Security
and Governmental Affairs, July 21, 2009. Available from http://hsgac.senate.gov/
public/index.cfm?FuseAction=Files.View&FileStore_id=3d506d4b-47ab-4a28-
ad27-46daaefeb1cb.

13. See Michael Masters's Senate subcommittee testimony.

14. "To date, there is no statistically significant evidence that the position
changes of any category or subcategory of traders systematically affect prices. This
is to be expected in well-functioning markets. On the contrary, there is evidence
that non-commercial entities alter their position following price changes. This is
also expected because new prices convey information affecting the prospects and
the risks of those entities. This being an interim report, the Task Force intends to
examine these findings further as it continues its work. However, to this point of
the examination, the evidence supports the position that changes in fundamental
factors provide the best explanation for the recent crude oil price increases. Ob-

served increases in the speculative activity and the number of traders in the crude oil futures market do not appear to have systematically affected prices. Moreover, if speculative activity has pushed oil prices above the levels consistent with physical supply and demand, increases in inventories should emerge as higher prices reduce consumption and investment in productive capacity is encouraged. Although this process may take time to unfold, inventories of crude oil and petroleum products, according to available data, have declined significantly over the past year. The view that financial investors have pushed prices above fundamental values is also difficult to square with the fact that prices for other commodities that do not trade on established futures markets (such as coal, steel, and onions) have risen sharply as well." Interagency Task Force on Commodity Markets, *Interim Report on Crude Oil* (July 2008). Available from http://www.cftc.gov/ucm/groups/public/@newsroom/documents/file/itfinterimreportoncrudeoil0708.pdf.

Chapter Fourteen

1. The credit spread between Baa bonds (the standard credit rating for investment-grade corporate bonds) and U.S. Treasury bonds hit 6.21 percent on December 16, 2008. It fell slightly in the first two months of 2009, but then jumped again as the depth of the global recession became apparent, peaking at 5.9 percent on March 23, 2009. Before 2008, this spread had only ever exceeded 5.9 percent for eight months between November 1931 and July 1932, when it peaked at 7.2 percent, before falling to 4.8 percent by early 1933. Data available from the Federal Reserve: http://www.federalreserve.gov/releases/h15/data/Monthly/H15_BAA_NA.txt.

See also Roger Aliaga-Díaz and Joseph H. Davis, *Research Note: Wide Credit Spreads and Future Corporate Bond Returns*, Vanguard Group, Inc. (March 2009). Available from https://institutional.vanguard.com/iam/pdf/RPD2.pdf.

2. Jessica Holzer, "A Loophole for Poor Mr. Paulson," *Forbes*, June 2, 2006. Steve Gelsi, "Paulson Files to Sell $500 mln of Goldman Stock," *MarketWatch*, June 30, 2006. Available from http://www.marketwatch.com/story/paulson-files-to-sell-500-mln-in-goldman-stock.

3. This situation was anticipated and clearly explained by Bernanke in his 2002 "Helicopter Ben" speech, when he argued that in a deflationary situation, the U.S. government could print money without limit—and if necessary drop it out of helicopters—to ensure that prices did not continue to fall: "Under a fiat (that is, paper) money system, a government (in practice, the central bank in cooperation with other agencies) should always be able to generate increased nominal spending and inflation, even when the short-term nominal interest rate is at zero. . . . The U.S. government has a technology, called a printing press (or, today, its electronic

equivalent) that allows it to produce as many U.S. dollars as it wishes at essentially no cost. By increasing the number of U.S. dollars in circulation, or even by credibly threatening to do so, the U.S. government can also reduce the value of a dollar in terms of goods and services, which is equivalent to raising the prices in dollars of those goods and services." Ben Bernanke, "Deflation: Making Sure 'It' Doesn't Happen Here," Remarks Before the National Economists Club, Federal Reserve Board, Washington, DC, November 21, 2002. Available from http://www.federal reserve.gov/boardDocs/speeches/2002/20021121/default.htm.

4. Arthur Burns, *Prosperity Without Inflation*, 30-31 and 69.

5. I have already mentioned the 85 percent tax rates that prevailed for most of the Eisenhower era. Although no one liked to pay these absurdly high taxes, neither were they seen as incompatible with American free enterprise or identified with outright communism. Compare this with today's political reaction to the possibility of an increase in the top U.S. tax rate from 39 percent to 44 percent.

Chapter Fifteen

1. Germany and Japan have experienced several episodes of economic recovery fizzling out without a hit from higher interest rates. These double-dip recessions were also attributable to policy changes—generally big fiscal tightening not compensated by looser monetary policy.

2. The rate on long-term bonds is arguably even more important than the overnight rate, and many financiers believe this to be the central bankers' Achilles heel. Bond rates, unlike short rates, are set by private investors in a competitive market. These investors are supposedly focused on the risks of inflation and government bankruptcy. They are often called "bond market vigilantes" because they can override the decisions of bureaucrats and take ultimate control over financial conditions. These issues are discussed further on pages 215–218 when we consider inflation and currency depreciation. In trying to work out who actually controls long-term interest rates, both theory and experience suggest that the overnight rate set by the central bank is more important than bond marker sentiment. This was spectacularly confirmed in December 2008, when the Fed's decision to print and push overnight rates down to zero was widely denounced as an inflationary debasement of the dollar, but Treasury bond yields, instead of rising as the bond-market vigilantes had expected, dropped almost immediately from 3.9 percent to 2.1 percent. For a remarkably frank admission by one of the world's top monetary theorists of the astonishing confusion in academic economics about the respective roles of central banks and private investors in setting short-term and long-term rates, see Ben Friedman, "What We Still Don't Know about Monetary and Fiscal Policy," *Brookings Papers on Economic Activity* 2 (2007).

3. The exceptional size of the output gap is partly a result of unusually deep recessions in every major economy and partly due to the fact that these recessions occurred at the same time. The post-Lehman seizure dragged all economies down at the same time. In the deep U.S. recessions of the 1970s and 1980s, by contrast, Europe and Japan continued to grow quite strongly while the U.S. economy collapsed. In the early 1990s, Europe was enjoying a postreunification boom when the United States went into recession. By the time Europe suffered its postunification bust, the United States was already recovering.

4. "It's the levels, stupid." Fielding questions after the latest Bank of England Inflation Report, Governor Mervyn King stooped to this inelegant phrase to emphasize an important point: Britain's recession has been so severe that the level of output will remain depressed even when growth resumes. In the governor's view, high unemployment could persist, putting downward pressure on inflation. The prospect looms of a long period of low interest rates and special measures to boost the money supply. Bill Martin, "We're Between a Rock and a Hard Place, and Need a Soft Pound," *The Guardian,* August 23, 2009.

5. These three conditions were reductions in excess capacity, accelerating inflation, and clearly deteriorating inflationary expectations: "The Committee will maintain the target range for the federal funds rate at 0 to 1/4 percent and continues to anticipate that economic conditions, including low rates of resource utilization, subdued inflation trends, and stable inflation expectations, are likely to warrant exceptionally low levels of the federal funds rate for an extended period." Board of Governors of the Federal Reserve System, Press Release, November 4, 2009. Available from http://www.federalreserve.gov/newsevents/press/monetary/20091104a.htm.

6. This lesson is thoroughly understand by central bankers from the history of the 1930s and from the more recent experience of Japan in 1997 and Germany in 2006. In 1997, after a year of strong recovery, Japan simultaneously raised taxes and reduced the growth of its money supply. As a result, Japan relapsed into recession and the deficit grew, instead of narrowing.

7. See Chen Shiyin and Bernard Lo, "U.S. Inflation to Approach Zimbabwe Level, Faber Says," *Bloomberg News,* May 27, 2009.

8. See Milton Friedman, *The Counter-revolution in Monetary Theory: Wincott Memorial Lecture,* September, 16, 1970.

9. It is unlikely that academic economists would ever have submitted themselves to such a rigorous scientific standard as evidenced in the next two paragraphs.

10. Milton Friedman, *The Counter-revolution in Monetary Theory* (my italics above).

11. The most detailed academic study, covering 160 countries during the last thirty years of the twentieth century, shows a strong correlation between money growth and inflation in countries with high inflation or hyperinflation, but a very

weak correlation in countries with inflation below 10 percent. Thus, high inflation implies monetary growth but monetary growth does not necessarily imply high inflation. Paul De Grauwe and Magdalena Polan, "Is Inflation Always and Everywhere a Monetary Phenomenon?" *Scandinavian Journal of Economics* 107:2 (June 2005): 239–259.

12. Friedman, in his classic statement of monetarist doctrine in 1970 (cited in footnote 10 above) actually presented eleven major qualifications to his bald statement of the invariable link between inflation and monetary policy. These are discussed in Ben Bernanke's equally classic lecture: "Friedman's Monetary Framework, Some Lessons," *Journal of the Federal Reserve Bank of Dallas* (October 2003): 207–214.

13. For a critical review, see Benjamin Friedman, "The Rise and Fall of Money Growth Targets as Guidelines for U.S. Monetary Policy," in Iowa Kuroda, ed., *Towards More Effective Monetary Policy*. See also James Tobin, "The Monetarist Counter-Revolution Today—An Appraisal," Cowles Foundation Paper No. 532 (Yale University, 1981). Available from http://cowles.econ.yale.edu/P/cp/p05a/p0532.pdf.

14. "I am the Lord your God and you shall have no other gods before me." See also Bernanke speech in footnote 13: "Friedman's monetary framework has been so influential that, in its broad outlines at least, it has nearly become identical with modern monetary theory and practice. I am reminded of the student first exposed to Shakespeare who complained to the professor: 'I don't see what's so great about him. He was hardly original at all. All he did was string together a bunch of well-known quotations.' The same issue arises when one assesses Friedman's contributions."

15. "The professors contrive new rules and methods . . . whereby all the fruits of the earth shall increase a hundredfold more than they do at present, with innumerable other happy proposals . . . The only inconvenience is that none of these projects are yet brought to perfection and in the meantime the whole country lies miserably waste, the houses in ruins and the people without food or clothes." Jonathan Swift, Part III, "A Voyage to Laputa," *Gulliver's Travels*, 166.

16. Bernanke, "Friedman's Monetary Framework, Some Lessons."

17. The only alternative would be a much higher rate of domestic inflation in China than in America and Europe, an alternative that the government and people would doubtless prefer to avoid.

Chapter Sixteen

1. James Tobin, "Stabilization Policy Ten Years After," *Brookings Papers on Economic Activity* 1 (1980): 19–71. See also Martin Feldstein and James H. Stock, "The Use of Monetary Aggregate to Target Nominal GDP," NBER Working Paper 4304.

2. In January 2009, Paul Krugman described the last stand of the anti-Keynesian fundamentalists against the worldwide fiscal stimulus programs with his characteristic combination of acerbic eloquence and academic rigor: "First Eugene Fama, now John Cochrane, have made the claim that debt-financed government spending necessarily crowds out an equal amount of private spending, even if the economy is depressed—and they claim this not as an empirical result, not as the prediction of some model, but as the ineluctable implication of an accounting identity . . . What's so mind-boggling about this is that it commits one of the most basic fallacies in economics—interpreting an accounting identity as a behavioral relationship . . . How is it possible that distinguished professors believe [this]? The answer, I think, is that we're living in a Dark Age of macroeconomics. Remember, what defined the Dark Ages wasn't the fact that they were primitive—the Bronze Age was primitive, too. What made the Dark Ages dark was the fact that so much knowledge had been lost, that so much known to the Greeks and Romans had been forgotten by the barbarian kingdoms that followed. And that's what seems to have happened to macroeconomics in much of the economics profession." Paul Krugman, "A Dark Age of Macroeconomics (wonkish)," *The Conscience of a Liberal, New York Times Blog,* January 27, 2009. Available from http://krugman.blogs.nytimes.com/2009/01/27/a-dark-age-of-macroeconomics-wonkish/.

3. Best estimates for 2010 general government borrowing relative to GDP were: United States 10.7 percent, Japan 8.2 percent, Germany 5.3 percent, France 8.6 percent, Italy 5.4 percent, UK 13.3 percent, Canada 5.2 percent. Organisation for Economic Co-operation and Development (OECD), *OECD Outlook* 86 (November 2009).

4. There has been a long history of debt defaults by sovereign governments, and in every case creditors have been left with no legal or political redress. See Anatole Kaletsky, *The Costs of Default,* and Carmen M. Reinhart and Kenneth Rogoff, *This Time Is Different: Eight Centuries of Financial Folly.*

5. The figures for Treasury securities exclude the notional holdings owned by the federal government itself through the Social Security Trust Fund and other purely notional accounting entities. Federal Reserve Board, "Flow of Funds Accounts of the United States: Flows and Outstandings, Third Quarter 2009," December 10, 2009.

6. Strictly speaking, the current account deficit is slightly different from the trade deficit, as explained in the text.

7. The current account deficit for the first three quarters of 2009, annualized, was $407 billion.

8. To be precise, real incomes sixty years from now will be 3.2 times higher if U.S. growth averages 1.96 percent per head, as it has since 1950, and 1.8 times higher if growth slows to 1 percent per head.

9. This assumes real economic growth of 3 percent real and 2 percent inflation.

10. International Monetary Fund, "Fiscal Implications of the Global Economic and Financial Crisis," IMF Staff Position Note SPN/09/13, June 2009.

11. Japan suffered five recessions in the twenty years since 1990, while the United States had three recessions and Britain and the eurozone suffered two each.

12. Reinhart and Rogoff, *This Time Is Different*.

13. Kaletsky, *The Costs of Default*.

14. See "Continental Illinois and 'Too Big to Fail,'" in FDIC Division of Research and Statistics, *History of the Eighties—Lessons for the Future*, vol. 1, 235–257. Available from http://www.fdic.gov/bank/historical/history/235_258.pdf.

15. Similarly, the near-collapse of the British banking system in the so-called secondary bank crisis of 1974 was accompanied by only a brief, though sharp, recession, whereas the recession that followed the U.S. savings and loan debacle in 1989–91 was the mildest and shortest on record.

16. This term was first used by the French economists Charles and Louis Gave. See Charles Gave, Anatole Kaletsky, and Louis-Vincent Gave, *Our Brave New World*.

17. Spain is not often recognized as a major force in the world economy, but its trade deficits throughout the precrisis period were second only to America's in dollar terms and almost twice as large in relation to its GDP. Spain is the only country apart from the United States ever to have experienced annual current account deficits of $100 billion.

18. International Monetary Fund, *World Economic Outlook (WEO)*, September 2009.

19. In its most recent global forecasts (November 2009), the OECD projected an increase in China's surplus from $300 billion in 2009 to $320 billion in 2011.

20. $148 billion in 2011, compared with $213 billion in 2007. OECD, *OECD Outlook* 86 (November 2009): 104.

21. Omnibus Trade and Competitiveness Act 1988 (H.R. 3). Available from http://www.treasury.gov/offices/international-affairs/economic-exchange-rates/authorizing-statute.pdf.

22. U.S. Treasury Secretary Timothy Geithner repeatedly made the following statement during his Senate confirmation hearings: "President Obama—backed by the conclusions of a broad range of economists—believes that China is manipulating its currency. President Obama has pledged as president to use aggressively all the diplomatic avenues open to him to seek change in China's currency practices. While in the U.S. Senate he cosponsored tough legislation to overhaul the U.S. process for determining currency manipulation and authorizing new enforcement measures so countries like China cannot continue to get a free pass for undermining fair trade principles." Timothy Geithner, Treasury Secretary Confirmation Hearing before the U.S. Senate Committee on Finance, January 21, 2010. Available from

http://www.finance.senate.gov/sitepages/leg/LEG%202009/012209%20TFG%20 Questions.pdf. See also Robert Aliber, "Tariffs Can Persuade Beijing to Free the Renminbi," *Financial Times*, December 8, 2009, and Martin Wolf, "Why China's Exchange Rate Policy Is a Common Concern," *Financial Times,* December 9, 2009.

23. The most important and successful of these interventions was the Plaza Agreement of September 22, 1985, which resulted in a 40 percent devaluation of the dollar over the following eighteen months. This was followed by the Louvre Accord of February 22, 1987, which helped to stabilize the dollar-yen exchange rate for the next five years in the range of 125–150, but was subsequently blamed for contributing to the 1987 crash on Wall Street and the Japanese bubble economy of 1988–89.

24. A good summary of recent thinking is John Williamson, "The Choice of Exchange Rate Regime: The Relevance of International Experience to China's Decision," Lecture at the Central University of Finance and Economics in Beijing on September 7, 2004. Available from the Institute for International Economics, Washington, DC, at http://www.iie.com/publications/papers/williamson0904.pdf.

A more detailed study is Kenneth Rogoff et al., "Evolution and Performance of Exchange Rate Regimes," IMF Occasional Paper 229, May 2004.

25. Michal Kalecki, Political Aspects of Full Employment, *Political Quarterly* 14 (1943), reprinted in Michal Kalecki, *Selected Essays on the Dynamics of the Capitalist Economy.*

Chapter Seventeen

1. International Monetary Fund, "Fiscal Implications of the Global Economic and Financial Crisis."

2. Ibid.

3. Ibid. The disproportion between the long-term costs and the cost of the crisis is greater in the United States than any other country. The IMF found the average ratio between demographic costs to crisis costs to be nine to one.

4. Aneurin Bevan in a speech at the Labour Party Conference, Blackpool, 1949.

5. Committee for a Responsible Federal Budget (CRFB), "CRFB Analysis of Congressional Budget Office's 2010 Baseline," January 26, 2010. Available from http://crfb.org/document/crfb-analysis-cbo's-january-2010-baseline.

6. "The country needs and, unless I mistake its temper, the country demands bold, persistent experimentation. It is common sense to take a method and try it: If it fails, admit it frankly and try another. But above all, try something." FDR, Oglethorpe University Commencement Address, May 22, 1932.

7. U.S. Environmental Protection Agency, *2000 Community Water System Survey*, vol. 1. Available from http://www.epa.gov/ogwdw/consumer/pdf/cwss_2000_volume_i.pdf.

8. OECD, "OECD in Figures 2009," *OECD Observer*, Supplement 1, 2009. Available from http://browse.oecdbookshop.org/oecd/pdfs/browseit/0109061E.PDF.

9. David Carey, Bradley Herring and Patrick Lenain, "Health Care Reform in the United States," OECD Economics Department Working Paper No 665, February 2009. Available from http://www.olis.oecd.org/olis/2009doc.nsf/linkto/eco-wkp(2009)6.

For detailed statistics on cancer and cardiac survival rates and other indicators of health care outcomes, see also OECD, *Health at a Glance 2007*, 100–116.

10. CRFB, " CRFB Analysis of Congressional Budget Office's 2010 Baseline."

11. A much higher proportion of health spending is included in government consumption in these other countries, which also explains why the size of their public sectors appear to be so much larger than the public sector in the United States. OECD, *Health at a Glance 2007*, 88–89.

12. OECD, *Growing Unequal? Income Distribution and Poverty in OECD Countries*, Table 4.5.

13. Roughly half the increase in all these figures was not caused by an actual expansion of public spending but simply by the shrinkage of GDP, which resulted in a smaller denominator in these ratios.

14. This German increase was not due to higher taxes but again to the arithmetic effect of the falling GDP denominator.

Chapter Eighteen

1. Alan Murray, Interview with Paul Volcker, "Paul Volker: Think More Boldly," *Wall Street Journal*, December 14, 2009.

2. Adair Turner, "How to Tame Global Finance," *Prospect* 162 (August 27, 2009).

3. In the United States, a permanent increase in the monetary base equivalent to 7 percent of GDP could generate seignorage revenue for the government (or save the government debt interest costs) equivalent to 0.21 percent of GDP, or $30 billion a year, assuming an average interest rate of 3 percent on U.S. Treasury debt. In the UK, an increase in the monetary base has been 9 percent of GDP. Assuming an average interest rate of 3 percent, the creation of additional central bank money could reduce government interest costs by 0.27 percent of GDP, or £4 billion per year.

4. Edmund Andrews, "Greenspan Concedes Error on Regulation," *New York Times*, October 23, 2008.

5. Economists Claudia Goldin and Lawrence Katz found in a recent study that Harvard graduates who went into finance "earned three times the income of other graduates with the same grade point average, demographics, and college major." See Claudia Goldin and Lawrence Katz, "Transitions: Career and Family Life Cycles of the Educational Elite, *American Economic Review: Papers and Proceedings* 98:2 (2008): 363–369.

Chapter Nineteen

1. For a detailed discussion of the growth potential of the biggest developing countries, the BRICs—Brazil, Russia, India, and China, plus smaller developing countries coming up behind them—see Dominic Wilson and Roopa Purushothaman, "Dreaming with BRICs: The Path to 2050," Global Economics Paper No. 99, Goldman Sachs Global Research, October 2003. Available from http://www2. goldmansachs.com/ideas/brics/book/99-dreaming.pdf. See also Goldman Sachs Global Economics Group, *BRICs and Beyond,* November 2007. Available from http://www2.goldmansachs.com/ideas/brics/book/BRIC-Full.pdf.

2. Summarizing the conclusions of April 2009 G20 summit in London Gordon Brown declared: "The old Washington Consensus is over." See Jonathan Weisman and Alistair Macdonald, "Obama, Brown Strike Similar Note on Economy," *Wall Street Journal,* April 3, 2009. See also a 2009 article by John Williamson, who coined the phrase: John Williamson, "The 'Washington Consensus': Another Near-Death Experience?" Peterson Institute for International Economics, April 10, 2009. Available from http://www.iie.com/realtime/?p=604. See as well Dani Rodrik, "Is There a New Washington Consensus?" *Business Standard,* June 12, 2008.

3. Unattributable interview with the author in Anatole Kaletsky, "We Need a New Capitalism to Take on China, *The Times,* London, February 4, 2010.

4. "'China's Spirit,' a 'Great Wall' at Heart Built to Ward Off Global Crisis," *People's Daily,* July 30, 2009.

5. Joshua Cooper Ramo, *The Beijing Consensus.*

6. Two of the best recent books are Will Hutton, *The Writing on the Wall: China and the West in the 21st Century,* and Bill Emmott, *Rivals: How the Power Struggle Between China, India and Japan Will Shape Our Next Decade.*

7. If China continues to grow at an average annual rate of 8 percent without any interruption, its living standards will catch up with those in Portugal, the poorest western European country, by around 2030. For details see footnote 10 below.

8. An excellent recent exposition of this argument is in Hutton, *Writing on the Wall.* Hutton argues that China's economic model is unsustainable because of the contradictions between an authoritarian state and a market economy, and he offers numerous examples of the dysfunctions that result.

9. "Since 1950 only thirteen economies have managed to grow at 7 percent or faster for at least 25 years. However, once one strips out three offshore financial centers and ports that are not fair points of comparison (Hong Kong, Singapore, Malta), an oil field, and an enormous diamond mine with small populations (Oman, Botswana), there are really only eight case studies of interest. Of these, four economies grew and then stalled: Indonesia, Thailand, Malaysia, and earlier, Brazil. One is a huge, fast-growing, lower middle-income state, where everyone is just now trying to decide whether it will keep growing or stall: China. And the last three economies define the true gold standard of development: Japan, Korea, and Taiwan." Joe Studwell, "Nurturing the Chinese Economy," *Far Eastern Economic Review* (December 2009). See also Michael Spence et al., *The Growth Report: Strategies for Sustained Growth and Inclusive Development.* Available from www.growth commission.org/index.php?option=com_content&task=view&id=96&Itemid=169.

10. Data refer to the year 2009. IMF, World Economic Outlook Database, October 2009. Available from http://imf.org/external/pubs/ft/weo/2009/02/weodata/index.aspx.

11. Kishore Mahbubani, *The New Asian Hemisphere: The Irresistible Shift of Global Power to the East.*

12. J. K. Galbraith, *The New Industrial State.*

13. See Gave, Kaletsky, and Gave, *Our Brave New World.*

14. Also described by Larry Summers as a balance of financial terror. See James Fallows, "The $1.4 Trillion Question," *The Atlantic* (January/February 2008).

15. The same may apply to food because agricultural demand for water and emissions of carbon and other toxic by-products from agriculture are doing as much damage to the environment as industrial or transport pollution.

16. See Tim Jackson, *Prosperity Without Growth: Economics for a Finite Planet.*

17. See Chapter 12, p. 198.

18. See footnote 2 in Chapter 1.

19. The annual transfer to OPEC countries that results from an increase of $100 a barrel in the price of oil is $1 trillion, or more precisely $1.07 trillion. This figure is based on OPEC oil output of 29.3 million barrels a day estimated by the International Energy Agency Oil Market Report for February 2010.

20. Average fuel economy in 2005 was 24.7 mpg in the United States and 37.2 mpg in the EU. U.S. road transportation consumes approximately 10.5 million barrels a day. If U.S. fuel economy were raised to the European standard, U.S. consumption would be reduced by 34 percent, or 3.6 million barrels per day (mbpd). Oil consumption by Chinese motor vehicles was estimated by Argonne National Laboratory at 108.6 million metric tons in 2005 and projected to grow to approximately xx tons in 2010. This is equivalent to 2.2mbd in 2005 and 3.4mbd in 2010. See Feng An and Amanda Sauer, "Comparison of Passenger Vehicle Fuel Econ-

omy and Greenhouse Gas Emission Standards Around the World," Pew Center on Global Climate Change, December 2004. See also M. Wang, H. Huo, and L. Johnson, "Projection of Chinese Motor Vehicle Growth, Oil Demand and CO_2 Emissions Through 2050," U.S. Department of Energy, 2006.

21. According to the International Energy Agency, OECD oil consumption fell from 44.7 million barrels a day (mbd) in 2000 to 43.2mbd in 2008 and will keep falling to 41mbd in 2015 and 40mbd in 2030. Meanwhile, non-OECD consumption is rising from 26.6mbd in 2000 to 35mbd in 2008, 40mbd in 2015, and 56mbd in 2030. International Energy Agency, *World Energy Outlook 2009*.

22. Yamani recently repeated this warning to his Saudi countrymen in slightly different words: "Thirty years from now there will be a huge amount of oil—and no buyers. Oil will be left in the ground. The Stone Age came to an end not because we had a lack of stones, and the oil age will come to an end not because we have a lack of oil." Gyles Brandreth, "Farewell to Riches of the Earth," *Daily Telegraph*, London, June 25, 2000. See also Bill Emmott, "OPEC's Greed Will Herald the End of the Oil Age," *The Times*, London, August 20, 2009.

23. Nicholas Stern, *The Stern Review: Economics of Climate Change*, 355.

Although energy research was officially listed as a "high priority national need" in repeated budgets, the U.S. government spent only $3 billion a year on energy research and development, largely on nuclear power, in the first decade of the twenty-first century. This was roughly one-third of government spending on energy R&D in the early 1980s (adjusted for inflation) and one-tenth of government spending on health research in 2004. The British government spent just £40m, one-thirtieth of the spending in 1985. Public and private R&D spending on energy fell as a proportion of total U.S. R&D spending from 10 percent in 1980 to 2 percent in 2005. "In the early 1980s, energy companies were investing more in R&D than were drug companies; in 2005, drug companies invested ten times as much in R&D as do energy firms. Total private-sector energy R&D in 2005 was less than the R&D budgets of individual biotech companies such as Amgen and Genentech. . . . Using emissions scenarios . . . and a framework for estimating the climate-related savings from energy R&D programs developed by Robert Schock from Lawrence Livermore National Laboratory . . . energy R&D spending of $15–$30 billion/year would be sufficient to stabilize CO_2 at double pre-industrial levels." Daniel M. Kammen and Gregory F. Nemet, "Reversing the Incredible Shrinking Energy R&D Budget," *Issues in Science and Technology* (Fall 2005).

See also Jim Skea, "The Renaissance of UK Energy Research," lecture on behalf of the UK Energy Research Centre given at Cambridge University, January 17, 2006. More information available from www.ukerc.ac.uk.

24. According to estimates quoted by the Chicago Mercantile Exchange: "International carbon trading could reach $1 trillion in the United States by 2020 and

$5 trillion globally." See "United States Still Early in Carbon Reduction Process," *CME Group* (Fall 2009).

25. China is adding as much new coal-fired electricity generation capacity every year as Britain has built in its entire history. Britain's total coal-fired capacity is approximately 30 gigawatts (GW). Between 2006 and 2010, China has added 192 GW, or 38GW per year, of coal-fired capacity according to U.S. government statistics. China is expected to add an additional 30 GW every year until 2030. U.S. Energy Information Administration, *International Energy Outlook 2009*, 49–50. See also Parliamentary Office of Science and Technology (POST), "Electricity in the UK," *Postnote* 280 (February 2007). Available from http://www.iop.org/activity/policy/Publications/file_21079.pdf.

26. CFC refrigerants whose elimination from the atmosphere under the 1989 Montreal Convention began to restore the earth's ozone layer in just twelve years. See footnote 3 in Chapter 1.

27. Joseph Stiglitz, "Chasing GDP Growth Results in Lower Living Standards," *The Observer*, London September 13, 2009.

28. Nicolas Sarkozy, "Opening Address to the 40th World Economic Forum," Davos, Switzerland, January 27, 2010. Available from http://www.weforum.org/pdf/Sarkozy_en.pdf.

Epilogue

1. S. C. Gwynne, Thomas McCarroll, William McShirter, and Richard Woodbury, "The Long Haul: The U.S. Economy," *Time*, September 28, 1992.

2. Robert Skidelsky, "For a New World, New Economics," *New Statesman*, August 30, 2010.

3. Review of *Capitalism 4.0*, "Magic by Numbers: Looking at the Past and Predicting the Future," *Economist*, July 8, 2010.

4. Gordon Brown, *Beyond the Crash: Overcoming the First Crisis of Globalization* (New York: Free Press, 2010), 13.

5. Andy Sullivan, "US Public Strongly Opposes Debt Level Increase," *Reuters News Service* January 12, 2011.

6. Conservative Conference, "David Cameron Speech," *The Guardian*, October 8, 2009, www.guardian.co.uk/politics/2009/oct/08/david-cameron-speech-in-full.

Bibliography

Aarseth, Sverre J. *Gravitational N-Body Simulations.* New York: Cambridge University Press, 2003.

Abdallah, Ahmad. *Peak Demand.* Hong Kong: GavcKal Research, 2009. Available from http://gavekal.com/Publication.cfm?rT=1&filetoopen=3805.

Aliaga-Díaz, Roger, and Joseph H. Davis. *Research Note: Wide Credit Spreads and Future Corporate Bond Returns.* New York: Vanguard Group, 2009. Available from https://institutional.vanguard.com/iam/pdf/RPD2.pdf.

An, Feng, and Amanda Sauer. "Comparison of Passenger Vehicle Fuel Economy and Greenhouse Gas Emission Standards Around the World." Pew Center on Global Climate Change, December 2004.

Aristotle. *Politics.* Translated by Ernest Barker. New York: Oxford University Press, 2009.

Arrow, Kenneth. *Social Choice and Individual Values.* New York: John Wiley & Sons, 1951, 1963.

Artis, M. J., and Mark P. Taylor. "Abolishing Exchange Control: The UK Experience." Discussion Paper No. 294. Centre for Economic Policy Research, February 1989.

Bagehot, Walter. *Lombard Street: A Description of the Money Market.* New York: Charles Scribner's Sons, 1897.

Bank of England. *Quarterly Inflation Report,* February 11, 2009. Available from http://www.bankofengland.co.uk/publications/inflationreport/conf090211.pdf.

Bardo, Michael, and Barry Eichengreen, eds. *A Retrospective on the Bretton Woods System: Lessons for International Monetary Reform.* Chicago: University of Chicago Press, 1993.

Bell, Daniel. *The Coming of the Post-Industrial Society.* New York: Basic Books, 1973.

Benedick, Richard. *Ozone Diplomacy: New Directions in Safeguarding the Planet.* Cambridge, MA: Harvard University Press, 1991.

Benen, Steve. "What Has Government-run Health Care Ever Done for Us?" *Washington Monthly,* July 29, 2009.

Bernanke, Ben. "Deflation: Making Sure 'It' Doesn't Happen Here." Remarks before the National Economists Club. Federal Reserve Board. Washington, DC, November 21, 2002.

———. "Friedman's Monetary Framework, Some Lessons." *Journal of the Federal Reserve Bank of Dallas* (October 2003): 207–214.

———. "The Great Moderation." Remarks at the meetings of the Eastern Economic Association. Federal Reserve Board. Washington, DC, February 20, 2004.

———. Statement before the Senate Committee on Banking, Housing, and Urban Affairs, September 23, 2008. Transcript available from http://banking.senate.gov/public/index.cfm?FuseAction=Hearings.ByMonth&DisplayDate=09/23/08.

Blanchard, Olivier, and John Simon. "The Long and Large Decline in U.S. Output Volatility." *Brookings Papers on Economic Activity* 1 (2001): 135–64.

Brittan, Samuel. *The Treasury Under the Tories, 1951–1964.* Baltimore: Penguin Books, 1964.

Brown, Douglass, et al. *The Economics of the Recovery Program.* New York: McGraw Hill, 1934.

Buchanan, James. *Public Choice: The Origins and Development of a Research Program.* Fairfax, VA: Center for Study of Public Choice, George Mason University, 2003.

Buenker, John D. "The Ratification of the Federal Income Tax Amendment." *Cato Journal* 1:1 (Spring 1981): 183–223.

Burns, Arthur. *Prosperity Without Inflation.* New York: Fordham University Press, 1957.

Burns, Arthur, ed. *The Frontiers of Economic Knowledge.* Princeton, NJ: Princeton University Press, 1954.

Butterfield, Herbert. *The Whig Interpretation of History.* New York: W.W. Norton and Company, 1931, 1965.

Caballero, Ricardo J. "Sudden Financial Arrest." Mundell-Fleming Lecture. IMF, November 2009. Available from http://www.imf.org/external/np/res/seminars/2009/arc/pdf/caballero.pdf.

Cannadine, David. *Mellon: An American Life.* New York: Knopf, 2006.

Carey, David, Bradley Herring, and Patrick Lenain. "Health Care Reform in the United States." OECD Economics Department Working Paper No 665. Paris: OECD, February 2009. Available from http://www.olis.oecd.org/olis/2009doc.nsf/linkto/eco-wkp(2009)6.

Cassidy, John. "After the Blowup: Laissez-faire Economists Do Some Soul-Searching—and Finger-pointing." *New Yorker,* January 11, 2010, 28–33.

Chernow, Ron. *House of Morgan.* New York: Grove Press, 2001.

Cheyney, Edward Potts. *A Short History of England.* New York: Ginn and Company, 1919.

Clarke, Peter. *Keynes: The Twentieth Century's Most Influential Economist.* London: Bloomsbury, 2009.

Coolsaet, Rick. "The Business of Terror: Anarchist Outrages." Translated by Barbara Wilson. *Le Monde Diplomatique, English Edition* (September 2004).

Cooper, Mark. "Excessive Speculation in Commodity Markets and the Collapse of Market Fundamentalism." Statement before Senate Committee on Homeland Security and Governmental Affairs, July 21, 2009. Available from http://hsgac. senate.gov/public/index.cfm?FuseAction=Files.View&FileStore_id=3d506d4b-47ab-4a28-ad27-46daaefeb1cb.

De Bary, William, and Richard Lufrano, eds. *Sources of Chinese Tradition: From 1600 Through the Twentieth Century,* vol. 2. New York: Columbia University Press, 2001.

De Grauwe, Paul, and Magdalena Polan. "Is Inflation Always and Everywhere a Monetary Phenomenon?" *Scandinavian Journal of Economics* 107:2 (June 2005): 239–259.

De Klerk, F. W. *The Last Trek—A New Beginning: The Autobiography.* New York: St. Martin's Press, 1999.

De Long, J. Bradford. "Liquidation Cycles and the Great Depression." NBER Working Paper, June 1991. Available from econ161.berkeley.edu/pdf_files/ Liquidation_Cycles.pdf.

Debreu, Gerard. "The Mathematization of Economic Theory." *American Economic Review* 81:1 (March 1991): 1–7.

Eichengreen, Barry, and Peter Temin. "The Gold Standard and the Great Depression." *Contemporary European History* 9:2 (2000): 183–20.

El-Erian, Mohamed. *When Markets Collide: Investment Strategies for the Age of Global Economic Change.* New York: McGraw Hill, 2008.

Emmott, Bill. *Rivals: How the Power Struggle Between China, India and Japan Will Shape Our Next Decade.* London: Allen Lane, 2008.

Epstein, Edward Jay. "Hidden Stake in Financial Weapons of Mass Destruction." *Vanity Fair* (February 2009).

Evans, Eric J. *Parliamentary Reform, c. 1770–1918.* New York: Longman Publishing Group, 1999.

Fallows, James. "The $1.4 Trillion Question." *The Atlantic* (January/February 2008).

FDIC Division of Research and Statistics. *History of the Eighties—Lessons for the Future,* vol. 1. Washington, DC: Federal Deposit Insurance Corporation, 1997. Available from http://www.fdic.gov/bank/historical/history/.

Federal Reserve Board. "Flow of Funds Accounts of the United States: Flows and

Outstandings, Third Quarter 2009." Washington, DC: Board of Governors of the Federal Reserve System, December 10, 2009.

Feldstein, Martin, and James H. Stock. "The Use of Monetary Aggregate to Target Nominal GDP." NBER Working Paper 4304. Boston: National Bureau of Economic Research, 1993.

Ferguson, Niall. *Ascent of Money: A Financial History of the World.* New York: Penguin Press, 2008.

Frankel, Jeffrey. "The Japanese Cost of Finance: A Survey." *Financial Management* 20:1 (Spring 1991).

Frieden, Jeffrey, and David A. Lake. *International Political Economy: Perspectives on Global Power and Wealth.* New York: Routledge, 1999.

Friedman, Ben. "What We Still Don't Know about Monetary and Fiscal Policy." *Brookings Papers on Economic Activity* 2 (2007).

Friedman, Milton. *The Counter-revolution in Monetary Theory: Wincott Memorial Lecture, 16 September 1970.* London: Institute of Economic Affairs, 1970.

———. "Inflation and Unemployment." Nobel Memorial Lecture, December 13, 1976.

Friedman, Milton, and Anna Jacobson Schwartz. *A Monetary History of the United States, 1867–1960.* Princeton, NJ: Princeton University Press, 1971.

Galbraith, John Kenneth. *The New Industrial State.* Princeton, NJ: Princeton University Press, 1967, 2007.

Gamble, Andrew. *The Spectre at the Feast: Capitalist Crisis and the Politics of Recession.* New York: Palgrave Macmillan, 2009.

Gave, Charles, Anatole Kaletsky, and Louis-Vincent Gave. *Our Brave New World.* Hong Kong: GaveKal Research, 2005.

Geithner, Timothy. Treasury Secretary Confirmation Hearing before the U.S. Senate Committee on Finance, January 21, 2010. Available from http://www.finance.senate.gov/sitepages/leg/LEG%202009/012209%20TFG%20Questions.pdf.

Gilbert, R. Alton. "Requiem for Regulation Q: What It Did and Why It Passed Away." *Federal Reserve Bank of St. Louis Review* (February 1986): 22–37.

Glaeser, Edward, and Janet Kohlhase. "Cities, Regions and the Decline of Transport Costs." NBER Working Paper 9886. Cambridge, MA: National Bureau of Economic Research, 2003.

Goldin, Claudia, and Lawrence Katz. "Transitions: Career and Family Life Cycles of the Educational Elite." *American Economic Review: Papers and Proceedings* 98:2 (2008): 363–369.

Goldman Sachs Global Economics Group. *BRICs and Beyond.* New York: Goldman Sachs Global Research Centre, November 2007. Available from http://www2.goldmansachs.com/ideas/brics/book/BRIC-Full.pdf.

Goodhart, C.A.E. "Monetary Relationships: A View from Threadneedle Street." *Papers in Monetary Economics*, vol. 1. Sydney: Reserve Bank of Australia, 1975.

Greenspan, Alan. "The Challenge of Central Banking." Remarks at the Annual Dinner and Francis Boyer Lecture of the American Enterprise Institute for Public Policy Research. Washington, DC, December 5, 1996. Available from http://www.federalreserve.gov/boarddocs/speeches/1996/19961205.htm.

Gresh, Alain. "Understanding the Beijing Consensus." Translated by Stephanie Irvine. *Le Monde Diplomatique English Edition* (November 2008).

Groenewegen, Peter. "Thomas Carlyle, 'The Dismal Science,' and the Contemporary Political Economy of Slavery." *History of Economics Review* 34 (Summer 2001): 74–94.

Harrod, Roy. *The Life of John Maynard Keynes*. New York: Macmillan, 1951.

Hawtrey, Ralph G. *A Century of Bank Rate*. London: Longmans, Green & Co., 1938.

Heilbroner, Robert. *The Worldly Philosophers*. New York: Touchstone, 1953, 1999.

Hobbes, Thomas. *On the Citizen*. Edited by Richard Tuck and Michael Silverthorne. New York: Cambridge University Press, 1998.

Hoover, Herbert. *The Memoirs of Herbert Hoover: Vol. 3, The Great Depression*. New York: Macmillan Company, 1952.

Hutton, Will. *The Writing on the Wall: China and the West in the 21st Century*. New York: Little, Brown, 2007.

Interagency Task Force on Commodity Markets. *Interim Report on Crude Oil* (July 2008).

International Energy Agency. *World Energy Outlook 2009*. Paris: IEA, 2009.

International Monetary Fund. "Fiscal Implications of the Global Economic and Financial Crisis." IMF Staff Position Note SPN/09/13. Washington, DC: International Monetary Fund, June 2009.

———. *World Economic Outlook* (September 2009).

Jackson, Tim. *Prosperity Without Growth: Economics for a Finite Planet*. Sterling VA: Earthscan, 2009.

Johnson, Paul. *A History of the American People*. New York: Harper Perennial, 1997.

Joint Committee on Taxation. "Overview of Present Law and Economic Analysis Relating to Marginal Tax Rates and the President's Individual Income Tax Rate Proposals" (Order Code JCX-6-01). Public hearing before the Senate Committee on Finance, March 6, 2001.

Kalecki, Michal. *Selected Essays on the Dynamics of the Capitalist Economy*. Cambridge, England: Cambridge University Press, 1971.

Kaletsky, Anatole. *The Costs of Default*. Twentieth Century Fund Paper. New York: Priority Press, 1985.

Kammen, Daniel M., and Gregory F. Nemet. "Reversing the Incredible Shrinking Energy R&D Budget." *Issues in Science and Technology* (Fall 2005).

Kay, John. *Culture and Prosperity: The Truth About Markets—Why Some Nations Are Rich but Most Remain Poor.* New York: HarperCollins, 2004.

Keynes, John Maynard. *The Economic Consequences of the Peace.* New York: Penguin Classics, 1995.

——. *The Economic Consequences of Mr. Churchill.* London: Hogarth, 1925.

——. "The End of Laissez-Faire" (pamphlet). London: Hogarth Press, 1926.

——. *Essays in Persuasion.* New York: W.W. Norton, 1963.

——. *The General Theory of Employment, Interest, and Money.* Amherst, NY: Prometheus Books, 1997.

King, Mervyn. "Speech to the CBI Dinner." January 20, 2009. Available from www.bankofengland.co.uk/publications/speeches/2009/speech372.pdf.

Knight, Frank. *Risk, Uncertainty, and Profit.* Boston, MA: Hart, Shaffner & Marx, 1921.

Kuroda, Iowa, ed. *Towards More Effective Monetary Policy.* New York: Macmillan, 1997.

Laing, Jonathan R. "Welcome to Sizzle Inc.: The 'Platform Economy'—a Business Model Focused on Knowledge While Outsourcing Production—Heralds an Age of Unprecedented U.S. Prosperity" (cover story). *Barron's,* December 25, 2006.

Landes, David S. *Unbound Prometheus: Technological Change and Industrial Development in Western Europe from 1750 to the Present.* New York: Cambridge University Press, 1969, 2003.

Lundgren, Nils-Gustav. "Bulk Trade and Maritime Transport Costs: The Evolution of Global Markets." *Resources Policy* 22:1–2 (March–June 1996): 5–32.

Lynch, Thomas, ed. *Contemporary Public Budgeting.* Washington, DC: Transaction Books, 1981.

Macaulay, Lord. *History of England.* New York: Continuum, 1848, 2010.

Machiavelli, Nicolo. *The Prince.* Rockville, MD: Arc Manor, 2007.

Maddison, Angus. *Growth and Interaction in the World Economy: The Roots of Modernity.* Washington, DC: AEI Press, 2005.

Mahbubani, Kishore. *The New Asian Hemisphere: The Irresistible Shift of Global Power to the East.* New York: PublicAffairs, 2008.

Mandelbrot, Benoit, and Richard Hudson. *The (Mis)behavior of Markets: A Fractal View of Risk, Ruin and Reward.* New York: Basic Books, 2004.

Masters, Michael. Testimony before the Senate Committee on Homeland Security and Governmental Affairs, May 20, 2008. Available from hsgac.senate.gov/public/_files/052008Masters.pdf.

Means, Howard. *Money & Power.* Hoboken, NJ: Wiley & Sons, 2001.

Mill, John Stuart. *Principles of Political Economy.* New York: Oxford University Press, 2008.

Naisbitt, John. *Megatrends.* Clayton Vic, Australia: Warner Books, 1982.

Newman, Paul A., et al. "When Will the Antarctic Ozone Hole Recover?" *Geophysical Research Letters* 33 (2006).

Organisation for Economic Co-operation and Development (OECD). *OECD Outlook 86* (November 2009).

———. *Growing Unequal? Income Distribution and Poverty in OECD Countries.* Paris: OECD, 2008.

———. *Health at a Glance 2007.* Paris: OECD, 2007.

———. "OECD in Figures 2009," *OECD Observer* Supplement 1 (2009). Available from http://browse.oecdbookshop.org/oecd/pdfs/browseit/0109061E.PDF.

Olson, Mancur. *The Logic of Collective Action: Public Goods and the Theory of Groups.* Cambridge, MA: Harvard University Press, 1965, 1971.

———. *Rise and Decline of Nations: Economic Growth, Stagflation, and Social Rigidities.* New Haven, CT: Yale University Press, 1982.

Ormerod, Paul. *The Death of Economics.* Hoboken, NJ: Wiley, 1997.

Parliamentary Office of Science and Technology (POST). "Electricity in the UK." *Postnote* 280 (February 2007). Available from http://www.iop.org/activity/policy/Publications/file_21079.pdf.

Pascal, Blaise. *Pensées.* Translated by A.J. Krailsheimer. New York: Penguin Books, 1966, 1995.

Paulson, Henry. *On the Brink: Inside the Race to Stop the Collapse of the Global Financial System.* New York: Business Plus, 2010.

Persky, Joseph. "Retrospectives: The Ethology of Homo Economicus." *The Journal of Economic Perspectives* 9:2 (Spring 1995): 221–231.

Plato. *Republic.* Translated by Robin Waterfield. New York: Oxford University Press, 2008.

Pope, Mildred. *Studies in French Language and Medieval Literature.* Manchester, England: Manchester University Press, 1939.

Purdum, Todd. "Henry Paulson's Longest Night." *Vanity Fair* (October 2009).

Ramo, Joshua Cooper. *The Beijing Consensus.* London: The Foreign Policy Centre, 2004.

Raphael, D. D., Donald Winch, and Robert Skidelsky. *Three Great Economists: Smith, Malthus, Keynes.* New York: Oxford University Press, 1997.

Rand, Ayn. *The Objectivist Newsletter: 1962–1965,* Third ed. New Milford, CT: Second Renaissance Books, 1990.

Reed, Christopher. "'The Damn'd *South Sea*': Britain's Greatest Financial Speculation and Its Unhappy Ending." *Harvard Magazine* (May–June 1999).

Reinhart, Carmen M., and Kenneth Rogoff. *This Time Is Different: Eight Centuries of Financial Folly.* Princeton, NJ: Princeton University Press, 2009.

Ricardo, David. *The Works of David Ricardo.* Edited by J.R. McCulloch. Charleston, SC: BiblioBazaar, 2009.

Rogoff, Kenneth, et al. "Evolution and Performance of Exchange Rate Regimes." IMF Occasional Paper 229. Washington, DC: International Monetary Fund, May 2004.

Rowthorn, Robert. "The Political Economy of Full Employment in Modern Britain." Kalecki Memorial Lecture, Department of Economics, Oxford University, October 19, 1999.

Sarkozy, Nicolas. "Opening Address to the 40th World Economic Forum." Davos, Switzerland, January 27, 2010. Available from http://www.weforum.org/pdf/Sarkozy_en.pdf.

Sawyer, Malcolm C. *The Economics of Michal Kalecki.* London: Macmillan, 1985.

Schumpeter, Joseph. *Capitalism, Socialism and Democracy.* New York: Harper and Row, 1942.

Seabright, Paul. *The Company of Strangers: A Natural History of Economic Life.* Princeton, NJ: Princeton University Press, 2004.

Sewell, Keith. *Herbert Butterfield and the Interpretation of History.* New York: Palgrave Macmillan, 2005.

Skea, Jim. "The Renaissance of UK Energy Research." Lecture on behalf of UK Energy Research Centre given at Cambridge University, January 17, 2006. Available from www.ukerc.ac.uk.

Shvedov, Maxim. "Statutory Individual Income Tax Rates and Other Elements of the Tax System: 1988 through 2008," (Order Code RL34498). Congressional Research Service, May 21, 2008.

Skidelsky, Robert. *Keynes: The Return of the Master.* New York: PublicAffairs, 2009.

Smith, Adam. *The Wealth of Nations, Books 1–III.* New York: Penguin Classics, 1982.

Sorkin, Andrew Ross. *Too Big to Fail.* New York: Viking Adult, 2009.

Soros, George. *The Alchemy of Finance: Reading the Mind of the Market.* Hoboken, NJ: John Wiley & Sons, 1994.

———. *The New Paradigm for Financial Markets: The Credit Crisis of 2008 and What It Means.* New York: PublicAffairs, 2008.

———. *The Soros Lectures: At the Central European University.* New York: Public Affairs, 2010.

Spence, Michael, et al. *The Growth Report: Strategies for Sustained Growth and Inclusive Development.* Washington, DC: World Bank, 2008. Available from www.growthcommission.org/index.php?option=com_content&task=view&id=96&Itemid=169.

Stern, Nicholas. *The Stern Review: Economics of Climate Change.* New York: Cambridge University Press, 2007.

Stiglitz, Joseph. "Incentives and the Performance of America's Financial Sector." Testimony at Hearing on Compensation in the Financial Industry. House Committee on Financial Services, January 22, 2010. Available from www.house.gov/apps/list/hearing/financialsvcs_dem/stiglitz.pdf.

Stiglitz, Joseph, Jaime Jaramillo-Vallejo, and Yung Chal Park. 'The Role of the State in Financial Markets." *World Bank Research Observer* Annual Conference on Development Economics Supplement (1993): 19–61.

Studwell, Joe. "Nurturing the Chinese Economy." *Far Eastern Economic Review* (December 2009).

Swift, Jonathan. *Gulliver's Travels.* New York: Penguin Classics, 2003.

Taleb, Nassim Nicholas. *The Black Swan: The Impact of the Highly Probable.* New York: Random House, 2007.

———. *Fooled by Randomness: The Hidden Role of Chance in the Markets and in Life.* New York: W.W. Norton, 2001.

Tobin, James. "The Monetarist Counter-Revolution Today—An Appraisal." Cowles Foundation Paper No. 532. Yale University, 1981. Available from http://cowles.econ.yale.edu/P/cp/p05a/p0532.pdf.

———. "Stabilization Policy Ten Years After." *Brookings Papers on Economic Activity* 1 (1980): 19–71.

Toffler, Alvin. *The Third Wave.* New York: Morrow, 1980.

Turner, Adair. "The Financial Crisis and the Future of Financial Regulation." The Economist's Inaugural City Lecture, January 21, 2009. Available from www.fsa.gov.uk/pages/Library/Communication/Speeches/2009/0121_at.shtml.

———. "How to Tame Global Finance." *Prospect* 162 (August 2009).

U.S. Energy Information Administration. *International Energy Outlook 2009.* Washington, DC: US EIA, 2009.

U.S. Environmental Protection Agency. *2000 Community Water System Survey,* vol. 1. Washington: EPA Office of Water, 2002. Available from http://www.epa.gov/ogwdw/consumer/pdf/cwss_2000_volume_i.pdf.

"United States Still Early in Carbon Reduction Process." *CME Group* (Fall 2009).

Waldrup, M. Mitchell. *Complexity: The Emerging Science at the Edge of Order and Chaos.* New York: Simon & Schuster, 1992.

Wang, M., H. Huo, and L. Johnson. *Projection of Chinese Motor Vehicle Growth, Oil Demand and CO_2 Emissions Through 2050.* Oak Ridge, TN: U.S. Department of Energy, Office of Scientific and Technical Information, 2006.

Weber, Max. *The Protestant Ethic and the Spirit of Capitalism.* Translated by Talcott Parsons. New York: Routledge Classics, 2001.

Wessel, David. *In Fed We Trust: Ben Bernanke's War on the Great Panic.* New York: Crown Business, Random House, 2009.

Whatley, George and Ben Franklin. *Principles of Trade.* London: Brotherton and Sewell, 1774.

Wiebe, Robert H. *Business Men and Reform: A Study of the Progressive Movement.* Cambridge, MA: Harvard University Press, 1962.

Williamson, John. "The Choice of Exchange Rate Regime: The Relevance of International Experience to China's Decision." Lecture at the Central University of Finance and Economics in Beijing, September 7, 2004. Available from the Peterson Institute for International Economics, Washington, DC, at http://www.iie.com/publications/papers/williamson0904.pdf.

———. "The 'Washington Consensus': Another Near-Death Experience?" Peterson Institute for International Economics, April 10, 2009. Available from http://www.iie.com/realtime/?p=604.

Williamson, John, ed. *Latin American Readjustment: How Much Has Happened.* Washington: Peterson Institute for International Economics, 1990.

Williamson, John and Roberto Zagha. "From the Hindu Rate of Growth to the Hindu Rate of Reform." Working Paper #144. Center for Research on Economic Development and Policy Reform. Palo Alto: Stanford University, 2002.

Wilson, Dominic, and Roopa Purushothaman. "Dreaming with BRICs: The Path to 2050." Global Economics Paper No. 99. New York: Goldman Sachs Global Research Centre, October 2003. Available from http://www2.goldmansachs.com/ideas/brics/book/99-dreaming.pdf.

Wolf, Martin. *Why Globalization Works.* New Haven: Yale University Press, 2004.

Wood, John Cunningham, and Michael McLure, eds. *Vilfredo Pareto: Critical Assessments.* New York: Routledge, 1999.

Zietz, Joachim. "A Note on Tests of Efficient Market Hypotheses: The Case of the Forward Exchange Rate." *Atlantic Economic Journal* 23:4 (December 1995): 310–317.

Acknowledgments

Many of the people who made this book possible were not aware of their contribution and some might prefer to remain unacknowledged, since they will disagree with my conclusions. But that is the occupational risk of befriending people who write books.

Firstly, I must thank the editors who have made my career as a journalist possible since 1976—James Harding, Robert Thomson, Sir Peter Stothard and Simon Jenkins at *The Times,* Sir Geoffrey Owen and the late Fredy (sic) Fisher at the *Financial Times* and Andrew Knight at the *Economist.* Colleagues on the *Times* to whom I must express special gratitude are Danny Finkelstein, Anne Spackman, Robbie Millen and Tim Rice, who had to put up with many stretched deadlines as I was rushing to finish this manuscript. I would also like to pay tribute to my two early mentors in the newspaper business—Brian Reading and John Plender on the *Economist* and Anthony Harris on the *Financial Times.* They introduced me to the fascinating world of economic policy and taught me far more about economic reality than all the books I had read at Cambridge and Harvard.

Secondly, and even more importantly in terms of the inadvertent intellectual inspiration they provided and the time and resources they made available for me to research and write this book, I must thank Charles and Louis Gave, my founding partners in the GaveKal group of companies. Since we first met in Singapore in 2001 and then started working together on the most tragic and memorable day of the new century, September 11, the Gave family have proved an inexhaustible fount of new ideas. Along with Pierre Gave, Steve Vannelli, Arthur Kroeber, Will Denyer, Ahmad Abdallah and the other colleagues who have contributed to GaveKal's growth and success, Charles and Louis have been wonderful sparring partners, especially on the many occasions when our political and economic views have sharply diverged.

Better still, the GaveKal team have been responsible for the expansion of our business, which has brought me into intellectual contact with several thousand of the brightest and most creative people in finance, business and public policy. When we founded GaveKal, Charles Gave said that many of our best ideas would come from clients and this has been equally true of the ideas in this book, even though most of the clients who unwittingly helped me with their challenges and counter-arguments will doubtless continue to disagree with my conclusions.

Further unintended assistance came from an even more distinguished group—the galaxy of renowned economists who gathered at George Soros's house outside New York to launch the Institute for New Economic Thinking (INET) in September 2009. The discussions that memorable weekend about the subversion of economics by academic politics—and especially the contributions of Joseph Stiglitz, George Akerlof, Axel Leijon-hufvud, Roman Frydman, John Kay, and, of course, our convenor George Soros—corroborated at the highest possible level my longstanding belief that academic economics had degenerated into a form of political propaganda and would need to be reinvented along with the capitalist system itself.

Then, of course, there were the people who made this book possible in the literal sense: My agent, Andrew Wylie, by expressing enthusiasm for the project when I first presented it to him in May 2009, helped to maintain my confidence through the summer of 2009, when the economic indicators still seemed to be pointing to a very different outcome of the crisis from the one my book proposal described. In PublicAffairs and Bloomsbury, I was lucky to find two justly celebrated publishers. Susan Weinberg and Peter Osnos at PublicAffairs and Michael Fishwick at Bloomsbury were bold and imaginative enough to appreciate a line of argument that defied the conventional wisdom after the crisis. But the willingness of Public Affairs and Bloomsbury to produce this book on an accelerated schedule would have come to nothing had it not been for the sharp insights, hard work and rapid responses of Lindsay Jones, my editor; Christine Marra, the project manager; and Susan Pink, the copy editor. Even their efforts would have proved futile had it not been for my eleventh-hour discovery of Evan Joiner, my omni-competent researcher and annotator in New York.

I should also thank Natascha McElhone for the use of her lovely cottage in Wiltshire for the two months of isolation I needed to collect and organise my thoughts, and Charles Jencks, the polymath architect and chronicler of postmodern thinking, for our many fascinating conversations and particularly the one at his house in Scotland that produced the title of this book.

Finally—and most importantly—I must acknowledge the contribution of the people who made me what I am: my late parents, to whom this book is dedicated, and my wonderful children and wife.

All, in their way, had a hand in this book's creation. Kitty, my daughter, offered me tremendous intellectual stimulation, as well as emotional encouragement, through the political ideas she encountered at Georgetown and on the Obama campaign—and also found Evan. Misha, my older son, threatened to disinherit me unless I managed to finish this book and set a fine example with his sudden burst of dynamism in Oxford. Sasha, the third of my children and the only one still at home, was often my sharpest and most perceptive critic and his interest in my ideas, as well as his jovial, enthusiastic presence, made all the effort seem worthwhile.

Above all, of course, I must thank my wife, Fiona Murphy, whose many sacrifices in her career as a filmmaker and writer have allowed me the freedom to work in the way I wanted. Even more than that, her extraordinary intelligence, all-encompassing interests and relentless determination to get to the root of any argument have influenced my way of looking at the world even more than she imagines.

Without all these people's contributions, this book could not have been written. I hope that some, at least, will consider the outcome to have been worthwhile.

Index

ANATOLE KALETSKY is editor-at-large of *The Times*, where he writes weekly columns on economics, politics, and international relations. Kaletsky is also a founding partner and chief economist of GaveKal Capital, a Hong Kong–based investment company with a controlling interest in Dragonomics, one of China's leading economic research businesses. He is on the governing board of the New York–based Institute for New Economic Theory (INET), a nonprofit created after the 2007–2009 crisis to promote and finance academic research in economics outside the orthodoxy of "efficient markets." From 1976 to 1990, Kaletsky was New York bureau chief and Washington correspondent of the *Financial Times* and a business writer on *The Economist*.